Perversion and Utopia

Perversion and Utopia

A Study in Psychoanalysis and Critical Theory

Joel Whitebook

The MIT Press
Cambridge, Massachusetts
London, England

This book was set in New Baskerville by DEKR Corporation and printed and bound in the United States of America.

Earlier versions of parts of this book have appeared in the following journals and books. Chapter 1: "Perversion and Utopia: A Study in Psychoanalysis and Social Theory," *Psychoanalysis and Contemporary Thought* 11 (1988); "Perversion—Destruction and Reparation: On the Contributions of Janine Chasseguet-Smirgel and Joyce McDougall," *American Imago* 48 (1991); Excursus: "Reconciling the Irreconcilable?: Utopianism after Habermas," *Praxis International* 8 (1988); Chapter 2: " 'A Scrap of Independence': On the Ego's Autonomy in Freud," *Psychoanalysis and Contemporary Thought* 16 (1993) [German translation: "Das Problem der Ich-Autonomie bei Freud," *Psyche* 46 (1992)]; Chapter 3: "Reflections on the Autonomous Individual and the Decentered Subject," *American Imago* 49 (1992); "From Schoenberg to Odysseus: Aesthetic, Psychic and Social Synthesis in Wellmer and Adorno," *New German Critique* 58 (Winter 1993) [German translation: "Von Schoenberg zu Odysseus: Aesthetische, psychische und soziale Synthesis bei Adorno und Wellmer," *Zur Verteidigung der Vernunft gegen ihre Liebhaber und Verachter,* ed. Christoph Menke and Martin Seel (Suhrkamp Verlag: Frankfurt am Main, 1993)]; and "Hypostatizing Thanatos: Lacan's Critique of the Ego," *Constellations* 1 (1994); Chapter 4: "Intersubjectivity and the Monadic Core of the Psyche: The Unconscious in Habermas and Castoriadis," *Revue européenne des sciences sociales* 86 (1989); Chapter 5: "Sublimation: A Frontier Concept," *The Spectrum of Psychoanalysis: Essays in Honor of Martin S. Bergmann,* ed. Arlene Kramer Richards and Arnold D. Richards (International Universities Press: New York, 1994).

Library of Congress Cataloging-in-Publication Data

Whitebook, Joel.
  Perversion and utopia : a study in psychoanalysis and critical
  theory / Joel Whitebook.
    p.   cm.
  Includes bibliographical references (p.   ) and index.
  ISBN 0-262-23178-6
  1. Frankfurt school of sociology. 2. Philosophy. 3. Psychoanalysis. 4. Utopias.
I. Title.
HM24.W483   1994
301'.01—dc20   94-22307
                                                                                   CIP

To the memory of my mother
Caroline Whitebook
(1921–1992)

Contents

Acknowledgments

I would like to thank the many friends and colleagues—the distinction is for the most part impossible to maintain—with whom I have discussed the issues addressed in this book during the years I have been working on it: Andrew Arato, Kenneth Baynes, Seyla Benhabib, Murray Bookchin, Susan Buck-Morss, Hauke Brunkhorst, José Casanova, Cornelius Castoriadis, Massimo Cellerino, Andrew Charwat, Halina Charwat, Janine Chasseguet-Smirgel, Jean Cohen, Petra Eggers, Alessandro Ferrara, Jürgen Habermas, Dick Howard, Dan Hill, Elliot Jurist, Louise Kaplan, Danielle Knafo, Gertrud Koch, Leo Lowenthal, Martin Löw-Beer, Joyce McDougall, Ramona Naddaff, Marion Oliner, Carla Pasquinelli, I. H. Paul, Emilia Steurmann, Mariana Wainer, Albrecht Wellmer, Richard Wolin, and Ivan Vejvoda.

The following colleagues who were generous enough to take the time from their already overburdened schedules to read the manuscript, either in whole or in part, deserve a special word of thanks: Dick Bernstein, Peter Dews, Ferenc Feher, Agnes Heller, Axel Honneth, Martin Jay, and Donald Kaplan. The sort of honest and incisive criticism they have offered is the most beneficial gift a writer can receive.

Something more needs to be said about Dick Bernstein and Donald Kaplan. I have been repeatedly touched by the consistent intellectual, professional, and personal support these two senior colleagues have given me over the years. I am grateful indeed for their unusual generosity.

Kitty Ross did me the invaluable favor of pushing me to continue to clarify my thoughts at a point when my spirits were sagging. Because of that, she deserves credit for contributing immensely to whatever coherence this book can claim.

Zoe Waldron is to be thanked for the conscientiousness and doggedness of her editorial assistance.

I am grateful to Claire Martin, the secretary of the New School Philosophy Department; she has been an inexhaustable source of assistance as well as gossip.

Finally, I would like to thank Thomas McCarthy and Larry Cohen of The MIT Press for having supported this project when it was little more than a germ cell.

Introduction

In response to a query from Leo Lowenthal asking how to describe
Freud's significance for the Frankfurt school, Max Horkheimer gave
the following answer: "I think you should be simply positive. We really are deeply indebted to Freud and his first collaborators. His
thought is one of the *Bildungsmächte* [foundation stones] without
which our own philosophy would not be what it is."[1] As this book
represents an attempt to reinvigorate the psychoanalytic dimension
of Critical Theory, it is important to recall how deep the rapport
between psychoanalysis and Critical Theory once was. The intimacy
between the two movements—which resulted, in part, from the fact
that both were the products of the traumatic and fertile encounter
between central European Jewry and the German Enlightenment—
was embodied in the fact that the Frankfurt Psychoanalytic Institute
was originally established in 1929 as a "guest institute" within the
Institute for Social Research. They were literally housed in the same
building—indeed shared the same classrooms—on Frankfurt's Vik-
toria-Alee, where, it might be added, such distinguished analysts as
Paul Federn, Hans Sachs, Siegfried Bernfeld, and Anna Freud offered lectures to the general public.

This arrangement, which at the time caused something of a sensa-
tion in proper academic circles, allowed the still-disreputable discipline of psychoanalysis to establish its first official tie, albeit indirect,
to the conservative German university system. Freud himself was so
appreciative of this affiliation that he wrote Horkheimer two letters

thanking him for his assistance.[2] The Critical Theorists also played a significant role in promoting Freud's candidacy for the Goethe Prize, which he received in 1930. Lowenthal recalls that "at the time, no one wanted to grant Freud an official prize; psychoanalysis was a despised and scorned science; it was anathema—extreme and avant garde. For that reason, for the city of Frankfurt to grant Sigmund Freud the Goethe Prize was quite extraordinary."[3]

Theoretically, the Frankfurt school's attempts to treat Freud on a par with such unquestionable masters of German thought as Kant, Hegel, and Nietzsche and to effect a synthesis between Freud and Marx were themselves no less "extreme and avant garde." Today, as Martin Jay has observed, "it is difficult to appreciate the audacity"[4] of these undertakings.

In the thirties, under the tutelage of the psychoanalyst Erich Fromm, at that time a member of both institutes, the Critical Theorists turned to psychoanalysis to make up for a fundamental deficiency in Marxian theory, namely, its lack of a psychology and its almost total disregard for the so-called subjective dimension. The turn to Freud, however, was not motivated by theoretical considerations alone. As the decade continued to unfold, the task of explaining why the proletariat had failed to fulfill its historic mission when the objective conditions were presumably ripe, and why Europe was racing headlong toward catastrophe became increasingly urgent. As Jay has observed, it was "no accident that growing pessimism about the possibility of revolution went hand in hand with an intensified appreciation of Freud's relevance."[5] In an attempt to address these questions, the members of the Institute for Social Research, equipped with the resources of psychoanalysis, undertook their pathbreaking investigations of authority, the family, the individual, and culture.

These interrelated studies in turn formed the empirical basis for the metahistorical analysis of *Dialectic of Enlightenment*, which would not only become the magnum opus of the Frankfurt school but would also articulate the problematic to which future Critical Theorists would, in one way or another, have to respond. With its elucidation of the self-vitiating dynamic of the civilizing process, its theory of negative anthropogenesis, *Dialectic of Enlightenment* bears strong structural similarities to Nietzsche's *Genealogy of Morals,* Weber's *Protestant Ethic and the Spirit of Capitalism,* and Freud's *Civilization and Its Discontents.* And because its position is reinforced by philosophical, sociological, and anthropological arguments, *Dialectic of Enlightenment* is perhaps even more implacable in its pessimism than Freud's late great work. The same analysis that shows that only a utopian solution—namely, the reconciliation of the species with external and internal nature—can break the dialectic of enlightenment also shows that such a reconciliation is structurally impossible. The assimilation of psychoanalysis provided the Frankfurt school with the concepts needed not only to comprehend the central dynamics and pathologies of modern rationality, individuality, and culture but also to elucidate the impasse of modernity in exquisitely aporetic detail. The coincidence between Critical Theory's turn to psychoanalysis and the emergence of the utopian or redemptive motif should also be noted. As we shall see, it is in no way accidental.

After the Second World War, two major works on Freud emerged in Critical Theory—Herbert Marcuse's *Eros and Civilization* and Jürgen Habermas's *Knowledge and Human Interests*—and the substantial differences between them are determined, to a large extent, by the authors' differing responses to *Dialectic of Enlightenment.* Marcuse accepts the fundamental premises of Horkheimer and Adorno's analysis and is therefore saddled with a radical formulation of the dilemma. He must then attempt to formulate an equally radical—which is to say, utopian—way out. Specifically, Marcuse accepts the premise that the ego and reason are intrinsically repressive or violent—in this, like Adorno, he anticipates many poststructuralist and postmodern themes—and then attempts to locate the good Other of instrumental reason and the autocratic ego. As psychoanalysis was used to diagnose the repressiveness of reason and the ego in the first place, it could also be used in the attempt to formulate a solution. Marcuse enlists Freud's early theory of perversions (later revised) in order to construe sexual perversions as the relatively direct expression of unconscious id impulses that have circumvented socialization and the reality principle. As such, they can be viewed as the preserve of an uncontaminated inner nature that could be investigated as a way of deciphering a utopian form of life beyond the (repressive) reality principle.[6]

In this book, I will not be particularly interested in criticizing Marcuse's romantic search for an uncorrupted first nature. Rather, I will be concerned with interrogating the notion of utopia itself, insofar as it has been formulated with psychoanalytic categories. The events of the past several decades, indeed the events of the century, have engendered a suspicion of omnipotence and grandiosity in political life and a new respect for finitude in all of us. Reading *Eros and Civilization* in this context—and knowing what psychoanalysis has learned about narcissism in the years since it was written—what emerges as objectionable is not its naiveté, recklessness, or impracticality but its hubris. Whereas Freud sought to devise a scheme for mastering omnipotence and coming to terms[7] with our finitude, Marcuse still wanted to escape it. This is the deep point of contention between them.

Nevertheless, having criticized Marcuse, we will still have to inquire into the fate of the utopian impulse—which will exist as long as humans continue to dream[8]—after the critique of utopianism. This question is virtually absent from recent Critical Theory and will comprise a central concern of this book. It will, in turn, lead us to a reconsideration of the concept of sublimation, a concept that has, for reasons we will examine, fallen into disuse in recent years.

Narcissism is another topic we will repeatedly encounter in our investigations. Freud himself admitted that he was uneasy with, and had little aptitude for, the archaic layers of the psyche but nevertheless recognized the existence of a narcissistic-preoedipal period of development—which he compared to the "Minoan-Mycenean civilization" that was unearthed "behind" the oedipal civilization of classical Greece[9]—and predicted that it would become a major focus of psychoanalytic research. He also speculated that women analysts might be better suited than himself for exploring these archaic strata of psychic life. He turned out to be more or less correct on both counts, for it could easily be argued that the major discoveries in psychoanalysis since Freud's death have been made in the Minoan-Mycenean realm of narcissistic-preoedipal development, and many of them were indeed made by women, specifically, Melanie Klein and Margaret Mahler. In a landmark article written in 1978, which attempts to assess the ramifications of these discoveries for classical psychoanalytic theory, Hans Loewald has pointed to two meanings of the phrase, "the waning of the Oedipus complex," namely, the weakening of oedipal structures in contemporary society and the "decline of psychoanalytic interest in the oedipal phase and oedipal conflicts and the predominance of interest in research in preoedipal development, in the infant-mother dyad and issues of separation-individuation and of the self and narcissism."[10] We examine the connection between the two meanings below.

Whereas Freud tended to view narcissism in a predominantly negative light—as the opponent of object love and reality testing and as a source of severe psychopathology[11]—recent psychoanalytic research has given us a more differentiated picture of this thoroughly ambivalent phenomenon. With respect to its malignant side, the research into early development has perhaps shifted the focus of psychoanalytically oriented social theory. While our predecessors in the field were primarily concerned with the challenge that the death drive and aggression posed for social theory,[12] a topic that, to be sure, continues to be a focus of interest, the problem of omnipotence has assumed a new centrality in recent discussions, because of our greater attunement to the narcissistic register. For example, any psychoanalytically oriented discussion of democracy must address the question of how that omnipotence can be decentered in order to foster a democratic character. At the same time as we have become increasingly aware of the dangers of omnipotence and grandiosity, Hans Loewald has pointed to the other side of "the waning of the oedipus complex":

The more we understand about primitive mentality, which constitutes a deep layer of advanced mentality, the harder it becomes to escape the idea that its implicit sense of and quest for irrational nondifferentiation of subject and object contains *a truth of its own,* granted that this other truth fits badly with our rational world view and quest for objectivity.[13] (emphasis added)

An important element in the dramatic and unexpected resurgence of religion in the last two decades in both the developed

countries and the developing world, as well as in the more recent
reappearance of militant nationalism, is the failure of modern, secular, and increasingly atomistic society to meet adequately the striving
"for unity, symbiosis, fusion, merging, or identification" that was formerly satisfied by religion.[14]

Habermas, in contrast to Marcuse, contests the totalizing monism
of *Dialectic of Enlightenment.* In opposition to Horkheimer and
Adorno, who see history developing only in the dimension of instrumentalization—the development of rationality and of the subject are
two complementary aspects of that process—Habermas introduced
the second dimension of intersubjective communication. The theoretico-political ramifications of this innovation were manifold. Because it allowed him to conceptualize forms of rationality and
identity that were not altogether violent—that is, were not altogether
corrupt—Habermas did not have to embark on a search for the good
Other of instrumental reason and the autocratic subject. (The unconscious and the drives, therefore, did not have to fulfill that function in his interpretation of Freud.) Similarly, because the
distinction between instrumental and communicative reason allowed
him to clarify the moral, legal, and democratizing advances of modernity, Habermas was able to counteract the Weberian antimodernism and concomitant political quietism of the Frankfurt school. The
recognition of certain universal normative principles in modernity,
he argued, makes it unnecessary to look outside the structure of the
modern world for the standards of critique. Indeed, contrary to the
dire assessments of *Dialectic of Enlightenment* and *One Dimensional
Man,* Habermas maintained that, as a result of the recognition of
those principles, immanent critique became significantly more prac-
ticable in modern society than it had been in any form of premodern, traditional society.[15] The idea that eventually emerged as the
centerpiece of Habermas's labyrinthine enterprise in the late seventies, and that continues to play that role, is the defense of "the project of modernity."[16] Everything turns, of course, on what one takes
that project to be.

These innovations were not without their price. While it avoids the
impasse of the early Frankfurt school, the Habermasian turn, as has
often been noted, also results in a certain domestication of Critical

Theory; the utopian or redemptive moment (as well as the bodily dimension) seems to have been lost completely. To put the problem differently: Habermas has effected a necessary and salutary encounter with liberalism—for which Horkheimer and Adorno had a deep aversion—within Critical Theory. After its working through of liberalism, however, the question arises whether Critical Theory has anything distinct to offer beyond the liberal program. Or has it simply come to represent one position on the left wing of the liberal spectrum?[17] In that case, the only thing that would distinguish Habermas from Rawls, for example, would be their *strategies* for justifying the basic principles of liberalism; the underlying vision would itself be basically the same. In other words, in what sense, if any, can the distinction between Traditional and Critical Theory be maintained today?

Habermas's general domestication of Critical Theory is duplicated in his deradicalization of what was perhaps Freud's most subversive discovery, the unconscious—or the psychic imaginary, as Cornelius Castoriadis has called it. An emphatic notion of the unconscious constituted an encumbrance to Habermas's program in two respects. First, as I will try to demonstrate, a nonlinguistic or prelinguistic unconscious, which Freud went so far as to call "the core of our being,"[18] would constitute an obstacle to Habermas's linguistifying program. As it does for Jacques Lacan, the linguistic turn also requires a linguistification of the unconscious for Habermas. I would add, moreover, that Habermas's later move from psychoanalysis to the nondynamic, cognitivist learning theory of Jean Piaget and Lawrence Kohlberg was already anticipated by the evisceration of the unconscious in *Knowledge and Human Interests*. Second, insofar as Habermas sought to correct the thoroughgoing antiprogressivism of Horkheimer and Adorno by elucidating the advances of modernity, the unconscious, in all its admittedly unsettling regressiveness, presented a problem for his program as well. As we shall see, this too helps to explain the turn to the tidier theories of Piaget and Kohlberg. Habermas believed that their formal learning schemes would enable him to demonstrate the sort of progress he was seeking. The transgressive phantasms of the unconscious, however, not only are a source of regression but also provide the *imagos* of a different reality.

Whereas Marcuse wanted to translate those imagos into social reality in too direct a fashion, Habermas seems to have deprived himself of access to them almost completely.

This is especially unfortunate given that today we are witnessing an "atrophy of the political imagination" [19] on a massive scale. At the same time as we have become reticent about utopian speculation, developments in various regions of the world—from the countries of the Southern Hemisphere to the North Atlantic community, from the Far East to the former Soviet Union—seem to be surging ahead without a vision to inform them. At best, technocratic planners in Brussels and elsewhere try to steer the course of development to ensure the conditions of stable economic growth while avoiding crises of catastrophic proportions. At worst, the most ominous elements of the past rush in to fill the void. [20] For this reason, and others, I am suggesting that a renewed encounter with psychoanalysis can be fruitful for Critical Theory at this juncture.

I would submit, moreover, that a reexamination of Freud's *mode* of defending "the project of modernity" can also prove instructive in counterbalancing the excessive formalism and rationalism of the Habermasian approach. It has often been observed that the distinctive power and fascination of Freud's enterprise results, in no small part, from its synthesis of rationalism and irrationalism, of the Enlightenment and romantic traditions. [21] (Romanticism has led a contrapuntal existence within the Enlightenment since its inception.) Thus, to be sure, Freud was, as Albrecht Wellmer has observed, "still a representative of European rationalism and the Enlightenment," who ultimately sought to strengthen "the power of reason and the power of the Ego." [22] But he also sought to do justice to the Other of reason—to give the horse its due, to use one of his favorite metaphors. Hence the romantic element in his thinking. Indeed, even further, Freud sought to strengthen rationality and the ego precisely through a deep and sustained encounter with the Other of reason, namely, with the unconscious, dreams, taboos, perversions, symptoms, *Thanatos,* narcissism, psychosis, and so on. That is what the regressive experience of the transference neurosis is all about. In this endeavor, Freud was pursuing a program, initiated by Hegel, of "exploring the irrational and [integrating] it into an expanded reason." Maurice Merleau-Ponty's observation that "this remains the task of our century" is as correct today as when he made it in 1946, despite the deformities of the Hegelian system and the decline of Hegel's philosophical fortunes vis-à-vis Nietzsche's over the past several decades.[23]

Habermas too subscribes to this Hegelian program. In fact, he believes that his own theory of communicative action, which consists in a reinterpretation of the central intuitions of German Idealism in terms of an intersubjective theory of communication, at last provides the means of fulfilling it.[24] I will attempt to show, however, that, while his programmatic intentions are essentially correct, he, in fact, rationalistically short-circuits reason's communication with its Other. As a result, Habermas—the communications theorist par excellence—ironically proffers a limited conception of communication. He therefore loses the element of tension between romanticism and Enlightenment that gave Freud's defense of "the project of modernity" its complexity and appeal. As I have already indicated, one place where these deficiencies are particularly apparent is in Habermas's original rationalizing *qua* linguistifying interpretation of psychoanalysis, which we will examine in detail, and his eventual retreat from psychoanalysis to cognitivist learning theory. Indeed, for many it was a sad day in Frankfurt when Lawrence Kohlberg replaced Sigmund Freud as a *Bildungsmacht* of Critical Theory.[25]

These considerations point to a curious phenomenon in Habermas's career. In his controversies with Karl Popper, Hans-Georg Gadamer, and Niklaus Luhmann, Habermas was exemplary in fulfilling the Hegelian injunction to enter into the strength of an opponent's position; he learned extensively from these debates, and, in each case, his position was markedly altered as a result. However, in his encounters with poststructuralism, postmodernism, and what he calls the Counter-Enlightenment *(Gegenaufklärung)* in general, his position has remained conspicuously external to theirs. Unlike Adorno, who at times is separated from the Counter-Enlightenment by only a hair's breadth[26]—and for whom Nietzsche constituted a central figure on the same *niveau* as Kant and Hegel—Habermas seems to have difficulty identifying with the deeper and often darker impulses that animate the poststructuralist project. As a result, he continually withdraws to the level of formal argumentation to defend "the project of modernity." Again and again, Habermas translates the old logical argument—that the relativist skeptic is involved in a self-referential contradiction—into communicative terms and attempts to demonstrate that his Counter-Enlightenment adversary is guilty of a "performative contradiction." But, as Adorno already recognized, such a procedure leaves "the fiber of relativistic thinking more and more untouched."[27] The formal refutation, in short, possesses an air of emptiness and also prevents Habermas from more fully enrolling "all the reactionary arguments against Western culture in the service of progressive enlightenment."[28]

In relation to his latter-day Nietzschean opponents, Habermas appears to repeat the difficulties that another Kantian, Heinrich Rickert, had in defeating the existentialism and *Lebensphilosophie* of his day. Indeed, Gadamer's explanation of Rickert's inability "to come anywhere near the influence of Nietzsche and Dilthey," despite the formal validity of his arguments, could be applied to Habermas's difficulties with the poststructuralists:

Thus the question arises of the degree to which the dialectical superiority of reflective philosophy corresponds to a factual truth and how far it merely creates a formal appearance. . . . However clearly one demonstrates the inner contradictions of all relativist views, it is as Heidegger has said: all these victorious arguments have something about them that suggests they are attempting to bowl one over.[29]

Because Habermas's arguments do not establish adequate contact with the "fiber" of the Counter-Enlightenment position, his better arguments often do not carry enough force.

The appeal of poststructuralism and postmodernism in this context is twofold. Their greater affinity for the irrational and transgressive speaks to and is, at the same time, a symptom of the widespread sense of irrationality, of generalized groundlessness, that permeates contemporary life. Stanley Rosen has observed that "Postmodernism is the Enlightenment gone mad,"[30] by which I take him to mean the following: the Enlightenment, propelled in part by the dynamic of capitalist development, initiated a relentless critique of all empirically existing norms. That critique was itself predicated on a specific conviction, namely, that the ground of that critique could be provided and that norms could be reestablished on a nondogmatic basis. If, however, that conviction proves false and the process of critique cannibalizes its own foundations, as it does in postmodernism—if, in other words, all that is solid melts into air with nothing to replace it—then the madness to which Rosen refers is the result.[31] Whatever the philosophical merits of discourse ethics, it is not clear that Habermas's defense of modernity in predominately formal and procedural terms has enough bite to address the anxieties associated with the general slide into groundlessness. To take one example, the institutionalization of formal procedures, however essential, means little if the (affective) commitment, the political will, to enforce them is lacking; the fact that enlightened Europe can again tolerate genocide on its continent only fifty years after the Holocaust gives one pause to wonder about the depth of its own resolve.[32]

The other side of the appeal of poststructuralism and postmodernism is more positive. Let us not forget, after all, that the radicality, vitality, and exhilaration of modernist culture resulted in large part from its unprecedented exploration of the irrational and the transgressive, which became possible after the closures of classical bourgeois art and the rigidly integrated ego were breached. And poststructuralism, whose identifications lie more with aesthetic modernism than with the normative advances of the Enlightenment, retains a certain advantage in the controversy with Critical Theory, insofar as it has attempted to continue this aspect of the project of the avant-garde. To be sure, aesthetic modernism is assigned its place in the Habermasian tripartite schematization of the modern worldview (in the aesthetic-expressive realm).[33] But unlike Walter Benjamin or Theodor Adorno, who had the experience of the Berlin and Viennese avant-garde behind them respectively, Habermas's manner of theorizing is not informed in any fundamental way by the impulses of aesthetic modernism. For understandable historical reasons, he is apprehensive about the regressive potential of the transgressive and the aestheticization of politics, and he seeks to contain them within his formal construction. While he may avoid the dangers of the irrational and transgressive to the extent that he isolates himself from them, his project is, I will argue, depleted to the same extent. From the other side, if Habermas tends to isolate himself from the transgressive, poststructuralism—which enshrines "the 'black' writers of the bourgeoisie,"[34] such as Nietzsche, Sade, Artaud, and Bataille, in its pantheon—tends to *idealize* it in the tradition of the *poète maudit*. In this case, the tension between romanticism and the Enlightenment, which is characteristic of Freud, is also collapsed, but in the opposite direction. Again, I shall argue that sublimation represents a third alternative to the romantic idealization of the irrational and the rationalist isolation from it.

Freud represents something of a test case for both prongs of the postmodern attack on the Enlightenment—the critique of reason and the critique of the subject. The question is, does Freud's skeptical defense of the Enlightenment result in a strengthened—that is, a more comprehensive and more flexible—notion of reason and the subject, as Wellmer maintains? Or does it release unintended consequences that ultimately overwhelm rationality and the ego, as the postmoderns, who read Freud against himself, contend?

With respect to the psychoanalytic critique of reason, it can be argued that Freud provides if not lethal, at least powerful new weapons to the skeptic's armamentarium. The relevant concept in this context is the Freudian notion of distortion *(Entstellung)*. After Freud's demonstration of the pervasive and systematic distortions that the past, the unconscious, and transference—or desire and power, if one wants to use that vocabulary—inevitably cause in conscious mental life (and language), including the mental life (and language) of the psychoanalyst, it becomes virtually impossible to retain the aspiration that reason might achieve the purity that first philosophy, from Parmenides through Kant to Husserl, had demanded of it. It becomes apparent, in other words, that a degree of distortion and contamination are uneliminable from rationality.[35] In a move that remains strangely loyal to the purist requirements of first philosophy, if only in the breach, Freud's demonstration of the inevitability of distortion is regularly adduced to invalidate reason as such. There is, however, another possibility, namely, to contest those purist requirements themselves. And here Freud can be of service by providing a psychological account of the wish for purity. Although this account does not have the status of a strict philosophical argument, it can nevertheless serve a "therapeutic" function in working through the end of metaphysics. Freud undoubtedly had something like this in mind when he spoke of transforming "*metaphysics* into *metapsychology*."[36] And, in conjunction with this softening of the demand for purity, a theory of sublimation can serve to explain how the genetic factors, which are the source of distortion, can be transformed so that distortion is overcome to a satisfactory degree. I will attempt to show, in other words, that a theory of sublimation can provide an account of the relation between genesis and validity, which can avoid the traps of both an unattainable idealistic purism and a self-destructing genealogical reductionism.

The claim that Freud was opposed to the Enlightenment ideal of an autonomous individual and was a champion of the decentered and split subject has become an article of the postmodern catechism. As far as the decentered subject is concerned, this claim can only be maintained by ignoring the distinction between two forms of decentration. The first is the Piagetian, in which decentration refers to the process through which children's egocentrism is dislodged and they are compelled to reorient themselves in a world of multiple perspectives. Far from being opposed to enlightenment and autonomy, coming to terms with the relativity of one's viewpoint contributes to, indeed, is an essential precondition for, their achievement. The second form of decentration is the structuralist and poststructuralist model. Decentration in this case refers to the reduction of the ego to an effect of a more basic phenomenon—for example, the unconscious, *la langue,* power, and so on—which operates behind its back. The intention in this case is not to strengthen the ego but to disparage it as an epiphenomenon, deluded about its actual power.

Freud is a proponent of decentration in the first, Piagetian, sense of the term. What he adds to the basically cognitive, Piagetian account of the shift from egocentrism is the affective component—the displacement of infantile narcissism. Somewhat paradoxically perhaps, decentering in this sense actually strengthens the ego by making it more reflective, flexible, and autonomous. Let us not forget that the fantasied strength of the narcissistic register, omnipotence, is in fact a defensive sham.

The claim that Freud propounded the theory that the human subject is essentially split is even more problematic. For Freud, as David Macey correctly points out, "the splitting of the ego and the disturbance of its synthetic function" are symptoms resulting from the defensive struggle against "a powerful but prohibited instinctual demand." Contrary to Lacan's claim, "at no point does Freud imply that splitting is a characteristic of human subjectivity as such."[37] We shall see, moreover, that Freud explicitly states that the goal of psychoanalytic treatment is to heal those splits and to restore or, better yet, to enlarge, the unity of the ego to the greatest extent possible. That enlargement occurs through the facilitation of the ego's communication with, and integration of, all the instinctual forces it was previously forced to ward off. This is not to deny the existence of disturbances of the synthetic function and pathological forms of unification, such as one finds in obsessive-compulsive neurosis and paranoia. But this is precisely the point: these are *disturbances* and not intrinsic aspects of the ego's synthetic function.

Critics of the ego, like Adorno and Lacan, prompted by a philosophical suspicion of synthesis, tend to hypostatize pathological, rigidified forms of ego formation into the ego as such. As a result, they are left only with a choice between two poisons, namely, violent unification or no unification at all. The alternative is, as I have already suggested, to attempt to conceptualize nonviolent forms of ego synthesis. We shall see that there are already quite detailed suggestions along these lines in Freud himself, if one examines *Inhibitions, Symptoms, and Anxiety,* a text that is rarely discussed these days, rather than the posthumous, fragmentary, inconclusive, and overworked "Splitting of the Ego in the Process of Defense."

The stakes in the controversy over the narcissistic genesis of the ego are high; indeed, it raises the question of whether the center will hold. That is the reason it has figured so prominently in the postmodern critique of the subject. Just as, empirically, the bourgeois faith in reason and progress collapsed in the trenches of World War I, so, theoretically, did the distinctions that made that faith tenable threaten to collapse into an undifferentiated "night . . . in which all cows are black"[38] when Freud introduced the concept of narcissism into psychoanalytic theory in 1914. When the ego "found its position among the sexual objects,"[39] as it did in "On Narcissism," it became increasingly difficult, if not impossible, for Freud to maintain the distinction between the sexual instincts and the ego instincts. The philosophical import of that difficulty is immense: if the distinction between the sexual and the ego instincts cannot be maintained, then the ego, the presumed subject of reason, is reduced to the status of one natural object among many. This would mean, in turn, that the distinctions between reason and its Other, between the knowing subject and its object—which are absolutely necessary in some form if a notion of scientific rationality, however it is conceived, is to be maintained—would be in danger of being lost as well. One's faith in scientific objectivity and progress (as well as autonomous action) would, at that point, become indefensible.

Let me be clear. I do not mean to imply that the Enlightenment's concept of autonomy is acceptable as it stands. Indeed, one of the closures of the Enlightenment that most requires criticism is the Kantian conceptualization of autonomy.[40] For Kant, autonomy is achieved through the suppression of heteronomous desire, that is to say, the repression of inner nature. And it is indeed possible to construe Freud, and especially certain strands of ego psychology, as Kantian in this sense. Put in psychoanalytic terms, this would mean that the autonomy of the ego is established by its dissociation from and repression of—to use Foucault's term, "confinement" of—the id.

On this reading of Freud, which is more or less that of the early Frankfurt school and poststructuralism, the autonomous ego would indeed stand condemned of rigidity, constriction, violence, and repression. And given such an indictment, moreover, the valorization of perversion as the representative of the heteronomous drives, as the good Other of the repressive ego, does indeed become plausible. There is, however, another way to read Freud in which autonomy is construed in exactly the opposite manner. In this case, autonomy is not achieved through the repression of inner nature but, on the contrary, through the maximization of "free intercourse"[41] with it. As Castoriadis argues, autonomy, far from comprising a "power grab" by the ego, would consist in *another relation* between the conscious and the unconscious, between lucidity and the function of the imaginary, in *another attitude* of the subject with respect to himself or herself, in a profound modification of the activity-passivity mix, of the sign under which this takes place, of the respective place of the two elements that compose it. . . . Desire, drives—whether it is Eros or Thanatos—this is me, too, and these have to be brought not only to consciousness but to expression and existence. An autonomous subject is one that knows itself to be justified in concluding: this is indeed true, and: this is indeed my desire.[42]

Habermas also toyed with a more robust notion of autonomy when he considered adding a seventh stage to Kohlberg's scheme of moral development, in which inner nature would be brought into relatively unfettered communication with the ego. But, for systematic reasons that we will examine in detail, he eventually backed away from this position.

My reexamination of the concepts of decentration, splitting, and autonomy should be situated in their larger political context. The controversies over the psychoanalytic theory of the ego are obviously part of the broader controversy concerning the modern subject, initiated, to a large extent, by Heidegger's philosophy. Recently, with the renewed appreciation of democracy, thinkers in the Heideggerian tradition have found themselves in an embarrassing dilemma. One the one hand, they feel compelled—undoubtedly because of Heidegger's dubious political credentials—to support the democratizing movements that are struggling for recognition throughout the world and that are perhaps the last refuge for progressive politics after the demise of socialism. On the other hand, because of their critique of the subject (and of rationality), the neo-Heideggerians have deprived themselves of the theoretical resources necessary to support these movements consistently. They are therefore compelled, for example, to try to extract a theory of democracy from the concepts of difference and otherness alone.

Luc Ferry and Alain Renaut have perceived the situation clearly. They argue that because Heidegger viewed the technological domination of the globe, which he took as the essential feature of modernity, as the inescapable outcome of modern subjectivity—because he equated subjectivity with the will to power—he was forced to condemn subjectivity in general. Modernity, however, consists not only in the tendency toward omnipotent domination but in another, equally fundamental tendency in the opposite direction, namely, toward democratization and the critique of omnipotence itself. But as a result of its blanket rejection of the subject, Heidegger's criticism of modernity is "radically incompatible with the minimum of *subjectivity* needed for *democratic* thinking, in whatever form we conceive it." Ferry and Renaut therefore pose the following question to the neo-Heideggerians: "In short, how can we think democracy without imputing to man the minimal will and mastery that Heidegger denies him because will and mastery in some sense already contain the seeds of the world of technology conceived of as the 'will to will'?" They argue that if the idea of democracy is to have any meaning, it requires a conception of subjectivity in which "human beings" are understood, to the minimally requisite degree, as "the authors of the choices they make, or should make, in common." They do not mean to suggest, however, that we should return to "the idea that man is the owner and controller of the whole of his actions and ideas." Such a return is not only "dangerous," because of the salutary effect the decentering of the subject has had on tempering our grandiosity and omnipotence, but impossible "after Marx, Nietzsche, Freud and Heidegger."[43] The real task for the contemporary theorist, according to Ferry and Renaut, is not to "coolly [deconstruct] subjectivity" but to "rethink the subject" after its critique.[44] One of the central aims of this book is to use the resources of psychoanalytic theory to contribute to this effort.

Finally, it is not only the case that Critical Theory has retreated from psychoanalysis over the past two decades. It is also the case that analysts themselves—who have, for understandable reasons, become increasingly preoccupied with clinical questions concerning the so-called widening scope of psychoanalysis—have evinced little interest in the broader cultural issues that had fascinated Freud and earlier generations of analysts. Indeed, in the past, these issues were not simply relegated to the more peripheral status of applied analysis but were seen to be essential pillars of the psychoanalytic enterprise. It is my hope, therefore, that this book will not only contribute to the revitalization of the psychoanalytic dimension of Critical Theory but will help to rekindle an interest in social and cultural theory within psychoanalysis as well.

1

"I Can Offer Them No Consolation": Freud's Ambivalent Critique of Civilization

Freud, Horkheimer, Adorno and the Critique of Civilization

While Freud has come to be viewed as the unwavering partisan of civilization, indeed, as the virtual incarnation of "phallogocentrism" itself, an examination of a crucial passage in *Civilization and Its Discontents* reveals how skeptical he could be:

> For a wide variety of reasons, it is very far from my intention to express an opinion upon the value of human civilization. I have endeavored to guard myself against the enthusiastic prejudice which holds that our civilization is the most precious thing that we possess or could acquire and that its path will necessarily lead to heights of unimagined perfection. I can at least listen without indignation to the critic who is of the opinion that when one surveys the aims of cultural endeavor and the means it employs, one is bound to come to the conclusion that the whole effort is not worth the trouble, and that the outcome of it can only be a state of affairs which the individual will be unable to tolerate. My impartiality is made all the easier to me by my knowing very little about all these things. . . . I have not the courage to rise up before my fellow-men as a prophet, and I bow to their reproach that I can offer them no consolation.[1]

This skepticism with respect to the value of civilization is consistent with the thoroughly materialistic, immanentist, and disillusioned account Freud gives of its function: the domination of external and internal nature. In the first instance, civilization includes "all the knowledge and capacity that men have acquired in order to control the forces of nature and extract its wealth for the satisfaction of human needs." Secondly, as "every individual is virtually an enemy of civilization," owing to the instinctual (especially aggressive) character of his or her inner nature, "civilization has to be defended against the individual, and its regulations, institutions and commands are directed to that task."[2] A major function of social institutions is, in short, to regulate inner nature, either through direct "measures of coercion" or "other measures that are intended to reconcile men to [civilization] and to recompense them for their sacrifices."[3] And, in one of his most Marxian remarks, Freud notes that "the two trends of civilization are not independent of each other,"[4] that is, the level of material progress determines, to an extent, the range of possibilities for instinctual gratification and the institutions necessary for regulating them in a given society.

Despite the carnage of the First World War, 1930 was perhaps still too early a date to entertain seriously an unequivocally negative verdict on the value of civilization and to undertake a search for an alternative, whatever that might mean. Moreover, like Max Weber, who argued there was no acceptable alternative to the "iron cage" of modernity, Freud was skeptical about the possibility of finding a nonregressive alternative to civilization: "But how ungrateful, how short-sighted after all, to strive for the abolition of civilization! What would then remain would be a state of nature and that would be far harder to bear."[5] Any alternative that could be envisioned would necessarily be more costly than the high price of civilization that Freud himself had done so much to document.

Some fifteen years after the publication of *Civilization and Its Discontents*, however, the situation had changed so dramatically that it became increasingly plausible to argue not only that "the whole effort is not worth the trouble" but that the continued development, if not of civilization in general, at least of modernity, could in fact prove calamitous; the very enormity of the events made the search for an extreme solution at least theoretically entertainable. It could be maintained that fascism, Stalinism, total war, the Holocaust and the bomb (and later the ecological crisis), far from representing transient historical aberrations, resulted from the innermost dynamics of civilization itself. The conclusion was drawn in certain circles—on the Right as well as on the Left—that nothing short of a radical reevaluation of the premises of civilization would be commensurate with the crisis that had befallen Western modernity and adequate for formulating a solution to it. It became at least plausible to argue that, given the totalized nature of the crisis, nothing short of an equally totalized solution, a holistic transfiguration of civilization itself, would work. And indeed one wonders what Freud's attitude would have been had he lived to witness the events of the Second World War.

Interestingly, the basis for a distinction between the radical reformer, who accepts the basic structure of civilization and rebels against particular injustices *within* it, and the transfigurative utopian, who rebels against civilization *as a whole,* can already be found in Freud. In *Civilization and Its Discontents* he makes the following observation:

The liberty of the individual is no gift of civilization. It was greatest before there was any civilization, though then, it is true, it had for the most part no value, since the individual was scarcely in a position to defend it. The development of civilization imposes restrictions on it and justice demands that no one shall escape those restrictions. What makes itself felt in a human community as a desire for freedom may be the revolt against some existing injustice, and so may prove favorable to a further development of civilization; it may remain compatible with civilization.

He goes on to consider the transfigurative utopian: "But it may also spring from the remains of the original personality, which is still untamed by civilization and may thus become the basis in them of hostility to civilization. The urge for freedom, therefore, is directed against particular forms and demands of civilization or against civilization as such."[6] That Freud traces the urge to transgress the fundamental strictures of civilization to "the remains of the original personality," that is, to perverse impulses, is consistent with both his theory of perversion as the atavistic continuation of infantile sexuality into adult life and his account of the origins of civilization.

In *Totem and Taboo* he had argued that the primal murder and its sequelae, which constitute the founding acts of civilization, result in an arrangement of renunciation that provides civilization with its basic structure. The entire episode culminates, in a thoroughly Hobbesian manner,[7] in the social contract between the brothers through which they mutually renounce the right to full expression of their sexual and aggressive drives in return for the benefits of civilized social life. The central renunciations of the social contract are simultaneously the two taboos of totemism and the two prohibitions of the Oedipus complex, that is, the prohibitions against incest and patricide. The establishment of these prohibitions is, for Freud, the constitutive act through which a law-governed social world is created, namely, the oedipally structured social ontology of civilization. The first type of rebel, then, who revolts "against some existing injustice," basically accepts the oedipally structured world of mutual renunciations and only objects to the fact that the burden of these renunciations is not distributed equitably. He or she seeks to reform civilization, in the name of justice, from within its basic structure. The second type, on the other hand, the transfigurative utopian, rejects the entire oedipally structured framework itself. He or she does not seek a more equitable distribution of renunciations but, rather, an end to the system of renunciation altogether.

In their main work of the forties, *Dialectic of Enlightenment,* which was to become the magnum opus of the first generation of Critical Theory, the social theorists of the Frankfurt school undertook the radical reevaluation of civilization from which Freud had abstained. The Critical Theorists had concluded that their analysis, which had been essentially Marxian, albeit of a very esoteric sort, had to be radicalized to fathom all that had happened. For Horkheimer and Adorno, this radicalization consisted in a move from the more traditional critique of political economy to the critique of the domination of nature and instrumental reason. In a manner not dissimilar from their arch nemesis on the Right, Heidegger, they sought to trace the crisis of the twentieth century not merely to the dynamics of capitalist development but to the project of Western Enlightenment, which had begun when the Greeks first attempted to replace *mythos* with *Logos,* indeed when the concept was first separated from the object.

The question that Horkheimer and Adorno posed themselves was the following: how was it that the process of Enlightenment and the conquest of nature, which, according to both the liberal and the Marxian traditions, were intended to emancipate humanity from centuries-old bondage, had resulted in a new and historically unprecedented form of barbarism? They answered that although the entire modern tradition, from Bacon to Marx, agreed that the mastery of the external environment and the creation of sufficient social wealth was at least a necessary precondition for the betterment of humanity's estate, it had failed to realize one crucial point: namely, that humanity had to dominate its own inner nature in order to undertake the domination of external nature. And the analysis of the domination of inner nature provided the point of entrée for the systematic incorporation of Freud's thinking into Critical Theory.

To carry out the conquest of the material environment, Horkheimer and Adorno maintained that human beings had to transform themselves into disciplined, purposive agents and society into a totally bureaucratized and administered system. As we will see, they identify the unity of the "autocratic" ego with the unity of instrumental reason (or "identity thinking") and argue that both impose an abstract, forced unification on the heterogeneous, the different, and the Other. Toward the inside, the autocratic ego represses the polymorphous perversity of the individual's instinctual makeup to forge a unified self. And toward the outside, the same ego imposes instrumental reason on the particularity and diffuseness of external nature to control and manipulate it. This double process of domination *qua* unification issues in a central thesis of the book: the reification of external nature and the reification of internal nature mutually entail each other: "The subjective spirit which cancels the animation of nature can master a despiritualized nature only by imitating its rigidity and despiritualizing itself in turn."[8] The problem is, then, that the entire process is self-vitiating: to the extent that the conquest of external nature has been completed—and the presumed objective conditions for human emancipation thereby created, as Horkheimer and Adorno (as well as Marcuse) rather naively assumed they had been by mid-twentieth century—the human subject has been so deformed and reified in the process that it cannot appropriate the fruits of its own labor: "With the denial of nature in man not merely the *telos* of the outward control of nature but the *telos* of man's own life is distorted and befogged."[9] The domination of inner nature, which was supposed to provide a means to human emancipation, ultimately makes that emancipation impossible. It would seem, on the basis of the logic of Horkheimer and Adorno's totalized diagnosis, then, that only the utopian transfiguration of civilization could provide a solution. Like Freud and Weber, however, they could not envision any alternatives to civilization whose regressive features were not more disturbing than the given historical prospects themselves. For the Critical Theorists the only escape from this fateful logic was to be found in esoteric works of art and philosophy—nothing with a more encompassing social trajectory could be located in the current historical setting. This was the impasse that Horkheimer and Adorno bequeathed Critical Theory, an impasse to which each subsequent Critical Theorist has had to respond in his or her own way.

Eros and Civilization Reconsidered

Eros and Civilization represents an attempt on Marcuse's part to break the deadlock of *Dialectic of Enlightenment* by playing the utopian gambit, which Horkheimer and Adorno refused to play, at the level of the book's psychoanalytic stratum.[10] Marcuse subscribed to the thesis that the barbaric events of this century were not transient historical aberrations but resulted from the internal and totalizing logic of modern civilization:

Throughout the world of industrial civilization, the domination of man by man is growing in scope and efficiency. Nor does this trend appear as an accidental, transitory regression on the road to progress. Concentration camps, mass exterminations, world wars and atom bombs are no 'relapse into barbarism,' but the unrepressed implementation of the achievements of modern science, technology and domination.[11]

At the same time, however, writing in the economically booming but spiritually puerile fifties, and in line with *Dialectic of Enlightenment,* he also believed that all significant oppositional forces had been efficiently neutralized through their absorption into a seamlessly running system in which a preestablished harmony existed between artificially generated needs and the consumeristic fulfillment of those needs so that domination was not even experienced as domination. Short of an economic collapse, which was unforeseeable, this absorption could apparently continue indefinitely. Indeed, the fact that *Eros and Civilization,* the most utopian of Marcuse's major works, was written at a time when the possibilities of meaningful political action appeared at their lowest is one instance of the not uncommon connection between utopian speculation and political despair. (Another is, of course, the conjunction of a negative philosophy of history with messianism in the work of Walter Benjamin.)

Eros and Civilization's stated intentions are purely theoretical, namely, to contribute "to the *philosophy* of psychoanalysis,"[12] by demonstrating the theoretical possibility of "a nonrepressive civilization, based on a fundamentally different experience of being, a fundamentally different relation between man and nature, and fundamentally different existential relations."[13] It could not, however, locate any empirical dynamics moving in that direction. At most, Marcuse could only point to the tension caused by the discrepancy between the current repressive reality and the potential for "a qualitatively different, nonrepressive reality principle"[14] which had been created by the scientific and technological achievements of civilization itself.

It was only after the political explosions of the sixties that *Eros and Civilization* was discovered as a major text for the self-understanding of the utopian movements that had sprung up. During the heady exuberance of those days, moreover, Marcuse himself began to treat the speculative ideas of *Eros and Civilization* as the basis for a concrete political program. Declaring that utopia had ended as a "noplace," as a mere phantasm, he argued it could now be achieved as a historical reality.[15] Using strictly Marxian arguments against the Marxian critique of utopia, he maintained that, contrary to Marx's prediction, the forces of production had matured under capitalism, rather than under socialism, to the point where an eschatological break in the continuum of history had become possible. What had formerly been considered a purely idealist utopian society could, therefore, be realistically placed on the historical agenda. This being the case, Marcuse, in language that resonated with the slogans of May, 1968, called for a move from Marx back to Fourier, and from socialist realism to socialist surrealism.[16] In one of the final paroxysms of Marxian-Enlightenment hubris, Marcuse proclaimed that "today any form of the concrete world, of human life, any transformation of the technical and natural environment is a possibility." For him, only "the total mobilization of existing society against its own potential for liberation" prevented that possibility from being actualized in a progressive direction.[17] And he derived the concrete filling for that utopia from his investigations in psychoanalysis.

Like the poststructuralist and feminist appropriators of Freud who came after him, Marcuse sought to uncover a "hidden trend in psychoanalysis"[18] that would undo Freud's pessimistic and paternalistic liberalism. In *Eros and Civilization,* he attempts to demonstrate that "Freud's own theory provides reasons for rejecting his identification of civilization with repression,"[19] in the hope of dissolving the seemingly immutable opposition between the instinctually embodied individual and society. Such a demonstration would have refuted, at least in principle, the self-vitiating logic of civilization as Freud described it in *Civilization and Its Discontents* and as Adorno and Horkheimer took it over in *Dialectic of Enlightenment.* Marcuse's strategy is to historicize Freud's notion of the reality principle, to show that the reality principle, at least today, is mostly a matter of convention. Against Freud, who maintains that the (repressive) reality principle is by *physis,* that is, transhistorical and intrinsic to the human condition, Marcuse argues that it is historically contingent and therefore mutable: "Freud . . . believes that the pleasure principle and reality principle are 'eternally' antagonistic. The notion that a nonrepressive civilization is impossible is a cornerstone of Freudian theory."[20] Freud therefore hypostatizes "a specific historical *form* of civilization as the *nature* of civilization."[21]

To make his case, Marcuse introduces two correlated sets of distinctions: between the reality principle and the performance principle, on the one hand, and between necessary repression and surplus repression, on the other. Regarding the first, Marcuse admits there is a transhistorical dimension of the human condition—a basic reality principle, as it were—but construes it in such a way as to minimize its ultimate importance. The basic reality principle is by *physis* and refers to the renunciation, however minimal, that will always be necessary to negotiate the metabolism between humanity and external nature. Regardless of how thoroughly external nature may be mastered, that is, how thoroughly automated technology may become, it will always remain necessary to exert some effort and, therefore, to practice some instinctual renunciation, to extract the goods of life from it. The kernel of truth, according to Marcuse, in Freud's ontologization of a repressive reality principle results from the fact that *to date* "a repressive organization of the instincts" has underpinned "*all* historical forms of the reality principle in civilization." [22]

The "performance principle," in contrast, is a term Marcuse introduces to designate "the prevailing historical form of the *reality principle*" [23] that operates in advanced societies. In such societies, where modern science and technology have the potential to create abundance, shorten the working day, and pacify the struggle for existence, the extensiveness of actual renunciation is enforced not because of physical necessity but because of the necessity to maintain a system of political and economic domination.

The point of departure for Marcuse's distinction between necessary repression and surplus repression is Freud's Marxian observation, mentioned above, that "the mutual relations of men are profoundly influenced by the amount of instinctual satisfaction which the existing wealth makes possible." The distinction is meant to provide a quasi-quantitative concept for measuring the degree of historically unnecessary renunciation that operates in a given society. That is, it is meant to measure the difference between the "amount of instinctual gratification" that could be permitted if the existing forces of production were utilized to their fullest and the amount that is actually permitted on the basis of their repressive organization. Repression *simpliciter,* which pertains to the phylogenetic dimension of human existence, refers to the degree of renunciation necessitated by the basic reality principle, and surplus repression refers to the superfluous renunciation imposed by the performance principle. Surplus repression, then, obviously modeled on Marx's notion of surplus labor, could be used as a psychoanalytic measure for determining the exploitation in a given society:

Within the total structure of the repressed personality, surplus-repression is that portion which is the result of specific societal conditions sustained in the specific interest of domination. The extent of this surplus-repression provides the standard of measurement: the smaller it is, the less repressive is the stage of civilization. The distinction is equivalent to that between the biological and the historical sources of human suffering. [24]

Marcuse maintains—and this is one of the assumptions that undoubtedly strikes us as naive today—that the forces of production have developed to the point where surplus repression constitutes by far the commanding share of renunciation exacted in modern society. If science and technology were directed to ends other than maintaining the current socioeconomic order, so the argument goes, surplus repression could be eliminated. In this "Marxification" of Freud, Marcuse is also drawing on Marx's distinction between the realm of necessity and the realm of freedom, without mentioning it by name. As Marx puts it in a famous passage:

In fact, the realm of freedom actually begins only where labor which is determined by necessity and mundane considerations ceases; thus in the very nature of things it lies beyond the sphere of actual material production. Just as the savage must wrestle with Nature to satisfy his wants, to maintain and reproduce life, so must civilized man, and he must do so in all social formations and under all possible modes of production [in other words, the basic reality principle]. . . . [T]he true realm of freedom, . . . can blossom forth only with this realm of necessity as its basis.[25]

Unlike Marx, however, who maintained they would only be developed in a future socialist society, Marcuse believes that the material conditions now exist to make possible the historical transition—which would amount to a rupture in the continuum of domination—from the realm of necessity to the realm of freedom, and from human prehistory to history proper. He links these Marxian themes to his Freudian categories by arguing that the scientific and technological accomplishments, which are themselves the fruits of the performance principle, already have "created the preconditions for a qualitatively different, nonrepressive reality principle."[26] Moreover, Marcuse, as opposed to Marx, as well as Adorno and Habermas, who abstain on principle from utopian speculation, believes it is legitimate and possible to provide positive content for that utopia. Indeed, *Eros and Civilization* can be seen as an attempt to use psychoanalysis to fill Marx's intentionally empty notion of the realm of freedom.

Marcuse sets out then to validate "the hypothesis of a nonrepressive civilization" by demonstrating "the possibility of a nonrepressive development of the libido under the conditions of mature civilization,"[27] that is, under conditions in which surplus repression had been eliminated. If this could be done, if he could show that the domination of internal nature was not necessary for the maintenance of mature civilization, then the impasse articulated in *Dialectic of Enlightenment* would have been overcome. The basic conceptual move that allows his demonstration to proceed—which is, in fact, the basic and problematic move of Marcuse's entire Marxifying reconstruction of Freud—is the identification of material scarcity *(Lebensnot)* with reality or necessity *(Ananke)* as such: "Behind the reality principle lies the fundamental fact of Ananke or scarcity *(Lebensnot)*, which means that the struggle for existence takes place in a world too poor for the satisfaction of human needs without constant restraint, renunciation, delay."[28] If necessity were equivalent to scarcity, and if scarcity were historically contingent and therefore eliminable, then Ananke itself could be averted and the "repressive modification of the instincts"[29] eliminated as well. Marcuse argues that, because Freud always assumed that the existence of material scarcity is an immutable condition, he viewed the opposition between the pleasure principle and the reality principle as an ontological fact. But for Freud, as we shall see, there is also an essential connection between Ananke and temporality in the form of transience; Ananke presents itself to us in the figure of loss, the ineluctable result of the fleeting existence of all things, that is, the inexorable unidirectional flow of time and the loss that inevitably results from it.[30] And the difference between the treatment of time in Freud and Marcuse, for whom it is also a central concern, is telling.

The argument of *Eros and Civilization,* moreover, like the argument of Marx's *Capital,* centers on the distribution of time in another one of its modalities, namely, the length of the working day. For Marx, whose "guiding model," at least in his Left, Aristotelian, nontechnocratic vein, "was doubtless the Athens of Pericles,"[31] modern science and technology could reduce the length of the working day to an absolute minimum. This reduction could in turn qualitatively increase the amount of leisure time, which is the necessary precondition for pursing the "higher" activities beyond the struggle for existence. In the polis, which was based on a slave economy and the subjugation of women, that leisure and those activities were only available to the small male elite. In a future communist society, however, where automated technology would replace slavery, where "the shuttle would weave and the plectrum touch the lyre without a hand to guide them,"[32] they could become the possession of the population at large. Communism, in short, would resemble something like the polis writ large, in which the status of citizenship would be universalized. All citizens would be free to pursue higher activities.

Marcuse's Freudian variations on these Marxian themes both adopt the basic scheme and radicalize it. With Marx, Marcuse maintains that although the realm of material production can itself "never be a realm of freedom and gratification," it "can release time and energy for the free play of human faculties *outside* the realm of alienated labor."[33] However—and this is a mark of his eschatological radicalism—the form of activity he envisions for the realm of freedom differs from that of Marx: "Because they belong to the cultural household of the performance principle itself"—to the "old Adam," as Bloch calls it—the "higher values" of the cultural tradition are inappropriate for an emancipated society. Therefore, instead of being generalized to the population as a whole, they must be transfigured. (To be sure, the aesthetic dimension continues to play a central role in this transfiguration.) To use our earlier distinction, Marcuse is not advocating the radical reformation of civilization, as Marx in some sense still was, but the utopian transfiguration of it.[34]

The nonrepressive restructuring of the instinctual organization comprises a principal feature of the transfigurative radicalization of the Marxian scheme. "Men," Freud observes, "are not spontaneously fond of work."[35] Economic necessity requires therefore that they be transformed from the "libidinal subject-object[s]," which they originally are, into "instruments of alienated labor" (cf. Foucault's notion of disciplinary culture), and "the distribution of *time* plays a fundamental role in this transformation." Against the timelessness of the id and the absolute hedonism of the pure pleasure ego, which left unchecked themselves would make disciplined labor impossible, pleasure must be temporally dismembered so that it can be doled out in "small separate doses" outside the workday—after hours, as it were.[36] Moreover, "the temporal reduction of the libido" in the service of alienated labor is "supplemented by its spatial reduction."

In an ambiguous discussion of genitality, Marcuse argues that the dismemberment of pleasure and disciplining of the organism requires "the socially necessary desexualization" of the originally polymorphous-perverse body and the concentration of the capacity for pleasure in the genitals. He begins by acknowledging, in agreement with Freud and in line with his own distinction between necessary repression and surplus repression, a biological and thus transhistorical substratum for "the primacy of the genital zone,"[37] which results from the internal maturation of the organism: "The 'containment' of the partial sexual impulses, the progress to genitality belong to this basic layer of repression which makes possible intensified pleasure: the maturation of the organism involves normal and natural maturation of pleasure." He goes on to argue, however, that "the mastery of instinctual drives may also be used *against* gratification" and that "in the history of civilization, basic repression and surplus repression have been inextricably intertwined, and the normal progress to genitality has been organized in such a way that the partial impulses and their 'zones' were all but desexualized in order to conform to the requirements of a specific organization of human existence."

Marcuse seems to be suggesting something like surplus genitalization, so to speak, which is superimposed on the maturational process by the requirements of particular social formations, namely, "the monogamic-patriarchal family" and the "hierarchical division of labor."[38] Although he acknowledges the existence of a basic maturational substratum, it tends to drop out of his historicizing analysis, and the weight of his argument shifts almost completely to the socially imposed stratum of repression. The integration of the partial instincts under the dominance of genitality is explained as a product of the division of labor: genitality is a necessity, because the "unrepressed development" of the pregenital instincts "would eroticize the organism to such an extent that it would counteract the desexualization of the organism required by its social utilization as an instrument of labor."[39] Along these same lines, the "unification of the partial instincts and their subjugation under the procreative function" also restrict the scope of sexuality for functional reasons: "from an autonomous 'principle' governing the entire organism it is turned into a specialized temporary function, into a means for an end."[40]

Echoing what is an essential theme of *Dialectic of Enlightenment,* Marcuse argues that the " 'unification' of the various objects of the partial instincts into one libidinal object of the opposite sex, and . . . the establishment of genital supremacy" corresponds to the "centralization" of the organization of society under the performance principle. And for Marcuse, this "unifying process is repressive. The partial instincts do not develop freely into a 'higher' stage of gratification which preserves their objects, but are cut off and reduced to subservient functions."[41] That is, the unity of the self, like the unity of the repressive rationality of the performance principle, is not achieved through the integration of the part instincts and their objects, but through their repression and exclusion. We return to these themes when we consider Adorno's notion of forced unification.[42]

The diagnosis of the repressive unity of the self (and its object), which excludes and represses the polymorphous dimension of inner nature—and which is concomitant with the repressive unity of "the logic of domination"—initiates a search for the good Other of the repressive ego. Marcuse locates that good Other in sexual perversions and in fantasy life with which they are intimately connected. Insofar as they represent "adherence to the *status quo ante*"[43] of pregenital sexuality and its prolongation into adult life, which they do at least for the early Freud, Marcuse argues that the sexual perversions seem to have eluded and rejected "the entire enslavement of the pleasure ego by the reality ego" and to "place themselves outside the dominion of the performance principle and challenge its very foundation." Because they lie beyond the regime of repressive reason, they can be taken as ciphers that point to the contours of social and psychic formations on the other side of the performance principle. In the current social order that equates the "normal, socially useful and good" and therefore stigmatizes pleasure for its own sake, the perversions must, according to Marcuse, appear as *"fleurs du mal."*

In contrast to Chasseguet-Smirgel, whose position we examine below, Marcuse maintains that the darker aspects of perverse sexuality, "the hideous forms so well known in the history of civilization," are not intrinsic to perversion itself but "seem to be linked with the general perversion of the human existence in a repressive culture." For the same systematic reasons as the poststructuralists, Marcuse valorizes the *poète maudit,* and he argues that the *fleurs du mal,* when deciphered from a utopian perspective beyond the performance principle, can assume a *"promesse de bonheur."*[44]

Furthermore, because they remain both "free from the reality principle"[45] and faithful to the pleasure principle, the perversions, Marcuse argues, "show a deep affinity to phantasy."[46] As Freud noted: "With the introduction of the reality principle one species of thought-activity was split off; it was kept free from reality-testing and remained subordinated to the pleasure principle alone. This activity is *phantasying.*"[47] Judged from within the categorical framework of the repressive reality principle, fantasy—"the psychic imaginary" to use Castoriadis's term—must of necessity appear retrogressive, false, and unrealistic. But precisely because it preserves "promises and potentialities which are betrayed and even outlawed by the mature, civilized individual,"[48] fantasy possesses "a truth value of its own"[49] that the established reality principle must dismiss as utopian in the bad sense. Marcuse argues, however, that the very achievements of civilization at its maturest stage, which make the "nonoppressive distribution of scarcity"[50] possible, also make it possible ipso facto to redeem the truth value of fantasy and to reverse the negative meaning of "utopia." In this changed context, "regression assumes a progressive function" that can yield "critical standards which are tabooed by the present," and "the *recherche du temps perdu*" can become "the vehicle of future liberation."[51]

In accordance with Marx's basic scheme, but now expressed in psychoanalytic terms, Marcuse attempts to show how the "the general reduction of the necessary labour of society to a minimum," that is, the radical reduction of the length of the working day, could provide the basis for the "free development of individualities":[52] "The reduction of the working day to a point where the mere quantum of labor no longer arrests human development is the first prerequisite for freedom."[53] Linking societal economics with libidinal economics, he explicates the notion of free human development in terms of the allocation of instinctual energy. The quantum of instinctual energy devoted to labor, which, owing to the length of the working day, has been the largest single portion of the total instinctual energy available under the performance principle, could be released for other purposes. In conjunction with the resexualization of the body, this quantum of liberated libido could in turn be reorganized in the nonrepressive manner Marcuse is seeking to demonstrate is possible. He refers to this reorganization of the instincts as "the transformation of sexuality into Eros":

No longer used as a full-time instrument of labor, the body would be resexualized. The regression involved in this spread of the libido would first manifest itself in a reactivation of all erotogenic zones and, consequently, in a resurgence of pregenital polymorphous sexuality and in a decline of genital supremacy. The body in its entirety would become an object of cathexis, a thing to be enjoyed—an instrument of pleasure. This change in the value and scope of libidinal relations would lead to a disintegration of the institutions in which the private interpersonal relations have been organized, particularly the monogamic and patriarchal families.[54]

And, with respect to "the quantum of instinctual energy still to be diverted into necessary labor," that is, with respect to the basic reality principle and basic repression, it would be "so small"[55] that its overall impact could be minimized and managed in such a way as not to jeopardize the larger scheme.

In addition to being automated and rationalized, the nature of work, Marcuse maintains, could itself be transformed into play in a way that would parallel the transformation of sexuality into Eros. Drawing on motifs in Kant and Schiller, he argues that, freed from the incessant pressure of toil, the purposeful purposelessness of play and other sublimatory activities could, in fact, lean on, to use Freud's term, "the satisfaction of the great vital needs."[56] For example, the challenges posed by demands of external nature could become an occasion for creativity rather than drudgery.

Anticipating what has become a familiar postmodernist reading strategy that looks to the margins for the key to interpreting texts and cultural objects, Marcuse attempts to extrapolate "a new relation between instincts and reason" from "a marginal trend in mythology and philosophy."[57] He maintains that as "reason is the rationality of the performance principle,"[58] indications of another reality principle must be pursued *beyond* the frontiers of rationality in the strict sense: "The culture of the performance principle makes its bow before the strange truths which imagination keeps alive in folklore and fairy tale, in literature and art."[59] As opposed to Prometheus, "the culture-hero of toil, productivity and progress through repression," Marcuse turns to Orpheus and Narcissus as "symbols of another reality principle."[60] Both heroes—Narcissus by definition, but Orpheus as well—belong to the earliest strata of experience and are associated with the promise and threat of Nirvana that emanates from the archaic mother. "In the beginning," as Simone Sternberg has observed, "there was the voice":[61] the mother's voice—with its particular melody, rhythm, and timbre, preceded by her heartbeat in the womb—not to mention the lullaby—*precedes the father's word,* that is, linguistic communication, and serves as a transitional object to soften the pain of the emerging separation between mother and child. It is also a fundamental source of music.[62] Marcuse sees Orpheus's ability to pacify the animals with his song as a symbol of the overcoming of "the opposition between man and nature, subject and object."[63]

Marcuse also prefigures Kohut's attempt to redeem certain aspects of narcissism from Freud's almost entirely negative assessment of it when compared to object love. To be sure, he acknowledges that "Narcissus appears as the *antagonist* of Eros," who "spurns love, the love that unites with other human beings," and that, as such, "he symbolizes sleep and death, silence and rest." But he also maintains that this does not constitute the rejection of Eros *per se,* but only the rejection of "one Eros for another."[64]

Like so many of the authors who came after Freud we are considering, Marcuse views the introduction of the concept of narcissism into psychoanalytic theory not simply as "the addition of just another phase to the development of the libido" but as a philosophical turning point in the development of psychoanalysis potentially so radical in its implications that Freud could not assimilate it. As we have seen, until the later work of Loewald, Kohut, and others, narcissism had, for the most part, been viewed almost exclusively as the "egoistic withdrawal from reality." It can also, however, be seen as signifying a deeper connectedness with external reality—a connectedness Freud at least intimated with his notion of the oceanic feeling. In this case, "beyond all immature autoeroticism, narcissism denotes a

fundamental relatedness to reality which may generate a comprehensive existential order. In other words, narcissism may contain the
germ of a different reality principle."[65]

His treatment of narcissism lies at the speculative and problematic[66] core of Marcuse's already unabashedly speculative work. The
"fuller Eros"[67] that he ascribes to Narcissus is thoroughly implicated
in "the terrifying convergence of pleasure and death" in the Nirvana
principle[68]—a convergence that makes Freud's thinking on the pleasure principle and the death drive so notoriously difficult to sort out.
The narcissistic promise of Nirvana, bliss, *jouissance,* is, at the same
time, the threat of de-differentiation, oblivion, and *Liebestod.* And this
fact presents a difficulty for his utopian appropriation of the theory
of narcissism. Marcuse attempts to solve the problem and redeem
Narcissus by undoing that convergence, by uncoupling pleasure
from death, so that Narcissus would represent "the redemption of
pleasure, the halt of time, the absorption of death; silence, sleep,
night paradise—the Nirvana principle *not as death but as life*" (emphasis added).[69]

Following an early article by Loewald,[70] Marcuse locates the origins of this convergence in the archaic mother "in whom the son
[sic] once had the integral peace which is the absence of all need
and desire—the Nirvana before birth."[71] During the early stages of
postnatal development, that experience of nondifferentiation continues to an extent: "At this primary stage of the relation between
the 'pre-ego' and reality, the Narcissistic and the maternal Eros seem
to be one, and the primary experience of reality is that of libidinous
union." The attitude toward (maternal) reality during the early narcissistic phases of development is not one of "defense and submission, but of integral identification with the 'environment.' " It is from
this "Narcissistic-maternal" attitude that Marcuse hopes to extrapolate a different relation to reality.[72] He argues that, because Freud
took the existence of scarcity to be uneliminable, he never asked
"whether the Narcissistic-maternal attitude toward reality cannot
'return' in less primordial, less devouring forms under the power
of the mature ego and in a mature civilization. Instead, the necessity of suppressing this attitude once and for all is taken for
granted."[73]

With the unfolding of the separation-individuation process, and especially with the increasing importance of the father and the entry into the oedipal phase,[74] the figure of the archaic mother begins to assume a dual aspect. It comes to represent not only the unsurpassable pleasure of Nirvana but also the risk of de-differentiation and "maternal engulfment," which would be tantamount to death for the incipient ego.[75] There is a similar duality in the father. On the one hand, paternal reality, that is, reality as we commonly think of it, is external and harsh, as opposed to maternal reality, which is associated with pleasure and connectedness. The father, with his prohibition on incest and threat of castration that force the child to renounce the mother as "a libidinal object," is experienced as "the representative of the demands of reality." Indeed, "the submission to the castration threat [is] the decisive step in the establishment of the ego as based on the reality principle."[76] In this context, Marcuse interprets the homosexuality of Orpheus and Narcissus as a protest against the law of the father and therefore against the historical continuum of domination: "Psychoanalytic theory sees in the practices that exclude or prevent procreation an opposition against continuing the chain of reproduction and thereby of paternal domination—an attempt to prevent the 'reappearance of the father.' "[77] On the other hand, insofar as reunion with the early mother has come to symbolize reengulfment and death, the father and the incest taboo constitute an antithanatonic—that is, a life—force: "Perhaps the taboo on incest was the first great protection against the death instinct: the taboo on Nirvana, on the regressive impulse for peace which stood in the way of progress, of Life itself. Mother and wife were separated, and the fatal identity of Eros and Thanatos thus dissolved."[78] As we will see, Odysseus can return to the home from which his journey originated, and to his wife Penelope, only after his travels have sufficiently distanced him from the regressive pull of the Sirens' song.

The image of reconciliation that Marcuse discovers in Narcissus and Orpheus is not confined to the mythological tradition alone. He also uncovers it as a countermotif within the mainstream of Western philosophy itself. While many philosophers, Nietzsche and Heidegger, for example, have sought to determine the point at which Greek thought became corrupted, whether it was with Parmenides,

Socrates, or Plato, Marcuse locates it relatively late, namely, with Aristotle. Whatever the previous meaning of Logos, "since the canonization of the Aristotelian logic the term merges with the ideal of ordering, classifying, mastering reason." It becomes "the logic of domination" (Marcuse's term for instrumental reason or identity thinking). As such, it is "increasingly antagonistic to those faculties and attitudes which are receptive rather than productive, which tend toward gratification rather than transcendence—which remain strongly committed to the pleasure principle."[79] Moreover, the ego of the philosophical tradition, the correlate of the Logos of domination, "reveal[s] itself as an essentially aggressive, offensive subject, whose thoughts and actions [are] designed for mastering objects. . . . This *a priori* antagonistic experience define[s] the *ego cogitans* as well as the *ego agens*."[80]

However, within the heart of Western philosophy, indeed within Aristotle himself, Marcuse identifies another logic, which he refers to as "the Logos of gratification" and maintains that "the effort to harmonize" the logic of domination and the logic of gratification "animates the inner history of Western metaphysics." It is on this point that "Freud's metapsychology meets a mainstream of Western philosophy."[81] The countermotif of reconciliation is not to be found in Aristotle's *Organon* but in his *Metaphysics:* "It obtains its classical formulation in the Aristotelian hierarchy of the modes of being, which culminates in the *nous theos*. . . . The ascending curve of being is bent in the circle which moves in itself; past, present, and future are enclosed in the ring."[82] The attributes that characterize the *nous theos*—in terms of which Aristotle praises it—*are thoroughly narcissistic:*[83] as thought thinking itself, Aristotle's god is a self-sufficient plenum, pure actuality, unburdened by privation, materiality, and otherness, and therefore in need of nothing beyond itself. The criteria in terms of which Aristotle recommends the contemplative life are the same: it is the best life for humans because it is "most closely akin"[84] to the life of god and "is a life such as the best which we enjoy but a short time."[85] Furthermore, the Aristotelian god, the unmoved mover, does not impart motion to the moved cosmos through mechanical causality, but through narcissistic desire, as it were: god, as "the object of desire and the object of thought . . . produces motion as being loved."[86] Like the lover after the beloved, the various onto-logical strata of the moved cosmos, which suffer from graduated degrees of privation, yearn after god, whose perfection consists in his "self-dependent actuality."[87] On the model of narcissistic object choice, he is what they would like to be. This might help to explain the curious inversion that has taken place in recent years: whereas for Marcuse, the logic of reconciliation is opposed to the logic of domination, for the postmodernists, the urge for reconciliation is at its source.[88] That is, for them, the unifying dynamic of reconciliation, which narcissistically reduces all otherness and particularity to a homogenizing subsumptive universal, is the source of instrumental reason. Their position, however, is based on the assumption that all unification is totalizing and violent, an assumption we will have ample occasion to challenge.

Marcuse is sufficiently honest in his thinking and thoroughgoing in his utopianism to confront the major obstacle opposing his program directly, namely, time. "But the fatal enemy of lasting gratification is *time,* the inner finiteness, the brevity of all conditions. The idea of integral human liberation therefore necessarily contains the vision of the struggle against time."[89] At this point, not just the banal unworkability of utopia but the profound philosophical flaws in Marcuse's position—as well as the deep differences between his project and Freud's—become fully apparent. The figure of Narcissus is once again relevant, for his captivation by his immobile image in the river, the Heraclitean symbol of all becoming, represents an attempt to arrest time and deny loss. Marcuse, it should be stressed, intends that the struggle against time be taken literally. He rejects the merely aesthetic exercise of remembrance, à la Proust, as just that, "artistic and spurious"; for "remembrance" to become "a real weapon" it must be "translated into history."[90] Citing an incident noted by Walter Benjamin, Marcuse writes that, in July of 1789, revolutionaries in Paris evinced at least an intuitive grasp of the need to conquer time by "simultaneously but independently at several places" shooting "at the time pieces on the towers of Paris."[91]

But would "the struggle against time"—assuming, that is, we can make sense of the notion—even be desirable? Here the thoroughly ambivalent nature of narcissism, to which we have repeatedly

referred, comes into play. While narcissism may point to a more connected, less distanced relation to reality in a perhaps overly oedi-
palized and scientized world, the register of narcissism contains its
dark side as well, having to do with the *omnipotent denial of reality*. The
classic psychoanalytic scheme envisages the encounter with transience—as well as the encounter with the Oedipus complex—as a
primary experience in which the decentering of infantile omnipotence occurs. As we will see when we consider Ricoeur, Ananke qua
the ineluctable, as opposed to Ananke qua scarcity, confronts us in
the figure of loss. And, ideally, in coming to grips with the inevitable
losses of childhood, the individual begins not only to renounce his
or her omnipotence and to acknowledge Ananke but, through
mourning and internalizing the lost objects, to develop the psychic
structure and capacity for symbolization to deal with that loss as well:
"reality, hard reality, is the correlate of . . . internalized absence."[92]
It is hard to imagine how an end to scarcity, even if that idea were
coherent, would eliminate an end to Ananke in this transhistorical
sense. Moreover, since the capacity for symbolization, which is to
say, the basis of human culture, results from loss, mourning, and
internalization, it is not clear that the struggle against time is even
desirable.

Nor is it clear that Marcuse's remarkably casual minimalization of
the significance of the Oedipus complex—which itself entails enormous loss and is the other experience in which omnipotence comes
to grief—is at all advantageous. The patriarchal arrangement of society has provided, if nothing else, an efficient but extremely costly way
of decentering human omnipotence. Any proposal for an alternative
arrangement of sexual and familial relations that would eliminate
the Oedipus complex must therefore provide an alternative means
for taming infantile omnipotence:

But the new-born will *always* have to be torn out of *his* world, without asking
him for an opinion he cannot give, and forced—under the pain of psychosis—to renounce his imaginary omnipotence. . . . This is the true signification of the Oedipal situation, for which, *in this respect*, the embodiment of
the patriarchal family is *at once* exemplary and accidental. We are justified
in imagining everything with respect to the transformation of social institutions; but not the incoherent fiction that the psyche's entry into society

could occur *gratuitously*. The individual is not the fruit of nature, not even a tropical one, but a social creation and institution.[93]

An earlier generation of Left Freudians had to confront the theory of aggression to counter Freud's political pessimism. Today, precisely because we are so aware of narcissistic-preoedipal development, progressive psychoanalysts have to take up the problem of omnipotence. Any scheme for radical social transformation that does not include a mechanism for decentering infantile omnipotence stands condemned of utopianism in the pejorative sense.

Freud's Two Theories of Perversion

Marcuse's claim that the sexual perversions represent the good Other of the logic of domination and the repressive ego, and can therefore be taken as a cipher for a utopian order beyond the performance principle, is based on the early Freud. (I will not take up here the question of this Rousseauean figure of thought, which seeks to find an untainted element of presocial nature as a fulcrum for social transformation.) Joyce McDougall has made the observation, however, that, in treating the Wolf Man, Freud came to appreciate more fully the significance of the primal scene—and its essentially traumatic nature—in the formation of perversions and revised his theory accordingly.[94] In his early writings before that celebrated case, Freud had indeed understood the perversions "as the persistence into adult life of id impulses that have escaped repression,"[95] and Marcuse, like much of the Freudian Left from Wilhem Reich to the French *désirants* of the seventies, bases his work on this formulation. Because he understands the perversions as being constructed from these presumably uncontaminated id impulses, Marcuse can construe them as phenomena that have evaded the effects of repressive socialization. But to do this means, among other things, that he fails to grasp the essentially *traumatic* nature of their genesis.[96] After the treatment of the Wolf Man—as well as the formulation of the structural theory that expanded his interest into the realm of ego and superego pathology and placed new emphasis on the function of aggression—Freud came to see that perversions were a counterphobic reaction to the trauma of the primal scene and that this trauma had implications for the formation of the individual's ego and for his or her relation to reality. It also meant that the perversions had an intimate connection with the economics of aggression. My thesis is that Marcuse can approach the perversions in a utopian manner because he excludes the problems of trauma, disavowal, and aggression from his analysis.

The difference between Freud's treatment of the perversions examined in *Three Essays on Sexuality* and in "Fetishism" encompasses the theoretical distance he had traveled between 1905 and 1927. In *Three Essays,* one of the founding texts of the topographic-economic model, Freud attempts to conceptualize the perversions on the model of drive-defense and repression. At this point, he saw no difference *in principle* between the formation of neurotic symptoms and of perversions. They are produced from the same raw material of sexual wishes and by the same formation process, and the main difference between them is one of degree: what the perversions express in a fairly direct form, the symptom expresses in a more disguised fashion. Or, to put it differently, what the perversion acts out more or less directly, the symptom symbolizes. This is the meaning of Freud's two statements in the *Three Essays* that "the symptoms constitute the sexual activity of the patient" and that "neuroses are, so to say, the negative of the perversions."[97]

With the introduction of the structural theory, however, Freud came to locate the mechanism of disavowal *(Verleugnung)* at the center of the perversions. In fact, it was largely through his study of fetishism, which he took as the paradigmatic case of the perversions, that Freud first recognized disavowal (and the splitting of the ego, which is a concomitant of it) as a mechanism distinct from neurotic repression *(Verdrängung)* on the one hand, and psychotic repudiation *(Verwerfung)* on the other. Indeed, he states that fetishism provides "a particularly favourable subject for studying the question" of disavowal.[98] While Freud never articulated a theory of disavowal on the level of, say, the theory of repression, nor systematically distinguished it from other "closely allied processes," Laplanche and Pontalis observe nevertheless that "there is . . . a definite consistency in the evolution of the concept, in his work."[99] While initially viewing disavowal as a basically psychotic phenomenon, Freud eventually came to see it as a more or less independent structure lying somewhere between the psychosis and the neurosis.

In his first attempts to define the specific difference between the psychosis and the neurosis in terms of their respective strategies *toward reality,* Freud suggests that disavowal constitutes the specifically psychotic approach:

In neurosis a piece of reality is avoided by a sort of flight, whereas in psychosis it is remodelled. Or we might say: in psychosis, the initial flight is succeeded by an active phase of remodelling; in neurosis the initial obedience is succeeded by a deferred attempt at flight. Or again, expressed in yet another way: neurosis does not disavow reality, it only ignores it; psychosis disavows it and tries to replace it.[100]

Laplanche and Pontalis point out that Freud had been searching throughout his career for a defense mechanism that was specific to psychosis, and it is significant that he introduces disavowal in a paper dealing with psychosis. Interestingly, however, at about the same time, Freud began to use the term in his discussion of childhood sexuality and to identify disavowal as the defense the child employs when confronted with the castration complex. Thus, in "The Infantile Genital Organization," Freud tells us:

We know how children react to their first impression of the absence of a penis. They disavow the fact and believe they *do* see a penis, all the same. They gloss over the contradiction and preconception by telling themselves that the penis is still small and will grow bigger presently; and they then slowly come to the emotionally significant conclusion that after all the penis had at least been there before and had been taken away afterwards.[101]

A certain ambiguity about the way the child processes what he sees, however, can already be detected in Freud's account, and the tension produced by that ambiguity will become a basis for the further development of the theory. On the one hand, he seems to be saying that children falsify the data of their perceptions and actually *hallucinate* a penis where there was none; this would be a "psychotic" solution. On the other hand, he seems to be maintaining that children perceptually *register* the penisless vagina and then attempt to formulate a theory to explain it away. Furthermore, Freud also asserted that the use of disavowal is "neither uncommon nor very dangerous"[102] in childhood but would become psychotic if extended into adult life.

It was in 1927 that Freud explicitly connected disavowal with castration anxiety and fetishism and—inasmuch as fetishism is taken as the prototype of the perversions—with perversion in general. His thesis in "Fetishism" is that, just as the little boy had to believe in the existence of his mother's missing penis to combat his castration anxiety, so the fetishist must create his fetish for exactly the same reason. To put it more precisely, "The fetish is a substitute for the woman's (the mother's) penis the little boy once believed in and—for reasons familiar to us—does not want to give up."[103] This interpretation would mean that perversion is a way of denying sexual difference. What is important in that article is that Freud rejects the term "scotomization" as a designation of the child's defensive activities vis-à-vis castration and explicitly counterposes "disavowal" to it: "If I am not mistaken, Laforgue would say in this case the boy 'scotomizes' his perception of the woman's lack of penis. . . .' [S]cotomization' seems to me particularly unsuitable, for it suggests the perception is entirely wiped out, so that the result is the same as when a visual impression falls on the blind spot in the retina."[104] Freud is thus explicitly repudiating the position he had himself ambiguously advanced earlier, namely that the child obliterates the content of his perception and replaces it with a hallucination, after rejecting the strictly psychotic interpretation of "disavowal."[105] How does he then understand it? In fact, his unsuccessful attempt to answer this question will lead him to introduce the notion of splitting. However, before considering splitting, let us examine those unsuccessful attempts. Freud writes:

In the situation we are considering . . . we see that the perception [of the vagina] has persisted and that a very energetic action has been undertaken to maintain the disavowal. It is not true that, after the child has made his observation, he has preserved unaltered his belief that women have a phallus. *He has retained that belief but also given it up.* In the conflict between the weight of the unwelcome perception and the force of counter wish, *a compromise has been reached,* as is only possible under the dominance of the unconscious law of thought—the primary process. Yet in his mind the woman *has* got a penis, in spite of everything; but this is no longer the same as before.[106]

The relative obscurity of this passage results from the fact that Freud had not yet found the conceptual terms to say more clearly what he would like to say.

After rejecting the strictly psychotic interpretation of "disavowal," he attempts to construe it on the model of the neurosis, that is, as a compromise formation. However, a neurotic compromise, because it involves repression, cannot *ex hypothesi* involve the *simultaneous* presence of two contradictory ideas in consciousness—namely, the woman does and does not have a penis. The problem for Freud is that, logically, fetishism constitutes a simultaneous admission of and a denial of the woman's "castrated" state. It is an admission insofar as the perception of the penisless organ must have been at least tacitly registered, or else there would have been no reason to fabricate the fetish. And it is a denial insofar as the fetish is supposed to be the missing penis. It was only after he introduced the distinction between repression *(Verdrängung)* and splitting of the ego *(Ichspaltung)*—or between horizontal and vertical splitting, as it is sometimes called today—that Freud could adequately articulate the ideas for which he was groping.

It was in large part to account for this fact, that in fetishism "two attitudes persist side by side . . . without influencing each other,"[107] that Freud introduced—or, since he had already used the notion in the 1890s, we should say reintroduced—the concept of splitting.[108] Freud had intentionally distanced himself early in his career from the notion of splitting when he had tried to distinguish his account of hysteria (and psychopathology in general) from Janet's and Breuer's. Freud came to view their account of hysteria in terms of splitting as superficial, which is to say, merely descriptive. He sought, in contrast, to provide a dynamic explanation in terms of *intersystemic* conflict between conscious and unconscious demands. The theory of repression could account for, indeed it posited, the presence of contradictory ideas in the different systems; but it could not accommodate their simultaneous presence in the same system. With the introduction of the structural theory, however, and the increased

investigation of "the ego's pathological states,"[109] it became necessary to account for the phenomenon of *intrasystemic* as well as intersystemic conflicts, that is, conflicts within the ego itself. And the
concept of splitting was rehabilitated for this purpose.

While fetishism perhaps provides the prototype for splitting, Freud
is quick to point out that to one degree or another, a split of sorts
accompanies all psychopathology. Though his usage is uncharacteristically ambiguous, we can interpret his meaning in the following
manner. First, it is necessary to distinguish between splitting in a
narrower and in a more general sense. The narrower sense would
refer to the splitting of the ego—intrasystemic splitting—that we
have just discussed. The more general sense of splitting would refer
to the fact that all psychopathology diminishes the unity of the self
in one way or another. The existence of splitting in all psychopathology can be observed in the way Freud distinguishes repression from
disavowal, namely, in terms of what each defends against. Whereas
repression defends against the drive demands of the id, disavowal
defends against the demands of external reality. In each case a split
occurs: with repression, between the ego and the id; with disavowal,
within the ego itself. To put it differently: whereas the price paid
with repression is the failure to integrate a portion of instinctual
life; with disavowal, it is the failure to integrate a portion of external
reality.

For Freud, in sum, the fetishist cannot tolerate the penisless state
of the woman because he takes it as evidence that she has been castrated and concludes that, as castration exists as a general possibility,
he too can be castrated as punishment for his forbidden wishes. It is
to combat this castration anxiety that he constructs the fetish, a tangible substitute for the missing penis. Freud argues that, as a child,
the fetishist-to-be, like all children, created the fantasy of the phallic
woman to disavow his mother's penisless state, which he took as evidence of castration, and to counteract the anxiety resulting from it.
The fantasy typically maintains that the mother's apparent castration
is not permanent: either she is hiding a penis inside her, which will
reappear, or the missing penis will grow back at a later date, or some
such similar fantasy. However, whereas other children relinquish—
or at least repress—this developmentally normal fantasy, the fetishist
maintains it as an active fantasy into adult life and acts it out in his

sexual practices. Through the fetish, he declares, as it were, that women are not castrated, that castration does not exist as a general phenomenon, and that therefore he cannot be castrated. This reassurance becomes a necessary condition for his achieving orgasmic potency.

Perversion, Aggression, and Disavowal: On the Contributions of Janine Chasseguet-Smirgel and Joyce McDougall

The last several decades have witnessed the production of a remarkable body of literature written by Janine Chasseguet-Smirgel and Joyce McDougall on the perversions. Just as the sexual repressiveness of the Victorian era provided the backdrop for Freud's original investigations of hysteria and obsessive-compulsive neurosis, I would suggest that the cultural transformations of the sixties and seventies provided the historical context for the theories of these two eminent Parisian analysts. Their work represents, in part, an attempt to respond, from within the classical Freudian paradigm, to the questions raised for psychoanalysis by the sexual revolution, feminism, and gay liberation. These movements have provided a stimulus for *both* authors—particularly Chasseguet-Smirgel, who is a political scientist as well as a psychoanalyst—to take up the question of the perversions, which has been central to psychoanalysis since its inception, and to readdress it. This time around, however, they have at their disposal all the knowledge about narcissism and preoedipal development that has been acquired since the Second World War. While the structure and even the content of Chasseguet-Smirgel's and McDougall's positions have much in common, a close comparison reveals a striking disparity in the ethical tone that colors their positions. Let me stress that I am not referring to an explicitly articulated ethical doctrine, for neither theory contains one, but rather to something like their overall intonation or trajectory. Each theory expands Freud's theory of disavowal, examines the preoedipal roots of perversion, and reconstructs the relationship between perversion and reality in a strikingly similar, indeed, almost homologous fashion. Nevertheless, despite these similarities, the dominant ethical flavor of the two theories is so different as to be almost opposed. Chasseguet-Smirgel's theory is characterized by politically conservative undercurrents—

which, to be sure, introduce an element of conflict into her writing. (Indeed, in important ways her conservatism is the mirror image of Marcuse's position.) McDougall's position, in contrast, has an undeniable liberal bias and contains an appeal to combat conventionalist tendencies within psychoanalysis. Not only has she identified a new nosological entity, "the normopath," but one of her books is entitled *Plea for a Measure of Abnormality*. The question must be asked, then, how could such similar arguments produce such different results? The answer, I would maintain, can be located primarily in their different treatments of the problems of aggression and creativity.

While Chasseguet-Smirgel and McDougall do not deny the importance of castration anxiety in the perversions, they expand the scope of the notion of disavowal to cover a wider range of phenomena. Before turning to Chasseguet-Smirgel's analysis of disavowal, however, which pertains to what she refers to as the "double difference," that is, the double difference between the sexes and between the generations,[110] it is necessary to examine her notion of the "archaic matrix of the Oedipus Complex."[111] Through this notion she introduces the preoedipal dimension into her account of the perversions. It is a central tenet of Freudian anthropology that, because the "intrauterine existence" of the human infant "seems to be short in comparison with that of most animals, . . . it is sent into the world in a less finished" and, therefore, more helpless "state" than the young of other species;[112] the human infant is, in short, born premature and helpless. Chasseguet-Smirgel argues that the distress that accompanies this helplessness is immensely compounded by the fact that it "follows hard upon an earlier state of completeness in which every need was automatically satisfied,"[113] namely, the state of primary narcissism (or the undifferentiated or symbiotic state, as it is more apt to be called today). In this plenumlike condition, which, so it is assumed, begins during prenatal existence and continues for a more or less brief period after birth, the child experiences no otherness, lack, or deprivation. Chasseguet-Smirgel, like Freud, maintains that, once the "departure from primary narcissism occurs," a wish arises to "recover that state"[114] of fusional utopia, which, in one form or another, will accompany the individual throughout life. The wish to recover that undifferentiated state perhaps provides the psychological underpinning for the philosophical quest for presence. As we will also see with Castoriadis, everything depends on how this wish—which, it must again be stressed, is fundamentally ambivalent—is pursued.

It is a major premise of Chasseguet-Smirgel's argument that incest between mother and son not only represents an attempt to possess the mother on a genital level but also constitutes the preeminent instance of the regressive attempt to recapture the fusional perfection of prenatal and early postnatal experience by literally reentering her. Chasseguet-Smirgel specifically endorses Ferenczi's "hypothesis that the return to intrauterine life constitutes a universal human fantasy and is eventually the biological underpinning of the Oedipal wish."[115] It is at this point that the concepts of prematurity and helplessness assume their central importance in her argument. Incestuous desire arrives on the developmental scene before the little boy is capable of fulfilling it. His immature, prepubescent penis makes it impossible for him to carry out his wish to enter his mother's mature womb and satisfy her, and, therefore, makes it impossible for him to recapture the lost paradise of intrauterine existence through incestuous intercourse. Chasseguet-Smirgel maintains that "the reality is not that the mother is castrated, but that the mother has a vagina that the little boy cannot fill."[116] She argues, moreover, in a revision of Freud that has important consequences for the theory of female sexuality, that the theory of phallic monism is devised *defensively*—by little boys and psychoanalytic theorists alike—to deny the existence of this frightening orifice.

It should be pointed out that although Chasseguet-Smirgel limits her analysis to little boys, parallel arguments could also be made for little girls. The point is that children of both sexes are inadequate sexual partners for the parents because of the immaturity of their genitals. This means, moreover, that they are excluded from a variety of prerogatives—symbolized primarily by the right to engage in sexual intercourse—that belong to the parental generation in virtue of children's physiological immaturity.

Confronted with the fact of his helplessness, then, the little boy has two alternatives open to him, one leading to the triadic solution and ideal-progressive development, the other to the dyadic solution, regression and perversion. In the first case, he can accept the fact that it is not his little "widdler"[117] but his father's phallus that is the complement of his mother's vagina and is capable of satisfying her, as well as the fact that the father possesses it in virtue of his maturity. That is, he can acknowledge the double difference between the sexes and between the generations. This alternative, however, requires a significant degree of strength, for it involves the toleration of considerable psychic pain: the mortification resulting from the recognition of his helplessness and inferiority vis-à-vis the father and the sense of exclusion from the sexually self-contained parental couple. If he can tolerate the psychic pain, it becomes possible to renounce incest[118] as an immediate means of seeking the recovery of omnipotent perfection, to project the reunion with the fusional object into the future and displace it onto a substitute, and to identify with the father and his mature phallus as a way of pursuing that projected goal. The little boy can, in other words, compensate himself for the psychic pain caused by the recognition of his helplessness and rejection with the aspiration to become like his father and enjoy the father's "prerogatives"[119] in the future. Furthermore, the ban on incest, by barring the dyadic solution, also offers enormous relief. As we saw with Marcuse, in addition to the temptation that the archaic mother holds for all of us, her engulfing characteristics can be terrifying, and the interdiction against incest offers protection from those "limitless demands."[120] The decided advantage of this alternative is that the boy elects the "long indirect road"[121] of development and the reality principle as opposed to the short path of immediate gratification and the pleasure principle; he invests, as Chasseguet-Smirgel puts it, in "development as such."[122]

If, on the other hand, he cannot tolerate the psychic pain that acknowledging the double difference would entail, the little boy can attempt to disavow this crucial piece of reality. In this case, he tries—often abetted by a seductive mother—to maintain the illusion that his penis is *already* an adequate sexual organ and, through the idealization of pregenitality, that pregenital sexuality is superior to the genital sexuality of the parents.[123] While this disavowal is perhaps "normal" at a certain stage of development, its continuation into adult life and enactment can produce perversion. As we shall see, anality, because of its protogenital and bisexual character, lends itself superbly to this disavowal and contributes to the destructive and illusory character intrinsic, Chasseguet-Smirgel maintains, to the perverse universe.

While Chasseguet-Smirgel's account of the genesis of perversion centers on the denial of the double difference, McDougall's focuses on the disavowal of the meaning of the primal scene. The two accounts are, needless to say, not incompatible: on the contrary, they complement each other to the extent that the child encounters and works through the double difference, in large part, in and through the encounter with the primal scene. More specifically, McDougall's understanding of the perversions—or the "neosexualities," as she calls them [124]—centers on the attempt to master the trauma caused by the child's encounter with the primal scene *through counterphobic, manic enactment.* She argues that perverse sexual activity constitutes an attempt to restage the primal scene in such a way as to eliminate its traumatic aspects. It can be compared to "a stage play in which some vital links are missing (and its air of theatricality is common to many a perverse scenario)." [125] Whereas in the original situation, the child passively suffered the agonizing realities of exclusion, incomprehensible and unmasterable excitation and narcissistic injury, in the reenactment the perverse individual becomes the active author—the master of ceremonies, as it were—of an alternative primal scene in which the traumatic elements of the original are excised and replaced with his "neosexual inventions."

According to McDougall's thesis, underlying all the manifest differences in perverse sexual practices, where "the decor, actors and objects may vary considerably," there exists a relatively invariant "perverse scenario." In fact, the meaning of wide variety of perverse sexual practices "may be reduced to the relatively simple proposition that there is no difference between the sexes. More precisely put, [the pervert's] secret is this: there are perceptual differences between the sexes, but these are without significance; and above all this difference is neither the cause nor the condition of sexual desire." [126] If "the genital organs of the parents are not intended to complete one another and mutual desire is nonexistent," [127] then the meaning of the primal scene, and the child's exclusion from it, is negated in toto. She argues, moreover, that the sadomasochism that seems to

be an inevitable element in perverse sexuality represents a counterphobic attempt to contain and master the rage and anxiety that
result from the child's exclusion from the primal scene and his in-
comprehension of it. The neosexual creator thus *plays with* cruelty,
pain, destructiveness, and fear in the desperate attempt to demonstrate that they are not dangerous or frightening. Ultimately, the
"dynamic motor of perversion is more closely linked with anxiety
than desire"; indeed, "when anxiety appears . . . it is . . . erotized and
[itself] becomes a . . . condition of sexual excitement."[128]

McDougall, expanding on Freud's analysis, attempts to delineate
the precise nature of perverse disavowal by locating it in terms of the
sexually mediated development of the child's sense of reality.[129] She
maintains that, developmentally and diagnostically, perversion lies
between the psychoses and the neuroses and, as such, constitutes a
"third structure," which partakes of elements from both. Unlike the
psychotic solution—which correlates with the earliest stages of the
encounter with sexual difference—the perception of the mother's
penisless state is not repudiated and then magically "remodeled"[130]
by hallucinating the missing penis. Instead, with the perverse solution, as with the neurotic, the "*affectively disturbing* . . . information
gathered from outer reality" is in fact registered. The two solutions
differ, however, with respect to what is done with that piece of information once it has been registered. The neurotic creates "autoplasti-
cally imaginative, internal fantasy ways of dealing with [the] painful
knowledge." For example, having acknowledged "the mother's open
sex," he may "counterinvest" it so that, rather than being "an object
of fascination," it becomes "a dirty or dangerous . . . place of dis-
quiet" that is to be avoided. He may, in short, develop a neurotic
phobia. The perverse individual, or neosexual individual, on the
other hand, *disavows* it.

McDougall argues that this disavowal consists in "a destruction of
meaning" that proceeds in two steps. In the first, the information is
registered, which is to say, it is avowed. In the second, the meaning
of that information—namely, "that the genitals of his parents are
different and complementary, that he is forever excluded from the
closed circle, and that, should his desire persist, he must face the
threat of castration"—is "denuded"[131] through "the cutting of asso-

ciative links."[132] For McDougall, these two moments correspond to the two sides of the splitting—of knowing and not knowing—that most authors who write on the subject agree is ubiquitous in perversion. The perverse practices, then, enter to fill the "gap" in meaning left in the associative network where the links have been severed. And, as with the psychosis, "what was abolished internally returns from without."[133] However, as what is abolished in the perversions is signification and not perception, it is not "recovered in the form of delusions" but is "retrieved through a form of *illusion* contained in an act," that is, through the perverse drama. It is, in other words, an enacted illusion, which the perverted person "controls and delimits."[134]

If the perverse individual makes "a considerable advance over the psychotic"[135] in creating an illusional rather than a delusional solution, it must be remembered that he or she has yet to master problems that are of a preoedipal nature and concern self-object differentiation. At this point, McDougall raises an issue that is absoutely essential for our entire understanding of the genesis of the perversions and of their relation to preoedipal and oedipal issues: "[I]t must be remembered that incestuous longings and the realization of their improbable fulfillment is part of the human lot, and is not sufficient explanation of the perverse sexual choice and organization."[136] Why, in other words, if the encounter with the Oedipus complex, the primal scene, and castration anxiety is "part of the human lot," does it prove to be traumatic and result in perversion for some individuals and not for others? She answers that the manner in which children traverse the separation-individuation process— "the first separation from the breast-mother"[137]—will determine their response to the anxieties of the phallic-oedipal stage and influence its outcome.[138] In other words, how children negotiate the dissolution of symbiosis; renounce omnipotence and magic; learn to tolerate privation, tension, anxiety, and the existence of otherness; and establish a relatively firm separate identity through the internalization of a good enough object will, in large part, determine how they manage the challenges of the oedipal crisis. If children do not adequately fulfill these developmental tasks, then they are exposed not only "to the castration anxiety of the phallic phase" but to the deeper threats of disintegration, annihilation, and psychic death. The "discovery of genital otherness and the forbidden incestuous wishes that this entails" would exacerbate the still-unresolved "drama of subjective otherness" as such and threaten the fragile sense of individual identity, thus becoming a disorganizing experience rather than the reverse.[139] At the same time, "sexuality" itself would run "the risk of becoming merely an instrument for repairing rifts in the feeling of identity."[140]

McDougall maintains that inasmuch as the transitional object is a symbolic creation that allows the child progressively to represent and accept the mother's otherness, the failure to create such objects, whatever the particular reasons, may prefigure the subsequent creation of a fetish as a concrete means of denying sexual difference. The fetish also "indicates" a distinct "failure in symbolization," namely, "an incapacity to render symbolic the difference between the sexes in the adult sexual relationship, along with the renouncing of omnipotent wishes that this entails."[141] The failure of symbolization becomes apparent when one considers the way perverse fantasy can be expressed in pornography. Contrary to the popular belief that the perverse fantasy world is unusually rich and imaginative, it can, in fact, be remarkably constricted, concrete, and impoverished, because it has to serve such a highly *defensive* function. Perverse fantasies, as they appear in pornography, as opposed to erotica, for example, are designed precisely to *constrict fantasy* in order to prevent certain thoughts from emerging:

It seems to me that one important differentiating factor [between pornographic and erotic art] is to be found in the extent of imaginative space that the artist leaves to the public. Erotica, if it is to be judged as art, should stimulate the fantasy of the onlooker, whereas pornographic inventions leave next to nothing to the imagination, whence their lack of artistic merit. In this case, it seems to me the fetishistic, voyeuristic, and other scenarios are pornographic rather than artistically erotic, which sheds some light on the psychic economy of those who invent sexual perversion. There is a conspicuous lack of fantasy and imaginative freedom in most perverse inventions; once created they tend to be stereotyped and to maintain their central theme and detail for decades as though the person were not permitted to imagine anything else.[142]

One need only think of the work of the Marquis de Sade, which, once the initial rush of novelty passes, often becomes tedious and boring. This is an unexpected fact with which almost all the major commentators on the divine Marquis have to grapple.

While McDougall attempts to locate the perversions in terms of the development of the sense of reality, Chasseguet-Smirgel enlists the theory of sexual stages to elucidate their essence. Her thesis is that the regression to anality, which is a central mechanism in the perversions, accounts, in large part, for the falsity, idealization, and destructiveness that are intrinsic to their essence. The proto- or pseudogenital character of anality—in which "the faecal mass or 'stick' foreshadows the genital penis, the production of stools becomes a prototype of childbirth. . . . [T]he daily separation from the faeces is a precursor of castration, and excrement in the rectum anticipates genital coitus"[143]—makes that libidinal phase a suitable vehicle for fleeing the unbearable anxieties of genitality. By utilizing the proto-genital characteristics of anality to create a semblance of genitality, the anxious child and the perverted individual can retreat from genitality and, at the same time, disguise their retreat. For example, the phallically shaped stool or "fecal penis," which is bisexual in virtue of the fact that both sexes possess it, can be used to deny the significance of the paternal phallus and the double difference between the sexes and between the generations, while retaining a semblance of the genital dimension. The falsity that Chasseguet-Smirgel maintains is intrinsic to perversion results from the attempt to pass this pseudogenitality off as the authentic thing. " 'Falsehood,' " she writes, "is built up by taking the equation, faeces = penis, literally."[144]

The process of idealization is closely linked with the theme of falsity, for idealization must be mobilized to combat and disguise the counterfeit and inferior nature of the fecal penis; shit, in short, must be passed off as gold. The compulsion to idealize, in turn, helps to explain the tendency toward aestheticism that, according to Chasseguet-Smirgel, also characterizes the perversions: "The sexual pervert is a man of good taste, an enlightened amateur, an aesthete more often than a real artist."[145] It is at this point that we arrive at one of the most problematic aspects of Chasseguet-Smirgel's entire theory.

On the one hand, she does not want to deny that the "role and importance" of perverted individuals "in the socio-cultural field can never be overestimated."[146] How could she, when, as she herself says, "examples are superfluous"?[147] On the other hand, it would seem to follow necessarily from her position that the perverted individual—because he or she has not recognized the paternal phallus—can never be an authentic creator but only a pseudocreator, dilettante, and aesthete. Ultimately, for Chasseguet-Smirgel, truth and authentic creativity are grounded "in nature"—taken in the specific sense of paternity, procreation, and filiation: "[T]he 'true' . . . is always engendered by its natural causes, in conformity with its essence, and in turn engenders according to the same law, whereas the 'false' is situated beyond any natural continuity . . . [and only] pretends to obey the principle of filiation."[148] In short, she collapses creativity into procreativity, culture into nature, and she argues that the work's inauthenticity derives from the fact that it is "fabricated" rather than begotten.

Moreover, Chasseguet-Smirgel attempts to buttress her essentialist position, which can only be viewed as philosophically naive, by revising Freud's metapsychology in a direction that is theoretically regressive. When she argues that the human drive has a "preformed object," she undoes the distinction, which is a cornerstone of the Freudian revolution, between an animal *Instinkt,* where such a preformed object exists, and the human *Trieb,* where the object is "accidental and variable."[149] As Laplanche and Pontalis point out, human sexuality is, in some sense, intrinsically perverse insofar as it only "leans on" the self-preservative instinct and therefore inevitably overshoots the requirements of mere biological existence.[150] It is precisely the "accidental and variable" nature of the *Trieb* that makes perversion *and* artistic creation coequal possibilities for human beings. To deny the polyvalent character of the human drive would be to dissolve the very question of the relationship between perversion and creativity that has fascinated and perplexed analysts from Freud to Loewald.

The regression to anality also serves to explain the fact that "perversion is," according to Chasseguet-Smirgel, "inevitably sadistic."[151] Her argument is not only based on the familiar aggressive and sadistic features of the anal phase originally delineated by Freud. It is also based on quasi-philosophic—if not quasi-ontological—arguments concerning the nature of reality and human sociation. In language that echoes central themes of French structuralist and poststructuralist thought, Chasseguet-Smirgel maintains that reality as such and social reality in particular are constituted as a system of differences. The regression to anality seeks to negate the "paternal universe," which is constituted through law and the double difference, and to create a counter "anal-sadistic universe," consisting in a homogeneous fecal matter "where all differences are abolished."[152] (At a still more primitive layer, lies the wish not simply to debase the differentiated paternal universe but to cast off the world of the father altogether and return to "a universe without obstacles, without roughness or differences, entirely smooth, identified with a mother's belly stripped of its contents, an interior to which one has free access.")[153] As reality is constituted through differentiation, this "fecalization" amounts to an attack on reality as such.

The intrinsic sadism of the perversions, then, does not result simply from the typical physiological features that impart an aggressive character to anality, for example, sphincter control—although it results from that too—but from a more fundamental ontological rage, so to speak, against the differentiated state of the paternal universe.

A place where this rage and its resulting destructiveness is perspicuous is in the work of "the author best placed to reveal the very essence of anality and sadism, the Marquis de Sade himself."[154] What one often finds in his oeuvre are sacrilegious orgies that systematically set out to violate all "natural" distinctions. Chasseguet-Smirgel's thesis is that the progression toward diabolical surgery, murder and dismemberment, which often characterize the Sadean orgy, is not accidental but, on the contrary, the logical outcome of the attack on differentiation. When the intention of the entire process is to "[eradicate] the essence of things,"[155] to reduce "everything that is highly differentiated . . . to homogeneous" fecal "particles from which all specificity have been subtracted," then murder and dismemberment, conceived of as the "mere rearrangement of cells," is its logical culmination.[156]

If there is a single point that accounts most for the difference in tone between the theories of Chasseguet-Smirgel and McDougall, it is perhaps the latter's persistent emphasis on reparation and "the eternal attempts of every child to effect some sort of self-cure for the inevitable psychic conflicts that will assail him."[157] For McDougall, every symptomatic phenomenon, including the perversions, must be viewed simultaneously as a piece of pathology and as a psychic creation that aims at self-cure and seeks to avert an even greater psychological catastrophe. Chasseguet-Smirgel, because she tends to reduce the perversions to their genesis in anality and does not understand them as multidetermined phenomena,[158] tends to see only the destructiveness and misses the struggle against it.

McDougall, on the other hand, views the sadism involved in "neosexual" enactments both as an expression of the hatred against the parents in the primal scene and the bad "breast-mother" that was its precursor, and as an attempt to contain that hatred and repair its fantasied consequences. Indeed, it is the capacity of neosexual creations "to contain and harmlessly discharge hatred and violence through erotization of the affects [which] delimits perverse organizations from psychotic ones."[159] In the neosexual enactment, "the fetish, the partner, or part object" can be used as a "container for the subject's destructive wishes toward the objects of his desire." If the individual is closer to the *depressive* mode of functioning, "the erotic act may include the fantasy of *repairing* the partner for imagined castrative or other attacks." If the individual is closer to the persecutory mode of thought, "the need to *control and master* the *partner* erotically in order to *protect [the] self* against attack may reveal itself." In this case "the orgasm of the partner is then felt to be equivalent to his castration, and the subject thus escapes the danger of finding himself the object and victim, able to be manipulated and influenced by sexual desire."[160] The point is that, except in the limiting case of the Sadean orgy—which Chasseguet-Smirgel takes as the essential case— "no one is castrated; no one is killed."[161] And as long as the perverted individual is successful at containing murderous and castrative impulses through these erotized enactments, a more complete form of psychic death, namely, psychosis, can be averted: to this extent, "Eros triumphs over death."[162]

The analysis of creativity is another area in which the differences between the two theories are pronounced. As we have seen, Chasseguet-Smirgel assimilates creation to procreation and stresses the internalization of the father, the renunciation of pregenitality, and the acceptance of the paternal universe as the necessary precondition for authentic creativity. McDougall, in sharp contrast, views artistic creativity as the preeminent sphere where the "deep bisexual longing in mankind," which "the genital sexual relationship cannot alone absorb," finds acceptable social expression. "Creative acts and processes . . . permit people to produce magically," which is to say, retain their omnipotent wish to be both sexes at once by being both father and mother to the artistic product. She observes, moreover, that "many work inhibitions and intellectual and artistic blocks are rooted in the unconscious refusal to accept bisexual wishes and conflicts." She also views masturbation, where the hand can function as the organ of the opposite sex and thereby create the illusion of bisexual completeness, as the other "quasi-universal" activity where the bisexual wish finds expression. However, unlike the essentially private activity of masturbation, artistic creation, while produced "magically,"[163] is, at the same time, directed toward an audience and must therefore conform to public requirements of aesthetic representation. Indeed, as Freud already noted, the artist's privileged status results, in part, from the ability to impose private preoccupations, which remain loyal to the pleasure principle, on an audience in such a way that they assume public significance.[164]

Similar and closely connected differences emerge in the analysis of anality and creativity. Rather than stressing the sadism of that psychosexual stage, McDougall emphasizes its productivity. Citing Picasso's dictum "that the only work that counts is the work that has not yet been accomplished," she argues that "to a truly creative individual, the production is always more important than the final product" and that this "pleasure-in-producing" can be traced to the sublimatory transformations of the child's "immense delight in the eliminatory acts that give birth to his first visible creations—his own body products."[165] And, once again, as in the case of bisexuality, many inhibitions and blocks in creativity can result form the taboos surrounding anal erotism as well as anal sadism. To be sure,

Chasseguet-Smirgel recognizes that, because it is idealized in the perversions, anality is not available for sublimatory transformation, and that the perverse work in fact suffers from a deficit of instinctuality.[166] However, because her position is weighted so heavily in the direction of the destructive side of anality, its productive contribution to creativity does not systematically enter her analysis.

I would like to raise a criticism of McDougall's position that pertains, as one might expect, to the flip side of her strong point. While she has effectively elucidated the various normative and perhaps normalizing presuppositions that have been operative in psychoanalysis since its inception, she is less persuasive when she attempts to clarify the standpoint from which she necessarily works. Like the rest of us, after Thomas Kuhn, she has learned that, whether we deny it or not, every clinical intervention, indeed even the decision when to intervene, is theory laden—and hence value laden. At the same time, she has also learned how difficult it is to justify the theoretical frameworks that necessarily inform those interventions.

McDougall attempts to grapple with this issue in her contribution to the symposium entitled "Perversions and Near-Perversions in Clinical Practice."[167] After exposing many of the value assumptions that inform psychoanalytic theory and practice in a variety of schools, she attempts to formulate her own version of "a fundamental value underlying our theories of psychic functioning and clinical practice." She argues that, just as society seeks to "safeguard *social* survival" and medicine attempts to "safeguard *biological* survival," psychoanalysis should "claim as its ethic the goal of safeguarding, above all, the factors that contribute to the *psychic* survival of human beings."[168] As we have already seen, McDougall approaches all pathological phenomena as "childlike attempts at self-cure in the face of unavoidable mental pain," that is to say, as unsuccessful attempts, made in childhood and continuing into adulthood, to survive "the universal traumata of human life."[169]

This attitude is undoubtedly indispensable in permitting analysts to empathize with patients' fantasies and behavior, however alien, foreign, and disturbing they may appear. As a "fundamental value" for psychoanalysis, however, psychic survival is inadequate for two reasons. First, as opposed to biological survival, psychic survival is not simply a functionalist concept with no normative reference. Except in the extreme case of certain forms of psychosis, in which something like psychic death becomes a possibility, humans always survive more or less adequately, and the notion of adequacy necessarily makes reference to a norm. Hence, we are back to all the problems of clarifying the norm that surround the more traditional candidates for a fundamental value. The normative question cannot, in fact, be avoided.

Second, I would argue that the notion of psychic survival is too weak. McDougall, like many of the best-intentioned analysts today, wants to avoid the dogmatic and sectarian excesses of the past and to appreciate the realities of the pluralistic world in which we live and practice. This laudable aspiration, however, has caused her, like many contemporary analysts, to become too apologetic and timid in the espousal of psychoanalytic values. Further, I would maintain that we do not simply have a notion of survival but of living well, which means, among other things, that it is better to know than not to know; that it is better to be creative than to be fallow; that it is better to face the unavoidable crises of life centering on separation, sexual difference, and death than to disavow them; and, although we appreciate the reality and the function of aggression in human life, that it is better to love than to hate.

The Freudian Left and the Freudian Right: Marcuse, Chasseguet-Smirgel, and the Limits of Utopia

It may be surprising, but it is not illogical, that Chasseguet-Smirgel, the psychoanalytic conservative, and Marcuse, the ultra-leftist, should concur so thoroughly in their description of the relation between the perverse and the utopian impulse. Both theorists maintain that a basic affinity exists between the two in that each represents the wish to circumvent the reality principle. They part company, however, when it comes to the assessment of the reality principle itself and, therefore, in their stance toward the impulse to bypass it. Chasseguet-Smirgel, on the one hand, views the reality principle as a transhistorical phenomenon, which exists by nature and which can be violated only at the cost of psychopathology at the level of the individual and of barbarism at the level of the collectivity.

Marcuse, on the other hand, sees it as a historically contingent fact, which exists by convention and which can and ought to be superseded. Indeed, as we have seen, he believes that the current configuration of the reality principle, the performance principle, *must* be surpassed in order to escape the dialectic of enlightenment. We have also seen that Marcuse explicitly looks to perversion as a phenomenon that has eluded reality testing and that can therefore be used to decipher the contours of a social order lying beyond the reality principle. Chasseguet-Smirgel draws a similar sociopolitical conclusion—one that had already been implicit in her more strictly clinical work: a "perverse core," consisting in a wish to transgress the human condition as it is delimited by the Oedipus complex, constitutes a ubiquitous feature of human psychic life:

Man has always endeavored to go beyond the narrow limits of his condition. . . . [P]erversion is one of the essential ways and means he applies in order to push forward the frontiers of what is possible and to unsettle reality. I do not see perversions only as disorders of sexual nature affecting a relatively small number of people, though their role and importance in the socio-cultural field can never be overestimated. I see perversions more broadly, as a dimension of the human psyche in general, a temptation in the mind common to us all.[170]

She observes, moreover, that this ubiquitous, perverse core often becomes unbound during periods of social and political upheaval—for example, during the time of imperial Rome, prerevolutionary France, and Weimar Germany, and, by implication, undoubtedly during our own time—when faltering institutions can no longer integrate it into social life. This observation leads her to suggest the following hypothesis: "Shouldn't we associate historical ruptures which give an inkling of the advent of a new world, with the confusion between sexes and generations, peculiar to perversion, as if the hope for a new social and political reality went hand in hand with an attempt at destroying sexual reality and truth?"[171] Unfortunately, a seeming contradiction exists in Chasseguet-Smirgel's thinking concerning the facts she has perceptively described: she recognizes, on the one hand, that the perverse-utopian impulse, taken as an urge "to push forward the frontiers of what is possible and to unsettle reality," is a universal feature of mental life that provides the motor for much progressive social and cultural development, indeed, that history would be a stagnant affair without it. As such, she wishes "neither to condemn perversion [nor] to sing its praises"[172] but to analyze its significance for cultural development. On the other hand, a generally apprehensive attitude toward this wish to unsettle reality, fueled by recent historical and cultural developments, often causes Chasseguet-Smirgel, as we have observed, to lose her psychoanalytic neutrality. As a result, she is unable to consider how the general loosening of character structures and the dramatic easing of sexual taboos that have occurred since the sixties might contribute to new, postconventional identity formations.

The link between the archaic and the ideal, the past and the future, the infantile and the utopian becomes conspicuous in her discussion of the ego ideal, perhaps her single most important contribution to psychoanalytic theory. It quickly becomes apparent that this discussion is closely linked with her theory of the archaic matrix of the Oedipus complex, that is, with the theory through which she attempts to integrate narcissism into the account of the perversions, considered above. Because he does not seem to have made a clear distinction between the superego and the ego ideal, Freud never developed a systematic theory of the latter.[173] Although he introduced the notion in 1914, "from 1923 the concept of the ego ideal was . . . literally absorbed by that of the superego," and, although he continued to discuss the phenomena to which the concept referred, "Freud [after 1923] only rarely mentions the concept [by name]."[174] Chasseguet-Smirgel therefore wants to maintain a firm distinction, on the basis of Freud's own texts, between the superego, as "the heir to the Oedipus Complex"[175] and the agency of prohibition within the psyche, and the ego ideal, as "the heir to the original narcissism in which the childish ego enjoyed self-sufficiency"[176] and the agency of aspiration. The concept of the ego ideal emerges for Freud within the context of a specific problem context: given his strong position on the conservatism of the instincts, namely, that "man . . . has shown himself incapable of giving up a satisfaction he had once enjoyed," it is difficult to conceive how de-velopment is possible. For it follows that man would not be "willing to forgo the narcissistic perfection of his childhood,"[177] and "station-ary infantilism"[178] would appear unavoidable. Freud's solution is to argue that the narcissistic pleasure and perfection of childhood are in fact not given up but projected into the future and, as such, be-come the ego ideal:

> The ideal ego is now the target of the self-love which was enjoyed in child-hood by the actual ego. The subject's narcissism makes its appearance dis-placed on to this new ideal ego, which, like the infantile ego, finds itself possessed of every perfection that is of value. . . . What he projects before him as his ideal is the substitute for the lost narcissism of his childhood in which he was his own ideal.[179]

Once posited, the ego ideal becomes, as it were, the institutionalized sense of perfection in the psyche. Freud maintains, moreover, that "the departure from primary narcissism . . . gives rise to a vigorous attempt to recover that state."[180] However, once again everything turns on how that attempt is pursued, for "the ego ideal is at the source of the best and the worst of things."[181] The ego ideal, as the past projected into the future, moreover, can be understood as fur-nishing the psychological basis for the motif, so prominent in mysti-cal, romantic, and utopian literature, of the origin-as-goal.[182] Similarly, this sense of perfection can also be understood as the psy-chological source of the sense of the Absolute, the pursuit of which can result in the most sublime as well as the most calamitous conse-quences in human affairs.

The ambivalence, then, that is an essential feature of the ego ideal for Chasseguet-Smirgel, refers to the manner in which the individual can seek to recover lost omnipotent perfection once primary fusion has dissolved and differentiation has been introduced: "Thus the ego ideal is characterized by its bipolarity. In order to be again united with the ego it can choose either the shortest route, the most regres-sive one, or the evolutionary route which includes the integration of each stage of development."[183] After the dissolution of primary narcissism, the child can pursue the dyadic, or regressive, solution by attempting to recapture the primary object directly. While actual incest—incestuous intercourse constituting, as we have seen, an attempt to remerge with the primary object as well as an attempt to possess the mother on a phallic level—represents the most direct form of the dyadic solution, it is not the only one. Chasseguet-Smirgel argues that various forms of psychopathology and perversion represent, at least in fantasy, attempts at direct reunion with the incestuous object. She argues, moreover, that such diverse phenomena as hypnosis, being in love, addiction, and mesmerization by a charismatic leader can be traced to this wish for a manic merger with the primary object. Alternatively, the child can pursue the triadic, or progressive, solution. In this case, the individual accepts the prohibition against incest, that is, against direct reunion with the primary object, and turns his attention to the "external world for the object of his desires" [184] and as the arena in which to pursue the ego ideal by refinding the primary object in a substitute form.

The tension experienced by the gap between the ego ideal and the actual ego becomes an important motor for development. As opposed to the super-ego, which operates through fear, castration anxiety, and guilt, and poses maxims in the form of "Thou shalt not. . . ," the motivational force of the ego ideal consists in "a sense of expectation, hope, and promise" [185] Its maxims are, accordingly, positive and progressive, for example, "Mature and become X." The anthropological significance of the incest taboo consists in the fact that it turns the child away from the closed world of the incestuous family toward external reality. Needless to say, to the extent that one can approximate the ego ideal through outer-directed activity, one can never match the grandiose perfection fantasied in the dyadic solution. While "satisfaction is brought about from fulfilling this ideal," [186] that satisfaction is always limited. This is simply an anti-utopian fact and a feature of human finitude.

As with Marcuse and Ricoeur, time also plays a central role in Chasseguet-Smirgel's account of reality. Insofar as it leaves the dyadic solution open, the failure to internalize the double difference between the sexes and between the generations entails the failure to schematize an adequate conception of time, of development, and, ultimately, of reality itself. For this reason, Chasseguet-Smirgel considers the internalization of the double difference—which, for her, constitutes a translhistorical deep structure of human sociation—as "bedrock"[187] for establishing a "firm basis"[188] in reality. Temporality is first encountered in the interval between the emergence of a wish and its fulfillment, so that the immediate gratification of the wish would preclude the experience of that duration. Furthermore, psychic elaboration and symbolization arise in that interval only as an attempt at mediating the gap between the wish and the object by providing a substitute means of gratification; first, the representation of pleasure and, later, pleasure in representation replace organ pleasure.

Freud recognized the relationship between symbolization and the absent object in his famous observation of the *"fort-da"* game his grandson had devised to symbolically master his mother's (and father's) absence. Freud's jocular reference to his grandson's "great cultural achievement"[189] is in earnest: the symbolic mastery of the absence of the object and the pain attached to it is the nucleus of all cultural development. The elimination of the gap between the wish and the object—which Marcuse's notion of "integral satisfaction" certainly would accomplish—would therefore eliminate symbolization and the cultural achievements for which it provides the basis:

In other words, access to reality, distance of the ego and secondary process are possible only in the absence of such wish fulfillment as union with the mother affords. All these acquisitions which have made us human beings would collapse like a house of cards if that which gave rise to them were abolished; that is to say, if instead of "projecting itself forward," the ego ideal sought only to be united with the ego in a regressive style.[190]

Building on earlier preoedipal experiences of absence, frustration, and loss, the resolution of the Oedipus complex forecloses the dyadic option of direct remerger with the primary object and opens the triadic option—and therewith progressive development—as the only viable route: "The odeipal phase, with its incest taboo, solidifies awareness of the 'third dimension.' Immediate satisfaction keeps us very close to the object, in fact immerses us in it. Progressive frustrations—which later acquire an oedipal meaning—and the triangular situation enable us to keep the object at a distance, *creating perspective.*"[191] It may seem peculiar to point out that for Chasseguet-Smirgel the notion of "all these acquisitions which have made us human beings," which are the products of symbolization as a response to transience, frustration, and loss, is not problematic: what these acquisitions are and why they ought to be preserved is axiomatic. But for an eschatological utopian like Marcuse, who wants to contest the structure of civilization as a whole, it is not self-evident at all: any traditional virtue can be indicted as belonging to the regime of "old Adam." That he can take "the struggle against time" seriously is therefore consistent with his suspiciousness toward the "higher values" of the cultural traditions.

Chasseguet-Smirgel is correct in her insistence that the pursuit of the ego ideal must be mediated and that the attempt to recapture the union of the original object in a regressive, unmediated fashion is fraught with danger: any viable psychic and social structure must renounce direct access to the primary object. However, when she extrapolates her findings to the political realm, her own analysis itself becomes too unmediated.

In applying her analysis of the perversions—which takes the Sadean orgy as their paradigm—to the political realm, she traces much of the barbarism of our century—from the ovens of the Holocaust to the killing fields of Cambodia—to the same fecalization of the paternal universe that she identified in the connection between perversion and anality. Auschwitz, she points out, where bodies were incinerated into undifferentiated ash, was referred to as "the anus of the world." [192] While the element of rage against the parental couple in the perversions should in no way be underestimated, nor should the perverse element of fascism be ignored, Chasseguet-Smirgel's analysis of the relationships among perversion, sadism, and politics, is itself not sufficiently differentiated. After all, there is a distinction as McDougall recognizes, between fantasy and symbolic enactment, however barbaric the content, on the one hand, and political action that seeks concretely to realize that content in the world, on the other.

Chasseguet-Smirgel's sometimes less-than-neutral attitude toward the perversions results from her failure to make that distinction adequately. Furthermore, she criticizes a number of the political and cultural movements of the last thirty years—including the French student movement of 1968, the women's movement, the Chinese Cultural Revolution, the fall of Cambodia, and the ecological and pacifist politics of the German Greens—in terms of their regressive tendencies, by which she means their attempt to circumvent the paternal law and reunite with the archaic mother directly. And, while her analyses of these movements are often perceptive, they tend to be too undifferentiated. She is so troubled by the regressive elements of these movements, by their "*fascination* with the primitive mother"[193] and concerned with constructing a "rampart against barbarity"[194] that, unlike Marcuse, she is unable to appreciate the other side, namely, the legitimate desire to rediscover the maternal voice in an overly bureaucratic, scientistic, and phallocentric civilization that threatens to destroy our natural habitat.

If, according to Chasseguet-Smirgel, the perverse individual idealizes pregenitality and immaturity, then, for her part, she tends to idealize a rather delimited notion of maturity and conformity to the (paternal) law, which she hypostatizes into an ahistorical phenomenon. Consequently, she does not distinguish between an autonomous and a heteronomous relation to the law, which would make a critical stance toward existing laws possible. This becomes apparent in her strangely unequivocally affirmative analysis of the superego. Chasseguet-Smirgel argues that, whereas the ego ideal "tends to reinstate Illusion," the superego tends "to promote reality."[195] It is undoubtedly true that, without an adequate *passage* through the developmental crucible of the Oedipus complex and the establishment of the superego, the child's access to reality will be compromised. The establishment of the superego is therefore a precondition, but only a precondition, of the individual's access to reality. To close the investigation at this point, however, as Chasseguet-Smirgel does, is to ignore the other side of the superego: namely, its archaic, primitive, and cruel aspects, which result from its close proximity to the id[196] and which can combine to give it its illusory (and instinctualized) character. Let us not forget that the superego can become "a pure culture of the death instinct."[197]

Ricoeur correctly observes that "one would fail to grasp . . . the specificity of the Freudian interpretation of morality if one passed too quickly over these archaic features of the superego."[198] The superego, along with the id, forms an "internal foreign territory" vis-à-vis the ego and, as such, confronts the ego as an alien institution with its own heteronomous laws. And because of the heteronomy of its laws and the cruelty of its demands, the superego can, at best, produce only an inadequate premorality, which is, at the same time, an antimorality: "Freud's contribution here consists in his discovery of a fundamental structure of ethical life, namely a first stratum of morality that has the function both of preparing the way for autonomy and of retarding it, of blocking it off at an archaic stage. The inner tyrant plays the role of premorality and antimorality."[199] Chasseguet-Smirgel, who confesses she is "not very familiar" with ego psychology,[200] never takes up the next developmental step, which is required for the move from premorality to morality in the proper sense, from heteronomy to autonomy, from immature conformity and idealization to *real* maturity. Instead, her analysis never moves beyond a heteronomous relationship to the law (acting in accordance with the law), and she never raises the question of how the ego can make the law its own. Therein lies a deep theoretical source of her conservatism. Like her nemesis Lacan, and in a similarly ahistorical fashion, she hypostatizes and valorizes the law of the father, lawfulness as such, and never asks how the individual, having internalized lawfulness, can adopt a critical stance toward any given law.

The problem becomes particularly acute in her analysis of Freud's Jewishness. She argues that Judaism's emphasis on the paternal law and differentiation allowed him to explore and chart the subterranean world of the unconscious without becoming engulfed by it. She fails, however, to take into account the other, equally important side of Freud: namely, in the name of the ego—perhaps in identification with the heretical Jewish tradition—he was a critical rationalist, who promulgated the autonomous critique of the paternal law and traditionalistic authority; after all, he set out to debunk the order of the fathers in *Totem and Taboo, The Future of an Illusion,* and *Moses and Monotheism.*[201] Indeed, it is impossible to conceive of Freud, the militant atheist and "the godless Jew," affirmatively quoting the Old Testament the way Chasseguet-Smirgel does.[202] To be sure, Freud understood the centrality of law and the social contract in the structuring of civilization and of the psyche, but, as a proponent of the Enlightenment, he also maintained that law should be subjected to the scrutiny of the ego and legitimated by autonomous reason.[203]

Because she does not introduce a distinction between autonomy and heteronomy—and hence a distinction between an ego and a superego solution to the problem of perverse sexuality—Chasseguet-Smirgel remains a stalwart of the "Party of the Superego." (Let us not forget that the authoritarian personality, with its masochistic submission to the superego, is itself a form of character perversion.) Were she to introduce the distinction I am suggesting, she could transfer her allegiances to the "Party of the Ego," while retaining her opposition to the "Party of the Id."[204]

Ricoeur: Ananke as the Cipher of Possible Wisdom

As I have already indicated, Ricoeur's treatment of the topic of Ananke—which he understands as the "inexorable" or the "ineluctable"[205]—is far more satisfactory than Marcuse's.

Ricoeur shows that the notion of the reality principle, like the concept of the reality that is its correlate, undergoes a transformation in Freud's thinking after the introduction of narcissism. In the beginning, the reality principle was simply understood in perceptual terms, as the principle of mental functioning introduced with the (relative) renunciation of hallucinatory wish fulfillment, the achievement of a sufficient quantum of bound cathexis for the ego to function, and the institutionalization of reality testing. Similarly, the concept of reality, prior to the introduction of narcissism, was neutral, simply the opposite of the hallucination: "Reality does not pose a problem, it is assumed as known; the normal person and the psychiatrist are its measure; it is the physical and social environment of adaptation."[206] Thus far, although the order and connection of the things do not necessarily correspond to the order and connection of our wishes, they do not necessarily oppose them either. Up to this point, "nothing in [Freud's] analysis bears a tragic accent: nothing foreshadows the world view dominated by the struggle between Eros and death."[207] However, after the introduction of narcissism—which provided Freud with both the motivation and the vocabulary to articulate what Kohut has called his "truth morality"[208]—the concept of reality acquires the connotation of *harshness*. As such, it becomes opposed to the nexus of our wishes and to our narcissism, that seeks to deny that harshness by creating consoling illusions. The most extreme formulation of this position is to be found in *Civilization and Its Discontents,* in which Freud states that the program of the pleasure principle "is at loggerheads with the whole world." [209] A direct line can be traced from the concept of narcissism, taken as desire's propensity to deny the harshness of reality; through the introduction of the death instinct, which represents the foremost instance of harsh reality; to the reformulation of the reality principle as Ananke. The reality principle develops from "a principle mental regulation" to "the cipher of possible wisdom." "Ananke does not merely pertain to reality testing, but to a wisdom that dares to face the harshness of life" and is, therefore, "the symbol of disillusionment." [210] The adoption of the Greek term to designate the concept indicates the expanded philosophical terrain Freud is now attempting to occupy. Furthermore, the reality principle, according to this interpretation, is not given once and for all but becomes a task, undoubtedly interminable, to be pursued throughout life.

To understand the meaning of Ananke as "the cipher of possible wisdom," we must, in turn, understand death as the ultimate cipher of a reality whose harshness results, in no small part, from its temporal constitution, that is to say, from transience. To this end, Freud's paper on narcissism should be considered in conjunction with his wartime triptych, "Thoughts for the Times on War and Death" (1915), "On Transience" (1916), and "Mourning and Melancholia" (1917). The first two "cultural" papers supply the broader philosophical meaning for the more strictly clinical "Mourning and Melancholia." Death, as the primary instance of transience and loss, is the supreme barrier to our omnipotence and the ultimate reminder of our "helplessness and . . . insignificance in the machinery of the universe." [211] As such, it constitutes the principal affront to our narcissism, which consequently mobilizes the innumerable strategies of illusion to deny transience in general and death in particular. If science or wisdom, and the two are indistinguishable for Freud, comprise the apprehension of reality shorn of the consoling illusions we project onto it, then "our incorrigible narcissism" [212] is indeed the opponent of wisdom in this sense. [213] This means that science prescribes not only a cognitive task but an affective one as well:

Resignation to the ineluctable is not reducible to a mere knowledge of necessity, i.e., to a purely intellectual extension of what we call perceptual
reality-testing; resignation is an affective task, a work of correction applied
to the very core of the libido, to the heart of narcissism. Consequently, the
scientific world view must be incorporated into the history of desire.[214]

A disturbing question, however, indeed the question on which the
entire Freudian enterprise turns, must be raised at this point: why
does this "resignation to the ineluctable" result in the erotic en-
hancement of life rather than depressive despair in the face of a
thoroughly disenchanted universe? What, in short, separates Freud's
vision from Beckett's? Or, as Ricoeur puts it: "Finally, what about the
reality principle, which seems indeed to usher in a wisdom beyond
illusion and consolation? How does this lucidity, with its attendant
pessimistic austerity, ultimately fit in with the love of life which the
drama of love and death seems to call for?"[215] Freud's answer to this
question is to be found in the concepts of mourning, symbolization,
and the formation of psychic structure.

In "Thoughts for the Times on War and Death," Freud offers a
personal observation that stuns the reader with its uncharacteristically provocative brutality. With the war, he writes, "life has, indeed,
become interesting again; it has recovered its full content." The reason for this is that "death will no longer be denied; we are forced to
believe in it. People really die."[216] While the strident tone of this
remark may result from Freud's struggle to master his own anguish
and disillusionment at the time, the meaning is, nevertheless, clear
here and throughout the triptych. Life is impoverished to the extent
that we practice denial to narcissistically defend ourselves from loss.

Freud elaborates this idea in "On Transience," a paper that can
be as philosophically serene as "Thoughts" can be brutal. During a
summer walk in the Dolomites, a young poet complained to Freud
that, although he recognized the beauty of the surrounding country-
side, he could not enjoy it, because "he was disturbed by the thought
that all this beauty was fated to extinction."[217] Freud explains this
condition as "a revolt . . . against mourning." Because the experience
gave the poet "a foretaste of mourning" and because he lacked the
confidence that he could tolerate "the extraordinarily painful"[218]
process of mourning—which, nevertheless, "comes to a spontaneous

end"—he abstained from investing his libido in the beauty of nature in an attempt to avoid the pain at its inevitable loss.[219] Denial, rather than insulating life from its inevitable pain, actually impoverishes it: "Life is impoverished, it loses in interest, when the highest stake in the game of life, life itself, may not be risked."[220] For Freud, denial, which clings to the pleasure principle, is not an efficient allotment of one's resources even with respect to the calculus of pleasure and pain. Finally, the link between mourning and "resignation to the ineluctable," goes further: mourning, in response to loss, results in the symbolization and psychic structure that make transience, and hence reality, tolerable. Thus, the intrinsic relation between Logos and Ananke. Considerations such as these lead Ricoeur, like Chasse-guet-Smirgel, to argue that "if man could be satisfied, he would be deprived of something more important than pleasure—symbolism which is the counterpart of dissatisfaction. Desire, qua insatiable demand, gives rise to speech."[221] The elimination of the gap between the wish and its object, "integral satisfaction" in Marcuse's terms, would preclude the conditions that make possible our existence as symbolizing animals.[222] And symbolization, we must insist, does not simply belong to "the cultural household of the performance principle."

Ultimately, then, the difference between Freud's skeptical realism and Marcuse's utopianism concerns the question of transience. Whereas Marcuse, who must be complimented for his speculative consistency, envisages the utopian "conquest of time," which would comprise an attempt at the omnipotent denial of Ananke, Freud formulates a program for the always-relative coming to terms with transience.

Excursus

The Suspension of the Utopian Motif in Critical Theory

Today the phrase "end of utopia" has come to mean exactly the opposite of what Marcuse intended in 1967, which is to say, it has come to mean that utopia has been exhausted as a project and discredited as a body of thought. Indeed, the idea of utopia is no longer regarded simply as softheaded, naive, or unattainable, it is viewed as *positively dangerous* as well. The political experiences of the last three decades have chastened the utopian sensibility and produced a new appreciation of human finitude—of difference, particularity, and plurality—as well as a suspicion of grandiose projects and the meta-narratives that have traditionally been associated with them. The postmodernists of the seventies and eighties rediscovered what Adorno and Horkheimer, who were deeply influenced by Nietzsche in this regard, had already recognized in the forties. Marxism, far from representing the negation of the Baconian legacy, was deeply implicated in its program of omnipotent domination. Authoritarian state socialism was not a contingent aberration of the Marxian project but a logical development of its innermost possibilities. Marx, Adorno observed, had wanted to turn the world into "a giant workhouse."[1] Leftist intellectuals of the postwar generation finally reacted to reports of the Gulag in the Soviet Union, the genocide in Cambodia, and the suppression of the Solidarity movement in Poland in the way they should already have reacted to the invasions of Hungary and Czechoslovakia, namely, with horror. At the same time the Hegelian insight, deriving from the conservative critique of the

French Revolution, that the attempt forcibly to impose abstract reason on an uncompliant world will result in violence of one form or another[2] has itself been abstractly generalized. In a form of theoretical anarchism, it has become fashionable to dismiss all ambitious theories that do not nominalistically cling to the particular as totalizing and, therefore, as potentially terroristic. The exception, of course, is the metanarratives that proclaim the end of the subject, meaning, history, and so on.

The demise of communism has rightfully engendered a new respect for liberalism, that sober philosophy that harbors no illusions about human perfectibility. Rather than devising a strategy for the perfection of humanity and society, liberalism seeks to formulate a scheme for rationally, which is to say, for justly negotiating the interactions of essentially flawed individuals, whose interests and desires might be in conflict at any given moment. The Marxian dismissal of so-called formal democracy rested on two assumptions: first, that Socialism could deliver on a superior, substantive form of democracy, which would eliminate the need for formal justice, and, second, that such a state of affairs, where conflict would be obviated in the reconciliation of the particular and general interest, is desirable. With regard to the first assumption, the indefinite deferment of the promissory note was, of course, only interrupted by the collapse of the Berlin Wall. And the second assumption is now seen as highly questionable. The Hegelian-Marxian idealization of the polis as the beautiful whole, where the general and the particular were reconciled, overlooked the fact that, far from being harmonized, a free society is argumentative even to the point of being fractious. As Hannah Arendt pointed out, the Athenians were perhaps the most contentious people that ever lived. If conflict is uneliminable, indeed, desirable, in a free society, then a method of negotiating conflicting points of views is required. Even Adorno, who is not famous as a champion of liberal democracy, argues that if we simply denounced the principles of formal justice as ideology, "we would be creating excuses for recidivism into ancient injustice." The element of rationality "which is inherent in the barter principle—as ideology, of course, but also as a promise—would give way to direct appropriation, to force."[3] When the barter principle is equated in toto with violence, the moment of promise is forgotten. And, empirically, when formal justice, whatever its limitations, is suspended, it only serves to benefit the powerful.

The current celebration of the West's victory over communism is, nevertheless, premature. We need only make note of the fact that in other regions of the world, from India to Argentina, the establishment of the principles of liberal democracy is often tenuous at best, and that, in certain cases, the most retrogressive features of the past, nationalism and chauvinism, are returning at an alarming rate. In the West itself, this self-congratulation elevates the conditions without which a better society cannot be established—that is, its necessary preconditions—into that better society. It overlooks the fact that our massive and perhaps intractable political, economic, environmental, ethnic, and cultural problems did not cease to exist with the demise of the Soviet Union. We simply possess the perhaps unsurpassable formal framework in which they can and must be confronted. The demise of actually existing socialism does not, in short, render the criticism of actually existing democracy obsolete.

The celebration of liberal democracy, moreover, for the most part disregards the vexing question of the market. There is no denying that, in the modern world, democracy has only existed in conjunction with the market. But at the same time, as the market appears to be a necessary condition for democracy, its destructiveness of cultural traditions, the environment, and, ultimately, democratic institutions themselves cannot be denied either. This is the truth content of Marx that should not be forgotten. Whether the connection between democracy and the market is necessary or contingent and whether the colonization of the lifeworld by the system can be contained, to use Habermas's vocabulary, remain open historical issues with profound consequences for the question of political and social renewal in developed and developing countries alike. Moreover, the formal principles of justice can accommodate an indefinitely wide range of historical content, of social forms; thus far, the public discourse in both the East and the West has exhibited a distinct "atrophy of the political imagination" concerning that content.[4] It is with respect to this content, I shall argue, that the utopian *imaginaire* can most productively be redirected after the end of utopia.

In turning to Critical Theory, we have seen that there is a systematic connection between the move to psychoanalysis and the move to utopian motifs in the early Frankfurt school. Both are motivated by the diagnosis of modernity as a dialectic of enlightenment. The sense of catastrophe, not of hope, initiated the search for redemption. Having inherited the problematic of reification from Lukács, who had himself inherited it from Weber, but being unable to accept his deus ex machina of the proletariat and the party, the Frankfurt school was left only with a totalizing, self-reinforcing logic of decline. Lukács without the party, after all, leaves one with the iron cage. Indeed, Horkheimer and Adorno, like Lukács before them and Foucault in his neostructuralist phase[5] after them, adopt a position that might be characterized as Weberian monism. Such a monism, despite the differences among its various adherents, identifies a tendency toward the totalization of *one* underlying process—for example, rationalization, commodification, technification, reification, instrumentalization, or power—as *the* essential dynamic of modernity and views all other developments, including the normative and democratizing innovations of modernity, as epiphenomenal to it. No positive, uncorrupted element exists within the totality that could provide the basis for immanent critique. Thus, unless one is stoically resigned to the inevitability of the iron cage, as Weber was, or can still believe in the existence of a class that is potentially transcendent, as Lukács did—and which the Frankfurt school could no longer do by the late thirties—then this totalizing, monistic analysis can instigate the search for the radical Other of instrumentalization. As we saw in Marcuse's case, it leads to an exploration of the unconscious and perverse sexuality as the good Other or repressive ego and the logic of domination. Since modernity is viewed as a corrupt totality that can only be holistically overcome—the Frankfurt school's contempt for the social democratic sensibility and hence for reformism enters in here[6]—and since, in principle, no positive feature can be located in it that could serve as a foothold for immanent critique, an uncontaminated element outside the totality, at least "a snippet of what differs,"[7] must be located that can serve as a fulcrum for the holistic transfiguration of that totality.[8]

This is not to say that Adorno is a utopian in any straightforward sense. Like everything else, he develops the utopian moment of his thinking in a dialectical manner that is defined by the following *aporia*. He insists that "the only philosophy which can be responsibly practiced in the face of despair is the attempt to contemplate all things as they would present themselves from the standpoint of redemption. . . . [A]ll else is reconstruction, mere technique." Epistemologically, so to speak, the very dissoluteness of the world requires the redemptive standpoint outside the "indigent and distorted" totality, for only the "messianic light" of redemption can adequately illuminate that fallen state in its fallenness. On the other hand, he recognizes that the adoption of the redemptive standpoint "is also the utterly impossible thing, because it presupposes a standpoint removed, even though by a hair's breadth, from the scope of existence."

To deny thought's conditioned status even "for the sake of the unconditional" and maintain that it can in fact remove itself from the world is to invite those conditioning elements to operate that much more blindly; it is, in fact, to deliver "thought up to the world."[9] Moreover, Adorno's acceptance of the *Bilderverbot,* the Jewish prohibition on representing God, reinforces his reluctance to speculate about the content of a possible utopian society. Not only is he suspicious of a false reconciliation that would soft-pedal the fallenness of the existing world, but, like the postmodernists, he is also concerned lest an abstract utopian design be violently imposed on the world and become one more template of domination. As we will see, similar aporetic inhibitions condition his thinking on the subject. Adorno, who defends the nonengaged intransigence of thought in the face of a bad reality,[10] makes it clear that his utopianism is not historical but an intratheoretical affair: "But beside the demand thus placed on thought, the question of the reality or unreality of redemption itself hardly matters."[11]

Habermas's initial systematic innovation against the older generation of Critical Theorists was to introduce a dualistic framework[12]—a third constituent would later be added—to counter their "anthropological and epistemological monism"[13] and avoid the resulting impasse. Interconnected theoretical and political considerations motivated his introduction of the distinction between practical or communicative rationality, on the one hand, and instrumental rationality, on the other. The dualistic framework provided Habermas with the resources he needed for his attempt to clarify the theoretical and normative foundations of Critical Theory, first as a transcendental anthropology of knowledge and later, after transcendental philosophy had come under increasing attack, as a reconstructive science. Whereas Horkheimer and Adorno had, for the most part, retained a disdainful distance from the methodological debates in the social sciences and academic philosophy, Habermas believed that with his revisions he could explicate Critical Theory's theoretical status and justify its normative standpoint to the larger community of investigators. Politically, he argued that, as science and technology had themselves become productive forces, it made sense to engage the scientific community more actively. Furthermore, the more differentiated theoretical scheme allowed Habermas to formulate a more discriminating assessment of modernity, including a diagnosis of its pathologies.

His rehabilitation of practical reason, reinterpreted in terms of an intersubjective theory of communication, allows him to elucidate the progressive, normative, democratizing advances of modernity. At the same time, he can still conceptualize a dialectic of enlightenment, now recast as the colonization of the lifeworld, which is no longer totalized. Instrumentalization becomes one—but only one—dynamic of modernity, coexisting alongside, and in tension with, its dynamic toward democratization. Whereas Adorno saw a totalized logic of decline, Habermas sees conflict and ambivalence, and this ambivalence provides the point of entry for political intervention. A more differentiated analysis "opens a perspective that does not simply obstruct courage but can make political action more sure of hitting the mark."[14] Habermas's strategy, then, is to assert modernity's democratizing dynamic against its instrumentalizing one by criticizing modern societies in terms of their own self-professed norms. He argues that, after the break with tradition, in which a system of taboos had structurally insulated the fundamental beliefs of the group from criticism, the requirement for the justification of basic norms has been incorporated into the self-understanding of modern societies. This does not mean that all norms are in fact rationally justified. It only means that, in principle, any given norm can be subjected to rational scrutiny and that the dogmatic appeal to tradition alone no longer counts as the final argument. This demand for justification constitutes "a piece of extant reason" [15] in the modern world that can serve as a foothold for immanent critique and a basis for radical reform. If this is true, then the search for an uncorrupted element outside the totality, which could provide the fulcrum for holistic rupture of that totality, is no longer necessary.

If the sense of catastrophe and the utopian *topos* go hand in hand with the early Frankfurt school, Habermas's less dire diagnosis of modernity results, as one might expect, in what Leo Lowenthal has called the "suspension of the utopian motif" [16] in Critical Theory. In contrast to Adorno's ultraradicalism, which remained confined to the theoretical and aesthetic planes, Habermas is a self-avowed "radical liberal," who has never regarded himself as avant-garde nor "dreamt of a revolutionary subject." [17] He rejects holistic revolutionary change in advanced societies, because our fallibilistic consciousness, reinforced by the lessons of history, should have deprived us of the requisite hubris for such an undertaking; because the unintended consequences of attempts at holistic transformation are simply too incalculable to be risked in complex societies; and, most importantly, because, as we have just seen, normative principles that ought not to be violated and that can become the basis for immanent critique have been institutionalized in modern societies.

As we might expect, moreover, the de-utopianization of Critical Theory was concomitant with the different uses Habermas makes of psychoanalytic theory, for he no longer utilizes psychoanalysis primarily for the diagnosis of the pathologies of modernity (as Adorno and Horkheimer did) nor for speculations about the contents of a utopian society (like Marcuse). Rather, as Thomas McCarthy points out, the single point that perhaps most separates Habermas from his predecessors in this regard is that "the lessons he derives from this reconstruction [of psychoanalysis] are largely methodological." [18] For Habermas "psychoanalysis is relevant . . . as the only

tangible example of a science incorporating methodical self-reflection." [19] Habermas, in other words, believed that psychoanalysis provided a model of the type of methodologically legitimate, self-
reflective science on which a critical theory of society should model
itself.

One of the main difficulties with the methodological appropriation of Freud, which Habermas himself came to realize, concerned
an ambiguity in the concept of self-reflection. That ambiguity would
become one of the sources for the transition from Habermas's theory of the sixties to his theory of the seventies and the move away
from psychoanalysis, which was concomitant with that transition.[20]
Self-reflection can mean the reconstruction of the presuppositions
of knowledge and action in the tradition of Kantian transcendental
philosophy, the aim being to determine and validate the fundamental norms of knowledge and action. Self-reflection can also mean, in
the tradition of psychoanalysis, the practical (and affective) reflection by a subject on, and struggle against, the ossified blockages to
insight and development that have been incurred in the self-formation process. The aim in this case is the practical emancipation from
those blockages. It is important to stress that the two involve very
different notions of the unconscious. The process of reconstruction
seeks to locate the structures, classificatory systems, schemata, and so
on, that underlie our knowledge and action but are not opposed
by any dynamic forces. They are therefore only unconscious in the
descriptive sense. This means that, in principle, they are "latent and
capable of becoming conscious" without sustained affective struggle,
although enormous cognitive effort may of course be required. Psychoanalytic reflection, in contrast, pertains to ideas that are unconscious in the dynamic sense, that is, they are unconscious because
"certain forces oppose them." Therefore a dynamic struggle is generally involved in their becoming conscious, and a specific means is
generally necessary—for example, psychoanalytic technique—for
combating those forces.[21]

Because he failed to distinguish between self-reflection and reconstruction, Habermas could assume that his reconstruction of the
universal presuppositions of the species' capacities for knowledge
and action, "transcendental anthropology," as he called it, was at

the same time emancipatory critique. When he recognized the distinction, the preponderance of the methodological motive in his thinking led him to more or less jettison self-reflection in the psychoanalytic sense, emancipatory critique, in favor of reconstruction. In conjunction with this, and in response to the criticism that the notion of a species-subject is untenable, Habermas moved away from transcendental anthropology, which presupposes such a subject, to a systems-theoretical approach. Axel Honneth describes the move: "From then on he no longer interprets the processes of rationalization, in which he attempts to conceive the evolution of society, as a process of the will-formation of the human species; rather, he understands them as a supra-subjective learning process carried by the social system."[22]

An impersonal learning process, not embodied individuals and groups, not struggling subjects, becomes the carrier of rationality on which Critical Theory could ground its hopes. One wonders to what extent the increasing move to the supra-subjective system as the carrier of reason was connected with the decline of the political movements of the sixties and the rise of neoconservatism in the seventies. In the late seventies, moreover, the defense of "the project of modernity,"[23] emerged as the theoretical and political organizing principle for Habermas's labyrinthine enterprise. The move from Freud to Piaget and Kohlberg must be understood in this theoretical context. Habermas believed the nondynamic theory developed by these two cognitive psychologists, with its formal development schemata, provided him with the means of explicating the supra-subjective learning process, with its purportedly progressive aspects, on which he now relied.[24] The transition from psychoanalysis to cognitive psychology had another consequence as well, that is, a decorporealization of Critical Theory. The move entailed a departure from the "underground" history of Europe, namely, the history of the body and "the fate of the human instincts and passions which are displaced and distorted by civilization,"[25] which had been so crucial for Horkheimer and Adorno. Honneth observes: "The investigation . . . is directed exclusively to an analysis of rules . . . so that the bodily and physical dimension of social action no longer comes into view. As a result, the human body, whose historical fate . . . Adorno . . .

had drawn into the center of the investigation . . . loses all value within a critical social theory."[26]

I will argue against Habermas (and Lacan) that Freud's drive theory is not a biologistic doctrine but a theory of the frontier between *soma* and *psyche*—a theory of the representation of the body in the mind—and that, as such, it can still provide a point of departure for reincorporating the body into Critical Theory.

Let us assume that the basic thrust of Habermas's reformulation of Critical Theory—the correction of the Frankfurt school's Weberian antimodernism, the chastening of its speculative excesses, and the narrowing of the project to render its findings more secure and its political aim more accurate—is correct. The following question would nevertheless remain: what is the fate of the transgressive-utopian impulse given the new sobriety? After all, it is safe to assume that human beings have continued to dream after the linguistic turn.

Habermas himself has intermittently tried to respond to the charge, often raised by sympathetic critics, that he has relinquished too much of the utopian (and aesthetic) content of the Frankfurt school. In his important (and transitional) essay on the thoroughly antiprogressivistic Walter Benjamin, in whom the conjunction of the sense of catastrophe with messianism is the most pronounced, Habermas raises a question against a position such as his own, which is characterized by a Hegelian acceptance of the basic structure of the modern world: must an appreciation of the progress in legality and morality that has occurred with modernity result in "a joyless reformism whose sensorium has long since been stunted as regards the difference between an improved reproduction of life and a fulfilled life"?[27] Indeed, the revisions in Critical Theory that enabled him to overcome the totalized negative philosophy of history and concomitant utopianism of the early Frankfurt school and that entail a separation of the question of justice and happiness appear to open a disturbing possibility, namely, "that one day an emancipated human race could encounter itself within an expanded space of discursive formation of will and yet be robbed of the light in which it is capable of interpreting its life as something good."[28] A just society could, in other words, be an empty one. It was largely in response to considerations such as these, I believe, that Habermas attempted, at several points in his career, to reintegrate utopian elements into his essentially nonutopian scheme and to add the aesthetic-expressive dimension to his formerly dualistic framework.[29]

I would like to consider two such points. In both cases, Habermas can be observed struggling against the constraints of his position. They involve the attempt to supplement the fundamental ethical norms of the Enlightenment, autonomy and maturity *(Mündigkeit)*,[30] with utopian content, while not violating the strictures of Kant's post-metaphysical standpoint nor conflating questions of the right with questions of the good. In 1969, perhaps in an attempt to differentiate himself from his mentor, Habermas was still willing to draw a strong distinction between himself, the Enlightenment philosopher of *Mündigkeit,* and Adorno, the utopian philosopher of reconciliation. Evincing no uneasiness at rejecting the utopian motif, Habermas argued that Adorno's commitment to the idea of reconciliation represented an unauthorized theological residue in his otherwise atheistic philosophy and that, had Adorno exchanged the norm of reconciliation for the norm *Mündigkeit,* he would have been able to escape the cul de sac of the dialectic of enlightenment: "Adorno, undeviating atheist that he was, . . . hesitated to moderate the idea of reconciliation to that of autonomy and responsibility."[31]

In *Theory of Communicative Action,* however, Habermas no longer argues that Adorno should have abandoned his utopian *desideratum* of reconciliation (and mimesis) for the concept of *Mündigkeit.* Now, in an attempt at *Aufhebung* ("sublation") rather than schism, he argues that Adorno should have retained it and moved from a philosophy of consciousness to a philosophy of intersubjectivity in order to have fulfilled it. Habermas, Wellmer, and Benhabib[32] all maintain that Adorno could have eluded the aporia of negative dialectics and achieved the solution he was seeking when he turned to *Aesthetic Theory* if he had moved to an intersubjective theory of communication. They argue that the nonreifying logic, the nonviolent synthesis of the manifold, which defined the concept of reconciliation for Adorno and which he believed was at least prefigured in the advanced work of art, actually obtains most fully in the dialogical relation of the identity of the identical and the nonidentical found in ordinary language communication. And communication, unlike the work of art, can become a basis for possible *social* synthesis. Moreover, the theory of communicative action reinterprets *Mündigkeit* in terms of socialization into an intersubjective community instead of in terms of the monological unfolding of individual development. As opposed to the 1969 article, reconciliation and *Mündigkeit* are now both conceptualized in terms of intersubjective communication, and there is, therefore, no essential conflict between them. As we will see, however, there is a problematic proviso in Habermas's suggestion that undoubtedly would have been unacceptable to Adorno, namely, that the concept of reconciliation be restricted to the relationship between subjects.

A second place where Habermas attempts to address the utopian concerns of early Critical Theory is in his critique of Lawrence Kohlberg's theory of moral development. Martin Jay correctly observes[33] that the early Frankfurt school had interpreted psychoanalysis as an empirical concretization of Kant's practical philosophy. Whereas Kant had formulated a purely philosophical account of autonomy, Freud provided an empirical theory that delineates the psychic structures that are the necessary conditions for autonomy and the developmental steps that must be successfully negotiated for those structures to be established. For Kant, as we have noted, autonomy is purchased through the renunciation of inclination, which is rooted in our empirical, bodily existence. For Freud—at least according to one well-known interpretation—it is achieved through the repression of our drives. On this reading, autonomy is achieved through the sacrifice of inner nature, and the conflict between duty and inclination or between the ego and the drives is absolutized. As early as 1938, Marcuse[34] challenged the absolutization of the conflict between reason and inner nature, and that challenge remained part of the materialist heritage of Critical Theory. Indeed, Marcuse's turn to Freud in *Eros and Civilization* and his attempt to conceptualize the emancipation of inner nature were motivated, in large part, by the desire to "deontologize" that opposition.

Habermas returns to this thematic, for a moment at least, when he criticizes Kohlberg's theory of moral development. Habermas initially enlists Kohlberg's cognitivist schema to help elucidate the progress in legality and morality referred to in the Benjamin article and thereby to demonstrate the advances that have occurred with the decentration of the modern worldview. He proceeds to argue, however, that Kohlberg's account of moral development does not go far enough. As it more or less corresponds to a Kantian ethics of universal principles, Kohlberg's ultimate stage (stage 6) suffers from the typical Kantian opposition of duty and inclination. Because needs are posited as naturally given, they are assumed to be inaccessible to cultural, rational, and communicative influence. Habermas therefore argues that the "model of autonomy" must be augmented by a "richer and more ambitious . . . model of unconstrained ego identity"[35] that would involve the unfettered communication—"free intercourse," to use Freud's term[36]—between the ego and the other regions of the personality. We should note that Habermas's politico-cultural motives for criticizing Kohlberg on this issue concern the contemporary politics of identity: if the decentered, postconventional subject is indeed to be more spontaneous, flexible, and open than the rigidly integrated bourgeois individual, and if needs are not going to be granted the fixed status of second nature, then it must be possible for inner nature to be more consciously drawn into the self-formation process. Thus, once the *formal* requirements of contemporary moral theory have been met by the first six stages of Kohlberg's schema, Habermas wants to remove "the restriction to the cognitive side"[37] and introduce *content* from the side of inner nature. Because of the initial Kantian separation of form and content, cognition and drive, that content, which was originally bracketed for the sake of autonomy, can only be brought in, if not as an afterthought, at least ex post facto. Logos and Eros, as it were, do not develop in tandem but in isolation from one another.

The dissociation of form from content, cognition from drive, is, however, not only a deficiency resulting from the Kantian restrictions of Habermas's approach—although it is certainly that, too. As with Kant, it has its positive, intentional aspect as well. It is precisely to guard against a prescriptive utopianism, which would dictate the substance of the good life from above, and to safeguard the possibility of plurality of individual and collective life-forms, that Habermas, following Wellmer, insists on a "gap" between the formal requirements of a just society and the concrete substance of the good life.

Justice would be the domain of discourse ethics, the good life of political practice:

Nothing makes me more nervous than the imputation—repeated in a number of different versions and in the most peculiar contexts—that because the theory of communicative action focuses attention on the social facticity of recognized validity-claims, it proposes, or at least suggests, a rationalist utopian society. I do not regard the fully transparent society as an ideal, nor do I wish to suggest any other ideal.[38]

For Habermas, what can at best be salvaged from the old substantive notion of the good life, after the decentering of the modern worldview, would involve some sort of contingent, flexible, and felicitous communication between and "balance among [the] moments"[39] within both collective and individual identities, which could not be specified before the fact. In the first case, that balance would pertain to the interplay of the aesthetic-expressive, the cognitive, and the normative realms; in the second, to put it psychoanalytically, to the interplay of the id, the ego, and the super-ego. (Given the concerns of this book, we will naturally concentrate on the possibility of a felicitous "balance" between the moments of the self.) And, ideally, that communication and balance would obtain between collective and individual identity as well.

Habermas argues that an additional stage (stage 7) must be added to the Kohlbergian schema that would cross the utopian threshold:

Need interpretations are no longer assumed as given, but are drawn into the process of discursive formation of will. Internal nature is thereby moved into a utopian perspective; that is, at this stage internal nature may no longer be merely examined within an interpretive framework fixed by the cultural tradition in a nature-like way. . . . Inner nature is rendered communicatively fluid and transparent to the extent that needs can, through aesthetic forms of expression, be kept articulable [sprachfähig] or be released from their paleosymbolic prelinguisticality.[40]

The return to the utopian motif and to the topoi of psychoanalysis converge on the concept of the linguisticality (Sprachfähigkeit) of inner nature. Programmatically, Habermas is correct in challenging the constricted Kantian notion of autonomy, which freezes the opposition between reason and inner nature, and in seeking a richer conception, where a more fluid process of communication would exist between the two. Today, as we have noted, real autonomy cannot mean the domination of the unconscious by consciousness, of the id by the ego, but must comprise, as Castoriadis maintains, the establishment of "another relation" between the two. But, as I have also indicated—odd as it may sound with respect to the communication theorist par excellence—Habermas's notion of communication is too restricted to carry out this program, and that restriction becomes particularly apparent in his discussion of the unconscious. Habermas can confidently argue for the discursive transformability of needs, because he believes he has already demonstrated the linguisticality of inner nature in his earlier interpretation of Freud.[41] As we will see, however, he asserts this linguisticality by denying Freud's fundamental distinction between word-representations and thing-representations. The articulability of inner nature can be casually maintained with little argumentation, because the linguisticality of inner nature is in fact presupposed from the start. In denying the existence of a preverbal, imagistic unconscious, Habermas also denies the existence of a psychic imaginary in Castoriadis's sense, a fact that he tries to hedge in the foregoing passage, as he must, with the cumbersome term "paleosymbolic prelinguisticality." Psychoanalysis, however, can be of service in avoiding "a joyless reformism" that is insensitive to the question of "a fulfilled life" only insofar as a robust notion of the unconscious is maintained. One essential source for visions of a better society—visions that could be debated in a just public sphere—is the psychic imaginary and its refashioning of the contents of cultural tradition. Without the input of the imaginary, any such debate, while possibly just, is in danger of being empty.

"The Modest Exegete": Freud and the Problem of the Ego

We have said previously, in our distinction of the various meanings of words, that "one" has several meanings.

Aristotle, *Metaphysics*

Much of the energy that Freud, in 1895, began to devote to the exploration of the psychical apparatus was sustained by a key idea in the back of his mind—an echo of his experience of the primal group [that is, his complicated and confusing extended family]: the need to reconcile the unity of that apparatus with its diversity, which, Freud thought was the purpose of psychical health, in contrast with the alienated unity of neurosis; and the need to find a transcription system between the various languages spoken by each of the psychical apparatus' subsystems, in order to prevent the eclipse of one of them and a "babelisation" of the whole.

Didier Anzieu, *Freud's Self Analysis*

Decentration and Enlightenment

Two of Freud's best-known, and seemingly opposed, epigrams define the force field in which his thinking on the ego unfolds. To under-emphasize either would be to simplify his thinking on the topic. On the one side is his observation *"The ego is not master in its own house."* [1] This epigram, along with the few suggestive but inconclusive remarks he makes in the unfinished paper "Splitting of the Ego in the Process of Defence," [2] is regularly adduced by proponents of the Counter-Enlightenment to demonstrate that Freud was a major figure in the

decentering of the modern subject. By maintaining that he was opposed to an autonomous, centered, and unified subject, they try to
appropriate him for their position. On the other side, however, is
another equally well known and no less essential dictum of Freud's,
namely, "Where id was, there shall ego become."[3] With the notable
exception of Lacan,[4] this latter epigram is almost universally taken
as exemplifying Freud's partisanship for "the project of enlightenment": it constitutes a programmatic call for the pursuit of autonomy
and emancipation through self-knowledge.

How, then, are these two seemingly opposed epigrams to be reconciled? For to be sure, if autonomy is understood as autarchic sovereignty—as *causa sui*—and if decentration is understood as the
dissolution or dispossession of the self, then the two are obviously
antipodes. The problem is often solved, or, better yet, dissolved by
the proponents of the Counter-Enlightenment by dismissing Freud's
advocacy of the Enlightenment program encapsulated in the second
epigram.

Instead of being viewed as the proper goal for character formation
and psychoanalytic practice, the autonomous individual is seen as a
symptom of the distorted, anthropocentric, atomistic, and entrepre-
neurial culture that produced it. However, I shall attempt to show,
largely through a close reading of Freud, that, far from being opposed to autonomous individuality, decentration can be understood
as an essential moment in its formation. This would mean that,
rather than subverting the Enlightenment, the decentration of the
subject is an essential moment in a project of enlightenment that is
consistent with its own concept.

Thus, while it is undoubtedly true that Freud's Copernican Revolution consists in the decentration of the subject, I must point to a
decisive fact concerning Freud's understanding of his position—a
fact already implicit in the reference to Copernicus—that will help to
determine the proper meaning of that decentration. Freud proudly
situates his discovery that "the ego is not master in its own house"
in the trajectory defined by two great achievements of the modern
scientific enlightenment, namely, Copernicus's claim that "our earth
[is] not the centre of the universe but only a tiny fragment of a
cosmic system of scarcely imaginable vastness," and Darwin's discov-

ery that "proved [mankind's] descent from the animal kingdom and his ineradicable animal nature." Freud, in other words, views the decentration of the subject not in opposition to, but as a major advance in, the "project of enlightenment." This fact can, in part, be overlooked because of a certain ambiguity in the concept of decentration. If the word is taken in the sense of dispossession *simpliciter,* then decentration would certainly stand in opposition to enlightenment. If, however, it is taken in the Piagetian sense of a *reorientation* that, by dislodging one's narcissistic egocentrism, increases one's perspective toward oneself and the world, then decentration is a necessary step in the process of enlightenment. As we shall see in the next chapter, dispossession of the naively centered ego is a necessary propaedeutic to the repossession of a more adequate ego.

The key to the deep and systematic connection between decentration and enlightenment in Freud's thinking is to be found in the theory of narcissism. Indeed, this is already evident in the fact that, by their very nature, Copernicus's cosmological, Darwin's biological, and Freud's psychological revolutions each dealt a major blow to humanity's "naive self-love," with psychoanalysis dealing perhaps the most severe injury to "human megalomania" of all.[5] The theory of narcissism—which Adorno "counts among Freud's most magnificent discoveries"[6]—constituted more than the delineation of another stage of psychosexual development in psychoanalytic theory. Because its discovery introduced "a veritable evil genius, to which must be attributed our most extreme resistance to truth,"[7] into the heart of psychic life, it compelled Freud to confront the problematic of truth and reality more directly. Ultimately, the theory of narcissism, formulated under the pressure of Jung's irrationalism, provided Freud with the provocation as well as the terminology to articulate his psychoanalytic *ethos,* "the ethic of honesty," in Rieff's terms, or Freud's "truth morality," as Kohut refers to it.[8]

In developing my thesis, I attempt a defense of two of Freud's perhaps most indefensible books, namely, *Totem and Taboo* and *The Future of an Illusion.* Now that the Enlightenment has fallen on hard times, these works cannot but appear hopelessly mired in nineteenth-century positivism, progressivism, Eurocentrism, and even utopianism. Nevertheless, I believe there is a redeemable kernel that can be extracted from these often painfully naive texts. Let me begin by examining Freud's attempt to translate a Comptean-style philosophy of history, with all its progressivistic and Eurocentric prejudices, into psychological terms.[9] Freud maintains that there are three stages of historical development—the animistic, the religious, and the scientific—and that these historical stages correspond to the three phases of individual development, namely, narcissism, object-love, and maturity. Ontogenetically and phylogenetically, the first phase, that is, the narcissistic-animistic, is characterized by the "omnipotence of thoughts" that results from the hypercathexis of the mind. In the case of both the infant and the primitive, the concentration of almost all the energy in the mind causes them to megalomaniacally "overvalue" their thoughts and, as it were, mistake the order and connection of their wishes for the order and connection of things. In the second phase, object-love and religion, the hypercathexis and resulting overvaluation is transferred from the self to the object, to the gods and parents respectively; using Kohut's terminology, we can say that omnipotence is not overcome but simply displaced from the grandiose self to the idealized object. According to Freud, only in the final, scientific stage, which "would have an exact counterpart in the stage at which an individual has reached maturity *(Reifezustand)*" would omnipotence as such have been surmounted: "The scientific view of the universe no longer affords any room for human omnipotence; men have acknowledged their smallness and submitted resignedly to death and to the other necessities of nature." Similarly, on the ontogenetic level, he maintains that the mature individual "has renounced the pleasure principle, adjusted himself to reality and turned to the external world for the object of his desires."[10] If the teleological philosophy of history, the ethnocentrism, and the energic explanations are disregarded, one crucial point nevertheless remains: for Freud, the desideratum is the mastery of omnipotence.[11] And he believes, correctly or incorrectly, that desideratum to have been achieved in the posttheological, postmetaphysical, scientific society created in the modern world, which represents the maturity of the species, and in the mature individual, who becomes at least a potential in that society and presupposes it as his or her precondition.[12]

A distinction can be introduced between Freud's commitment to science in the broad sense, as a *Weltanschauung* that embodies his truth morality, and his adherence to the specific tenets of nineteenth-century positivism. Science in the broad sense would consist in the *critique of illusion,* with "illusion" being defined not simply as error, such as "Aristotle's belief that vermin are developed out of dung," but as error "derived from human wishes."[13] Freud maintains, à la Feuerbach,[14] that the projection of our wishes causes us to form distorted representations of the world, with the most fundamental illusions—those of religion and, to a large extent, philosophy—growing out of one of the most elementary wishes, namely, the wish to be consoled in the face of an intrinsically harsh reality, which is almost intolerable and which "opposes human narcissism."[15] Science, thus conceived, not only defines a cognitive task, but, as we have noted, an affective one as well, "a work of correction applied to the very core of the libido, the heart of narcissism. Consequently, the scientific world view must be incorporated into a history of desire."[16]

At the same time, Freud rather naively believed that the specific procedures of nineteenth-century positivism by, among other things, de-anthropomorphizing the world picture, had finally provided the methodology for realizing the program of science in the broader sense: as Ricoeur observes, Freud, "like all his Vienna and Berlin teachers . . . sees and continues to see in [modern natural] science the sole discipline of knowledge, the single rule of all intellectual honesty."[17]

However, after the critique of positivism and the rise of the postempiricist philosophy of science, we now know—leaving the sense of the term "know" unspecified—that modern natural science did not provide a neutral, timeless methodology for the disinterested pursuit of truth but constituted nature from a particular perspective; we also know that perspective possessed technological domination, which is to say, omnipotent mastery, among its innermost possibilities. Modern positivism, in short, turned out to be another idol of the tribe that has fallen, at least in its hegemonic form. A further inference is, however, often drawn from the debunking of positivism, namely, that the project of science in the broader sense, qua the critique of illusion, has been invalidated as well. Freud's truth morality would thus fall with the debunking of the positivist doctrine in terms of which he attempted to explicate it. But a question can be raised against this self-liquidating dialectic, namely, does not Kuhn's metadiscourse about positivism, for example—regardless of how one explicates the validity of that discourse—itself constitute a step forward in the critique of illusion, which is also a step forward in an insufficiently radicalized project of enlightenment?

Strange as it may sound, there exists, as Castoriadis has recognized, a politically egalitarian and theoretically antifoundational dimension, albeit elaborated in a mythical form, in *Totem and Taboo:* "The surrounding imbecility, whether of the 'Right' or of the 'Left', cannot hide this fact: Freud, by virtue of his authorship of *Totem and Taboo* (and not just by virtue of that) belongs to the democratic and *egalitarian* tradition." [18] The connection between the antifoundationalism and egalitarianism is to be found in the renunciation of omnipotence. Conservative interpreters of the text often assign more weight to the murder of the omnipotent father than to the pact between the brothers. But "the 'murder of the father' is nothing and leads to nothing (apart from endless repetition of the preceding situation) without the 'pact of the brothers,' " [19] which, for Freud, constitutes the founding act of civilization. For our purposes, the significance of the pact—in which siblings are, as it were, transformed into citizens and association is placed on a nonkinship basis—consists in the following: to the extent to which they renounce two of the most imperious wishes of childhood, incest and patricide—the renunciation, needless to say, never being absolute—the brothers simultaneously renounce the right of narcissistic entitlement as such. Each standpoint is decentered vis-à-vis the others; the privileged center is left unoccupied and none claims absolute entitlement for his wishes. [20] Indeed, the significance of the Oedipus complex, as Lacan has emphasized, remains virtually the same today: infantile omnipotence comes to grief in the encounter with that "absolutely unmasterable situation," and, with the renunciation of their incestuous wishes, children are thrust into the law-governed world of equally decentered subjects. Any alternative form of gender arrangements that may be created in the future, as we have noted, will have to provide a means of dislodging infantile omnipotence, which, to date, has been accomplished—perhaps contingently but nevertheless effectively—by the patriarchal family. Similarly, the problematic of narcissistic entitlement also poses an ultimate limit to the right of otherness. While the "right to particularity"[21] has been recognized in a modern world that has become irreversibly pluralistic, no form of life can claim absolute entitlement for itself and its interpretation of the world without involving a potential for violence. The horrifying events in what was formerly Yugoslavia have provided an action critique, as the Situationists used to call it, of the unmediated politics of particularistic entitlement. The decentration of that entitlement, in the sense we have been discussing it, is a condition of the possibility of a plurality of macro- and microlifeworlds.

If we do not take the fiction of the social contract as a thought experiment that attempts to elucidate the founding of civilization in general, but, rather, of modern civil society[22]—and this is its historical significance in Hobbes, from whom Freud, of course, borrowed it[23]—additional light can be thrown on the thesis that modernity comprises the maturity of the species. The murder of the primal father would symbolize the fact that no Absolute is available outside the decentered structure of mutual interaction to ground either that interaction or the interaction between that structure and external nature, which is to say, no Absolute is available to ground either practical or theoretical reason. The phallus as the transcendental signifier is, as Lacan argues, an imaginary entity.

Modernity would be mature, then, insofar as it has in principle renounced the father, that is, insofar as it has structurally "stripped any paternal coefficient"[24] from its disenchanted worldview. *Mutatis mutandis*, immaturity would consist in the prolonged "longing for the Father"[25] as a source of ultimate authority and consolation in the face of meaningless, indifferent, and cruel Ananke. Freud tells us that his "sole purpose" in writing *The Future of an Illusion* is to promote the completion of this process of maturation qua disillusionment, which was structurally and programmatically initiated with modernity's critique of tradition, religion, and metaphysics, but which remains empirically unfinished. In his most utopian and perhaps—but only perhaps—most uncharacteristic passage, which has certainly been challenged by the recent rise of neofundamentalist movements, Freud declares that "infantilism is destined to be surmounted. Men cannot remain children forever." Someday, "like a child who has left the parental house where he was so warm and comfortable," they will "admit to themselves the full extent of their helplessness and insignificance in the machinery of the universe" and "go out into 'hostile life.' "[26]

Freud's ironical reference to "our God Logos"[27] indicates his awareness of the difficulty of justifying his adherence to the scientific Weltanschauung—of justifying his faith in reason, as it were—after access to the Absolute has been foreclosed. Indeed, Freud, "the master of suspicion,"[28] raises the possibility that he too may be "chasing an illusion."[29] He grasps the fact that discrediting religion and metaphysics makes it impossible to ground his adherence to science in the unconditional manner formerly required by the theological and ontological traditions. He does not, however, allow this lack of an ultimate ground let him fall into nihilism, in either its depressive or its manic form.[30] While he cannot provide a demonstrative deduction, he is satisfied to enumerate a number of good reasons, ranging from the progressive nature of science to the course of human evolution, to justify his adherence to the *Logos*. Chief among these is the fact that science, unlike religion, does not have "the character of a delusion"[31] and is capable of correction. It is, in short, fallible. Today, this strategy of justification may not satisfy postmodern skeptics, who, insisting that the foundations of science themselves be strictly scientific, often lodge their critique of the Enlightenment in its inability to provide an unconditional ground for its program. And, to be sure, an earlier, more naive, and more heroic stage of the Enlightenment—which sought to secure the "natural light of reason" with the same certainty as divine revelation—invited this criticism. An Enlightenment, however, that had become consistent with its own learning experience, that is, with its own maturity, would have worked through the fact its "god Logos is . . . not a very almighty one,"[32] and would not therefore seek to ground itself apodictically. Speaking psychophilosophically, as it were, the skeptic, who repetitiously insists on the criterion of the Absolute only to demonstrate that it cannot be fulfilled, continues to disappointedly "long for the father" rather than to mourn his loss.

The contemporary critique of rationality and the subject is abstract in its negativity to the extent that it fails to appreciate the residuum that remains at the end of the critique. Freud reminds us that, although the human intellect is weak, "there is something peculiar about this weakness,"[33] which means there is also something peculiar about its strength. And it is this peculiarity that seldom gets thematized in the current discussions. Thus with respect to Freud himself, the methods of psychoanalysis are often turned back against him to undermine the knowing subject and discredit psychoanalysis. However, reflection on the peculiar status of Freud's standpoint and the magnitude of his achievement can in fact produce a different result. As Ricoeur observes, "the same *doubter* who depicts the ego as a 'poor wretch' dominated by three masters (the id, the superego, and reality or necessity) is also the exegete who rediscovers the logic of the illogical kingdom."[34] The strength of the investigator who has the courage to document the weakness of the ego and map the kingdom of the night cannot itself be negligible. While the decentered ego of psychoanalysis may be humble in comparison to the more grandiose ego of idealist philosophy, it nevertheless requires austere strength of a certain order to tolerate the narcissistic injuries demanded by psychoanalytic knowledge and to come to terms with one's grandiosity to the extent it is possible. While the ego is no longer master in its own house, it has not been evicted either.

"The Ego in Its Strength and in Its Weakness"

Contemporary critics of the subject, insofar as they depict the ego as the passive effect of superior (instinctual, economic, linguistic, etc.) forces or structures that operate behind its back, are in a similar position to Georg Groddeck when he introduced the concept of the id—a position Freud accepts as correct but partial and attempts to assimilate to his own, more comprehensive theory. "Groddeck," Freud writes, "is never tired of insisting that what we call our ego behaves essentially passively in life and that, as he expresses it, we are 'lived' by unknown and uncontrollable forces."[35] Freud has no difficulty accepting the existence of this dimension of mental life, *as a dimension,* and assigning it a place in his scheme: "We have all had impressions of the same kind, even though they may not have overwhelmed us to the exclusion of others, and we need feel no hesitation in finding a place for Groddeck's discovery in the structure of science." Freud "propose[s] to take" this dimension of psychic life "into account" by distinguishing it from the ego and, following Groddeck, designating it with the term "id," which is meant to designate "whatever in our nature is impersonal and, so to speak, subject to natural law."[36] What Freud objects to, then, is not the *existence* of "unknown and uncontrollable forces" that operate behind the back of the ego—that would contradict the entire experience of psychoanalysis—but their hypostatization into the commanding factor in psychic life. If, however, the id is not to be assigned the dominant position in mental life, and if the ego is not to be construed as utterly passive and subservient to it, the essential question remains to be answered: what are the relative strengths of the ego and the id vis-à-vis each other? This is no easy question, and Freud's investigation of it has a complicated history.

The most extensive attempt to assess the nature of "the ego in its strength and in its weaknesses," occurs in *The Ego and the Id.*[37] I believe a close examination of this text reveals that *ultimately*—and, it would seem, contrary to Freud's inclinations and efforts in the opposite direction—the scale ends up rather heavily weighted on the side of the ego's "dependent relations," which is to say, on the side of its weaknesses. This fact creates a dilemma for Freud that he never satisfactorily resolves in *The Ego and the Id* and to which he must therefore return in *Inhibitions, Symptoms and Anxiety,* in part because of the demoralizing effect it was having on his followers; as we will see, the solution in that later work is itself not easy to interpret. On the one hand, Freud maintains that "psycho-analysis is an instrument to enable the ego to achieve a progressive conquest of the id"[38] by bringing "the influence of the external world to bear upon the id and its tendencies, and . . . [substituting] the reality principle for the pleasure principle which reigns unrestrictedly in the id."[39] On the other hand, he depicts the ego as such a "poor creature,"[40] subservient not only to the id but to external reality and the superego as well, that it is difficult to conceive how, given the analysis of *The Ego and the Id,* that conquest is possible. In other words, it is difficult to see how, on the basis of the ego's resources as they are enumerated by Freud, Groddeck's position can be avoided. Borrowing an image from *Phaedrus* of his "divine Plato," [41] Freud portrays the ego's subordination to the id in the following terms: "Thus in relation to the id [the ego] is like a man on horseback, who has to hold in check the superior strength of the horse." The question becomes, then, how the weaker ego can hold the superior strength of the id in check. Continuing the equestrian metaphor, he writes that "[whereas] the rider [tries] to do so with his own strength, . . . the ego uses borrowed forces. The analogy may be carried a littler further. Often a rider, if he is not to be parted from his horse, is obliged to guide it where it wants to go; so in the same way the ego is in the habit of transforming the id's will into action as if it were its own." [42] The term "borrowed forces" refers to the fact that the ego is formed *narcissistically*—that is, through the identificatory transformation of object libido into narcissistic libido—a fact regularly adduced by critics of the autonomous ego: if the ego is formed through the transformations of the drives, is it simply not itself a vicissitude of the drives? While it will be necessary to return to this point below, for the moment let us attempt to unpack Freud's metaphorical language into more conceptual terms.

Freud points to three attributes of the ego that provide its strength in contending with the superior forces of the id. First, the ego, in virtue of its relation to the perceptual system, organizes "mental processes" in time and subjects them to "reality testing." In this capacity, it mediates between intrapsychic and extrapsychic reality and, as such, is the agency on which the problematic truth devolves. Second, it interposes "the process of thinking" between the demands of the id and "motor discharges" and thereby "controls the access to motility." That is, it institutes a process of delay and transforms the id's pressure for immediate discharge into intentional action that seeks, "by means of muscular activity, to make the world fall in with the wishes of the id." Third, by transforming "the object-cathexes of the id into ego structures," it appropriates some of the id's energy for its own purposes; this is the process by which it acquires the "borrowed forces" referred to above.

However, no sooner has Freud enumerated these strengths than he begins to retract them. With respect to the first point, we will disregard the extreme case of psychosis in which the ego hallucinatorily reconstitutes external reality in a global fashion so that it complies with the demands of the id.[43] Instead, we will simply point to the more common situation in which "whenever possible" it engages in *rationalization* rather than reality testing—that is, it sacrifices the truth—so as to "remain on good terms with the id": "it clothes the id's *Ucs.* [unconscious] commands with its *Pcs.* [preconscious] rationalizations; it pretends that the id is showing obedience to the admonitions of reality, even when in fact it is remaining obstinate and unyielding; it disguises the id's conflicts with reality." Concerning the second point, Freud writes that the power to control access to motility is "a question more of form than of fact." With respect to action, the "ego's position is like that of a constitutional monarch," which is to say, while no wish can be transformed into action without the ego's "sanction," the ego "hesitates long before imposing [its] veto" on the id, just as the monarch is reluctant to exercise veto over the legislation of the parliament. In both the cases, then, the ego "only too often yields to the temptation to become sycophantic, opportunist and lying, like a politician who sees the truth but wants to keep his place in popular favour."[44]

The third point raises the much more profound problem of narcissistic or sexual monism.[45] Freud argues that the ego acquires the id's energy and thereby advances its own development qua structuralization seductively, which is to say, libidinously. By assuming the characteristics of the love object, that is, by *identifying* with it, and offering itself to the id as a substitute for that object, the ego cajoles, as it were, the id to abandon its sexual aims and relinquish its object cathexis: "When the ego assumes the features of the object, it is forcing itself, so to speak, upon the id as a love-object and is trying to make good the id's loss by saying: 'Look, you can love me too—I am so like the object.' "[46] This process is analogous to the transference love that develops in the course of an analysis. The ego, which is oriented to external reality "by virtue of its relation to the perceptual systems," presents itself to the id as a love object with a view to "making the id pliable to the world."[47] Likewise, "the physician . . . offers [himself], with the attention [he] pays to the real world, as a libidinal object to the id, and aims at attaching the id's libido to [himself]"[48] with a similar view in mind, namely, to bring "the influence of the external world to bear upon the id and its tendencies."[49] In both cases, the relationship to reality and, hence, to truth, at least in the perceptual-epistemic sense of reality testing,[50] is introduced via the medium of libido.

Earlier, in "Mourning and Melancholia,"[51] Freud had understood identification only as a specific and limited mechanism involved in the pathogenesis of melancholia and had failed to appreciate "the full significance of [the] process." In that "painful disorder," an object, which had been ambivalently loved, is lost and "set up again inside the ego—that is, . . . an object cathexis [is] replaced by an identification." And it is the noxious presence of this ambivalent, that is, hated as well as loved, object lodged inside the ego, so to speak, that accounts for the suffering of the melancholic. In *The Ego and the Id,* however, Freud came to understand identification not simply as a limited pathogenic process but as a "common" and "typical" one that plays a central role in normal development. More specifically, he came to view the "alteration" of the ego, which results from the internalization of abandoned love objects, as a central mechanism of ego formation itself: "the character of the ego is a precipitate of abandoned object-cathexes and . . . it contains the history of those object-choices."[52] While this process of transforming object libido into narcissistic libido through identification allows the ego to "obtain control over the id and deepen its relations with it" and is perhaps "the universal road to sublimation,"[53] there is nevertheless a price to be paid for that achievement. The ego must "to a large extent"—and the controversy concerning the ego centers on the magnitude of this extent—acquiesce "in the id's experience." It must, in other words, go in the direction the horse wants to go.

The expansion of the theory of identification from "Mourning and Melancholia" to *The Ego and the Id* thus implies "an important amplification of the theory of narcissism,"[54] especially with respect to the theory of ego formation. In his first formulation on narcissism, in

1914, Freud had maintained that, in the initial stage of development, primary narcissism, the ego itself is the "great reservoir"[55] in which all the libido is stored and "from which some is later given off to objects." However, at the same time as the ego can extrude some of its libido to objects, another portion of this "original libidinal cathexis . . . fundamentally persists" in the ego "and is related to the object-cathexes much as the body of an amoeba is related to the pseudopodia which it puts out." Because of the persistence of this original narcissistic investment, the "pseudopodia" can be "drawn back again" from objects and reinvested in the ego—as a form of secondary narcissism—whenever excessive danger or disappointment is experienced with objects in the external world,[56] for example, as in sleep, psychosis, and hypochondriasis. In this version of the theory, then, cathexis *emanates* from the ego in primary narcissism to the cathexis of objects and, finally, to the recathexis of the ego in secondary narcissism.

Two points should be noted concerning the conception of the ego in 1914. Although secondary narcissistic reinvestment in the ego *can* occur as a result of the withdrawal of cathexis from objects, it is preceded by an original narcissistic cathexis of the ego. The fact that it is stated in energic language should not obscure what is at stake philosophically in these passages: Freud is struggling to conceptualize the ego as subject and the ego as object. First, insofar as it has its own "ego-instincts" and energy *(Ichtriebenergie)* at its disposal, which are not derived from the sexual instincts, the ego is viewed as a subject or agent that can pursue its own "ego-interest" *(Ichinteresse)* of self-preservation and adaptation to the environment, an interest that is distinct from the aims of the sexual drives.[57] And second, insofar as the ego is cathected by sexual libido, that is, insofar as sexual energy is "aimed at the ego,"[58] the ego is an object; indeed, this was one of the momentous discoveries of the narcissism paper in which the ego "found its position among sexual objects and was at once given the foremost place among them."[59] Freud employed the term "ego libido" *(Ichlibido)*, as distinct from "ego instincts," to designate the attachment of libido to the ego qua object.

Throughout his career, and in polemical opposition to Jung's monism, Freud repeatedly insisted he was a dualist: the different versions of his instinct theory, whatever their varying content might be, always contained two opposed terms.[60] His primary reason for insisting on a dualist position was clinical: he wanted to maintain that psychopathology is the result of conflict, and conflict presupposes the existence of two terms that can conflict with one other. I will argue that there is a further, if implicit, philosophical reason as well for maintaining a dualistic position. For the moment, however, let us note that the concept of narcissism, which was introduced into psychoanalytic theory in part to usurp Jung's accounts of psychosis and animism in terms of a single undifferentiated psychic energy, threatens to undermine Freud's dualistic opposition between the ego instincts and the sexual instincts. In "On Narcissism" Freud raises the following objection against himself: if the ego can be an object of the sexual instincts, "why . . . is there any necessity for further distinguishing a sexual libido from a nonsexual energy of the ego instincts? Would not the postulation of a single kind of psychical energy save us all the difficulties . . . ?"[61] I believe an examination of the text reveals that Freud's attempt to meet this objection is ultimately inconclusive. Indeed, the very fact that he marshals so many arguments against Jung, none of which is sufficient in its own right, indicates the difficulty Freud is having in refuting him. And six years later, in *Beyond the Pleasure Principle*, he was still forced to admit that "the difficulty remains," namely, "that psycho-analysis has not enabled us hitherto to point to any [ego] instincts other than libidinal ones. That, however, is no reason for our falling in with the conclusion that no others in fact exist."[62]

The appeal, however, remains meager. Freud is only asserting the empty logical possibility that nonlibidinal instincts exist; he has not succeeded in establishing the actual existence of any such instincts. With the introduction of the distinction between the ego and the id three years later, the problem of monism is exacerbated still further. In the new scheme, as the id, not the ego, becomes the original reservoir of libido from which cathexes can be sent out to objects, the ego no longer has any independent sources of energy of its own. And, to make matters worse, the ego is now understood to be formed through the appropriation of those object cathexes for itself. Thus, whereas in the earlier scheme the ego *could become* the object of secondary narcissism, in the new scheme it is formed through, it is the product of, secondary narcissism: "The narcissism of the ego is thus a secondary one, which has been withdrawn from objects."[63] The ego itself appears to be a vicissitude of libidinal forces, with no independent origins of its own.

These considerations, although they may strike the reader as somewhat talmudic, have a significance that extends beyond the specialized domain of Freud scholarship. Indeed, as I have indicated, they raise philosophical problems of the first order. The discovery that the ego is formed through the dynamics of narcissism threatens, as we have seen, to collapse the distinction between the ego instincts and the sexual instincts, which would, philosophically speaking, collapse the distinction between reason and desire into a monism of desire: the ego—the supposed seat of rationality—would be engulfed by libido; there would be no extrainstinctual fundament on which psychoanalytic theory and practice, or the critique of reason for that matter, could stand. These considerations provide a point of departure for the totalized critique of reason insofar as it is formulated in terms of psychoanalysis.

On the Pathologies of the Synthetic Function

Thus, despite his efforts, Freud did not adequately resolve the difficulties raised by his analysis of the ego's strength and weakness within the framework of *The Ego and the Id*, where, as he later put it, he had drawn "a picture of [the ego's] dependent relationship to the id and to the super-ego and revealed how powerless and apprehensive it was in regard to both and with what an effort it maintained its *show* of superiority over them" (emphasis added). This depiction of the ego as weak and powerless was "widely echoed in psycho-analytic literature," and apparently had the effect of engendering a depressive-romantic Weltanschauung among certain of Freud's followers: "Many writers have laid much stress on the weakness of the ego in relation to the id and of our rational elements in the face of the daemonic forces within us; and they display a strong tendency to make what I have said into a corner-stone of a psycho-analytic *Weltanschauung*." It was in order to correct this "extreme and one-sided view," [64] in part, that Freud returned to the problematic of the ego's strengths and weaknesses in *Inhibitions, Symptoms and Anxiety*, where he argues that "the apparent contradiction" in his earlier assessment of the ego's dependent relations was "due to our having taken abstractions too rigidly and attended exclusively now to one side and now to the other of what is in fact a complicated state of affairs." [65] This "complicated state of affairs" pertains to the question of the unity and division of the subject, in this case to the intersystemic split between the ego and the id (although we will consider the intrasystemic split within the ego as well.) As far as I am aware, no one has studied Freud's immensely suggestive discussion in sufficient detail. We will return to it when we discuss Wellmer's attempts to locate Adorno's desideratum of nonviolent synthesis in the realm of the psyche. The one-sided understanding of the situation results from hypostatizing the split, that is, the disunity, between the ego and the id (and superego) into an absolute, when it is relative and variable. Freud argues that in fact there are "no sharp boundaries" within the psyche but only "artificial ones," like those "drawn in political geography," and that "we cannot do justice to the characteristics of the mind by linear outlines like those in a drawing or in primitive painting, but rather by areas of colour melting into one another as they are presented by modern artists. After making the separation [for the purposes of theory] we must allow what we have separated to merge together once more." [66] The division and integration in the psyche is, in short, always a matter of degree. Furthermore, it appears that, in order to approach adequately the question of the ego's relative strength and weakness, it must be reformulated in terms of the relative division and integration between the psychic agencies, a relation that "is subject to great variations in different individuals . . . and in the course of actual functioning." [67] Thus—in these passages, which are rarely emphasized by commentators—we rather unexpectedly find Freud arguing for a comparatively fluid picture of the boundaries between the psychic agencies. [68]

As one might expect in a thinker of Freud's depth, the content of his views on the nature of synthesis in the ego are reflected in his mode of theorizing; this is, of course, as it should be, for the products of the ego, especially one of its central cognitive products such as theory, ought to reflect its functioning. Although Freud never formulated a fully elaborated position on the degree of systematization appropriate to a theory, his many scattered remarks on the subject indicate that it was a matter to which he devoted some thought, and they make it possible to reconstruct, as Samuel Weber has done,[69] his position on the subject. To begin with, it is clear in his denunciation of Adler, that Freud was suspicious of too much systematization, which he likens to the secondary revision in dreams: "The Adlerian theory was from the very beginning a 'system'—which psychoanalysis was careful to avoid becoming. It is also a remarkably good example of 'secondary revision,' such as occurs, for instance, in the process to which dream-material is submitted by the action of waking thought."[70]

Like the other three forms of the dream work—condensation, displacement, and considerations of representability—the purpose of secondary revision is to distort the unconscious dream material so that it can elude the censor. However, in contrast to the others, secondary revision achieves its distortion in a somewhat paradoxical manner, namely, by making the manifest content too orderly; it introduces more coherence, intelligibility, and order, which is to say more synthesis, into the manifest content of the dream than is in fact present in the latent dream material itself: "As a result of its effort, the dream loses its appearance of absurdity and disconnectedness and approximates to the model of an intelligible experience." The facade of apparent meaning and coherence, however, falsifies the "true significance" of the dream, which lies in the presynthesized "mass of material present in the dream-thoughts."[71] Furthermore, the synthesizing function of secondary revision is one it shares with waking thought as well: "Our waking (preconscious) thinking behaves towards any perceptual material with which it meets in just the same way in which the function we are considering behaves towards the content of dreams. It is the nature of our waking thought *to establish order in material of that kind, to set up relations in it and to make it conform to our expectations of an intelligible whole*" (emphasis added). This process of synthesis, however, can go too far: "An adept in sleight of hand can trick us by relying upon this intellectual habit of ours. In our efforts at making an intelligible pattern of the sense-impressions that are offered to us, we often fall into the strangest errors or even *falsify the truth about the material before us*" (emphasis added).[72] Excessive synthesis on the part of the ego toward both inner and outer reality can, in short, "falsify" the material it receives from those sources by imposing more order on it than exists in the material *an sich.*

Already in *The Interpretation of Dreams,* Freud derisively compares secondary revision to the systematizing (and totalizing) impulses of the philosopher: "The philosopher," Freud notes, citing Heine, "seeks to fill 'the holes in the cosmic plan . . . with the bits and bonnets of his pyjamas,' just as secondary elaboration fills in 'the gaps in the dream-structure.' "[73] Later, in *Totem and Taboo,* Freud compares animism, which he considered the first system of thought, to secondary revision:

The secondary revision of the product of the dream-work is an admirable example of the nature and pretensions of a system. There is an intellectual function in us which demands unity, connection and intelligibility from any material, whether of perception or thought, that comes within its grasp; and if, as a result of special circumstances, it is unable to establish a true connection, it does not hesitate to fabricate a false one.[74]

Weber, one of the most sophisticated poststructuralist interpreters of Freud, argues that animism is "not merely a phylogenetic forerunner of systematic thinking," but insofar as it has a tendency " 'to grasp the whole universe as a single unity from a single point of view' " and " 'to explain the essence of the universe entirely,' " it is the "paradigm" of systematic thinking. "Unity and totality," he continues, "are the categories informing animism, and they make it the model of all systematic thinking: everything must be assimilated, with nothing left out."[75] Weber goes on to argue that the attempt to grasp the world in systematic thought, which is to say, in terms of unity and totality, results from the narcissistic ego's impulses, which we examine in detail in the next chapter, to impose its own artificial and rigid unity on the world. And, for reasons that will become immediately apparent, he terms this objectionable mode of theorizing "speculative": "The intellectual construct we call 'system' reveals itself to be narcissistic, in its origin no less than in its structure: *speculative,* in the etymological sense, as a mirror-image of the ego."[76] However, at the

same time as Freud objects to Adler's theory for being too systematic—too speculative, in Weber's sense—as Weber rightly points out,
he also objects to Jung's theory for not being systematic enough:

> Of the two movements under discussion, Adler's is indubitably the more
> important; while radically false, it is marked by consistency and coherence.
> Jung's modification . . . is so obscure, unintelligible and confused as to make
> it difficult to take up any position towards it. Wherever one lays hold of it,
> one must be prepared to hear that one has misunderstood it; one is thus at
> a loss to know how it should be properly understood. It presents itself in a
> peculiarly vacillating manner.[77]

Weber raises the obvious question, which is in fact at the center of
our investigation, but, because of his deconstructive suspicion of synthesis as such, never adequately addresses it: "If," as is apparent from
Freud's criticisms of Jung, "a modicum of coherence, consistency
and systematicity is indispensable to a theory, the question remains:
how much? or perhaps, also, of what kind?"[78] In other words, if
Freud equally rejects the extremes of totalized unification, on the
one side, and incoherence, on the other, what degree and what sort
of synthesis does his own nonspeculative and nontotalizing theory
possess? What degree and what sort of synthesis should a theory aim
at? (And this points to the larger question of a nonobjectionable
synthesis, which we examine in the next chapter.)

The form of Freud's theoretical discussion of synthesis and conflict within the psyche itself exhibits the content of his position on
the subject: he never attempts a final systematization or totalization
of his position,[79] but doggedly strives—almost in an internal struggle
with itself—to do justice to both moments of this "complicated state
of affairs." His procedure might be compared to Adorno's notion
of a "constellation," in which "concepts" are persistently gathered
"around the central one that is sought" in order to approach it more
closely without, however, reaching a final closure."[80] With respect to
the moment of unification, Freud attempts to correct the "one-
sided" view presented in *The Ego and the Id* by reminding the reader
that "the ego is identical with the id, and is merely a specially differentiated part of it,"[81] namely, "that part . . . which has been modified
by the direct influence of the external world through the medium of

the *Pcpt.-Cs* [perceptual consciousness]; in a sense it is an extension of the surface-differentiation."[82] In an uncharacteristically harmonistic vein, Freud maintains that "if the ego remains bound up with the id and indistinguishable from it, then it displays its strength." Indeed, "in many situations the two are merged; and as a rule we can only distinguish one from the other when there is a tension or conflict between them."[83] Freud argues—in a fashion which is strikingly similar to Kohut—that in so-called normal functioning, the ego and the id (as well as the superego) tend to act in accord with one another and that division into the tripartite psyche is pathological (cf. Kohut's notion of the pathological fragmentation of a normally "cohesive" self). In a statement that appears to contradict the picture of the "poor ego" beleaguered by three masters, he goes so far as to assert that "we should be quite wrong if we pictured the ego and the id as two opposing camps."[84]

On the other side, however, he maintains that, despite this moment of essential identity, "we were justified . . . in dividing the ego from the id, for there are certain considerations which necessitate that step,"[85] namely, the state of affairs that obtains in "psychical illness."[86] In other words, to the extent that the ego is divided from and opposed to the id, that is, to the extent that the subject is split, the situation is pathological and the ego displays its weakness accordingly. "If we think of this part by itself [that is, the ego as part of the id] in contradistinction to the whole, or if a real split has occurred between the two, the weakness of the ego becomes apparent"; the ego, in short, is weak, and the situation is pathological to the extent that it is *disassociated* from the id. This provides us with theoretical support in Freud for investigating a post-Kantian notion of autonomy based on the establishment of a different relation between the ego and the id, which is to say, reason and desire.

The situation regarding intrasystemic splitting, that is, splitting within the ego, which Freud did not begin to investigate methodically until the twenties, is more complicated, for in this case Freud locates both nonpathological as well as pathological splits. He begins his exposition of the ego in *New Introductory Lectures on Psycho-Analysis* with the following consideration, which, considered philosophically, is disarmingly uncomplicated: "We wish to make the ego the matter of our enquiry, our very own ego. But is that possible? After all, the ego is in its very essence a subject; how can it be made into an object?" Freud unhesitatingly offers an answer that brushes aside all the perennial conundrums concerning the possibility of transcendental reflection: "The ego can take itself as an object, can treat itself like other objects, can observe itself, criticize itself and do Heaven knows what with itself." It is simply a fact for Freud, and not a transcendental condition to be demonstrated, that the ego can and does take itself as an object of reflection, and it can perform this feat because of its capacity to split: "In this, one part of the ego is setting itself over against the rest. So the ego can be split; it splits itself during a number of its functions—temporarily at least. Its parts can come together again afterwards. This is not exactly a novelty, though it may perhaps be putting an unusual emphasis on what is generally known."[87] The fact that the ego can assume this dual position of subject and object derives, in large part, from the fact that it is "first and foremost a bodily ego." A person's body, "and above all [the body's] surface," occupies a "special position among other objects in the world of perception," for it can be experienced from the inside and from the outside at the same time: "It is *seen* like any other object, but to the *touch* it yields two kinds of sensations, one of which may be equivalent to an internal perception." I would suggest that when the ego is formed through the "projection" (it would perhaps be more accurate to say "internalization") of this surface into the interior of the psyche, this dual aspect is transferred from the body surface to the ego, where it is transformed into the ability to take itself as subject and object at the same time.

Although it is not the absolute ego of idealist philosophy, which Freud helped in no small measure to decenter, the more modest ego of psychoanalysis is not utterly powerless with respect to reflective knowledge. Clinically, classical psychoanalytic technique, at least as it is conceived in the tradition of ego psychology, uses this capacity of the ego to turn its gaze on itself to foster a nonpathological, therapeutic split in the psyche. This split becomes, in turn, a condition for forming a therapeutic alliance with the analyst's ego:[88] the existence of this observing ego makes it possible for the analysand both to undergo the regressive phenomena of the transference and to reflect on it. This alternation of experience and reflection is an essential feature of the psychoanalytic process. Without a sufficiently secure observing ego—whose scope and strength can vary dramatically over the course of an analysis, or within a single session—the analysand will, at best, not be able to use the experience of the transference and, at worse, be overwhelmed by it in a possible transference psychosis. The creation and use of this nonpathological, therapeutic split thus becomes a *sine qua non* for overcoming the pathological split that, according to Freud, is a feature of psychoneurosis as such.

In the discussion of the ego in *New Introductory Lectures,* Freud makes the familiar point that pathology, "by making things larger and coarser," can illuminate phenomena that in "normal conditions would otherwise have escaped us." In this case, this means that pathological splitting, which occurs for example in fetishism, and which "points to a breach or a rent," can illuminate something about the structure of the ego where "there may normally be an articulation present": "If we throw a crystal to the floor, it breaks; but not into haphazard pieces. It comes apart along its lines of cleavage into fragments whose boundaries, though they were invisible, were predetermined by the crystal's structure."[89] It thus appears that, both intersystemically (between the ego and the id and between the ego and the superego) and intrasystemically (within the ego), the psyche can split but not in an entirely random fashion. Rather, it splits along lines that are predetermined by its structure. The point for our purposes is that, although there are "no sharp boundaries" within the psyche, there are "articulations" that, while they do not always amount to a breach, can become the faults along which the psyche splits under conditions of pathology. I would suggest that, with this notion of articulation, Freud is attempting to formulate a concept of "soft" boundaries, that is, a concept that would account for the boundaries in the psyche but would not hypostatize them into rigid barriers.

From the other side, in addition to its ability to split, the ego can not only "come together again" but also "enlarge its organization,"[90] by forming associations with material from other portions of the psyche. I am referring, of course, to the synthetic function—which "is of such extraordinary importance"[91]—and which Freud defines as one of the essential features of the ego: "But what distinguishes the ego from the id quite especially is a tendency to synthesis in its contents, to a combination and unification in its mental process which are totally lacking in the id."[92] It is crucial to note that this synthetic function derives from the ego's genesis in sexuality, a point Loewald elaborates further: "Its desexualized energy still shows traces of its origin in its impulsion to bind together and unify."[93] The tendency of Eros to create ever larger unities is transferred to the ego when the ego is formed narcissistically, through the internalization of abandoned love objects, which we examined above.[94]

The libido that formerly bound the person to the love object binds the contents of the ego together when it is formed through the internalization of that object (or, more properly, object relation). While the fact that ego is formed libidinously or narcissistically is, as we shall see, adduced by Lacan and others in an attempt to debunk the ego's claims of autonomy and rationality—and to demonstrate its heteronomous embeddedness in instinctuality—this same fact can be viewed in an entirely different light. It can be used to elucidate the extent to which Eros itself can function as a vehicle for Logos. One can argue that the basic impulse toward rationality itself, "to find, across difference and otherness, manifestations of the same,"[95] that is, to synthesize, derives from the ego's erotic roots. The narcissistic or libidinous genesis of the ego only presents an epistemological problem, so to speak, if one insists on uncontaminated origins to guarantee its reality-testing capacities. If, on the contrary, one does not make such an idealist demand, and if, furthermore, one has a theory of sublimation to account for the *relative* disentanglement of the ego from the distorting conditions of its origins, then its libidinous genesis need not, in principle, present a problem. To be sure, this synthetic function of the ego is, as we have seen, "liable to a whole number of disturbances,"[96] the excessive and coercive synthesis of the obsessive-compulsive and the paranoid, for example. And reason is *mutatis mutandis* subject to a broad array of aberrations (for example, the theoretical and political totalitarianism in which "the monster of unifying madness"[97] seeks to reduce the social order and external nature to "a gigantic analytic judgment"[98] and thereby annihilate all alterity and particularity). The postmodernist critique of the ego and rationality are obviously directed at these aberrations. The problem with the postmodernist position, however, is that these aberrations are mistakenly identified with the ego and reason as such. As I have argued these disturbances constitute pathologies of the synthetic function and do not belong to its nature per se. The task will now be to distinguish between pathological and nonpathological forms of synthesis.

Deepening the Ego's Relation to the Id

Freud's introduction of the structural theory entailed a new, if not always recognized, conception of the relation between the ego and Eros. Where the earlier topographic model had depicted a fundamental opposition between the sexual instincts, on the one hand, and the ego or self-preservative instincts, on the other, the new theory viewed the ego's self-preservative function as itself derived from Eros: "[Eros] comprises not merely the uninhibited sexual instinct proper and the instinctual impulses of an aim-inhibited or sublimated nature derived from it, but also the self-preservative instinct, which must be assigned to the ego and which at the beginning of our analytic work we had good reason for contrasting with the sexual object-instincts."[99] With the structural model, the fundamental conflict no longer occurs between the ego and sexuality, as it had in the topographic, but is replaced by the conflict between Eros and Thanatos. One might say that, with the topographic model, Freud had been a Kantian in the sense that he had absolutized the opposition between inclination and understanding, to put it in Kant's language, or between the drives and the ego, to put it psychoanalytically. With the introduction of the structural model, things change. Although the new theory poses the danger of instinctual monism, it also contains, at the same time and for the same reasons, the potential for formulating a different relation between the ego and the drives, thereby overcoming that earlier Kantianism. In other words, while the fact that the id and the ego are depicted as undifferentiated at the outset produces the danger of instinctual monism, it also provides the conditions for a more intimate relation between the two.

Most authors stress the ego's seductiveness toward, and subservience to, the id when discussing the topics under consideration. The other side of Freud's formulation is rarely given equal attention: that the ego's use of "borrowed forces" in its dealings with the id not only forces it to "[acquiesce] to a large extent in the id's experience" but also causes the ego to "deepen its relation with the id." And it is this deepening that I want to investigate. As early as 1915, Freud had remarked with respect to the conscious and the unconscious that "a complete divergence of their trends, a total severance of the two systems, is what above all characterizes a condition of illness."[100] However, it was not until the introduction of the structural model that he began to indicate, but not work out in detail, the nature of a deeper relationship between the two systems, now conceptualized as ego and id.

In *Inhibitions, Symptoms and Anxiety,* Freud describes repression as a process of *dissociation* in which the ego refuses to communicate with particular contents of the id: "Repression proceeds from the ego when the latter . . . refuses to associate itself with an instinctual cathexis which has been aroused in the id."[101] It cannot be stressed strongly enough that the restricted unity of the ego (and, by implication, the unity of reason) when it results from repression is achieved through *exclusion.* This is the moment of insight in Foucault's argument that modern instrumental rationality was constituted through a massive act of exclusion. It is not generally recognized, however, that, for Freud, the content as well as the energic strength of the ego is impoverished to the extent that this exclusion has occurred. Indeed, much of the ego's energic resources must be engaged in "a tedious or interminable . . . struggle" to ward off the dissociated material, so that it is unavailable for other, nondefensive purposes. As we will see, this is a rigid form of ego unification that is hypostatized by Lacan and Adorno into ego unity as such. The warded-off material and "all its derivatives," which can return as symptoms, assume an "extraterritorial" status vis-à-vis the "ego organization," and a split is established in the psyche between the ego and this "internal foreign territory."[102] The ego, however, because of its essentially synthetic "nature," is "obliged" to "make what must be regarded as an attempt at restoration or reconciliation" *(Versöhnung)* with the excommunicated material:

> The ego is an organization. It is based on the maintenance of free intercourse and of the possibility of reciprocal influence between all its parts. Its desexualized energy still shows traces of its origin in its impulsion to bind together and unify, and this necessity to synthesize grows stronger in proportion as the strength of the ego increases. It is therefore only natural that the ego should try to prevent symptoms from remaining isolated and alien *(die Fremdheit und Isolierung des Symptoms aufzuheben)* by using every possible method to bind them to itself in one way or another, and to incorporate them into its organization by means of those bonds.[103]

Contrary to the Lacanian approach, which enshrines the split subject as the psychoanalytic equivalent of original sin, Freud views the healing of the splits in the psyche, through the undoing of these repressions qua excommunications, as one of the central therapeutic tasks of psychoanalysis: "In actual fact, indeed, the neurotic patient presents us with a torn mind, divided by resistances. As we analyze it and remove the resistances, it grows together; the greater unity which we call his *ego fits into itself all the instinctual impulses which before had been split off and held apart from it*" (emphasis added).[104] Again, we must stress that the expanded unity that results from undoing repressions in analysis is achieved through the "free intercourse" with the split-off foreign material. This expanded unity is, in short, achieved through the inclusion of what was previously foreign to the ego. This is a very different notion of unification than the one indicated above, and much of the confusion in the various critiques of the *principium individuationis* and the autocratic subject result from the failure to recognize this distinction.

It thus turns out, somewhat paradoxically, that the ego does not most effectively establish "mastery" over the id, as is often assumed, by dissociating itself from and suppressing the id's instinctual material. On the contrary, it achieves this end and enriches itself at the same time and to the same extent by establishing "free intercourse" with that material. On the basis of this formulation, Freud's metaphor of "draining the Zuider Zee,"[105] which is presented as an elaboration of the dictum "Wo es war, da soll Ich werden," can be misleading. If it is taken to mean a mere "power grab," in which the ego, consciousness, secondary processes, and rational thinking would usurp the id, the unconscious, primary processes, magical thinking, and so on, then it is not only rationalistically naive but grotesque and undesirable as well. As Castoriadis asks,

[H]ow can we conceive of a subject that would have entirely absorbed the imaginative function [his term for the id or the unconscious], how could we dry up the spring in the depths of ourselves from which flow both alienating phantasies and free creation truer than truth, unreal deliria and surreal poems, this eternally new beginning and ground of all things, without which nothing would have a ground, how can we eliminate what is at the base of, or in any case what is inextricably bound up with, what makes us human beings—our symbolic function, which presupposes our capacity to see and to think in a thing something which is not [i.e., which presupposes the imaginative function]?[106]

The "work of culture"[107]—for both the collective and the individual—should be conceived as precisely that, work. That is, it should not aim at an "attained state" in which an "ideal person who has become pure Ego once and for all . . . [proffers] a discourse all its own . . . [and] never produces phantasies." Nor should this "impossible state," which would in fact be "unhistorical" and constitute another "mystification," even be taken as a regulative ideal toward which the individual asymptotically strives. The goal of autonomy does not prescribe a state at all but an "active situation" in which a "real person would be unceasingly involved in the movement of taking up again what had been acquired" and reworking and reappropriating it. The autonomous subject would no longer be heteronomously, that is to say, passively, determined by the id, *a tergo*, as with Groddeck and Lacan, but would establish an active relation toward fantasy life that would no longer need to be defensively warded off. The autonomous subject would be "capable of uncovering phantasies as phantasies . . . [and not allowing] them to rule—unless he or she is so willing"—which is to say, capable of saying "this is indeed true, and: this is indeed my desire," and allow the latter to have free expression under the aegis of the ego.[108]

3

Synthesis as Violence: Lacan and Adorno on the Ego

Freud as the Heir to Classical German Philosophy

Stanley Cavell has made the observation that it was not the proletariat, as Marx and Engels had believed, but Freud who was the heir of classical German philosophy.[1] And, indeed, this is the way in which the Frankfurt school saw him: more specifically, they understood Freud's developmental theory as an empirical concretization of the Kantian practical philosophy. They argued that, while Kant had elaborated a theory of maturity (*Mündigkeit*) and autonomy in strictly philosophical terms, Freud formulated an empirical theory that specified the concrete developmental accomplishments necessary for their actual attainment.[2] These two intimately connected concepts are associated for Kant, as well as for Freud, with the emancipatory aspirations of modernity. In a text that has received much attention recently,[3] "What is Enlightenment?" Kant described the process of enlightenment as overcoming one's self-imposed immaturity (*Unmündigkeit*) and defined immaturity "as the incapacity to use one's intelligence without the guidance of another," that is, the incapacity to think for oneself without the direction of external authority.[4] In a separate but related text,[5] Kant similarly defined autonomy as self-determination qua self-legislation: one is autonomous to the extent that one is subject to laws of one's own making rather than determined by the heteronomous laws of nature. And the concept of nature can include the laws not only of outer nature but of inner nature and of society as well, insofar as the latter function in an unreflective, naturelike *(naturwüchsig)* fashion. For inner nature, too, is ruled by laws, albeit of a very peculiar sort, namely, the laws governing the discharge of the drives, the functioning of the pleasure principle and the "logic" of the primary process. As Laplanche and Pontalis put it, inner nature can impinge on us with "a consistency and resistance comparable to those displayed by material reality."[6] The larger issue involved in these considerations is Kant's characteristically, and perhaps uniquely, modern attempt to formulate a critique of traditional and dogmatic—which is to say, *heteronomous*—authority. Once this critique has been established, it is no longer acceptable to maintain that "the representations of the tribe"[7]—including its sacred core—are valid simply in virtue of the fact that elders, in the broadest possible sense of the term—that is, the parental generations—subscribed to them. Rather, it then becomes legitimate to demand that those representations be rationally accounted for. The establishment of this possibility constitutes a novel rupture in the course of human history, and it is simply a historical fact, not a piece of Eurocentrism, that this breakthrough occurred in the West.[8]

Although Freud's discussion of maturity is formulated in more prosaic, which is to say, more familial and less philosophical terms than Kant's, the two accounts are, nevertheless, ultimately congruent. Freud writes:

The liberation of an individual, as he grows up, from the authority of his parents is one of the most necessary though one of the most painful results brought about by the course of his development. It is quite essential that liberation should occur and it may be presumed that it has been to some extent achieved by everyone who has reached a normal state. . . . On the other hand, there is a class of neurotics whose condition is recognizably determined by their having failed in this task.[9]

The normative role that the concept of maturity plays in Freud's thinking should be apparent from this passage: separation from one's parents is a crucial task of so-called normal development, and, conversely, the failure to achieve that goal results in neurosis. In fact, it can be shown that, for Freud, pathology in general, on both the group as well as the individual level, is identified with *atavistic infantilism*.[10] Freud, then, provides the intrapsychic, developmental, and affective dimension that is missing by design, as it were, from Kant's a prioristic theory: maturity in the Kantian sense of thinking for one-self presupposes separation from one's parents not in any mundane physical sense but in the deep intrapsychic sense of relinquishing one's libidinal ties to incestuous objects. Only to the extent that individuals have undergone the painful process of relinquishing, mourning, and internalizing those infantile objects is their thinking (and action) sufficiently uncontaminated by conscious or unconscious parental imagos and familial dramas to be called their own.

Similar observations can be made with respect to the concept of autonomy. Indeed, as I have already suggested, Freud's epigram "Where id was, there shall ego become"[11] can be taken as a programmatic statement for the move from heteronomy to autonomy in the Kantian sense. The formation of ego structure not only frees individuals from the heteronomous determination of the id but, insofar as it also distances them from the ego's other "internal foreign territory," namely, the superego—which, as we have stressed, can be no less heteronomous and primitive than the id—it also frees them from the naturelike compulsions of society. Indeed, paraphrasing Freud, we might say that the dictum "Where superego was, there shall ego become" could be taken as a programmatic statement for the move from acting "in accordance with" the law to acting "out of respect for" the law.[12] Just as the sacred core of society is no longer systematically insulated from criticism in modernity, so postconventional identity formation no longer takes place through the quasi-automatic socialization into traditionally delineated roles, which is to say, through the quasi-automatic internalization of the collective superego. The creation of an enterprise such as psychoanalysis—in which no topic, however sacred, can in principle be made taboo for exploration, and which seeks to maximize an individual's autonomy—only becomes thinkable after this rupture with heteronomous tradition has occurred and perhaps only in a decadent city like fin de siècle Vienna, where the old order was disintegrating so rapidly.

Lacan and the Decentered Subject

This Enlightenment reading of Freud and psychoanalysis has, to say the least, not gone unchallenged in recent years. The post-modern critique, which combines elements from the philosophical discussion of alterity with elements from the psychoanalytic theory of narcissism, has challenged autonomy as a basic value not only for psychoanalysis but for ethical life in general. The central thesis is the following: the ego, far from being an agency of truth and emancipation, is in fact a defensive structure, a submissive slave, sycophant, opportunist, and liar [13]—a "symptom" as Lacan put it [14]—that narcissistically seeks to protect the individual from otherness and, in so doing, ultimately violates the otherness of the Other. Or, stronger yet, it may be that the very notion of emancipation is itself simply another guise for the will to power and one of the grandiose illusions of modernity that seeks to deny our finitude—that is, our inescapable embeddedness in nature, language, and tradition—through omnipotent mastery. According to this account, the ego and, as Derrida has observed, the desire for a center in general, [15] is a product of anxiety.

The work of the early Lacan has become a *locus classicus* for the psychoanalytically formulated critique of the autonomous ego. It should be noted that Lacan, in his earlier works at least (and undoubtedly under the impact of Kojève), employs the same vocabulary of reification and alienation—and even emancipation—as Hegelian Marxism to locate his critique of the ego. Indeed, much of the radical aura surrounding his position results from that rhetoric. [16] Lacan unequivocally situates his critique of the ego, as well as "our role as an analyst in a definite context in the history of mankind." [17] Indeed, for him the ego is no less a "historic result," [18] which is to say, a product of modernity, than it was for Marx. At the beginning of the *Seminar* on the ego, he warns his students against retrospectively projecting our modern conception of the ego into the past when we attempt, for example, to understand the Greeks:

It seems to us then that Socrates and his interlocutors must have had an implicit notion of this central function, that the ego must have had for them a function analogous to that which it occupies in our theoretical thinking, but also in the spontaneous apprehension we have of our thoughts, our tendencies, our desires, of what belongs to us and what does not, of what we admit to being expressions of our personality or what we reject as being parasitical on it. It is very difficult for us to imagine that the whole of this psychology isn't eternal. [19]

Rather than being eternal, "the register of the ego" has been "acquired over the course of history,"[20] and we can point to the particular point of its emergence, namely, with the rise of modernity and the philosophy of Descartes. Lacan, of course, does not view this acquisition in a positive light but sees it as the "fundamental illusion of man's experience, or at least of modern man." And he views the task of psychoanalysis, "the liberating, demystifying treatment of a human relation," as emancipating us from that illusion.[21] Moreover, in addition to its illusory character, the ego's pathological status—it is, as we have noted, "the human symptom par excellence"[22]—also derives from its reified nature. Homo psychologicus, whom psychoanalysis is charged to treat, is a "product of our industrial age" and "his relationship to this machine is so very intimate that it is almost as if the two were actually conjoined." More specifically, the machine's "emotional significance" for the modern individual "comes from the fact that it exteriorizes the protective shell of his ego." The machine, in short, constitutes an external reflection of the reified ego. "The psycho-analytical dialogue," as opposed to merely "psychotechnical procedures," aims at dissolving that reification: because, in the Lacanian technique at least, it bypasses the reified ego with its method of free association, it "can re-establish a more human relationship."[23]

For Lacan, Freud's "Copernican Revolution" consists in the "subversion" of the "pre-analytical notion of the ego," which is to say, the centered, self-present, and transparent ego more or less shared by common sense, Cartesian philosophy, and academic psychology.[24] This subversion consists, according to Lacan, in the decentering of the ego vis-à-vis the unconscious, that is, the demonstration that the unconscious, or the "subject of the unconscious," as he calls it, and not the ego, constitutes "the core of our being" [der Kern unseres Wesens].[25] Because it provokes such powerful resistances, later analysts have continually been tempted to recoil from Freud's utterly subversive discovery and to rehabilitate the pre-analytic ego. And it is precisely this temptation to which Hartmann and the ego psychologists succumbed. The introduction of autonomous ego functions, so Lacan maintains, amounts to turning back from Freud's Copernican Revolution and reinstating the ego of academic psychology: "Ah! Our *nice little ego is back again!"*[26] Lacan's polemic against ego psychology and his return to Freud are thus meant to reverse this regression. He insists that the disagreement with Hartmann is absolute, without possible mediation. If the ego psychologists are correct, "[W]e will have to abandon the notion I tell you to be the essence of the Freudian discovery, the decentering of the subject in relation to the *ego,* and to return to the notion that everything centres on the standard development of *ego.* This is an alternative without mediation—if that is true, everything I say is false."[27] I return to this lack of mediation below in discussing the latent absolutism in Lacan's position.

Drawing on Freud's theory of biological prematurity, Lacan traces the ego's origins to the manic attempt to deny infantile helplessness *(Hilflosigkeit).* For Freud, as we have noted in the discussion of Chasseguet-Smirgel, it is a fundamental anthropological fact that the human infant is born premature and helpless relative to the young of other species. Because "its intra-uterine existence seems to be short in comparison with that of most animals," the human infant "is sent into the world in a less finished" and, therefore, more helpless state than the young of other species.[28] Lacan locates that helplessness in the fragmented and unintegrated state of the child's bodily experience—what he calls "the body in bits and pieces"[29]—that results from its "anatomical incompleteness" and manifests itself in "the signs of uneasiness and motor uncoordination of the neo-natal months."[30] During the mirror stage, the child anticipates a future situation in which its helplessness would have been overcome. In contradiction to its actually fragmented and uncoordinated state, in the mirror—or, more precisely, in the mirroring experience—the child perceives a synthesized image of himself or herself as already integrated and no longer helpless: "The uncoordinated, incoherent diversity of the primitive fragmentation gains its unity"[31] in the fascination of the gaze. The child's "false" perception, moreover, is accompanied by a "flutter of jubilant activity,"[32] which Lacan takes to indicate the child's manic excitement at "believing" himself or herself to have escaped the helplessness qua fragmentation. The ego is constituted, in turn, through the identification with—that is to say, the internalization of—the unified imago. This internalized imago, now set up in the psyche, as it were, provides the trajectory for further "maturation," namely, the further unification of the self. Lacan's thesis is that this trajectory is "alienating" and "fictional"[33] in virtue of the fact that it imposes a rigid structure on, and thereby falsifies the actual state of, the child's corporeal and motoric experience, which is in fact fragmented, and projects an illusory image of the child as whole. The internalization of the imago leads "to the assumption of the armour of an alienating identity, which will mark with its rigid structure the subject's entire mental development."[34] It follows, for Lacan, that the "essential function of the ego," which he refers to as its imaginary function because of its specular origins, is not reality testing, but *méconnaissance*, that is, "very nearly the systematic refusal to acknowledge reality which French analysts refer to in talking about the psychoses."[35]

Human knowledge and activity, insofar as it is mediated by the ego, is thus not only capable of being deceived but is, "as such," "deceiving," "inauthentic," and "deluded."[36] He argues that as the ego, therefore, is itself the source of the systematic deception, it cannot be the agency for overcoming that deception. The standpoint of the ego is not simply a "mistake" or a "partial point of view" that can be corrected or expanded, but it must be circumvented or abandoned in toto if the truth of the unconscious subject (whatever that might mean)[37] is to be attained—"the truth lies elsewhere."[38] From the technical standpoint, this leads Lacan to reject the clinical value of the therapeutic alliance, which is a central tenet of the ego psychologists who seek to form and maintain an alliance between the ego of the analyst and the observing or healthy part of the patient's ego— that is, the part not embroiled in the transference and the pathology—so as to expand and strengthen the latter. How, Lacan asks, if "it is at the level of the ego that all the resistances occur"—if, in other words, the ego is involved in systematic deception throughout—can such an alliance make sense?[39] The important point to note for our purposes is Lacan's monolithic and completely undialectical view of the ego. The ego's functioning is not seen as a mixture of rationalization and insight, resistance and curiosity, deception and truth. Rather, it is seen as *méconnaissance*, and *méconnaissance* alone.

He terms the ego an "orthopaedic" entity because of its imposition of this rigid and artificial unity on "the turbulent movements that the subject feels are animating him,"[40] a unity it will also seek to impose coercively on the object. Finally, Lacan suggests that, if one were to use the language of traditional psychoanalysis, it might be more proper to refer to the ego thus conceived as an "Ideal [ego],"[41] as opposed to an ego ideal, in order to indicate its idealized, grandiose, and manic character. Today, we might compare it to Kohut's notion of the grandiose self.

The ego's relationship to the object is no less narcissistic than its own formation insofar as it only apprehends the object not in its own right but through "the grid of the narcissistic relation."[42] This is, of course, the psychoanalytically formulated counterpart to the central objection to the philosophy of reflection. The Cartesian subject constitutes the object according to its own internal schemata and can never reach the Other independently of those schemata. The being that "stands across from me in the circle of reflection" is, as Manfred Frank has put it, "*my* Being" and, in the Cartesian tradition, this "Being for-me" has been mistaken for Being as such.[43]

The difficulty, moreover, is not confined to the theoretical plane alone but has momentous consequences for practical life. In an analysis that, as we will see, is strikingly similar to Adorno's, Lacan argues that the object thus constituted is an object of domination, and the form of knowledge corresponding to this objectification—which he terms "paranoic," because of its projective character—is a form of power. When the narcissistic ego constitutes the object in its own image—"egomorphically"[44]—the orthopedic rigidity of the narcissistic ego is conferred on the object; as a result, this reified object becomes an object of possible technical manipulation: "That which constitutes the ego and its object with attributes of permanence, identity, and substantiality, in short, with entities or 'things' . . . extends indefinitely [man's] world and his power . . . by giving his objects their instrumental polyvalence."[45] Moreover, he traces the desire for knowledge and the roots of rationality to the will to power: "the passionate desire peculiar to man to impress his image in reality is the obscure basis of the rational meditations of the will."[46] As with Adorno, the reified subject and the reified object mutually entail one another, and the form of cognition that corresponds to this reification is one of technical control.

Lacan's Hypostatization of the Death Instinct

An objection can be raised against Lacan's account of the genesis of the ego. It pertains to the purportedly "fictional" and "alienating" status of the integrated imago. As we have seen, that imago and the developmental direction it defines are considered fictional because its unity is only "virtual" or "anticipatory" when measured against the actually fragmented state of the child's existence. But why, it may be asked, should the temporal, that is, the developmental, dimension be disregarded and the current fragmented state hypostatized into the true one? Why, in other words, should there be an essentialization of fragmentation? Lacan is, in fact, taking the "body in bits and pieces" as the child's essential state and any departure from it, a form of falsification. My thesis is that essentialization can be traced to Lacan's a priori "Heraclitean"[47] predilection for deficiency, discord, and fragmentation, and to his suspicion of all forms of finality, reconciliation, and synthesis. It is not simply that the infant's integrated self-image in the present is factually false that leads Lacan to object to it. He rejects any future integration and to the ego qua synthesizer, because he valorizes Becoming over Being and he objects to synthesis, which he equates with reification as such: "Here we see the ego, in its essential resistance to the elusive process of Becoming, to the variations of Desire."[48] To make a similar point from a more concrete perspective, we need only recall the other two major theorists of the mirror, Winnicott and Kohut. For them, the integrating experience of the mother's smile, far from situating the child on an alienated trajectory, provides a hope in a future when he or she would no longer suffer the pain and anxiety of infantile helplessness.

It cannot be denied, of course, that Lacan's argument also stems in part from a legitimate desire to prevent Freud's message of the plague, that is, of "the radical heteronomy . . . gaping within man,"[49] from being diluted by overly harmonistic and conformist theories of development. This is the valid moment in the by now familiar critique of fifties ego psychology that Lacan shares with the Frankfurt school. In addition to the sociological question, however, there is still an important theoretical issue at stake concerning synthesis. And it is clear that Lacan cannot assimilate the second moment of Freud's persistently and intentionally dualistic thinking,[50] namely, Eros, the other coequal combatant in the battle of Titans, into his theory. Because of his desire to preserve *only* the moment of conflict, darkness, and heterogeneity in Freud, and because of his a priori antipathy to synthesis, Lacan offers an extremely selective reading of Freud's theoretical revisions of the twenties, which, for him, consist almost exclusively in the introduction of the death instinct. Lacan concentrates on *Beyond the Pleasure Principle* and disregards *The Ego and the Id*, the tripartite model of the psyche, and Eros almost entirely. He argues that, in the period preceding the publication of *Beyond the Pleasure Principle*, there was a certain deradicalization occurring "in the circle around Freud," and "the meaning of the discovery of the unconscious," namely, the radical heterogeneity within humans, was being "pushed into the background." Therefore, "it was precisely in order to regain the sense of his experience [of that heterogeneity] that Freud wrote *Beyond the Pleasure Principle*" and introduced the death instinct. Whereas the unconscious had been the cipher for negativity, for the plague, in the early Freud, the death instinct became that cipher for the later Freud. What Lacan fails to recognize, however, is that the really novel element in the twenties was not the death instinct but Eros. The death instinct had, in fact, been present *in nuce* in Freud's thinking since he first introduced an entropic, tension-reducing force in the form of the constancy hypothesis in the *Project*.[51] What was radically new in the twenties—and we can ask why Freud had not thematized this before—was an anti-entropic force in the form of the life instinct. Loewald correctly stresses this point: "I cannot emphasize enough that it was the introduction of the idea of the life instinct (which encompassed different conceptions of pleasure and of the pleasure principle) that was a true and unsettling innovation in psychoanalytic theory—an innovation that Freud could no longer circumvent but with which he felt much less at home than he did with the death instinct."[52] We return to the "unsettling" consequences of the introduction of Eros and to the problem of pleasure and the pleasure principle in our discussion of sublimation in chapter five.

Lacan's inability to assimilate the concept of Eros becomes especially apparent in an interesting exchange with Hyppolite in *Seminar*

II. Lacan makes the peculiar claim—peculiar, given Freud's doctrine of Eros—that the notion of a tendency in nature to produce "superior forms, more and more elaborated, more and more integrated" was "alien to" Freud and "he explicitly repudiates it." Lacan traces this supposed aversion to a synthetic tendency to Freud's "medical experience," which "allowed him to locate the register of a certain kind of suffering and illness, of fundamental conflict, in man." Hyppolite raises the obvious objection to these observations:

I'm not at all challenging the crisis described by Freud. But he opposes the libido to the death instinct, and he defines it as the tendency of the organism to come together with other organisms, as if that constituted progress, integration. So, independently of this undeniable conflict of which you speak and which doesn't make him an optimist from the human point of view, we nevertheless find in him a conception of the libido . . . which asserts clearly the broader and broader integration of organisms. Freud says it quite succinctly in the text [of *Beyond the Pleasure Principle*] itself.

In short, what about Eros, which "holds together everything in the world"?[53] Lacan offers the following response: "The tendency to union—Eros to unite—is only ever apprehended in its relation to the contrary tendency, which leads to division, to rupture, to a redispersion, most especially of inanimate matter. The two tendencies are strictly speaking inseparable. No notion is less unitary than that."[54] This argument, however, does not demonstrate that Freud had an aversion to a synthetic dynamic in nature; it simply assigns that dynamic its coequal place in the battle of the Titans. Lacan's position involves a sophism: because Eros is never apprehended in a pure state, as absolute unity, but only in conjunction with Thanatos, the concept of a integrative dimension is discredited as such. It is possible to maintain, however, that Eros exists not absolutely but as a tendency in conjunction with, and in opposition to, the tendency toward disunification, and it is this tendency that Lacan refuses to acknowledge and conceptualize. Instead, he absolutizes disunity and, in some sense, ceases himself to be a conflict theorist, which is to say, he assigns an unmitigated victory to Thanatos. As Freud himself puts it in "Analysis Terminable and Interminable," which is certainly not one of his more upbeat works: "Only by the concurrent or mutually opposing action of the two primal instincts—Eros and the death-instinct—never by one or the other alone, can we explain the rich multiplicity of the phenomena of life."[55] Despite his apparent philosophical sophistication and his polemic against the Hegelian notion of absolute knowledge,[56] Lacan's own absolutism, albeit of a reverse sort, is apparent in the assertion that if Eros does not exist absolutely, it does not exist at all: he preserves the Absolute as his standard, if only to demonstrate that it cannot be fulfilled.

Similarly, as I indicated above, Lacan insists that between a completely unified, transparent, and self-present ego and complete decentration of the subject there is no possibility of mediation; no third term exists. Interestingly enough, Hartmann, whose position is often more subtle than he is sometimes given credit for, in fact provides the following, less monolithic description of the ego's characteristics:

Contrasts in the ego are many: the ego has from its start the tendency to oppose the drives, but one of its main functions is also to help them toward gratification; it is a place where insight is gained, but also of rationalization; it promotes objective knowledge of reality, but at the same time, by way of identification and social adjustment, takes over in the course of its development the conventional prejudices of the environment; it pursues its independent aims, but it is also characteristic of it to consider the demands of the other substructures of personality, etc.[57]

And from a more philosophical standpoint, Ricoeur provides the distinctions that make it possible to offer a more differentiated account of the ego, which is to say, to "deconstruct the false *cogito*"[58] and its self-deceptions, thereby preserving the subversiveness of the Freudian project without, at the same time, repudiating the ego as pure *méconnaissance*. Ricoeur, then, introduces the Husserlian distinction between apodicticity and adequacy. He argues that, while this distinction itself had already been implicit in the traditional philosophical distinction between the transcendental and the empirical, "before Freud, the two moments were confused." The advent of psychoanalysis, however, "drives a wedge between" them.[59] "Apodicticity" refers to the unassailable moment of my existence, which, for Descartes, cannot be denied even when I am systematically and totalistically deceived by so thoroughly paranoid and omnipotent a figure as the evil genius. It refers to the indubitable fact *that I am* insofar as

I mentate, regardless of how delusional that mentation may be, and is therefore the moment that survives any deconstruction of the naive cogito.[60] "This impregnable moment of apodicticity," however, "tends to be confused with the moment of adequation, in which I am *such* as I perceive myself."[61] The adequacy of my consciousness of myself, my self-knowledge, can no longer, to say the least, be taken for granted after psychoanalysis' documentation of the innumerable ruses of desire and especially after its discovery of narcissism, "the great screen between self and oneself."[62] On the contrary, after Freud's intervention in the history of Western rationality, we must assume "the possibility that I am deceived," to one extent or another, "in every ontic statement I pronounce about myself."[63] Thus, both the apodicticity of the "that I am" and the "indefinitely dubious character" of what I am "must be assumed together."[64]

With Lacan, and against the Cartesian tradition, Ricoeur thus maintains that psychoanalysis constitutes a "discipline of reflection,"[65] that demands the critique of the immediacy, pretentions, and self-deceptions of the naive, and therefore illusory, cogito: "Only the *cogito* which has passed through the critical test of psychoanalysis is no longer the one claimed by philosophy in its pre-Freudian naiveté." However, against Lacan and with Freud, Ricoeur insists that adequacy of consciousness and expansion of the ego remain the goal: "Psychoanalysis can have no therapeutic ambition other than enlarging the field of consciousness and giving back to the ego some of the strength ceded to its three powerful masters [the id, the superego, and external reality]." What had been "origin" in the idealist tradition, namely "conscious-being *(Bewusstsein)*," now "becomes task or goal." Thus, rather than abandoning the standpoint of the ego altogether, the deconstruction of naive consciousness can instead initiate a process of creating, through the work of psychoanalysis and in alliance with the analysand's observing ego, a more adequate—note, I do not say fully adequate—ego/consciousness: "becoming-conscious *(Bewusstwerden)*" remains the task, an interminable one, to be sure, but a task nonetheless.[66] Ricoeur can hold this position because, in contrast to Lacan, who, as we have seen, speaks of the intrinsic and systematic *méconnaissance* of the ego, he refers only to the "indefinitely dubious character" of the cogito. By this he means we know, in principle, that we can always be deceived, but we never know the extent to which we are in fact deceived at any given time.

Fundamentally distinct philosophical outlooks and practical projects are condensed in these different formulations. Both Ricoeur and Lacan reject, on the basis of the psychoanalytic revolution, the possibility of "total reflection" or "Hegelian absolute knowledge."[67] How could they fail to after Freud's discovery of the unconscious—a discovery that installs "the anteriority of instinct in relation to awareness and volition [and] signifies the anteriority of the ontic plane to the reflective plane, the priority of *I am* to *I think*"?[68] Indeed today, after the critique of idealism not only by psychoanalysis but by so many otherwise divergent philosophical traditions, the impossibility of total reflection has become a commonplace. The interesting question, in my opinion, which has prompted the enormous revival of interest in pragmatism, has become the following: how is valid knowledge and action possible without access to an absolute standpoint?[69]

Lacan, however, refuses to reject the other, equally untenable position, namely, that the ego as such is systematically and totally deceived. With Ricoeur we can agree that the extent of the ego's self-delusion is at any given time "indefinite" and, at the same time, insist that the distinction between delusion and nondelusion nevertheless be maintained. In other words, it does not follow from the fact that there always exists a possibility of delusion that we are always deluded.[70] Paraphrasing Lacan, we can say that the truth does not lie elsewhere, but in the middle of the two equally abstract and unstabilizable alternatives of total reflection and total delusion.[71]

Adorno's Aporetic Defense of the Autonomous Individual

We are generally not in the habit of grouping Adorno's aestheticized Hegelian-Marxism and Lacan's brand of surrealistic scientism together. Nevertheless, as I have already indicated, there exists a remarkable convergence between the two, up to a point, with respect to their critique of the ego. Indeed, Adorno and Lacan advance the same three interconnected theses:

1. The unity of the ego as such is rigidified, compulsory, and coercive.

2. The ego is a narcissistic (or paranoid) structure insofar as it can apprehend the object only in terms of its own reflection (or projections).

3. The rigidly integrated ego is deeply implicated in the will to power and the domination of nature.

These three theses are connected in that the structures the ego refinds in the object (including inner nature) reflect its own internal structures of forced unity and impose a violent synthesis on that object; this synthesis, in turn, constitutes the object as an object of possible technical domination.

The convergence between Adorno and the early Lacan's critique of the ego may not be as surprising as it at first appears. Both Habermas and Dews[72] have pointed out that, while Adorno veers away at the last possible moment and thus avoids the final, self-abnegating totalization of the critique of reason and of the subject, he nevertheless travels a long way down the road of that critique with the Romantics, Nietzsche and Heidegger. It is the considerable distance he traverses with the tradition of the Counter-Enlightenment that he shares with Lacan, who is, of course, deeply influenced by Heidegger in these matters.[73] But while Adorno shares much of the Counter-Enlightenment's diagnosis of reason and the subject, unlike the Counter-Enlightenment, he ultimately refuses to abandon the standpoint of rationality and the ego. And this refusal, in conjunction with the critique of the Enlightenment, generates aporia at the heart of Adorno's philosophy, which he is not only willing to accept, but which in fact furnish the perpetual dynamic for his theorizing. As he understands it, the insurmountable aporia are not the result of theoretical errors, as it were, but are generated by the historical circumstances themselves. Under those circumstances, the only trace of freedom that is historically available consists in not choosing between the poles of those aporia. Adorno insists that "a free man would only be one who need not bow to any alternatives, and under existing circumstances there is a touch of freedom in refusing to accept the alternatives."[74]

Thus, with respect to the self-destruction of reason, although his attack on identity thinking and the imperialism of the concept is relentless, he nevertheless insists that philosophy "must strive, by way of the concept, to transcend the concept."[75] In *Dialectic of Enlightenment,* he and Horkheimer describe in the following way the "dilemma that faced us in our work" and became "the first phenomenon for investigation": On the one hand, "we were wholly convinced—and therein lies our *petitio principii*—that social freedom is inseparable from enlightened thought"; on the other hand, "[we] recognized"—and this is the point they share with the Counter-Enlightenment—"that the notion of this very way of thinking ... already contains the seed of the reversal universally apparent today."[76] And while they intended their critique of enlightenment "to prepare the way for a positive notion of enlightenment which will release it from entanglement in blind domination,"[77] that positive notion was never forthcoming. Without such a positive notion, the grounds for their commitment to "enlightened thought" could never be adequately clarified. Instead, Adorno continued, as Habermas puts it, "to circle about within this *performative contradiction* and remain there"[78] for the next twenty-five years; on this central point, *Negative Dialectics* is no different from *Dialectic of Enlightenment.* Similarly, "Adorno's critique of the modern subject," the necessary corollary of the critique of reason, is as "implacable as any poststructuralist's and is based on not dissimilar grounds." But, again, rather than abandoning the standpoint of the subject, as poststructuralists do, Adorno insists that our only option is to " 'use the force of the subject to break through the deception of constitutive subjectivity.' "[79] As in the case of a positive doctrine of enlightenment, however, he never indicates in sufficient detail how this might be accomplished. All we are given is the admittedly enticing, but unfortunately abstract, call to be mindful of nature in ourselves: "By virtue of this mindfulness *[Eingedenken]* of nature in the subject, in whose fulfillment the unacknowledged truth of all culture lies hidden, enlightenment is universally opposed to domination."[80] I try to provide more content to this notion in the discussion of sublimation in chapter 5.

At the same time as he criticizes the notion of the autonomous individual, Adorno aporetically and obliquely retains it as a norm that is ambivalent in two senses. First, he objects to Kant's rigoristic, formal a priori formulation, which, as we have seen, purchases autonomy at the price of sacrificing what Kant called inclination, that is, empirical existence, inner nature, and pleasure. Freud, of course, provided "the report on the forces of destruction rampant in the individual" as a result of the sacrifice of inner nature.[81] While Kant's "timid bourgeois detestation of anarchy" may have matched "his proud bourgeois antipathy against tutelage" and allowed him to make a determined stand against it, that same hostility also caused him to miss the truth content in the moment of anarchy.[82] An adequate notion of autonomy would have to do justice to the claims of the drives and the pleasure principle, which were better accommodated in the hedonistic and eudaemonistic tradition in ethics. In the final paragraph of "On the Metacritique of Practical Reason," in *Negative Dialectics,* in which Adorno brings Kant into confrontation with Freud, he precisely formulates what is for him the unsurpassable aporia. First, the moments of truth and untruth in the Kantian clause of the aporia: "The subjects are free, after the Kantian model, in so far as they are aware of and identical with themselves; and then again, they are unfree in such identity in so far as they are subject to, and will perpetuate, its compulsion." And the corresponding moments of untruth and truth in the anarchistic clause: "They are unfree as diffuse, nonidentical nature; and yet, as that nature they are free because their overpowering impulse—the subject's nonidentity with itself is nothing else—will also rid them of identity's coercive character."[83] The true moment of this clause coincides with and *exhausts* the postmodern critique of the subject, which ignores the content of truth in the Kantian clause altogether. For the present, however, I only want to point out that, in this passage, identity is coercive per se.

The second ambivalence derives from the fact that the autonomous individual, both as a norm and as an inadequately realized empirical reality, was a product of the "short intermezzo of liberalism."[84] The old Frankfurt school argued that, for a brief historical—and necessarily self-liquidating—moment, classical bourgeois society had articulated a vision of autonomy in its philosophy and high culture (and for Adorno, this, above all meant Beethoven) such that it was necessary to retain the core of that vision despite its distortions, limitations, and ideological husk, and that that vision had been realized in a partial but distorted way among certain privileged sectors of the population. The new historical framework that made possible the emergence of the individual as a norm and a partial reality included the following: (1) *The creation of civil society* as a realm in which individuals could pursue their self-interest, economic and otherwise, as they determined it, their "subjective freedom," as Hegel called it, as long as they abided by the restrictions of formal law. (The market, of course, constituted the empirical core of civil society.) [85] (2) *The rise of the modern family.* As opposed to the premodern *household,* in which marriages were arranged by the parents or the collective for political or economic reasons, the modern family, unburdened of its direct productive functions,[86] became an "affectionate unit," to use Lawrence Stone's terms,[87] in which individuals were free, in principle at least, to enter into marriage and form families in order to pursue their own sexual, romantic, and emotional happiness. This affectionate unit, which bourgeois ideology could also sentimentalize as a "haven in a heartless world,"[88] was seen as an essential precondition for the creation of the inwardness *(Innerlichkeit)* necessary for the formation of the modern, highly individuated self.[89] (3) *The separation of the family from civil society.* For this affectionate unit to perform its function of character formation properly, it had to remain sufficiently insulated from the impersonal forces of civil society. (4) *A patriarchal society.* With more than a hint of idealizing nostalgia,[90] the Frankfurt school, especially Horkheimer, held that the strong father, who, as head of the family pursued its interests as an independent entrepreneur in the market, was an essential condition for the formation of autonomous individuality (at least for the boy). He possessed the habits of moral rectitude, cultivated taste, and critical thinking, which are the constituents of individual autonomy: "Admiration for nobility of character, fidelity to one's word, independence of judgment, and so forth, are traits of a society of relatively independent subjects who enter into contractual relationships with each other."[91] These habits and character traits, moreover, were internalized by the son through a direct oedipal struggle with the actual father. This mode of character formation, with its corresponding neurotic pathologies, created the sort of superego that, while perhaps excessively harsh and rigid, was nevertheless capable of the independent moral and political judgment necessary for resisting external authority. *Homo oeconomicus* and *Homo criticus* were not entirely unrelated. The old Frankfurt school maintained that the classical Oedipus complex, "the father complex" as Freud often calls it, pertains most properly to this historical period.

However, the continued unfolding of the very "atomizing forces of civil society" that had disembedded the individual from the precapitalist social substance and created the individual in the first place served, in the long run, to undermine it not just as an empirical reality but, with bourgeois society growing increasingly "cynical" about its own values,[92] as a norm as well. The members of the Institute for Social Research maintained that the transition from the liberal laissez-faire capitalism of the nineteenth century to the administered monopoly capitalism of the twentieth eroded the empirical basis for the individual. Among other things, the father was transformed from a self-employed entrepreneur, heading a family business and pursuing its interest in the market, into an employee of a firm. The new imperative was no longer to be independent but to fit into a large, bureaucratic organization, to become a cog in the machine. The pressure to conform and get ahead, though it may require strategic calculation, does not tend to promote habits of critical thinking:

Once the legal owners are cut off from the real productive process and lose their influence, their horizon narrows. . . . Under the conditions of monopolistic capitalism . . . even . . . a relative individual independence is a thing of the past. The individual no longer has any ideas of his own. The content of mass belief, in which no one really believes, is an immediate product of the ruling economic and political bureaucracies, and its disciples secretly follow their own atomistic and therefore untrue interests; they act as mere functions of the economic machine.[93]

As the father's actual position and independence in society declined, his authority in the home, from which he was moreover increasingly absent, also diminished. The decline of the family enterprise meant the father had less to offer in terms of the son's future well-being. The son would now have to find employment and make his own way in the world of the impersonal organization, and whatever know-how and wisdom the father might have to impart would quickly become obsolete in a world where everything, including the rate of change, was constantly being revolutionized. Furthermore, the vacuum created by the father's diminished authority and absence from the household was increasingly filled by the forces of civil society, thus breaching the insulation of the private sphere. The school, the peer group, and, above all, the culture industry came to play a progressively larger role in the socialization of the child. Previously, the internalization of societal norms and the formation of psychic structure had proceeded in and through a confrontation with an actual father who was the representative of the outside society, which is to say, the relation between psyche and society had been personally *mediated.* Now, however, the forces of civil society increasingly reached *directly* into the private sphere, indeed into the psyche itself, and assumed that function. With the direct socialization of the psyche, the unadministered area defined by the nonintersection of society and psyche, in which the child's individuality and autonomy could previously develop—"the spiritual breathing space that bourgeois existence grants at least its better-placed members"[94]—was eliminated. What has remained in the totally administered world is the exaggerated but empty appearance of individuality in the standardized forms of "self-expression" afforded by consumerism and the "personalities" of the culture industry. The narcissistic personalities that have resulted from this lack of internalized ego structures have suited this situation perfectly: the grandiose figures of the political world and the culture industry "mirror" directly the narcissistic needs engendered by this regression to narcissism, and "the social power-structure hardly needs the mediating agencies of ego and individuality any longer."[95]

For classical Critical Theory, the theses of the fatherless society, the overly socialized world, and the end of the individual go together. The political consequences of this constellation led Horkheimer and Adorno to a *qualified* defense of the individual and subjectivity as a last refuge of freedom in the face of the totalizing forces of modern society:

In the period of his decay, the individual's experience of himself and what he encounters contribute once more to knowledge, which he had merely obscured as long as he continued unshaken to construe himself positively as the dominant category. In the face of the totalitarian unison with which the eradication of difference is proclaimed as a purpose in itself, even part of the social force of liberation may have temporarily withdrawn to the individual sphere. If critical theory lingers there, it is not only with a bad conscience.[96]

Habermas, it should be noted, who is far more even-handed in assessing the ambivalence of modernity, sees positive potentials in the same phenomena in which the older critical theorists saw only the negative: he believes that the same transformations in family structure, socialization, and personality that have contributed to new forms of psychopathology and anomie also make the formation of new, reflexively accomplished, postconventional identities possible and necessary.

Considerations such as these led Adorno to the observation that "the prebourgeois world does not yet know psychology, the oversocialized one knows it no longer."[97] Psychology, as the science of the individuated psyche, did not exist in the prebourgeois world, because, prior to the emergence of the individual, its object had not yet come into existence: *Homo psychologicus* was created simultaneously with *Homo oeconomicus*. The postbourgeois world knows psychology no longer as that science, because its object is now in the process of being dissolved. Strictly speaking, for Adorno, the object and, therefore, the science of psychology only exist during the brief moment of equipoise when the atomizing forces of civil society had sufficiently dislodged the individual from the collective but not yet engulfed him or her completely,[98] the period during which Freud created psychoanalysis while trying to come to grips with his father's death.

We can reverse Adorno's quip that "in psycho-analysis nothing is true except the exaggerations"[99] and say that recent developments in psychoanalysis itself have given some credence to the element of truth in Adorno's exaggerations. As Adorno himself knew,[100] since the fifties, many of the most important controversies within psychoanalysis have centered on its "widening scope."[101] It is argued that, as opposed to the ideal-typical "classical patient" (whether such a patient ever existed is itself controversial), who suffered from oedipal-level neurotic pathology—for example, obsessions, hysteria, phobias, and inhibitions—and for whom classical psychoanalytic technique had supposedly been designed (this claim too has become controversial), a new type of patient has been appearing in the consulting room with increasing regularity. This patient typically suffers from preœdipal, narcissistic, and borderline character disorders— often centering on problems in separation-individuation and the coherence of the self—and must be treated with postclassical techniques. The more sociologically minded analysts trace these new disorders to transformations in the family, sexual roles, socialization, and child rearing that have occurred since the Second World War. Moreover, interest has also increased in the preœdipal stages of development and the relationship to the early mother in conjunction with the controversy over the widening scope.

Finally, despite the patriarchal and class basis involved in the notion of the autonomous individual, the ideological mystifications and hypocrisy that often surrounded it, and, perhaps most importantly, the toll it took on inner nature, in one important respect at least, the concept of the autonomous individual was nevertheless preferable to the more diffuse forms of identity that have followed it. Against the backdrop of the triumph of fascism and Stalinism in Europe, on the one side, and the apparently imminent victory of the spiritually bankrupt culture industry Adorno and Horkheimer thought they were witnessing under the palm trees of the Pacific Palisades, on the other, the autonomous individual, whatever the limitations and cost, appeared worth preserving as a form of character that could at least partially resist absorption into a totally administered world. The "common sense" of the bourgeois, "the correct assessment of situations, the worldly eye schooled by the market, shares with the dialectic a freedom from dogma, narrow-mindedness and prejudice. Its sobriety undeniably constitutes a moment of critical thinking." [102] This is the important political point that is missed in the manic and one-sided celebration of the end of the subject.

A Critique of Adorno's Theory of the Subject

Having sketched Adorno's position, I now raise the following question: is an aporetic and oblique defense of the autonomous individual the best that can be achieved? Habermas has suggested, for example, that there is an alternative to endlessly circling around in the aporia so heroically and relentlessly spelled out in *Dialectic of Enlightenment:* "The reader who resists being overwhelmed by the rhetoric" of that work and "steps back and takes seriously the thoroughly philosophic claim of the text" can criticize the hidden "abstractions and simplifications" that make those aporia appear so intractable.[103] Indeed, Habermas is puzzled at Adorno and Horkheimer's ability to treat the fate of Western rationality so nonchalantly:

It is still difficult to understand a certain carelessness in their treatment of, to put it quite blatantly, the achievements of Western rationalism. How can the two advocates of the Enlightenment (which they always claimed to be and still are) so underestimate the rational content of cultural modernity that they observe in its elements only the amalgamation of reason and domination, of power and validity.[104]

Following Habermas's general suggestion, I examine some of the assumptions pertaining to the psychoanalytic dimension of *Dialectic of Enlightenment.* I believe it can be shown that the aporia that result from Adorno's critique of the subject rest on abstract and oversimplified presuppositions concerning the nature of the ego. And these presuppositions are precisely the points he shares in common with Lacan. If those assumptions can be unearthed and criticized, then one will no longer be left with the two equally unsatisfactory alternatives the Lacan/Adorno diagnosis of the ego allows: abandoning the standpoint of the ego altogether (Lacan) or continuously circling about in the aporia (Adorno). This approach should, moreover, make it possible to formulate a more concrete notion of the "mindfulness of nature in the subject."

Horkheimer and Adorno, as we have seen, locate the roots of the crisis of modernity in the intrinsic and mutually implicating link between the domination of external nature and that of internal nature: "The subjective spirit which cancels the animation of nature can master a despiritualized nature only by imitating its rigidity and despiritualizing itself in turn";[105] the reification of inner and outer nature entail one another. They advance the thesis that, with the move from *mythos* to *logos,* from myth to enlightenment, "the world becomes chaos, and synthesis salvation."[106] Enlightened thought, in all its forms, preconstitutes Being as *unity* and dismisses the superabundance[107] that escapes its synthesizing grid as mere chaos and Nonbeing: "In advance, the Enlightenment recognizes as being and occurrence only what can be apprehended in unity; its ideal is the system from which all and everything follows. . . . To the Enlightenment, that which does not reduce to numbers, and ultimately to the one becomes illusion; modern positivism writes it off as literature. Unity is the slogan from Parmenides to Russell."[108] From the vantage point of enlightenment, with its drive toward unity and system, the "magical heritage," which "was not ordered by one identical spirit,"[109] was too diffuse, concrete, and particular. In magic, as the use of the technique of mimicry indicates, there was "specific representation."[110] Even its attempts to control the object through imitating it "really concerned the object":[111] "The magician imitates demons; in order to frighten them or to appease them, he behaves frighteningly or makes gestures of appeasement."[112] Because of the "holiness of the *hic et nunc*," the unique object was "unfit for exchange." In scientific thinking, on the other hand, "there is no specific representation" but only "universal interchangeability."[113] With the transition from myth to enlightenment, the concrete, unique, and nonexchangeable entity is reconstituted as the particular, that is, as a fungible instance of the universal under which it can be subsumed and thereby assigned a place in, and incorporated into, the hierarchical system: "Science in general relates to nature and man only as the insurance company in particular relates to life and death. Whoever dies is unimportant: it is a question of ratio between accidents and the company's liabilities. Not the individuality but the law of the majority recurs in the formula."[114] By disqualifying nature, that is, by rejecting all nonquantitative attributes of the object (for example, secondary qualities) as mere anthropomorphic projections, enlightenment "makes the dissimilar comparable by reducing it to abstract quantities," and "disqualified nature becomes the chaotic" yet manipulable "matter of mere classification."[115] This underlying (quantitative) substratum "constitutes the unity of nature"[116] as it is apprehended by enlightenment. Synthesis proceeds exclusively from the side of the "all powerful subject." The consequences of these transformations are not confined to the theoretical realm alone but have profound ramifications for practical life. Nature, thus constituted, becomes not only an object of possible scientific knowledge but, at the same time, an object of possible domination as well; enlightenment knows things "insofar as [it] can manipulate them."[117] Once it has been incorporated into the system, conceived of as the "hierarchical construction of concepts,"[118] the inferential-predictive power intrinsic to that system is conferred on nature as an object of possible scientific knowledge, thus transforming it into an object of possible technical manipulation at the same time: "Being is apprehended under the aspect of manufacture and administration."[119]

The absolute corollary of a "despiritualized nature" is, as I have already indicated, the autocratic self, the subject of the conquest of nature whose identity must be as spiritless, rigid, and abstract as the reified object it dominates. Horkheimer and Adorno identify that subject with the bourgeois individual, taken in the broadest possible sense: "The burgher, in the successive forms of slaveowner, free entrepreneur, and administrator, is the logical subject of the Enlightenment."[120] For Kant, whom Horkheimer and Adorno take as paradigmatic in these matters, the unity of the hierarchical system of reason and the unity of the object have "the synthetic unity of apperception,"[121] the abstract "I = I" that must accompany all empirical perceptions, as their correlate. The transcendental unity of apperception, which lies at the foundation of the unity of the self,[122] imparts its synthetic function to the forms of the understanding, which, in turn, *preconstitute* possible objects of experience *as unities,* thus establishing the "homogeneity of the general and particular"[123] in advance and excluding the unsynthesizable-in-itself—the "nonidentical" as Adorno liked to call it—from experience: "Intuitively, Kant foretold what Hollywood consciously put into practice: in the very process of production, images are pre-censored according to the norm of understanding which will later govern their apprehension."[124] "The unity of thought," both of the object and of the system of thought, is guaranteed a priori by the "unconscious operation of the intellectual mechanism which structures perception in accordance with understanding" so that what "subjective judgment" finds in the object is, in fact, a refinding of what has been "deposited" there in advance.[125] Put in psychoanalytic terms, this means that the ego only apprehends the object narcissistically, that is, in terms of its own reflection. And, what it encounters in the object is what it has already projected into it, in this case, its own abstract unity. The autocratic self, in short, "repressively shapes its Other in its own image."[126] In this sense, enlightenment is no less anthropocentric than myth.

While the unity of the subject, "on which the possibility of the logical form of all knowledge necessarily depends," is a priori in the sense that it organizes nature as an object of experience for the subject, it is at the same time also a posteriori: a "product of, as well as the condition for, material existence."[127] The unity of the subject is rooted in the metabolism with nature and the struggle for self-preservation: "The system the Enlightenment has in mind is the form of knowledge which copes most proficiently with the facts and supports the individual most effectively in the mastery of nature."[128] The constituting subject, which constitutes nature as an object of experience, has itself been constituted by the natural history of the species in its struggle for survival.[129] Enlightenment sought, first through Odyssean cunning and later through methodical science, to substitute the "subjection of nature to the self" for the mythical world's "subjection to nature"[130] and thereby to transcend the sheer repetitive, circular immanence of nature that is governed by the law of equivalence, that is, the law that states that "everything that happens must atone for having happened."[131] The flaw in this strategy, however, was the failure to recognize that this substitution, rather than transcending the law of equivalence, was itself simply another instance of that law and therefore still subject to it. Horkheimer and Adorno recognized that, like all hubris, the hubris of the attempt to master nature had to be paid for, and the price was commensurate with enlightenment's "insufficient righteousness."[132]

It should be pointed out, moreover, that the archaic terror evoked by the superior forces of nature, while better disguised, is no less intense with enlightenment than with myth, indeed, "Enlightenment is mythic fear turned radical." That fear manifests itself in the totalitarian tendency of enlightenment, which seeks to reduce the world to a "gigantic analytic judgment" and which—like the extreme narcissist who cannot tolerate the existence of the not-I—attempts to deny that existence by cannibalistically incorporating everything into its omnipotent orbit: "Nothing at all may remain outside, because the mere idea of outsideness is the very source of fear."[133]

Horkheimer and Adorno elucidate their "theory" of self-formation through an interpretation of the *Odyssey*. While Homer is a transitional figure between the archaic world and the enlightened world of the polis—and is perhaps a particularly revealing example because he is transitional—he is nevertheless already viewed as an enlightener qua unifier with respect to the popular tradition that preceded him. The Homeric *epos* takes the earlier *mythos* and "organizes" the diverse myths by imposing its narrative structure on them. In so doing, Homer also creates a national epic that helps to form a collective identity for the disparate tribes that populated the Hellenic world. With Odysseus himself, "the opposition of enlightenment to myth is expressed in the opposition of the surviving individual ego to multifarious fate."[134] Like his chronicler Homer, Odysseus is also a transitional figure, whose ego is only tenuously individuated, owing to its still-recent emergence from the archaic matrix. And as "the self is still so close to prehistoric myth, from whose womb it tore itself,"[135] it is constantly threatened with "reengulfment"[136] by those archaic forces: "The adventures of Odysseus are all dangerous temptations removing the self from its logical course"[137] of individuation and maturation. Read from a psychoanalytic perspective—which is by no means the only way to read this thoroughly overdetermined text— the relative lack of an *external* structure of the narrative parallels the relative lack of an internalized ego on the part of its hero. Just as the epic is held together in a picaresque fashion, that is, episodically, so Odysseus's self-development is portrayed as an external journey, with the tasks and conflicts of each intrapsychic stage represented as an encounter with one of "the old demons [who] inhabit the distant bounds and islands of the civilized Mediterranean."[138] Horkheimer and Adorno's methodological assumption, as it were, seems to be that the investigation of the self *in statu nascendi* reveals its true character. One might say this is separation-individuation theory before Mahler[139] and in a classicist vein.

For Horkheimer and Adorno, the mastery of inner nature, no less than the mastery of outer nature, consists in forms of violence. Toward the outside, as we have seen, the autocratic ego imposes its rigid unification on the diversity of external nature. Toward the inside, it attempts to impose that same compulsive synthesis on the manifold of inner nature, that is, on the polymorphous diffuseness of the id; the *principium individuationis* is violent per se. To be more precise, the ego is *formed* and maintains itself through that very imposition; it becomes "an entity only in the diversity of that which denies all unity."[140] The goal with respect to both outer and inner nature is the same, namely, self-preservation. Whereas the mythical world attempted to control the forces of outer nature, personified in the figures of the gods, by propitiating them through sacrifice, Odysseus seeks to escape the world of myth and its particular form of lawfulness altogether by self-sacrifice, which substitutes renunciation for external sacrifice. With his cunning, he attempts to elude mythical fate and achieve mastery over nature by rationally calculating the renunciation of his own internal nature. On the individual level, the history of this substitution constitutes the history of Odysseus's self-formation; on the collective level, it represents the history of the civilizing process itself.

Following in the tradition of Nietzsche's *Genealogy of Morals* and Freud's *Civilization and Its Discontents,* Horkheimer and Adorno argue that "the history of civilization is the history of the introversion of sacrifice. In other words: the history of renunciation."[141] Odysseus, the prototype of the bourgeois individual, forges his identity through violence and achieves "maturity through suffering": "Men had to do fearful things to themselves before the self, the identical, purposive, and virile nature of man was formed, and something of that recurs in every childhood."[142] The temptation—and threat— of each developmental stage qua adventure is the "allurement . . . of losing oneself in the past," that is, in the regressive bliss and terror of ego de-differentiation. By contrast, the completion of the "developmental task" posed by each stage/adventure—the successful "coming to terms" with the psychic pull of that stage/adventure— constitutes another step in the solidification of identity and the integration of the ego. Horkheimer and Adorno argue, moreover, not only that the original genesis of the ego occurs through violence but that the continued maintenance of that unity, once formed, also requires the constant expenditure of force: "The strain of holding the I together adheres to the I *in all stages;* and the temptation to lose it has always been there with the blind determination to maintain it" (emphasis added).[143] This assertion rests on the assumption that no achievement of ego integration—no sublimation—can assume relative stability over time, which is to say, no form of identity can possess the character of the relatively unforced naturalness of second nature, but must always involve the exertion of will: the central and continuous threat, against which the ego must constantly struggle, is disintegration.

At the same time, this threat contains, as has already been indicated, the promise of the "unfettered fulfillment"[144] (complete *jouissance,* to use the Lacanian vocabulary) of ego loss, de-differentiation, and merger—in short, the dissolution of the *principium individuationis.* And this threat poses a constant menace to civilization: "The dread of losing the self and of abrogating together with the self the barrier between oneself and other life, the fear of death and destruction, is intimately associated with the promise of happiness which threatened civilization at every moment."[145] The promise of happiness, it should be noted, is equated with the prospect of ego loss and merger. The story of the individual's compromise with that promise, which is perhaps the constitutive compromise of civilization itself and the cause of the ubiquitous ambivalence that characterizes civilized social life, is recounted in the Siren episode. Using his cunning, "defiance in a rational form," to defy the mythical order, Odysseus hits on a solution to evade the law of equivalence. Shrewd man that he is, Odysseus is not so grandiose as to underestimate the power of nature and allow himself "to listen freely to the temptresses," with their promise of ecstatic delirium, but "keeps to the contract of his thralldom and struggles in his bonds at the mast." However, like Portia in *The Merchant of Venice,* who also wields her cunning in the service of Shylock's survival, Odysseus "has found an escape clause in the contract, which enables him to fulfill it while eluding it. The primeval contract does not provide for the possibility of the seafarer listening bound or unbound to the bewitching voices."[146] Odysseus's "successful-unsuccessful" solution, which is "inimical both to his own death and to his own happiness,"[147] is to renounce the unfettered pleasure of the Sirens' song—merger with the primary object—in exchange for safe passage (i.e., survival) and the experience of their song *at a distance:* "The prisoner is present at a concert, an inactive eavesdropper like later concertgoers."[148] In Freudian parlance, he renounces the absolutistic but self-destructive demands of the unmediated pleasure principle for the diminished yet obtainable gratifications of the reality principle. The price he pays for this exchange is his bondage to the mast, that is, the constraints of civilized life and the degraded quality of his musical experience, which is to say, "the abasement and mortification of the instinct for complete, universal, and undivided happiness."[149] However, and here is the rub, the substitution of renunciation for sacrifice does not escape the law of equivalence—which means, the attempt to dominate nature does not transcend the natural context—but remains thoroughly trapped within it: "The dismissal of sacrifice by the rationality of self-preservation is exchange no less than sacrifice itself was." It was every bit as much hubris for Odysseus to think his cunning could altogether escape fate as it is for modern science to think it can transcend the natural environment—including inner human nature. The self-vitiating character of enlightenment results from this fact. The subject "is still imprisoned in the natural context as an organism that tries to assert itself against the organic." With the move from sacrifice to renunciation, the ritualistic rigidity, compulsiveness, and monotony of magic are exchanged for the rigidity of "the identically persistent self," which, having so deformed its inner nature, becomes incapable of enjoying the material fruits of the conquest of nature. The "sacrificial ritual that man celebrates upon himself" through the denial of inner nature is the "germ cell" out of which the dialectic of enlightenment inexorably unfolds.[150] The renunciation of internal nature, which was only supposed to be a mediate means to the mastery of external nature and the creation of the material preconditions for human happiness, in fact deprives the entire process of any intrinsic end, except self-preservation, and, in the long run, not only makes that happiness inaccessible but jeopardizes survival as well. Even the Sadean orgy, often taken to be the incarnation of, if not happiness, at least pleasure, is seen as nothing but the realization of the purposeless purposefulness of the industrial spirit: "The architectonic structure of the Kantian system, like the gymnastic pyramids of Sade's orgies . . . reveals an organization of life as a whole which is deprived of any substantial goal. These arrangements amount not so much to pleasure as to its regimented pursuit—organization . . . [T]he scheme of an activity was more important than its content."[151] Together with the progressive disenchantment of the sacred—and eventually the delegitimation of all realms of substantive normativity—the domination of inner nature renders the process of enlightenment *zwecklos:* "With the denial of nature in man not merely the *telos* of the outward control of nature but the *telos* of man's own life is distorted and befogged."[152]

At this point, we arrive at one of those theses referred to by Habermas that, because of the rhetorical power of the text, are not always fully conspicuous in *Dialectic of Enlightenment* but are nonetheless susceptible to philosophical scrutiny. The thesis concerns the nature of the self-formation process and contains Adorno and Horkheimer's philosophical appropriation of Freud in a nutshell:

Man's domination over himself, which grounds his selfhood, is almost always the destruction of the subject in whose service it is undertaken; for the substance which is dominated, suppressed, and dissolved by virtue of self-preservation is none other than that very life as functions of which the achievements of self-preservation find their sole definition: it is, in fact, what is to be preserved.[153]

To unpack the meaning of this passage, it is necessary to distinguish between three terms, namely, "subject," "self," and "substance." To begin with, "subject" is the most comprehensive term and can be compared, I would suggest, to Freud's "total subject" or *"GesamtIch."*[154] As such, it comprises the individual in all its aspects, objective as well as subjective, somatic as well as psychic; the other two terms represent aspects of it. "Selfhood" would refer to specifically subjective aspects of the *Gesamt-Ich,* and "substance" to the bodily dimension and inner nature. How, then, does the formation of subjective selfhood "almost always" destroy "the subject in whose service it is undertaken"? First, as happiness is the *telos* in which the subject's self-formation process finds its "sole definition," and as human happiness must lean on inner nature for its content, the formation of selfhood, insofar as it dominates and sacrifices inner nature, destroys the *telos* of the subject qua self. Second, even if we disregard the question of happiness and limit ourselves strictly to the question of survival, the strategy of sacrificing inner nature and happiness for the sake of self-preservation does not work: as the proliferation of nuclear power, the ecological crisis, and the like, indicate, this strategy does not even secure the survival of the subject as a *zoon biologon* but in fact jeopardizes it. Adorno and Horkheimer's thesis is that only the preservation of inner nature could prevent the whole self-vitiating dialectic of enlightenment from unfolding. It must be asked, however, preservation in what sense? Given their hostility to the idealization of first nature and all forms of *völkisch* longing for originary states, they undoubtedly would have rejected the following proposition had it been explicitly put to them. Nevertheless, the logical implication of their position is that inner nature must be preserved in an unmediated manner.

These two Hegelian philosophers[155] do not, at this crucial juncture at least, employ a notion of the sublation/sublimation[156] of desire but tacitly insist on the preservation of presocialized nature in an unmediated state. Indeed, they formulate Odysseus's basic problem in a remarkably blunt fashion: "He can never have everything; he has always to wait, to be patient, to do without."[157] Odysseus cannot in other words, remain in the preindividuated state of primary narcissism governed by the pleasure principle and hallucinatory wish fulfillment but must make the transition to object relatedness, delayed gratification, and the reality principle. If it is true that the origin remains the goal for the homesick Odysseus, neither the *oikos* to which he returns[158] nor the state in which he returns to it is the same as when he set out for Troy; they have been mediated by years of maturation through experience—by Aeschylean understanding through suffering *(pathonta gnonai)*. This is symbolized above all by the fact that, after having traversed the preoedipal stages/adventures of his journey, the consummation of Odysseus's homecoming consists in the identification of the olive-hewn conjugal bed. But on Adorno and Horkheimer's construction, as "everyone who practices renunciation gives away more of his life than is given back to him . . .

and more than the life that he vindicates," nothing short of remaining in that original state would appear to do: that is, nothing short of the unmediated preservation of inner nature, of "complete, universal, and undivided happiness"[159] can prevent the dialectic of enlightenment from unfolding. This is the unacknowledged hubristic-absolutist requirement that constitutes the psychoanalytically formulated bad utopianism on which the entire construction tacitly rests.

Unlike Marcuse, who viewed "primary narcissism" as "the archetype of another existential relation to *reality*"[160] and, as we have seen, sought to decipher a utopian vision in it, Adorno refrained, on principle, from any such utopian speculation. And, contrary to Deleuze and Guattari's attempt to formulate a psychologically grounded critique of capitalist society, in *Anti-Oedipus*—which, as Frank has shown, carries some of the central implications of Lacan's analysis of the ego to their logical conclusion[161]—Adorno never subscribed to the grotesque idea, popular within the Foucauldian element of the antipsychiatry movement, that the dissolution of the *principium individuationis* seen in schizophrenia constitutes a form of enlightenment or emancipation. While he agrees that "the identifying principle of the subject is itself the internalized principle of society" and hence a form of domination, Adorno nevertheless sees schizophrenia simply as a regression from the individual's domination by society to his domination by nature: "As schizophrenia, subjective freedom is a destructive force which incorporates men only so much more in the spell of nature."[162] Schizophrenia loses even the mediating moment of society.

Adorno, in general, never succumbed to the tempting simplification, common to so many strands of cultural radicalism, of viewing sickness in a sick society, of viewing deviation per se, as health: "And how comfortless is the thought that the sickness of the normal does not necessarily imply as its opposite the health of the sick, but that the latter usually only present, in a different way, the same disastrous pattern."[163] Nor did Adorno succumb to the often-connected notion that, because what passes as normal is so often sick, there is no distinction between sickness and health, reason and unreason— that these terms are simply conventional social constructions: "The dialectic cannot stop short before the concepts of health and sickness, nor indeed before the siblings reason and unreason." To be sure, once the dialectic "has recognized the ruling universal order and its proportions as sick . . ., then it can see as healing cells only what appears, by the standards of that order, as itself sick, eccentric paranoia—indeed, 'mad.' " In its immediacy, however, such madness is simply the abstract negation of that societal sickness and as such does not escape the generalized pathology. Thus, while "it is true today as in the Middle Ages that only fools tell their masters the truth, the dialectician's duty is thus to help this fool's truth to attain its own reasons, without which it will certainly succumb to the abyss of the sickness implacably dictated by the healthy common sense of the rest."[164] In other words, without enlightenment, sickness in a sick society is bound to repeat the logic of the sick system whose symptom it is.

Adorno and Wellmer on the "Nonviolent Togetherness of the Manifold"

Adorno's aporetic impasse is determined by his restricted concept of synthesis. What he said of Kant might well be said of himself, namely, that "his total conception will not let him visualize the conception of freedom otherwise than as repression."[165] This results from the fact that, like Lacan, Adorno—with one important exception—cannot visualize synthesis otherwise than as violence. In addition to sharing elements of Lacan's philosophical ("Heraclitean") and aesthetic suspicion of synthesis, Adorno also has good historico-political reasons for mistrusting false synthesis and premature reconciliation in a world where "the whole is" held to be "the untrue."[166] We will consider these later. For now, however, let us turn to the more philosophical incentives for his suspicion of synthesis, a problem that has been addressed most directly and comprehensively by Wellmer. In a series of important articles—"Reason, Utopia and the *Dialectic of Enlightenment*,"[167] "Truth, Semblance, and Reconciliation: Adorno's Aesthetic Redemption of Modernity," and "The Dialectic of Modernism and Post-Modernism: The Critique of Reason since Adorno"[168]—Wellmer has attempted to release the frozen potential of Adorno's thinking from its aporetic confinement and use it in order to undertake a renewed encounter with the postmodern critique of reason and the subject. Stated in its most general terms, Wellmer's thesis is that postmodernism, properly understood—that is, understood with the aid of his reinterpretation of Adorno—does not represent the negation of the project of modernity, as it is generally maintained, but rather its radicalization. As a "Gestalt" within modernity's immanently developing self-critique, postmodernity constitutes a moment in modernity's overcoming its own incomplete realizations and thereby becoming more consistent with its own essentially critical concept: "postmodernism at its best might be seen as a self-critical—a skeptical, ironic, but nevertheless unrelenting—form of modernism; a modernism beyond utopianism, scientism and foundationalism."[169] At the same time, Wellmer's analysis of Adorno also represents an attempt to affect a mediation between the old Frankfurt school and the second generation of Critical Theorists, of which he is a prominent member. From the one side, following the linguistic turn in Critical Theory, he brings the insights of the philosophy of language to bear on Adorno's thinking, in an attempt to ferret out the "residue of naiveté"[170] that attaches to its tacit adherence to the philosophy of the subject. That residue, he argues, determines Adorno's aporetic impasse from the outset, so that its elimination would serve to dissolve the seemingly intractable blockages in his thinking. From the other side, Wellmer seeks to retrieve the fundamentally aesthetic impulses that animate Adorno's thinking and incorporate them into Habermasian communication theory; for, despite the addition of the aesthetic-expressive sphere to the previously dualistic framework of instrumental and communicative reason, the relation of the Habermasian enterprise to aesthetic intuition has remained largely external.[171]

The one significant exception to Adorno's suspicion of synthesis, which I mentioned, is to be found, as Wellmer argues, in the advanced work of art:

The authentic, advanced work of art, which [for Adorno] virtually becomes the last residue of reason in a rationalized world ... represents a type of 'logic' and 'synthesis' which is markedly different from the repressive types of logic and synthesis characteristic for 'identifying' thought [and its correlate, the autocratic ego]. The aesthetic synthesis achieved by the work of art is different from that of conceptual thinking in that it does not do violence to the particular, the suppressed, the nonidentical. It is for this reason that the work of art becomes for Adorno the preeminent medium of a nonreified cognition and, at the same time, the paradigm for a nonrepressive integration of elements into a whole.[172]

Moreover, the advanced work of art being the only available example of "the nonviolent togetherness of the manifold"[173] (cf. Freud's notion of Eros), Adorno takes it as the only prefiguration, however circumscribed, that might provide a glimpse of the mode of social and psychic integration that would obtain in an emancipated society where reification had been sublated. While a nonreifying logic cannot in principle be discursively articulated in language because of the intrinsically reifying nature of conceptual thought, it can at least be intimated in the advanced work of art. It provides "a glimmer of messianic light glimpsed in the here and now, an anticipation of reconciliation in the real world."[174] Insofar as it embodies a nonimperialist logic—where the particular is not sacrificed to the universal nor the Other to the autocratic subject—Adorno believed that the truly advanced work of art stood as a cipher for possible social reconciliation. Hence the move from negative dialectics to aesthetic theory.

Wellmer, armed with the resources of the philosophy of language, attempts to link his redemptive critique of Adorno's aesthetic theory to his more ambivalently redemptive critique of postmodernism. He tries to show that, despite his relentless modernism, Adorno was unable to extrapolate the full consequences of aesthetic modernism for new forms of psychic and social synthesis, and he could not, therefore, fully recognize the nonreifying, emancipatory potential of other aspects of modernity. Aesthetic modernism had found the "*type* of unity and meaningful whole" exhibited in the "traditional synthesis" of the great works of bourgeois art to be, in fact, an "inauthentic unity" and a "fictitious totality of meaning," which, despite the secularization of culture, "remained analogous to a divinely created cosmos." "Aesthetic enlightenment discovers something violent, unreflected and inauthentic in the unity of the traditional work, as in the unity of the bourgeois subject, namely a type of unity which is only possible at the price of suppressing and excluding that which is disparate or cannot be integrated, that which remains unarticulated and repressed."[175] The modernists, therefore, sought to create new, more flexible, and more open forms of "aesthetic synthesis" that could, through "the expansion of the boundaries of the work of art" and of aesthetic experience, "gather" the diffuse, the nonidentical, and the split-off together into its domain.[176] And while "Adorno himself set the open forms of modern art in relation to a form of subjectivity which no longer corresponds to the rigid unity of the bourgeois subject," he could not draw the consequences of that relation. What prevented Adorno from "taking his thought one step further"—and this is Wellmer's thesis—was his inability to "concede to modern society what he had conceded to modern art, namely that enlightenment has liberated possibilities of 'extending the limits of the subject' . . . as well as unleashing possibilities of reification."[177] Adorno was blocked in his thinking at this point by the equation of subjectivization and reification (cf. Foucault), an equation which is, in turn, a consequence of his unreflected commitment to the philosophy of the subject. If the move from the philosophy of the subject to the philosophy of language can break the equation between subjectivization and reification, then the emancipatory potential of aesthetic modernism can be recouped for social theory. Making such a move, at any rate, is Wellmer's strategy.

Wellmer attempts to carry it out by disentangling three distinct yet often "intermingled" forms of the critique of reason and the subject. He begins with a consideration of "(1) the psychological critique (unmasking) of the subject and its reason."[178] The preeminent figure in this critique is, needless to say, Freud, who demonstrated "the *factual* impotence or nonexistence of the 'autonomous' subject . . . and the irrational nature of its putative reason." Far from being a quasi-autonomous agent, transparent to itself and in its intentions, "the decentered subject of psychoanalysis," which is "a meager remnant of the philosophical subject," turns out to be the *effect* of a nexus of opaque biological, psychological, and sociological forces operating behind its back rather than the master of those forces—"a poor creature"[179] indeed: "As embodied beings, as 'wish-machines' or even as 'will to power' (in the sense of Freud's great predecessor,

Nietzsche), human beings do not know what they want or what they are doing. Their 'reason' is merely an expression of psychic forces or an imprint of power relations, and the Ego . . . is at best a weak mediator . . ., a virtuoso of rationalization," rather than an agent of reality testing and truth. The psychological unmasking of the subject thus results in "the discovery of an *Other* of reason within the subject and its reason." [180] And it is with this discovery that the psychological critique of the subject joins up with "(2) the philosophical, psychological and sociological critique of 'instrumental' or 'identitary' reason and its subject." [181] Wellmer uses the notion of "the epistemological triad of subject, and object and concept" [182] to explicate the element of violent synthesis that, as we have seen, lies at the core of the instrumental reason and the autocratic subject for Adorno and Horkheimer. Instead of constituting an "organum of truth," [183] in any strong sense of the term 'truth,' conceptual thought is viewed as "an organ of adaptation for men just as claws and teeth are for animals." [184] The synthesizing force of the concept "suppresses and subjugates" the inner nature of the subject at the same time and to the same extent that it "suppresses and subjugates" outer nature, the object, in the interest of instrumental control. It was the fact, of course, that conceptual thought appeared so irredeemably implicated in domination that caused discursive rationality to be identified with instrumental reason as such, which sent Adorno on a quest for "the better Other of the instrumental spirit as a world beyond discursive reason" [185]—a quest that culminated with *Aesthetic Theory*.

It is Wellmer's contention, however, that the diagnosis and therefore the program and impasse that follow from it are themselves the result of an unexamined acceptance of the basic configuration of the philosophy of the subject. Indeed, this is already suggested by the reference to the epistemological triad. In this respect, the first two forms of critique we have already examined have more in common with each other than either does with the third form of linguistic critique, which we will turn to next. [186] Wellmer argues that both forms of critique suffer from the "forgetfulness of language" that has been "characteristic of European rationalism" throughout its history. That is to say, "the critique of discursive reason as *instrumental* reason" has "surreptitiously" remained as psychologistic qua *intentionalistic* as the psychoanalytically inspired unmasking of the subject insofar as "both [draw] on the model of a subject that is 'constitutive of meaning' and posits itself against a world of objects in transcendental singularity." Wellmer maintains that the "methods of linguistic philosophy," initiated by Wittgenstein in his later works, can be used to criticize the presuppositions of the philosophy of the subject and reveal "a communicative praxis even at the foundation of instrumental reason which . . . cannot be reduced either to a manifestation of a *self-preserving* subject, or to that of a subjectivity that is *constitutive of meaning.*"[187] Paraphrasing Adorno's statement concerning the "mindfulness *[Eingedenken]* of nature in the subject," which is the closest thing to a prescriptive statement in *Dialectic of Enlightenment*, Wellmer asserts, "It is only through the mindfulness of *language* in the subject that we can escape the thrall of the philosophy of the subject."[188]

Let us turn, then, to "(3) the linguistic critique of reason as transparent to itself, and of its subject as constitutive of meaning."[189] The Wittgensteinian critique is aimed at dislodging the name theory of meaning from the "preconsciousness" of Western philosophy, in which it is deeply entrenched, despite the manifest differences separating the various schools and traditions. This theory depicts meaning as the result of a constitutive act in which a monological subject confers meaning on linguistic signs. It can be termed "rationalistic" not only because it is based on a meaning-constitutive subject but "because it participates willy-nilly in idealizations characteristic of the rationalist tradition—especially the objectification of meaning as something 'objectively existing.' "[190] The Wittgensteinian position, in contrast, dissolves the notion of meaning as an independently existing entity, either in the ideal or psychological sense, and elucidates it instead in terms of an intersubjective language game in which it is embedded. It elucidates it, that is, in terms of the ability to follow a rule in a form of life praxis in which a speaker must be trained qua socialized. In so doing, the linguistic critique, like the other two forms of critique, dispenses with the "subject as ultimate arbiter of its own intentions"[191] and identifies an " 'Other of reason' *within* reason itself." It too, in other words, participates in the unmasking of the pretensions of rationalism. However, in this case—and this is the novel and fruitful twist with the linguistic critique—a different Other of reason [192] is identified. And, as a result, this version of the decentering of the subject, as opposed to the structuralist and neo-structuralist versions, is not necessarily a cause for skeptical, nihilistic, or cynical despair. Against "structuralist objectivism," which "ignores the pragmatic dimension of a signitive relation that is essentially open and not objectifiable," and against "neo-structuralist skepticism," which confuses that "openness and nonobjectifiability" with the complete indeterminacy and uncontrollability of "linguistic meaning," [193] post-Wittgensteinian pragmatism identifies the *determinable openness* of the applicability of a rule within a language game. And this determinable openness constitutes a potentially inexhaustible resource for generating meaning: "The 'interweaving' of the concepts of 'rule' and 'meaning' is shown in the fact that rules signify an intersubjective praxis for which someone has to be *trained*, in fact that meanings are essentially *open*." [194] In having uncovered this determinable openness of meaning, the linguistic critique has, at the same time, located the potentialities for the very expansion of the boundaries of meaning, experience, and identity that postmodernism is looking for.

The central thesis of Wellmer's "metacritique of the critique of identitary reason" [195] then is the following: Adorno mistook the reified and "dogmatically constrained" [196] uses of language, connected with the philosophy of the subject, for language as such and was therefore compelled to reject discursive rationality *tout court*. Combining the Weberian notion of rationalization as systematization with the Freudian notion of the totalizing dynamic of worldviews—for example, of paranoiacs, obsessives, religious prophets, and even philosophers—Adorno linked the "compulsion to systematize and the 'rage' toward all that is nonidentical" with the "ego principle." [197] The principle of contradiction, which is the basis of discursive thinking and, at the same time, "the system in a nutshell," [198] is the conceptual correlate of unitary self. Wellmer argues, however, that Adorno's "*psychological* explanations of the compulsion to systematize are more convincing than his attempts to explain it in terms of the *logic of concepts*." Adorno's mistake is to equate discursive rationality with the basically monological systems of formal logic and natural science, which are concerned with deductive relations between statements. This leads him to identify the "idealizations which are fundamental to formal logic—that is, the idealizing assumption of 'rigid meanings'—as a property peculiar to concepts themselves," and, therefore, to see "the rigidity of the deductive system as something inherent in the general concept as such." The results of linguistic philosophy have shown, however, that conceptual thought cannot adequately be characterized, monologically, "in terms of a deductive relationship between statements." To be sure, argumentation—which is by definition (at least) dialogical—contains an " 'identitary' dimension." It does not, however, "possess the linearity of deductive relationships between statements" nor "the stability of 'rigid meanings.' " Rather, it involves a more fluid "moving back and forth between concept and object" as well as "between one concept of an object and another"[199] within a framework of dialogical interaction. Moreover, the demythologization (which is simultaneously a de-demonization) of formal logic, mathematics, and physics by the neo-empiricist philosophy of science—itself a spin-off from the later Wittgenstein[200]—has demonstrated that these disciplines, the very paradigms of instrumental rationality, themselves rest on communicative practices with "fuzzy edges." As "the controversies about their foundations" show, the practice of normal science involves an objectification out of a backdrop of everyday communicative practices that themselves cannot be objectified and therefore cannot be comprehended scientistically. Wellmer takes Adorno's own notion of "mimesis," namely, "that which in 'true' reason goes beyond instrumental reason," and argues that it does not have to be pursued "extraterritorially," beyond "the sphere of conceptual thought." On the contrary—and this is Wellmer's strong claim—he argues that linguistic philosophy's decentering of the subject has shown the existence of "a communicative-mimetic" dimension *at the heart* of discursive reason, and that all that is required is "an unleashing of the potential *within* it to restrain the claims of instrumental reason and dispel the semblance of false totalizations."[201]

At this point, I would like to raise several criticisms of Wellmer's interpretation of Adorno. These criticisms concern the advantage claimed for the move to communication theory: particularly, the claim to have sublated Adorno's negative dialectics through the sublation of the philosophy of the subject in which it is embedded. I will try to show, to put it in Hegelian terms, that in certain important respects the presumed sublation of negative dialectics and the philosophy of the subject constitute more of an abstract negation than a true *Aufhebung;* which is to say, it misses part of the important truth content of the position to be sublated.

The charge that Wellmer brings against Jauss's, Burger's, and Bohrer's criticisms of Adorno can be directed at Wellmer's (and Habermas's) criticisms themselves: while "at least partially correct," they "nevertheless leave a sense that the conclusions arrived at are not commensurate with the object of their inquiries, as if the actual substance of Adorno's aesthetic eluded them."[202] As we have seen, Wellmer—along with Habermas[203] and Benhabib[204]—has accepted Adorno's desideratum of nonviolent synthesis as a way out of the aporia of identifying thought and has argued that Adorno could have eluded the aporia of negative dialectics and have better realized the solution he was aiming at in his *Aesthetic Theory* if he had moved to an intersubjective theory of communication. Adorno's attempt to extrapolate an indication of nonreified social synthesis from the aesthetic synthesis of the advanced work of art is misdirected, because the work of art, owing to its *essentially monological* character, can never indicate the logic for social synthesis, which is *irreducibly intersubjective.* However "nonrepressive," the work of art cannot provide a model for reconciliation at the societal level. Wellmer maintains, furthermore, that the nonreifying logic that defines the desideratum for Adorno, while perhaps intimated in the work of art, actually obtains most fully in "dialogical relationships *between* individuals, who recognize each other in their individuality, as equals and as absolute others both at the same time."[205] If this logic of "the nonviolent togetherness of the manifold" defines the condition of a solution, then it is to be found most completely not in aesthetic experience but in intersubjective communication.

I mentioned in the excursus that Adorno might not have recognized Habermas's putative *Aufhebung* of his position as an *Aufhebung,* and I believe the same difficulty repeats itself with Wellmer's argument. Using Wellmer's own formulation, we must ask whether this solution is, in fact, "commensurate with the object of [Adorno's] inquiries" or whether "the actual substance of Adorno's" theory has "eluded" it? Has, in other words, the notion of reconciliation become so attenuated in the move from negative dialectics and aesthetic theory to communication theory that it no longer sufficiently resembles the original desideratum to count as a solution? After all, Adorno had a concept of reconciliation between subjects available to him in the Hegelian notion of mutual recognition. Indeed, in 1969, the very year Habermas's first article on Adorno appeared, Adorno explicitly considered the notion of communication between subject and subject as an adequate notion of reconciliation and emphatically rejected it. Intersubjective communication still suffers from all the deficiencies of subjective reason—it does not achieve a mediated reconciliation with the object:

If speculation on the state of reconciliation were permitted, neither the undistinguished unity of subject and object nor their antithetical hostility would be conceivable in it; rather, the communication of what was distinguished. Not until then would the concept of communication, as an objective concept, come into view. The present one [which is essentially the same as the Habermasian] is so infamous because *the best there is, the potential of an agreement between people and things,* is betrayed to an *interchange between subjects* according to the requirements of subjective reason. In its proper place, even epistemologically, the relationship of subject and object would lie in the realization of peace among men as well as between men and their Other.[206] (emphasis added)

What is "partially correct" in the Habermasian-Wellmerian aufhebung "leaves the best there is" for Adorno untouched: despite the potential reconciliation between subjects, nonspeaking being, as it were, remains the object of an objectivating attitude. But that objectivating attitude occurs within the interaction between "two subjects [who] agree *with each other about something* that exists," rather than within a singular representing consciousness.[207] For the sublation to be more sufficient, it would have to be shown that this has consequences for the relation between "people and things," including the thinglike dimension of our own bodies.

Wellmer argues that Adorno, despite his adherence to Rimbaud's admonition "*Il faut être absolument moderne,*" never fully tapped the emancipatory potential of cultural modernity for a theory of expanded subjectivity in the same way in which he drew on it for his theory of art; in this respect, at least, the postmodernist discussions appear more promising. The new forms of aesthetic synthesis, which for Adorno characterize the truly advanced works of art, could have been seen to "correspond formally"[208] to possible new forms of psychic synthesis. The advanced works expand the boundaries of art by integrating material that was formerly split off and excluded by the "closed unity" of great bourgeois art. However, "a more flexible unity of an individual self"[209]—which, along with new forms of anomie and psychopathology, is made possible by the socioempirical dissolution of the "classical" bourgeois individual—can be envisioned in which the boundaries of the self are expanded and become more permeable so as to integrate meanings that were previously confined to the "archaic dimension"[210] of dreams, parapraxes, psychoses, jokes, and neurotic symptoms. Adorno, however, never speculated about the possibility of a "nonrepressive configuration of" *intrapsychic* "elements," that is, of "being-oneself in a nonrepressive sense."[211] This would be, of course, quite close to the new "*relation* between the conscious and the unconscious" that Castoriadis talked about. Again, Wellmer attributes this failure on Adorno's part to his entrapment in the philosophy of the subject and his failure to appreciate the fundamental advances made by twentieth-century philosophy of language.

As we have seen, because he is wedded to the philosophy of consciousness, Adorno is also more or less explicitly wedded to two of its major corollaries, namely, the rigidity of meaning and the inevitable inadequacy of the concept to the particular. As we have also seen, Wellmer argues that, when the philosophy of consciousness is sublated by the philosophy of language, those two corollaries are dissolved. This means that for Adorno, with respect to inner nature, there existed a necessary "disproportionality between intuition and concept," and he feared that we become *"alienated"* from "our own private nature" when we attempt to articulate it in language. It was this fear that led Adorno to attach "such immense importance . . . to all forms of literary usage and aesthetic objectification as *correctives* of the discursive use of language." Through such forms, "that which is locked within the muteness of individual experience becomes accessible and communicable." Wellmer argues, however, that if we examine "how our language works in reality and what its possibilities are"—and do not retain Adorno's metaphysical-messianic criterion of "a 'true language' in which 'content itself' is revealed"—our language does not have to be regarded as "hopelessly inadequate." Ordinary language, although it may not be capable of capturing inner experience *an sich,* nevertheless, *because of its openness,* contains "the resources . . . which *recurrently* enable us—with greater or lesser success—to transcend the speechlessness of language"[212] and to articulate our inner intuitions. Needless to say, it can also fail us in that effort and force us to fall silent. Wellmer's thesis is that these resources of ordinary language, the essential openness of meaning, constitute the conditions of the possibility of resynthesizing the historically disintegrating elements of the "classical" bourgeois individual and the novel modes of experience that accompany them into new configurations of the self.

The openness of meaning in ordinary language, however, constitutes only one of the two necessary conditions for establishing the possibility of " 'communicatively fluid' ego identity."[213] The other condition is the linguisticality *(Sprachfähigkeit)* of inner nature. It is not enough for Wellmer simply to argue that the openness of ordinary language provides the resources for the articulation of inner nature. He must also show that inner nature is itself *sprachfähig,* capable of such articulation, and the nature of that articulability must be elucidated. Although Wellmer's Wittgensteinian insistence on the openness of meaning is a necessary rejoinder to Adorno's essentially frozen position, ordinary-language communication, even with its openness of meaning, inevitably runs up against an obstacle when it encounters unconscious mentation. The demonstration of the openness of meaning does not per se establish the linguisticality of inner nature; additional arguments are required. This is a problem that Wellmer never takes up directly and that Habermas solves by fiat when he denies the distinction between thing-representations and word-representations in his interpretation of psychoanalysis.

Wellmer affirmatively cites Adorno's observation that in doing philosophy—especially, I would add, in doing great philosophy—we butt up against the boundaries of language: "[I]n doing philosophy we are operating at the frontiers of language; we are neither wholly inside language nor, as we might like to be, outside its borders."[214] My objection is that Critical Theory, after the linguistic turn, does not push up against the boundaries of language strenuously enough. While to transgress those boundaries completely would be to regress into either precritical metaphysics or delirious discourse,[215] the theory of communication remains too comfortably ensconced in the interior regions of the linguistic realm, well on this side of the border.

One point where that failure to push harder becomes particularly apparent is in the rather casual way in which both Habermas and Wellmer have assumed the possibility of rendering inner nature "communicatively fluid." Whereas Adorno fashioned an idiosyncratic dialectico-aesthetic discourse to press against the boundaries of the sayable, Freud formulated a theory of the drives to the same end. Again we must stress that the psychoanalytic notion of the "drive" is not a biological concept, as both Habermas and Lacan incorrectly suggest for similar systematic (linguistifying) reasons, but is a concept "on the frontier between the mental and the somatic."[216] As such, it represents a struggle to conceptualize the border between body and psyche, image and word, unsayable and sayable. It was precisely this pressing up against the boundaries of the sayable that caused Freud to fashion such an odd vocabulary—for example, Repräsentanz, Vorstellung, Vorstellungsrepräsentanz, Triebrepräsentanz, and psychische Repräsentanz—that has caused the commentators so much consternation. In rejecting drive theory and the distinction between word-representations and thing-representations, Habermas has abandoned—except for his flirtation with stage 7— the frontier region between the sayable and unsayable, never adequately to return to it again. The philosophy of language does not, however, sublate the philosophy of consciousness without remainder. It is the struggle to approach this residue, this moment of nonlinguistic otherness, that has dropped out of recent Critical Theory.

Linguistic Turn or *Bilderverbot?:* Wish, Image, and Word in Psychoanalytic Theory

Situating Habermas's Critique of Castoriadis

How one conceptualizes the communication between the psychic agencies, and hence the integration of the self, will, needless to say, be determined by how one conceives of those agencies in the first place. With Habermas and Castoriadis, we find two radically opposed conceptions of the unconscious, and that difference, with its important consequences, helps to explain Habermas's otherwise curious attack on Castoriadis.

Habermas's animosity toward Nietzsche, Heidegger, Derrida, and Foucault in *The Philosophical Discourse of Modernity* is easily understood. For him, these thinkers constitute the major representatives of the Counter-Enlightenment, who, because they raise the specter of irrationalism, nihilism, and political regression, must be refuted. A central thrust of the book, which consists in a series of lectures, is a polemic in that direction. The attack on Castoriadis, however, is at first more difficult to fathom, with respect to both its vehemence and its externality to Castoriadis's position. If he had wanted to properly criticize Castoriadis's theory of the monadic core of the subject—which, to be sure, is not immune from criticism—Habermas should have, once again, at least fulfilled Hegel's requirement of stepping into the strength of an opponent's position. Instead, we are given a superficial "excursus" that hardly does justice to Castoriadis's deep and original appropriation of Freud. If it is to be criticized, a theory of this depth deserves a more serious critique. The situation is all the more curious given that, vis-à-vis poststructuralism, postmodernism, neoconservatism, and so on, Habermas and Castoriadis are, as it were, on the same side of the theoretical barricades, despite the fact that the latter makes his home in Paris. Indeed, with respect to their most general intentions, Habermas and Castoriadis perhaps have more in common with each other than either has with many of the central currents of contextualist relativism that dominate the contemporary political-philosophical landscape. In this context, their stubborn defense of what Habermas calls "the project of Enlightenment" and Castoriadis refers to as "the project of autonomy"—the two are, at their core, almost indistinguishable—borders on the eccentric.

Castoriadis's doctrine of the monadic core of the subject, however, touched a theoretical raw nerve in Habermas, because it poses a profound challenge not only to his interpretation of Freud in *Knowledge and Human Interests*[1] but to the very heart of Habermas's general philosophical construction (of which the Freud interpretation is one paradigmatic aspect). The centerpiece of that construction, including the earlier reformulation of Critical Theory and the more recent defense of modernity, has been the "linguistic turn,"[2] that is, the move from the philosophy of consciousness and "subject-centered reason" to the philosophy of intersubjectivity and communicative rationality.[3] Anything that would challenge a thoroughgoing philosophy of intersubjectivity, as a monadic core of the psyche certainly would, poses a threat to the heart of Habermas's theory.

Let me develop this point by contrasting the (modified) Kantian transcendentalism of Habermas to the, if not fully Hegelian at least anti-Kantian, realism of Castoriadis. Habermas's linguistic reworking of Kantian philosophy—which attempts to establish the scope and validity of the different spheres of rationality through a reflection on the conditions of the possibility of the types of communicative action—predictably results in the quintessential Kantian problem: the *Ding-an-sich,* now recast in linguistic terms. Toward the outside, Habermas's linguistic transcendentalism prevents him from adequately reaching the extralinguistic reality of external (especially living) nature.[4] Considered from the other direction, toward the inside, I will try to show that it also prevents him from adequately reaching the prelinguistic reality of inner nature, which is to say, the unconscious.[5] In general, the move from the philosophy of consciousness to the philosophy of language, despite its successes in resolving certain philosophical problems concerning the relationship of subject to subject, does not prove to be the all-encompassing philosophical solution that Habermas and his followers often hope it will be. It would be naive to think that much of the old, that is to say, perennial, baggage would not have come along in the transition. Just as the philosophy of consciousness had difficulty transcending the circle of subjectivity and reaching the othersidedness of consciousness, to paraphrase Marx, so the philosophy of language has difficulty surmounting the larger circle of intersubjectivity and contacting the othersidedness of language in inner and outer nature. As I have noted, the problem of reference in the philosophy of language is exactly parallel to the problem of perception in the philosophy of consciousness. Habermas's statement that language "is the only thing whose nature we can know," which he made in his Frankfurt inaugural address in 1965, holds for him every bit as much today as it did then.[6] The problem becomes particularly apparent in his treatment of a prelinguistic unconscious and, a fortiori, of a monadic core of the primal subject. He is compelled for systematic reasons simply to dismiss the notion of a prelinguistic unconscious ex cathedra. Such a thicket of nonlinguisticality at the center of the subject would be anathema to his entire philosophy.

If Habermas is content to remain at the Kantian moment, that is, to remain on this side of language, and is not particularly troubled by the difficulties that result, Castoriadis, in contrast, is preoccupied with, and repeatedly returns to, the question that necessarily arose the instant the transcendental move had been made: what are we to make of this *Ding-an-sich*, which we are forced to posit but about which we can say nothing? A central thesis that, in this respect, sets Castoriadis in opposition not only to Kantianism but to contemporary contextualism as well—which, in any case, is basically the Kantian problematic of the categorical scheme, the framework, writ large—is the following: it is incoherent to maintain that extraconceptual or extralinguistic reality is pure chaos, "amorphous clay,"[7] on which we can impose the order, synthesis, form, and so on, of our conceptual/linguistic grids at will. After all, the history of science demonstrates that nature "rejects" some of our grids. It follows from the fact that we can impose only some of our conceptual/linguistic grids on the object, can organize it in specific ways, that the object is *amenable* to certain forms of organization, is in some sense *determinately organizable*. Thus, the attempt to maintain that all synthesis is on this side of thought/language cannot itself be sustained and already, to a certain extent, propels us to the other side of thought/ language. For example, the fact that the history of science proceeds through a succession of relatively incommensurate paradigms is, of course, often adduced as a prime piece of evidence for contextual relativism. Castoriadis, however, goes further and inquires into the conditions of the possibility of this fact itself, thus raising the anticontextualist question that underlies it: what must the organization of nature be "that allows [the succession of paradigms] to exist and makes them occur in the order that they do, and not in some other quite arbitrary order"?[8] This is not to imply that Castoriadis attempts to speak about the object in itself in a direct, pre-Kantian, and naively metaphysical manner. The point rather is this: unlike Habermas, who abstains from speaking about the object altogether for fear of a regression into precritical metaphysics, Castoriadis attempts to forge a discourse that would allow him to posit that which would be incoherent not to posit about the object in itself, but to do so in a nonmetaphysical fashion. This is the mode of theorizing he calls elucidation. As we will see, then, these general philosophical differences that separate Habermas and Castoriadis apply *mutatis mutandis* to their analyses of the unconscious. It represents a test case, of sorts, for their different philosophical approaches.

Castoriadis: From the Unconscious to the Psychic Imaginary

Habermas and Castoriadis turned to psychoanalysis, as Adorno, Horkheimer, Marcusc, and others had before them, partly in response to the crisis of Marxism. Both men sought to overcome the impasse of Marxian thought by adding a second dimension to Marx's materialistic monism; the theory each elaborated, however, reflects the differences in philosophical temperament separating the two thinkers. Whereas Habermas sought to locate that second dimension in a communicatively conceived notion of practical reason, Castoriadis sought to locate it in fantasy, or what he terms the psychic imaginary. As we have seen, Habermas is primarily interested in psychoanalysis for methodological reasons—as a "tangible example" of a successful self-reflective emancipatory science that combines communicative rationality with explanatory procedures and, as such, can be used to clarify the foundations of critical theory.

Castoriadis, on the other hand, is primarily concerned with Freud's discovery of the unconscious, which he seeks to develop into a theory of the imagination. He uses the doctrine of the psychic imaginary, in turn, to counter the reductionism not only of orthodox Marxism but also of orthodox Freudianism, which, of course, is structurally not dissimilar.

Each thing, insofar as it attempts to reduce the symbolic to the real (i.e., economic and biological-corporeal reality, respectively), excludes the possibility of authentically autonomous thought and action and of genuine historical creation, which is to say, the emergence of radically novel meanings in history. To the extent that the psychic imaginary intervenes between the real and the symbolic as a potentially inexhaustible source of new meanings, that reduction is impossible. The psychic imaginary consists in a largely self-generated stream of unconscious representations or images that are "not subject to determinacy," that is, not subject to time and contradiction.[9] (In this respect it differs from Lacan's specular notion of the imaginary, which does not consist in intrapsychically generated representations but in representations reflected from an external mirror.) These representations provide the material not only for the daydreams of the average person but for the florid hallucinations of Senatspräsident Schreber as well. In sublimated form, however, they can also be injected into public institutions and discourse and become the source of radically novel historical innovations, that is, of "new figures of the thinkable."[10]

Castoriadis's theory of the psychic imaginary differs from Freud's theory of unconscious fantasy in the degree of independence it assigns to the formation of those fantasies vis-à-vis biological-corporeal reality. Fantasy formation is much less rooted in the biological-corpo-real, and therefore much more spontaneous, for Castoriadis than for Freud. This allows Castoriadis to appropriate Freud to radicalize so-cial theory by offering a theory of historical creation while avoiding the conservative tendencies of orthodox psychoanalysis, which tends to view fantasies (and the social institutions deriving from them) as the eternal repetition of an "old medley"[11] based on a few drive-related motifs. To pull this off, however, Castoriadis must face an-other, complimentary difficulty: how to maintain the degree of inde-pendence for the psychic imaginary required by his theory of historical creation without altogether losing its moorings in the real. He remains too much of a Marxist and a Freudian—and rightfully so—to dissociate the psychic imaginary from the real completely. As we will see, he enlists Freud's doctrine of "leaning-on" (German: *An-lehnung;* Greek: *anaklisis*) in an attempt to solve this difficulty.

For the moment, however, let us note that Castoriadis's central criticism of Freud is that he devoted "a large part of his work" to trying to mitigate the radicalness of his breakthrough, which con-sisted in the "discovery of the imaginary element in the psyche," by seeking " 'real' factors, biology, infantile seduction, the primal scene, historical events, that would account for the history of the psyche, its organization, and finally, even its being."[12] Against this tendency, Castoriadis wants to assert "the *relative* independence and autonomy of phantasizing"[13] vis-à-vis the real. Everything turns, of course, on how the relative autonomy is understood.

The dilemmas Castoriadis encounters in trying to determine that relative autonomy are not his alone but "have a venerable tradition in philosophy."[14] On the one hand, if too much independence is assigned to the productive imagination, one runs the risk of a psy-choanalytic version of subjective idealism: "If the psyche produces everything out of itself, if it is sheer and total production of its own representations with respect to their form (organization) and to their content, we can wonder how and why it should ever meet any-thing other than itself and its own products."[15] While Castoriadis is certainly aware of this danger, as the foregoing passage indicates, I will argue that he is not entirely successful in avoiding it. If, on the other hand, the psyche "borrows" the material and organization for its representations from the real, the question arises as to how the real can make an impression on, or register in, the psyche, which is heterogeneous to it. To address this, Castoriadis maintains that the answer to the paradox of representation cannot be found "outside representation itself" and that an "original representation" must be posited that, as a schema of "figuration," would "contain within itself the possibility of organizing all representations" and, as such, would be the condition of the possibility of all further representations in the psyche.[16]

Freud, as we know, maintains that the real first announces itself in the psyche through the unpleasurable affect associated with hunger. The child, drawing on previous experiences of satisfaction, which is to say, drawing on traces of the real, forms a hallucinatory representation of the breast in an attempt to restore the "state of psychical tranquillity" that existed prior to the intrusion of the real through the unpleasurable affect. This hallucinated breast becomes, for Freud, the original phantasmic representation, and hallucinatory wish fulfillment becomes the prototype for all further fantasy and dream formation. Castoriadis argues, however, that the hallucinated breast is already a secondary or "constituted" fantasy, which itself presupposes a prior " 'constituting' phantasy-phantasmatization."[17] He maintains that we cannot rest content with hallucinatory wish fulfillment as an ultimate datum but must inquire into that state of psychic tranquillity that obtained prior to the intrusion of the unpleasurable affect and which the child seeks to restore through the hallucination. Castoriadis posits the existence of an original *"Ur-Vorstellung,"* "protorepresentation" or "phantasmatization," which cannot be traced to the real nor be a representation in the ordinary sense, for it is not the representation *of* anything. Rather, it is a "phantasmic scene," or a "unitary subjective circuit,"[18] which does not admit any externality, and in which the difference between inside and outside, subject and object, infant and breast and so on, has yet to emerge. After all, "The 'discovery' of the breast as absent . . . is made only in relation to and on the basis of the requirement that nothing is to be absent, nothing is to be lacking."[19]

How, then, does this "monadic core of the primal subject" or state of "initial autism,"[20] as he calls it, "contain within itself the possibility of organizing all representations"? Castoriadis argues that the requirement for complete unification "posited by [this] original representation,"[21] continues to operate after the breakup of the initial state—and we will have to inquire into the nature of that breakup—when it is transferred to the "monadic pole" of the psyche. The monadic pole[22] exerts a "tendency towards unification" over the rest of psychic life that has the most diverse and even contradictory effects, ranging from the complete irrationality of the unconscious to the highest achievements of reason. On the level of unconscious mentation, where the demand for complete unification continues to "reign in the fullest, rawest, most savage and intractable manner,"[23] it accounts for the utter indeterminacy of the primary processes: on this level, the monadic pole attempts to "short-circuit" all difference "in order to carry it back to an impossible monadic 'state' and, failing to do so, the monadic pole substitutes hallucinatory satisfaction and phantasizing."[24]

In the more conscious, socialized strata of the psyche, the unifying drive of the monadic pole is enlisted to synthesize the manifold of contents emanating from the outside into the relative unity of experience. It is in this sense that it provides the schemata for assimilating all representations entering the psyche from the outside; it is not simply the synthetic function of the ego but of the psyche in general. In a manner similar to the transcendental unity of apperception, it is the source of the "I think" that accompanies all representations and makes them *my* representations. And, like the transcendental unity of apperception, as it is the precondition for all other representations, it cannot itself be represented; we only infer it through its effects. At an even higher, more socialized level, "if the madness of this [earlier] stage is transformed into the reason of the adult"—into, among other things, the demand for "universal cognitive connection" and "universal significance"[25]—it can become a source of the highest achievements of mental life.

As I have already indicated, Castoriadis's discussion of the ambivalence of this demand for unification bears comparison with Chasseguet-Smirgel's notion of the "bipolarity" of the ego ideal. This results, of course, from the fact that both discussions derive from the problematic of Freud's theory of primary narcissism. Whereas Castoriadis maintains that a human being is neither a "sick animal" nor a "rational animal" as such, but has the equipotentiality for both sickness and reason by virtue of the monadic core of the psyche, Chasseguet-Smirgel maintains that "as in Aesop's adage the ego ideal is at the source of the best and the worst of things."[26] For Castoriadis, "the monster of unifying madness" lies behind not only the clinical madness of psychosis in the strict sense but the intellectual madness of an identifying thought and the political madness of totalitarianism as well. At the same time, however, it cannot be denied that:

[T]he sperm of reason is also contained in the complete madness of the initial autism. An essential dimension of religion—this goes without saying—but also an essential dimension of philosophy and of science derive from this. One does not put reason where it should be, and, what is even more serious one cannot reach a reasonable attitude with respect to reason . . . if one refuses to see in it something other than, of course, but *also*, an avatar of the madness of unification. Whether it is the philosopher or the scientist, the final and dominant intention—to find, across difference and otherness, manifestations of the *same* . . . is based on the same schema of a final, that is to say, primal unity.[27]

The most monstrous and the most sublime have their origins in the same source. As we have also noted, Chasseguet-Smirgel views the ego ideal, as Freud did, as the heir to the plenumlike perfection, that is, the undifferentiated unity of primary narcissism. And although the ego must strive to recapture that perfection qua unity of the ego ideal, too close a proximation to it, not to mention its actual attainment, would result in the de-differentiation of manic psychosis. As we have seen, Chasseguet-Smirgel traces not only severe forms of psychopathology to the attempt to capture the perfection of the ego ideal directly, but the most barbarous social and political pathology of the century as well. While too great a distance between the ego and the ego ideal, too little unity, results in lethargy, cynicism, complacency, depression, and lack of esprit—cf. "joyless reformism"—its attainment, reunification, were it possible, would cause "all [the] acquisitions which have made us human beings [to] collapse like a house of cards." As I have already mentioned, with both thinkers, it is not a question of unification versus lack of unification, as the question is often abstractly posed. The question is, rather, how much unification, and of what sort?

This entire problematic, in turn, invites comparison with Kant's notion of regulative ideas, which, through its role in the history of German Idealism and Marxism, worked its way into the development of utopian theory and practice. In fact, we might say that the Freudian notion of the ego ideal is the psychoanalytic counterpart of the philosophical concept of the regulative idea. Both concepts, moreover, exhibit a similar paradox.[28] Kant maintains that the human mind, "by the very nature of reason itself," has the "peculiar fate" of positing ideas of finality, totality, systematicity, and consistency, that is to say, ideas of unity, which "it is not able to ignore, but which . . . [transcend] all its powers to achieve."[29] As finite mind, it is constrained to pursuing them asymptotically, for any attempt to achieve them directly, that is, without the mediation of the understanding, will necessarily result in insuperable dialectical impasses. These impasses, resulting from the hubristic attempt to transgress the limitations of the finite mind, can be viewed as the pathologies of reason. Insofar as we consider its philosophical line of development, then, utopianism worked its way into the Marxian tradition through a progressive detranscendentalization of the Kantian regulative ideas. Whereas with Kant these finalistic ideas were to remain thoroughly transcendental and approached only asymptotically, with Hegel they assume an ambiguous middle ground somewhere between the transcendental and the empirical. And finally with Marx they become legitimate goals, for example, the end of prehistory and the establishment of the realm of freedom, to be attained in the real world. Kant already evinced a strong intuition about the dangers surrounding this detranscendentalization. And while it may not lead directly to the Gulag, its political consequences can be treacherous indeed: "the coldest and meanest of all deaths, with no more significance than cutting a head of cabbage," as Hegel dramatized in the chapter of the *Phenomenology* entitled "Absolute Freedom and Terror."[30] The paradox in the case of both Kant's regulative ideas and Freud's ego ideal, then, is that we are compelled to pursue something whose attainment would be undesirable; *to achieve these goals would be just as inhuman as not to strive after them.* Just as psychic well-being requires the maintenance of the proper distance between the ego and the ego ideal, so theoretico-political wisdom, as it were, requires the proper tension between the utopian urge toward completeness and the diffuseness of experience.

Thus far we have examined Castoriadis's attempt to conceptualize the autonomous aspect of the psyche's functioning vis-à-vis the real. We must now examine the problem from the other direction, namely, with respect to its nonautonomous relationship to extrapsychic reality. To conceptualize the relationship between the psychic imaginary and the real or, more specifically, between fantasy formation and biological-corporeal reality, Castoriadis, as I have already indicated, employs Freud's notion of "leaning-on," which he expands into an almost quasi-ontological category. To be sure, Laplanche and Pontalis have pointed out that the central and pervasive role of the notion of *Anlehnung* in Freud's thinking is often missed by the non-German reader, who generally associates it only with a type of object choice.[31] But Castoriadis wants to go further still. He insists that the concept of "leaning-on," along with the notion of the psychic imaginary, is both "as original and irreducible" a concept as that of cause or symbol, and absolutely necessary for "[thinking] otherwise." The simultaneous relatedness but nonreducibility that characterizes the "gaps" separating the various regions of being[32]—for example, between vital and inanimate phenomena, society and nature, and psyche and soma—cannot be conceptualized within the "inherited logic-ontology"[33] but requires the concept of leaning on. In each case, the first member of the pair leans on the second.

With respect to our topic, then, what does it mean for the psyche to lean on biological-corporeal reality? In the first instance, the psyche's independence vis-à-vis the biological-corporeal is not absolute, because "there can be no oral instinct without the mouth and the breast, no anal instinct without an anus." By this statement, Castoriadis does not mean simply that the bodily organs are mere external conditions without which the drive and its related fantasies cannot exist:

[T]he existence of the mouth and breast, or of the anus, is not a mere 'external condition,' without which there would be no oral or anal instinct, or more generally, no psychical functioning as we know it—in the same way as it is clear that without oxygen in the atmosphere or circulatory system there would be no psyche, no phantasies or sublimation. Oxygen contributes nothing to phantasies, it 'allows them to exist.'

He means, rather, that the morphology and mode of functioning of the pertinent organs and zones contribute to the drive-related fantasies in that they delineate the range of possible forms those fantasies can assume: "The mouth-breast, or the anus, have to be 'taken into account' by the psyche and, what is more, they support and induce [the fantasy]. . . . The privileged somatic data will always be taken up again by the psyche, psychical working out will have to 'take them into account,' they will leave their mark on it."[34] From the other side, however, while these biological-corporeal factors necessarily "support and induce" the fantasy, they do not cause or determine it. It is therefore impossible, within the "identitary frame of reference of determinacy" to state with "which mark and in what manner" these "privileged somatic data" will affect the fantasy. A gap of underdetermination separates the biological-corporeal substratum from the drive-related fantasy, and it is precisely in this gap that the "creativity of the psyche" functions. This gap also makes the reduction of the drives to the biological-corporeal impossible. Thus, while we know that every individual and society will necessarily take up these privileged somatic factors and rework them in his/her/its formation, we can predict nothing about the determinate form they will assume in a given individual or society. The attempt to comprehend the relationship of the drive to its biological substratum from within the identitary logic thus leads to the paradoxical violation of one of the central canons of scientific thinking: "In the name of the scientific and rigorous mind, one ends up once again with this scientific monstrosity as a consequence: constant factors produce variable effects."[35]

Finally, we must address the question of the breakup of the psychic monad. Castoriadis's thesis stated in its sharpest (or most rhetorical) form—and this is where Habermas lodges his main objection—is as follows: the "social institution of the individual," which is simultaneously a process of psychogenesis *(idiogenesis)* and sociogenesis *(koinogenesis),* consists in the "imposition on the psyche" by society "of an organization which is essentially heterogeneous with it."[36] As the psyche is "in no way 'predestinated' *[sic]* by nature" for socialization, this imposition "amounts to a violent break, forced [on it] by its 'relation' to others."[37] Stated in this form, however, the thesis is incoherent: if the heterogeneity between psyche and society were as complete as Castoriadis suggests in these, his most extreme, formulations, the socialization process would not simply be violent, it would be impossible: it would be impossible to explain how "stationary infantilism" was ever overcome and development initiated. In this respect, a tension exists between the heterogeneity thesis and Castoriadis's use of the doctrine of anaclisis. At the same time as he asserts the essential heterogeneity between psyche and society he also asserts—as he must—that the social order " 'leans-on' the being of the psyche."[38] But this would mean that there is already something immanent in the monad on which socialization can lean, that is, it is not the absolute Other of society. Indeed, this follows from Castoriadis's anti-Kantian use of anaclisis as a central doctrine of his philosophy: in order for any region of being to lean on another, we must posit something within the second region that, while *"not thoroughly or ultimately congruent"* with the first, nevertheless *"lends itself to"* that anaclisis.[39] Concerning our topic, Castoriadis never, however, adequately "elucidates," to use his methodological term, that element within the psyche that "lends itself to" socialization.

Empirically, as it were, the breakup of the monad commences at the point where hunger first announces itself into the monad. However, hunger, in and of itself, "explain[s] nothing," for "the 'canonical' response to need is hallucination and phantasmatic satisfaction."[40] To illustrate the relative strength and independence of the imaginary factor in this context, Castoriadis adduces the example of anorexia: "To be sure, the imagination does not provide calories and if nothing else were to take place the infant would die—as indeed he does die as a result of his imagination and despite the food he is offered, if he is anorexic."[41] Somewhat ironically, the example of anorexia points to the very difficulties in Castoriadis's position that I have been attempting to bring out. For if he has not located something within the monad that makes it capable of opening up to and registering external reality, he cannot explain how hallucinatory wish fulfillment is ever renounced. Castoriadis's difficulty, in short, is explaining why we are not all anorectic. To be fair, this is not Castoriadis's problem alone but one he shares with Freud, who begins with an equally monadic starting point.[42] Freud could never explain how a "psychical apparatus," operating according to the pleasure principle alone, could renounce hallucinatory wish fulfillment and "decide to form a conception of the real circumstances in the external world and endeavor to make a real alteration in them."[43] A psyche operating according to the pleasure principle alone cannot decide anything.

There is, however, a less extreme formulation in Castoriadis in which he does not assert that psyche and society are radically heterogeneous but only that the psyche "can never generate" sociability "out of itself," which is a different story indeed. The more extreme formulation is the result of a faulty inference from the weaker formulation: Castoriadis wants to conclude from the fact "that the psyche's entry into society could never occur gratuitously"[44] that the psyche is "in no way 'predestinated' [sic] by nature" for socialization. All that follows, however, from the fact that the psyche can never autochthonously generate a socialized individual out of itself is that a "facilitating environment"[45] is necessary for socialization to unfold. Indeed, there are passages in Castoriadis himself that deny the inherent asociablity of the psyche: "This is the history of the psyche in the course of which the psyche alters itself and opens itself to the social-historical world, depending too, on its own work and its own creativity."[46] This statement presupposes the existence of a potentiality immanent in the psyche—dare we say an *Anlage*—which not only "lends itself to" socialization but which, to use Castoriadis's own phrase, can also "support and induce it" as well. There are two possible reasons why he could not incorporate into his theory, as he should have, the significance of these Anlagen that lend themselves to socialization. The first is the general hostility in the French psychoanalytic tradition (both Lacanian and non-Lacanian) toward American psychoanalysis and its emphasis on ego psychology,[47] for ego Anlagen constitute one of the central *topoi* of classical ego psychology. The second is his commitment to the monadic starting point, which he apparently feels he has to defend in a radical form in order to defend, in turn, the autonomy and creativity of the radical imagination.

Habermas, Lacan, and the Linguistification of the Unconscious

For Castoriadis, then, the starting point is monadic isolation, and the "great enigma" that has to be accounted for "[o]nce we find ourselves within . . . the imaginary-representative magma of the unconscious" is "the emergence of separation."[48] He begins with isolation and asks how communication is possible. Beginning from within an original and irreducible "representative/affective/intentional flux"[49] of the unconscious, Castoriadis must, like Freud, explain, first, how that self-enclosed stream of representations could possibly communicate with an extrapsychic reality that is heterogeneous to it and, second, how those imagistic representations could be translated into words.

Habermas's starting point is precisely the opposite: he begins with the fact of communication and asks how it can become deformed into the privatized unconscious. For him, the unconscious is a derivative phenomenon.

Support for these differing interpretations can be found in Freud himself, for, as Loewald, following Gill, has observed, the tension between the conception of the unconscious as originary and as derivative already exists in Freud:

The primary process, on the one hand, is 'motivated' [Gill's term] by defense, is due to the impact of repression on standard rational, secondary-process thinking. On the other hand, primary process is assumed to be the original form or mode of mentation according to the pleasure principle, which secondarily becomes changed by the exigencies of life, by "reality," resulting in a secondary-process mentation guided by the reality principle.

Loewald goes on to observe that "in a manner the ambiguity is resolved by introducing the concept of regression." Defense brings about regression from secondary- to primary-process thinking, which is " 'primary' because it is the first and more primitive. Defense, [that is,] repression, leads to a regression to this old mode of mental functioning: it does not *create* primary process."[50] In Habermas's interpretation of psychoanalysis, however, the primary process and the unconscious are strictly derivative; they result from, are created by, the deformation of secondary process, ordinary-language thinking, and do not predate it. There is, in short, nothing like an original "representative/affective/intentional flux," to which regression could return because of defensive functions, in his scheme. Indeed, it is inimical to it.

Habermas's criticisms of Castoriadis, and especially of the psychic imaginary, could have been predicted on the basis of the Freud interpretation in *Knowledge and Human Interests,* where he emphatically rejects the canonical distinction between word-representations *(Wortvorstellung)* and thing-representations *(Sach-* or *Dingvorstellung)* and ipso facto the existence of a nonlinguistic unconscious consisting in a stream of pictorial representations: "Now the distinction between word-representations and asymbolic ideas is problematic, and the assumption of a nonlinguistic substratum in which these ideas are severed from language are 'carried out,' is unsatisfactory."[51] By denying the distinction between word-representations and thing-representations, Habermas obeys a prohibition on images, a *Bilderverbot,* as it were, which, if it is of a somewhat different but related nature, is nevertheless as stringent as any in Benjamin and Adorno. In so doing, he not only denies a source of the political imaginary but rejects one of the fundamental tenets of Freud's metapsychology:

The system *Ucs.* contains the thing-cathexes of the objects, the first and true object-cathexes; the system *Pcs.* comes about by this thing-representation being hypercathected through being linked with the word-presentations corresponding to it. It is these hypercathexes, we may suppose, that bring about a higher psychical organization and make it possible for the primary process to be succeeded by the secondary process which is dominant in the *Pcs.*[52]

In Freud the point is thoroughly unambiguous: the unconscious is characterized by the primary process and thing-representations; the preconscious and consciousness, by the secondary process and word-representations. Indeed, the border between the unconscious and the preconscious is traversed by the addition of word-cathexes to thing-cathexes and is, therefore, at the same time, the border between the prelinguistic and the linguistic. As Freud maintains in his discussion of the "considerations of representability" *(Rücksicht auf Darstellbarkeit),* imagistic mentation, because of its plasticity *(Bildhaftigkeit)* and fluidity, because of the fact that "concrete terms . . . are richer in associations than conceptual ones,"[53] and because it can present wishes scenically as fulfilled, is much better suited for the anarchic purposes of the primary process and the pleasure principle than are the syntactically and energically bound secondary processes of linguistically mediated thought.

At this point we encounter another unexpected convergence between the work of a Critical Theorist and Lacan. In this fundamental respect at least, Habermas is remarkably close to Lacan; indeed, they represent the two foremost "linguistic reformulators," to use Ricoeur's term,[54] of Freud. Habermas and Lacan attempt to combat Freud's supposed biologism and argue that he did not have the conceptual tools available to him in his day to formulate his theory properly. As Habermas puts it, for Freud to have adequately conceptualized the phenomena he was encountering in the consulting room, "he would really have needed a theory of language, which did not exist at the time and whose outlines are only just beginning to take form today."[55] Both Habermas and Lacan argue, moreover, that with the development of the study of language in the twentieth century, they now possess the conceptual tools to articulate what Freud could express only inadequately and thereby to eliminate the crude biologism from psychoanalytic theory. Where Freud stammered, they can provide fully articulate science. Habermas draws on the tradition of hermeneutics, pragmatics, and ordinary-language philosophy to rectify Freud's shortcomings; Lacan turns to the school of structuralist linguistics.

The overly linguistifying tendency of Lacan's position leads him, just as it does Habermas, to obviate the distinction between thing-representation and word-representations: both are subsumed under the larger category of signifier, and the distinct nature of images, as opposed to words, is lost. As Laplanche puts it in his well-known critique, Lacan reduces "the specificity of the Freudian Unconscious and [forgets] the fundamental difference between the interplay and nature of representations on the unconscious level, on the one hand, and the preconscious-conscious one on the other."[56] Indeed, with his central thesis that "the unconscious is structured like a language," Lacan does not simply return to Freud but stands Freud on his head, in much the same manner that Marx stood Hegel on his. For Freud, the unconscious is imagistically structured, and the ego is mediated by language; for Lacan, it is just the opposite: the "unconscious is structured like a language," and the ego is an imaginary entity. To his credit—and in an uncharacteristic display of rigor—Lacan takes up the central and obvious phenomenon that stands as a counterexample to his thesis, namely, the rebus, the prototype of unconscious, pictorial thinking: "The first sentence of the opening chapter [of the *Interpretation of Dreams*] announces what for the sake of the exposition could not be postponed: that the dream is a rebus." That is to say, Freud's claim that a dream is "a psychic structure which has a meaning and which can be inserted at an assignable point in the mental activities of waking life"[57] and that dreams are therefore interpretable requires that the question of the rebus be addressed. Lacan continues: "And Freud goes on to stipulate what I have said from the start, that it must be understood quite literally." Lacan is employing the word 'literally' quite literally, indeed, more literally than Freud. He insists that the dream image must be understood like any other "letter," in his technical sense of the term, in the discursive grid:

This derives from the agency in the dream of the same literal (or phonematic) structure in which the signifier is articulated and analyzed in discourse. So the unnatural images of the boat on the roof, or the man with a comma for a head, which are specifically mentioned by Freud, are examples of dream-images *that are to be taken only for their value as signifiers,* that is to say, in so far as they allow us to spell out the 'proverb' presented by the rebus of the dream. (emphasis added)

Images, in other words, are to be analyzed in exactly the same manner as phonemes in structural linguistics, that is, in terms of their "value," their mere location in a structure that is itself meaningless and consists only in a system of pure oppositions. As "signifiers," images possess no meaning of their own and are indistinguishable in their intrinsic nature from any other signifier. To continue: "The linguistic structure that enables us to read dreams is the very principle of the 'significance of the dream,' the *Traumdeutung.*"[58] The linguistic nature of the unconscious, which is no different in principle from any other linguistic structure, in Lacan's structuralist sense of linguisticality, makes the "reading" of dreams possible. Because Lacan defines the unconscious as "linguistic" *ab initio* (as does

Habermas), the conditions of the possibility of "reading" the unconscious—which Freud had to account for theoretically—is in fact no
problem at all for him. Lacan is quite correct, moreover, to use the
term 'reading' to distinguish this activity from interpretation:
whereas hermeneutical interpretation is concerned with the "explication of meaning by meaning,"[59] structuralist reading aims at "the
[reduction] of meaning to nonmeaning."[60] Finally, Lacan explicitly
rejects another of the central tenets of the Freudian theory of the
unconscious, namely, that images are particularly "appropriate" for
representing instincts. He considers this a mistake that could be corrected by proper "linguistic training."[61]

Habermas is, of course, often criticized for his excessive rationalism. There is, however, a deep—if not rationalistic, at least scientistic—tendency in Lacan that often goes unnoticed, because it is
camouflaged by his dissociated mode of theorizing and by the subversive aura that surrounds his project. The fact that he is antisystematic is not the issue here—Nietzsche and Adorno are antisystematic
yet absolutely rigorous.[62] Lacan's ability to combine his surrealistic
shenanigans with the worst sort of scientism requires a form of splitting that confirms his thesis about the split nature of the subject in
the extreme—at least in his own case. His later turn to the formaliza-
tion of mathemes, where the scientism becomes fully manifest, was
no accident; it was already latent in the linguistification of the unconscious, which purged the analysis of all meaning and, as Dews observes, opened "up the objectivist perspective of conventional
structuralism."[63] Indeed, despite Lacan's polemics against the
Cartesian subject, the turn to linguistics, which was motivated by an
anything but subversive wish to make psychoanalytic theory scientifically kosher, was determined by an a priori commitment to the
Cartesian-mathematical standard of scientificality: "To pinpoint the
emergence of linguistic science we may say that, as in the case of all
sciences in the modern sense, it is contained in the constitutive moment of an algorithm that is its foundation."[64]

For Habermas, who has no aspirations toward theoretical avant-
gardism but who in fact seeks to temper the hyperradicalism of the
earlier generation of Critical Theorists, the charge of rationalism
poses no problem. For Lacan, however, whose avowed purpose is to

preserve the radicalism of Freud's discovery, it does. He misses precisely what was subversive, in the strict sense, in Freud's discovery, namely, the imagistic nature of archaic mentation driven by memory and the pleasure principle. As Lyotard observes, the dream work that "transforms" discourse into images is not itself another text, another discourse, but is precisely that form of work *(Arbeit)* that "by manhandling a text . . . does not speak" but "does violence to the order of utterance." It is, in other words, work on the order of utterance that is not of the order of utterance. This mistreating of the text, in turn, creates "a qualitatively different though still meaningful object,"[65] and the task of psychoanalytic theory is to account for both the magnitude of that mistreatment and the meaningfulness of the new object at the same time.

In a similar vein, Habermas's rejection of the distinction between thing-representations and word-representations is closely connected with one of the central theses of his Freud interpretation, namely, that repression is an intralinguistic phenomenon in and through which the unconscious is constituted. Habermas bases this thesis on the fact that repression is undone and the unconscious is translated into consciousness in the actual process of psychoanalysis.[66] He argues that "the ego's flight from itself is an operation that is carried out in and with language. Otherwise it would not be possible to reverse the defensive process hermeneutically, via the analysis of language."[67] Habermas conceives of repression as a process of excommunication. When, in the course of development, "the infantile ego" is confronted with the social prohibition of forbidden wishes personified in the form of frightening parental figures, it has no choice, because of its inherent weakness, but to take "flight from itself and objectivate itself in the id."[68] (To the detriment of his analysis, Habermas does not systematically distinguish between the unconscious and the id.) This flight consists in the excommunication of the representation of those wishes from public, intersubjective communication through their degrammaticization and privatization: "The psychically most effective way to render undesired need dispositions harmless is to *exclude from public communication the interpretations* to which they are attached."[69] As a psychic realm, the unconscious is constituted as the repository for all those excommunicated qua distorted, degrammaticized, and privatized representations and, as such, assumes the character of an internal foreign territory. Its foreignness, however, is only relative and not absolute, for, despite the distortions, it remains essentially a linguistic domain. "The communication between the two systems," as Freud called it,[70] is, for Habermas, in principle at least, not a problem; whatever technical difficulties such translation may present, the talking cure consists in the regrammaticization of those excommunicated but essentially linguistic representations and their reintegration into public communication.

Habermas's commitment to the linguistic position is so strong that he is compelled to systematically eliminate the existence of any putatively prelinguistic phenomena by assimilating their apparent prelinguisticality to the linguistic, just as Lacan eliminates the particular character of the rebus by assimilating it to the signifier. In both cases, the result of this linguistic reformulation is a thoroughgoing linguistic monism that cannot accommodate the otherness of the unconscious. This strategy is evident in the following passage from Habermas, which not only is so inaccurate as to be almost bizarre but also points to the fundamental difficulty with his approach:

Only in the medium of language is the heritage of man's natural history articulated in the form of interpreted needs: the heritage of a plastic impulse potential, which, while preoriented in libidinal and aggressive directions, is otherwise undefined, owing to its uncoupling from inherited motor activity. On the human level, instinctual demands are represented by interpretations, that is, by hallucinatory wish-fulfillments *[sic]*.[71]

Habermas, then, instead of attempting to theorize the hierarchy of frontiers between the nonlinguistic (somatic) and the prelinguistic (unconscious) and between the prelinguistic and the linguistic proper (preconscious-conscious), that is, rather than theorizing the coming to be of language, remains on this side of the categorical divide and extends the web of intersubjectivity so far as to incorporate the putatively prelinguistic into it. The strange equation of hallucinatory wish fulfillments with interpretations—the most that could possibly be said is that they are both representations—can only be explained by this extension. Were such an equation correct, a central distinction of Freud's entire theoretical construction, namely, between the progressive and regressive functioning of the psyche, would be lost. When it operates in a "progressive" direction, excitation moves through language toward the "motor end of the apparatus," and the individual seeks gratification through intentional action in the external, public, linguistically mediated world. Hallucinatory wish fulfillment, however, is the result of the psyche's tendency to work in "a *backward* direction."[72] Excitation moves toward the "sensory end" of the apparatus; the individual eschews the external world as a source of gratification and seeks pleasure through private, asocial phantasms.

Habermas ignores "the most general and the most striking psychological characteristic" of a dream (the prototype of hallucinatory wish fulfillment), namely, that "a thought of something that is wished is represented" not as a statement but, pictorially, "as a scene."[73] Insofar as they are linguistic, and therefore public and intersubjective, then, interpretations are exactly the opposite of pictorial, private, and autistic hallucinations. However, if wishes were, in fact, linguistically interpreted via their hallucinatory representation, as Habermas asserts, they would ipso facto be linked with public, culturally defined interpretations, and the requirements of his philosophical program would be met: drive representations would be included in the web of intersubjectivity and "rooted in the meaning structures of the lifeworld, no matter how elementary"[74] from the start.

To be sure, it would be meaningless to refer to a preinterpreted inner nature. Nevertheless, despite the enormous, intrinsic difficulties, Freud's entire drive theory consists precisely in the attempt not to conceptualize inner nature *an sich* but to elucidate the "frontier" *(Grenze)*[75] between soma and psyche (as well as the frontier between the image and the word): "an 'instinct' *(Trieb)* appears to us as a concept on the frontier between the mental and the somatic, as the psychical representative of the stimuli originating from within the organism and reaching the mind, as a measure of the demand made upon the mind for work in consequence of its connection with the body."[76] Habermas's and Lacan's charge of biologism against Freud is unfounded, for Freud distinguishes between an animal *Instinkt,* which is squarely within the realm of the somatic, and the human *Trieb.* Although the latter has its "source" in the body, it is taken as a "frontier concept," on the border between the somatic and psychic, precisely to distinguish between the object of biological and the object of psychoanalytic investigation. Indeed, it would not be excessive to assert that Freud was essentially a theorist of frontiers.[77] And, as Hegel already argued against Kant, the attempt to determine the limit of a frontier already begins to cross over it.

What is true of the work of all great thinkers, namely, "that difficulty and obscurity are the result of the struggle which thought, to achieve expression, must wage with the thing, with language and with itself,"[78] is compounded in this case for Freud; for "the thing" with which he is here struggling is the very "intersection of the 'natural' and the 'signifying.' "[79] The strain of Freud's encounter with the limits of signification forces him, as it has many philosophers, to formulate a specialized and sometimes even peculiar vocabulary, as we saw.[80] The ambiguity and terminological obscurity of the theory of instinctual representation mark the point where the enterprise strains against its intrinsic limitations.

At the same time, however, another point must be insisted on. Although Freud did as much as anybody to demonstrate the limits of signification and, in so doing, both reflected and contributed to the modernist crisis of language, he himself, as Yerushalmi observes, seems "to have remained singularly untouched by the general agitation."[81] And this in spite of the fact that he inhabited the same *Dorf* as Karl Krauss and Ludwig Wittgenstein. Indeed, Yerushalmi goes so far as to maintain that, against the overwhelming current of our age, Freud remained a "linguistic optimist" but not, to be sure, of a naive sort: "Although Freud, to my knowledge, never offered a comprehensive theory or even a systematic discussion of language, he retained throughout his life a primal belief in the potency of words, whether as a vehicle for his conscious thoughts and teachings or as a means of access to the unconscious."[82] The wrong conclusion is often drawn from the fact that Freud identified "the dream's navel," which consists in "a tangle of dream-thoughts which cannot be unravelled" and represents "the spot where [the dream] reaches down into the unknown,"[83] that is, the spot where signification dissolves into opacity. Rather than appreciating what a triumph of articulation it was to have expanded the domain of meaning to include the

formerly inviolable realm of the nocturnal and, in fact, to have elucidated the point at which meaning trails off into obscurity—all of
which took place in language[84]—the existence of a "navel," of an
opaque core deep in the psyche, is adduced to substantiate the hope-
less deficiency of all our communications, not just those at the
boundaries of the sayable.

Clinically, Freud's linguistic optimism pertains to the reliance of
psychoanalysis on "the watered-down magic" of words for its therapeutic effectiveness; the talking cure presupposes the potency of language, which, in its prescientific form, was associated with the
omnipotence of thoughts. In response to the charge that psychoanalysis is magical, and therefore ephemeral insofar as it relies on words,
Freud responds, "Quite true. It *would* be magic if it worked rather
quicker. . . . But analytic treatments take months and even years:
magic that is so slow loses its miraculous character. And incidentally
do no let us despise the *word*. After all it is a powerful instrument.
. . . [O]riginally the word was magic—a magical act; and it has retained much of its ancient power."[85] And, theoretically, Freud, while
no transcendental idealist, never ceased to believe that "even in its
caprices," with which he was intimately familiar, "the usage of language remains true to some kind of reality."[86] How could he believe
otherwise, if he wanted to maintain even a shred of legitimacy for his
clinical work or his theoretical formulations? At a more general level
bearing on the question of a psychoanalytic ethos, Freud—in opposition to Lacan's obstinate, narcissistic, and self-serving obscuran-
tism—strove with every sentence to communicate with his audience
or reader. As he attested, "I believe that I did everything possible to
render accessible to the other that which I knew and had experienced."[87]

Returning to Habermas, the failure to appreciate the psychism's
inherent tendency to "work in a *backward* direction" is only one aspect of his larger difficulty in dealing with regressive phenomena;
indeed, when it comes to regressive phenomena, he is unmusical.
Unlike Adorno, Castoriadis, and Chasseguet-Smirgel, who view regressive phenomena as thoroughly ambivalent, Habermas tends to
view them only negatively, if at all. This accounts, in part, for the lack
of a developed aesthetics in his philosophy as well as for its generally

progressivistic tenor. Adorno sees both the threat and the promise in the Sirens' song; Habermas—undoubtedly because of the disastrous regressive political events of this century—tends to see only the threat.

While both are regularly mistaken for hermeneutical monists in the psychoanalytic literature, Habermas's professed position is, like Ricoeur's, dualistic: where Ricoeur maintains that psychoanalysis, to be the discipline it is, must employ a mixed discourse that combines the language of force and the language of meaning, energics, and hermeneutics, Habermas argues that "psychoanalysis joins hermeneutics with operations that genuinely seemed to be reserved to the natural sciences," that it "unites linguistic analysis with psychological investigations of causal connections."[88]

In the details of his argument, however, Habermas equivocates on the dualistic thesis to such an extent that it is ultimately difficult to distinguish his position from a strictly hermeneutical one, as will become clear when we discuss his controversy with Gadamer. This becomes particularly apparent with Habermas's claim that repression is strictly an intralinguistic affair, that "the ego's flight from itself is an operation that is carried out in and with language." Habermas correctly maintains that psychoanalytic theory must take psychoanalytic experience not only as its point of departure but as its touchstone for verification as well. Thus he acknowledges that "the starting point of psychoanalytic theory is the experience of resistance, that is the blocking force that stands in the way of free and public communication of repressed contents." And he proceeds to draw the proper anticognitivist implications from this fact:

The analytic process of making conscious reveals itself as a process of reflection in that it is not only a process on the cognitive level but also dissolves resistances on the affective level. The dogmatic limitation of false consciousness consists not only in the lack of specific information but in its specific inaccessibility. It is not only a cognitive deficiency. . . . That is why the mere communication of information and the labelling of resistances have no therapeutic effect.[89]

He distinguishes "reflection" from a purely cognitive activity so as to designate a procedure that, as distinct from a pure hermeneutics, not only involves the translation of one text into another, of meaning into meaning, but contends with dynamic forces that resist that translation as well.

Unfortunately, the significance of this essential observation does not systematically enter into Habermas's metatheoretical considerations. His complete rejection of energic language—supposedly on the basis of the communicative experience of psychoanalysis—deprives him of the conceptual resources to specify what he means by "reflection," as an activity distinct from hermeneutical translation proper:

> This correlation of mentalistic expressions (such as impulse, stimulation, pain, pleasure, wish) and physical processes (such as energy quanta, energy tension and discharge, and, as a system property the tendency toward the afflux of energy) suffices to sever the categories of the conscious and the unconscious, which are primarily derived from communication between physician and patient, from the frame of self-reflection and transfer them to the energy-distribution model.[90]

But a central feature of "the communication between physician and patient" is, as Habermas himself has observed, the experience of resistance. And any metatheory of psychoanalysis, if it is to do justice to the phenomena, must account for that experience. While Habermas, as far as I can determine, rejects the traditional language of energy and force, he does not formulate an alternative language to replace it.

Although Ricoeur does not mention Habermas by name in this context, what he asserts with respect to the hermeneutical, phenomenological, and linguistic reformulators of psychoanalysis, all of whom reject the language of energy and force, applies to Habermas. Why, Ricoeur asks, do these "reformulations which attempt to meet the requirements of the theory of science . . . not satisfy us any more than they satisfy the operationalists?" To which he answers: "because they betray the very essence of analytic experience."[91] Ricoeur is not, however, proposing a precritical or objectivist interpretation of psychoanalysis. On the contrary, it is precisely "an epistemological critique" in the Kantian sense, that is, a critique that seeks to determine the conditions of the possibility of the phenomena that we encounter in psychoanalytic experience, that leads him to posit "the reality of the id." He argues that Freud's "naturalism" is not simply a residue of his positivist training, as the popular catechism often has it, but is in fact "well grounded" in "the thing aspect, the quasi nature aspect, of the forces and mechanisms in question." Any account that "does not go that far" is bound to slip "sooner or later" into idealism, which is to say, into the transparency of language or "the primacy of immediate consciousness." [92] It is bound, in other words, to lose "the priority of the *I am* over the *I think*." [93] (To be sure, programmatically Habermas argues that a moment of objectifying theory is required in psychoanalysis to account for, and aid in, the dissolution of the objectified, naturelike *(naturwüchsig)* parts of the personality; but because he rejects energic language and attempts to conceptualize those objectifications only in terms of split-off symbols, Habermas cannot fulfill his own programmatic intentions.)

The correlate of the ubiquitous experience of resistance in analysis is the experience of work *(Arbeit):* "Primarily and essentially because analysis is a struggle against the patients' resistances," [94] it is a "work to work relation," [95] experienced as work by both parties. To the work of the patient and the analyst must be added a third form of work to which they both correspond, namely, the mechanism of the neurosis itself through which desire is disguised. If, ultimately, "man behaves like a mechanism in order to accomplish by deception the aims of wish fulfillment," [96] that deception is achieved through distortion *(Entstellung).* The prototype of that distortion is, of course, the dream work *(Traumarbeit),* with its specific modes of functioning, the work of condensation *(Verdichtungsarbeit),* and the work of displacement *(Verschiebungsarbeit).* [97] Even if it is granted that the final goal of analysis remains purely hermeneutical, that is, self-understanding—although that, too, is not unproblematical—work in the opposite direction and of equal intensity to the work of distortion is nevertheless required to undo that distortion and make the hermeneutical goal of understanding attainable.

This is why "the art of interpretation is subordinated to technique" in analysis: "psychoanalysis is an arduous technique, learned by diligent exercise and practice"—not a technique in the sense of the natural sciences, but a technique nonetheless. Thus, whereas Habermas, because of his aversion to the energic vocabulary, equivocates with the term "reflection," Ricoeur wholeheartedly embraces the notion of technique and praises Freud's "amazing audacity" at "treating the intersubjective relationship *as technique*":[98] "It is not," as Freud says in an allusion to Hamlet, "easy to play upon the instrument of the mind."[99] Indeed, Ricoeur argues that the *Papers on Technique* "suffice to open an abyss between everything that reflection can draw out of itself and that which only a craft can teach."[100] While the hermeneutical correction of the positivist self-misunderstanding of psychoanalysis has been absolutely necessary, there is nevertheless a limit to how useful "the model of the text" can be in elucidating the experience of psychoanalysis. Unless one wants to speak in the most preciously metaphorical way, a text, unlike a patient, cannot miss hours or fail to pay the bill, become depressed or elated, fall in love, suffer from premature ejaculations or vaginismus, master a phobia, commit suicide, get better, masturbate, bleed, cry, and so on.

The pervasiveness of work and the necessity of technique in the analytic situation finds its metapsychological reflection in the bar of repression that separates the two systems: "The justification for the topographic differentiation into systems is to be found in praxis; the 'remoteness' between the systems and their separation by the 'barrier' of repression are the exact pictorial transcription of the 'work' that provides access to the area of the repressed."[101] This fact leads Ricoeur, like Lyotard, to explicitly reject the thesis, central to Habermas's position, that repression is strictly an intralinguistic affair. The linguistic reformulations of psychoanalysis have the merit of highlighting the languagelike nature of the unconscious, of showing "that the unconscious is related to the conscious as a particular kind of discourse to ordinary discourse." However, "the economic explanation is what accounts for the separation of the two discourses"; that is to say, "the distortion . . . which turns that other discourse into a quasi-language is not itself achieved by language" but by a force working on language.[102] Without the bar of repression, all talk of the unconscious, technically speaking, remains on the level of the preconscious and never reaches the dynamic unconscious of psychoanalysis, for example, the discussions by Chomsky, Piaget, and Lévi-Strauss. While Freud's attempt "to interrelate the modes of knowledge and the modes of desire and effort" was prefigured in the history of philosophy—by Nietzsche and Schopenhauer, but especially by Spinoza and Leibniz—the "originality" in Freud's contribution "consists entirely in the role played by the barrier between the systems." Thus Spinoza investigated the relation between idea and bodily grounded endeavor, and Leibniz examined the relation between perception and effort and the extent to which the latter can distort the former and produce illusion. But only Freud formulated a dynamic point of view and a technique that corresponded to it in order to explain the relationship between the two orders of representation, the two systems. To miss this point is to miss not only what is unique to his contribution but what is a defining feature of the psychoanalytic experience as well.

Given the foregoing considerations, Habermas's criticisms of Castoriadis in *The Philosophical Discourse of Modernity* should have come as no surprise. He argues that, having posited "the stream of the imaginary dimension" and the "monadic core of subjectivity," Castoriadis cannot solve the problem that plagued "the philosophy of consciousness from Fichte to Husserl," namely, "the intersubjectivity of social praxis that is compelled to begin from the premise of isolated consciousness." He proceeds to argue that, in Castoriadis's conception, "socialized individuals do not enter into intersubjective relationships with one another in any genuine sense of the term." Ultimately—and this is Habermas's main point—"Castoriadis cannot provide us with the figure of mediation between the individual and society." In Castoriadis, the socialized individual remains "divided into monad and member of society," and "psyche and society stand in a kind of metaphysical opposition to one another."[103]

The main charge Habermas levels against Castoriadis, namely, that he cannot provide the mediation between individual and society, and which is not entirely unfounded, can, however, itself be turned against Habermas, but from the opposite direction. Habermas himself does not provide a genuine account of the mediation of individual and society, because he solves the problem, at least in principle, in advance through the preestablished harmony between an already linguistic unconscious and a linguistically mediated social world. The problem of mediation only arises when there is a sufficient difference to be mediated. Habermas, in short, purchases the mediation between psyche and society by deradicalizing Freud's notion of the unconscious. Habermas is correct in arguing that "language functions as a kind of transformer"[104] that draws the individual into the intersubjective social world. But it does not do so without a residuum of private in-itselfness—without which we would all be precoordinated clones—and it is this residuum that does not adequately appear in Habermas's account. Paraphrasing Adorno, we might say that the child does not go into the intersubjective web without remainder. Adorno, as we know, moreover, praised the orthodox psychoanalytic theory of the drives, even with its biologism, for preserving the moment of nonidentity between individual and society. Whereas Adorno as well as Castoriadis, after having dramatized the moment of difference, have difficulty accounting for the moment of identity between psyche and society, Habermas is in danger of losing sight of the moment of nonidentity altogether. Habermas believes he has solved the problem by rejecting Castoriadis's *techne* model of socialization, in which social form is imposed on asocial matter, in favor of a model that views socialization as simultaneously a process of individuation:

Language has to be conceived of as a medium that both draws each participant in interaction into a community of communication, as one of its members, and at the same time subjects him to an unrelenting compulsion toward individuation. That is to say, the integration of perspectives of speaker, hearer and observer, as well as the intermeshing of this structure with a system of world perspectives that coordinates the object world with the social and the subjective worlds, are pragmatic presuppositions of a correct use of grammatical sentences in speech acts.[105]

The concept of individuation employed in this passage remains on the surface: it consists merely in the external mapping of one's viewpoint against a variety of other viewpoints, which is undoubtedly an important cognitive component of decentering and individuation. However, it fails to consider the deeper unconscious meaning of individuation, namely, "the strain of relating [self-representatives and object-representatives] that no human being is free from."[106] As always, Habermas's account "screens out the psychodynamics"[107] of the situation; it disregards the psyche's "monadic pole," its inherent tendency to "work in a *backward* direction," which is to say, the tendency to resist integration into the intersubjective net. While Habermas may be correct in arguing that Castoriadis tends to turn the relationship of "psyche and society" into a "kind of metaphysical opposition,"[108] Habermas leaves the dimension of private subjective interiority completely unexplored. Communication theory does not sublate the philosophy of consciousness without a remainder of subjective in-itselfness.

Habermas's error of equating hallucinations and interpretations results from the overextension of the translatability thesis. Like all the linguistic reformulators of Freud, Habermas argues from the fact that psychoanalysis is a "talking cure"—that is, that the unconscious can be made conscious via speech—that the unconscious must already be linguistic ab initio. This argument, while possessing a certain plausibility, infers too much: logically, all that is required to account for the *factum* of the talking cure is the assumption that the unconscious is amenable to translation into words, not that it is wholly linguistic at the start. As Ricoeur argues, it does not follow from the fact that unconscious discourse is translatable into conscious discourse that the unconscious is already linguistic, any more than the fact that French is translatable into English establishes that French is already English: "That these [unconscious] complexes should have an affinity for discourse, that they are sayable in principle is not to be doubted. Therefore the analytic situation itself establishes a semiotic aspect. . . . But none of this proves that what thus comes to language—or better, is brought to language—is or must *be* language."[109] The central contribution of Habermas and the reformulators has been to elucidate that semiotic aspect of psychoanalysis, that is to say, to elucidate the element of homogeneity between the two systems that makes the translation from unconscious to conscious possible. The corresponding shortcoming is to overextend their discovery and undervalue the moment of heterogeneity between the two systems.

By simply dismissing thing-representations as "asymbolic," Habermas, like Lacan, fails to make a crucial distinction that would have allowed for a more differentiated treatment of the problems at hand. Ricoeur, in contrast, makes such a distinction, and the greater adequacy of his Freud interpretation can, in large part, be traced to this fact. Ricoeur distinguishes between "a signifying power that is operative prior to language," on the one hand, and language *strictu sensu*, which is a subspecies of that larger category of signification, on the other: "The form by which an instinct reaches the psychism is called a 'representative' *(Repräsentant);* this is a signifying factor, but it is not yet linguistic. As for the 'presentation' properly so-called *(Vorstellung)*, this is not, in its specific texture, of the order of language; it is a 'presentation of things,' not a 'presentation of words.' "[110] Against the linguistic reformulators, Ricoeur maintains that "it is mistaken to believe that everything semiotic is linguistic": " 'meaning' does not," as Castoriadis puts it, "signify *logos*."[111] Ricoeur argues "that the universe of discourse appropriate to the analytic experience is not that of language but that of the image," which, of course, is not entirely unrelated to the realm of language.[112] This allows him to account for both the moment of identity and that of difference in the mediation between unconscious and conscious, private and public. Insofar as it is already significant, the pictorial language of the unconscious would be homogeneous with the language *strictu sensu* of consciousness in that it could potentially be translated into the latter. But insofar as it is not yet language *strictu sensu*, and insofar as it requires an enormous amount of work by both analyst and analysand to translate the language potential of the unconscious into language *strictu sensu*—a fact that is, as we have seen, largely underappreciated by the linguistic reformulators—the language of the unconscious is heterogeneous with the language of consciousness and, again, is separated from it by a bar of repression, that is, by force.[113] Hence the necessity of economic and dynamic categories.

Castoriadis, the Productive Imagination, and the Problem of Subjective Idealism

In an earlier discussion of Castoriadis's appropriation of psychoanalysis,[114] I argued that his problem is precisely the opposite of Habermas's. Because Castoriadis refuses to theorize adequately how the psyche "lends itself" to socialization, because socialization only comes violently from outside, he cannot ultimately provide the moment of identity in the mediation between psyche and society. I maintained that Castoriadis's repeated return to one of the central scandals of Kantian philosophy is suggestive, for, ultimately, he shares Kant's problems.[115] I raised the question of whether Castoriadis's preoccupation with this scandal indicates that he was intuitively struggling with one of the central difficulties of his own thinking under the guise of a discussion of Kant. The problem for Kant is the following: in *The Critique of Judgment,* he is forced into the embarrassing admission that the fit between the categories of our thinking (and language) and the being-thus of the world rests on no more than a "lucky accident" *(glücklicher Zufall).*[116] After God could no longer be invoked to underwrite that fit, as he still could in Descartes and Leibniz, it proved impossible to find an equally reliable transcendental guarantor. Although Castoriadis adduces this remarkable admission to rub Kant's nose in the ultimate shortcomings of his critical philosophy, a similar criticism can be made of his own position: as long as he completely abstains from examining how the psyche lends itself to socialization, the fit between psyche and society also rests on no more than a "lucky accident."

Freud, who, as Castoriadis observes, "never doubted the rational factor of the physical world"[117] and who displays his characteristic impatience with the "empty abstraction[s]" of the philosophers, addresses this question in the final paragraph of *The Future of an Illusion.* Although the answer is prosaic and would certainly be considered unsatisfactory from the standpoint of "transcendental purism,"[118] it is nevertheless rather plausible. In that paragraph, Freud argues that the attempt "to discredit scientific endeavor in a radical way, on the ground that" it is tied to the subjective organization of our "mental apparatus" is mistaken on the following count: the organization of our mental apparatus "has been developed precisely in the attempt to explore the external world, and it must therefore have realized in its structure some degree of expediency."[119] There must, in other words, be some fit between the organization of our mental apparatus and the world, because that organization has developed in the course of evolution in order to adapt to that world. I have pointed out that this idea became the point of departure for a research program of the ego psychologists, who went on to investigate the "preadaptiveness" of the psyche to the world.[120] Much has been made, within both the Frankfurt school and Lacanian psycho-analysis, of how this concentration on adaptation provided the theoretical underpinnings for the social and cultural conformism of the American ego psychologists, who stressed the moment of identity in the mediation between psyche and society to the almost complete exclusion of the moment of difference. There is undoubtedly truth to this objection. A conformist attitude, however, does not necessarily follow from a theory of adaptation, and the question of the fit between psyche and society remains unsolved without it or, at least, without an alternative theory to carry the same conceptual load.

I have also maintained that in his treatment of the unconscious, Castoriadis is not sufficiently faithful to the anti-Kantian element of his philosophy as it is formulated in the theory of leaning on. The reason for this is undoubtedly his legitimate eagerness to preserve the radicalness of Freud's discovery of the unconscious, which has been rendered "infinitely flat" [121] by the linguistic reformulators who try to assimilate "the operations of the unconscious to *secondary* modes of functioning belonging to waking life." [122] While Castoriadis objected to the excessive "constitutivism" of both the Kantians and the contextualists, who view the object as no more than "amorphous clay" on which our conceptual/linguistic grids can be imposed at will, his notion of the magma, which must be posited at the base of the unconscious and which is approached at the navel of the dream, itself resembles such amorphous clay: "A magma is that from which one can extract (or in which one can construct) an indefinite number of ensemblist organizations." [123] Castoriadis does not identify any potentiality toward language and sociability within the magma; it merely passively tolerates their (violent) imposition on it. Finally, I have suggested that Ricoeur's "archeology of the subject" results in a similar posit at the deepest layer of the psyche, namely, the posit of what he terms "desire." And, in fact, the characteristics Ricoeur ascribes to desire come closer to fulfilling the requirements of Castoriadis's philosophical construction than does Castoriadis's own notion of the magma; Ricoeur defines desire, "which is at the origin of language and prior to language," as the "potency to speech." If, like the magma, "desire is the unnameable," we must nevertheless posit that "it is turned from the very outset toward language" [124] and can therefore "support and induce" socialization. Philosophically, this posit of "potency to speech" provides a minimal notion "predetermined by nature," which Castoriadis's position requires.

Castoriadis has responded to my criticisms with the following objections. Like another illustrious Greek who preceded him by over two millennia, Castoriadis has a knack for the well-turned epithet: with respect to the question of the "fit" between mind and the world, he accuses me (following Freud) of offering a "Darwinio-Kantian" [125] solution to the problem. I do not, however, find the label objectionable per se: once one realizes that genealogical positivism, which seeks to dissolve reason into any of the various (anthropological, psychological, economic, or linguistic) powers that operate behind its back, is incoherent and a moment of transcendentality is unavoidable, on the one side, and that a completely purified transcendental position is unobtainable—that the a priori has a history—on the other, then it seems to me that a "Darwinio-Kantian" strategy is at least plausible.

Let me begin by examining the "Kantian" term of the epithet, both because it is the more philosophical and because it clarifies what Castoriadis takes himself to be doing. Against my claim that his preoccupation with the question of the "lucky accident" in Kant suggests that his position suffers from difficulties similar to Kant's, Castoriadis replies that "this nonresponse creates a problem for Kant but it does not create one for me." He argues that the notion of an " 'accident,' whether lucky or unlucky," only "creates a disagreeable surprise" within the framework of Kant's program of transcendental philosophy, which demands the isolation of the a priori and necessary conditions of experience and which locates them solely on the side of the subject. As for himself, however, who "would certainly never pretend to be able to bring the ultimate facts (that there is a world, that there is an in-itself) under the yoke of some kind of 'necessity,' " Castoriadis argues that the nonnecessary relation between mind and world is not a problem. And, technically speaking, he is of course correct. He never claims to provide a transcendental proof or deduction of the necessity of that fit in the Kantian mode but only to "elucidate" (his "methodological" term) a " 'correspondence,' in the vaguest sense of the term," between mind and world.

For him it is "a fact, a pure fact, a hard fact (and one which conditions an infinity of other facts, for example, the existence of the philosopher) that this correspondence exists."[126]

It is not on this level, however, that my difficulties with Castoriadis's position are to be located, for I am in general sympathy with his detranscendentalized elucidatory approach. Rather, I have difficulties with some of the details of that elucidation. What I had in mind in comparing him to Kant with respect to the "lucky accident" does not pertain to the details of the argument, but to a general problematic that he shares not only with Kant but, as Habermas recognized, with the entire philosophy of consciousness, stretching from Descartes through Kant to Husserl and Freud. The problem, stated in its most general terms, is as follows: how, beginning from a completely self-enclosed, monadic starting point, in which all that is ever encountered is the flow of internal representations, can the external world ever be reached? The problem is exacerbated in Freud, who posits a dynamic within the psyche, the tendency toward the narcissistic disavowal of reality and hallucinatory wish fulfillment, which actually opposes the opening up to the external world. To be sure, Castoriadis is correct when he argues that he has never stopped trying to "enumerate" the mediations between psyche and society;[127] indeed that is what his theory of sublimation is all about. I do not contest this. My objection pertains to one particular and crucial point in his elucidation, namely, the point of "the break-up of the monad" and its "open[ing] to the social-historical world." My thesis is that he has, for reasons I have tried to explain, drawn the productive power and tendency toward monadic self-enclosure of the imagination so strongly that he cannot elucidate that breakup; in other words, despite his efforts and his awareness of the problem, he cannot ultimately avoid a psychoanalytically formulated version of subjective idealism.

What about the "Darwinian" term of the epithet? I have come to recognize, in light of both Castoriadis's reply and a subsequent paper that further clarifies his position, that the Darwinian interpretation, while true, misses, in one sense at least, what is really new as a result of Freud, namely, the psychic imaginary. Indeed, Castoriadis's point is that Freud's own Darwinism—which is an element of his larger yearning for a realistic grounding of the imaginary (for example, in the historical reality of childhood seduction, of the murder of the archaic father, and of the primal scene)—obviates the originality of his own discovery. The Darwinian moment, in the narrowly adaptive sense, pertains only to "the first natural stratum," that is, to the stratum we more or less share with the rest of the animal kingdom, and not to what makes us distinctively human. As he puts it in a self-proclaimed act of irreverence that is in fact not all that irreverent, "the 'transcendental aesthetic' is good for dogs—and, of course, also for us, to the degree that, and it is immense, that we share a kinship with dogs."[128] Insofar as it synthesizes experience in terms of space and time, and therefore makes it possible to pick out relatively stable objects from "within the Heraclitean flux of representation," this "transcendental aesthetic" accounts for the "fit" between the mind and the physical world qua *res extensa* and, therefore, for the applicability of identitary-ensemblist logic—that is, *Verstand,* identity thinking, or instrumental reason—to that world. This endowment, moreover, which allows for surprisingly sophisticated calculations, is sufficient "as far as need and usage are concerned,"[129] that is to say, it is sufficient from the standpoint of survival and adaptation: "A dog probably does not have what we call the concept of a rabbit, yet it knows quite well that it is the same rabbit that it is chasing along a trajectory (which is, moreover, the solution to a differential equation, that of the curve of pursuit, which minimizes at each instant the space which remains to be covered in relation to the moving prey.)"[130] "The living being," then, "possesses an 'elementary' imagination, which contains an 'elementary' logic," and which constitutes and mediates its relation to its world. The difference, however, between this imagination and world and the human imagination and world—which also contains this rudimentary substratum as one of its components—is that the animal world is characterized, first and foremost, by closure. The relation between the subjective world of the living being and its environment is hereditarily predetermined by the adaptational demands of a specific biological niche and is relatively invariant for all the members of that species: "Nothing can enter into it—save to destroy it—except in accordance with the [genetically determined] forms and laws of the 'subjective' structure . . .

of the self." This solution is at the same time and for the same reason both adaptationally efficient and necessarily limited and inflexible. This characterization of closure is, as we have already noted, another way of formulating the Freudian distinction between a fixed animal *Instinkt,* which is efficiently preadapted to a specialized niche, and the human *Trieb,* which is malleable, open-ended, and at least adaptationally inefficient, if not radically afunctional, as Castoriadis maintains.

Castoriadis's thesis is that humanity's "essence is not to be found" in what it shares with the animal world but in precisely what emerges on "the ruins of [its] animality."[131] He argues that "we must postulate that a break in the psychical evolution of the animal world occurs when human beings appear." This break consists in "a monstrous development of the imagination, this psychical neoformation," through which "the human psychical world becomes *a-functional*"—that is, nonadaptive. "The inordinate swelling of the imagination" bursts the instinctually regulated adaptive closure "of the animal psychism" and—by disconnecting the imagination from functionality, representational pleasure from organ pleasure, and sexuality from reproduction—creates the quasi-autonomous human imaginary. Because of the evolutionary breakthrough of the radical imaginary, this "strange biped" (which used to be) known as man, is, according to Castoriadis, "radically unfit for life"[132] and requires the institutions of society to survive. By imposing its closure, its logic and imaginary significations on the child, society reintroduces, now from the outside, the closure that was lost in the evolutionary cleavage between *Instinckt* and *Trieb* and in and through that imposition "fabricates" the social individual. This means that it "fabricates, first and foremost—and exclusively, in the overwhelming majority of societies—closed individuals." In the individual, moreover, this closure operates by "cutting off communication between the subject's radical imagination and its 'thought,' "[133]—or, the communication between the two systems, as Freud called it. Most "thinking," in the reality-oriented, pragmatic, everyday sense of the term, takes place under this condition of closure, while, at the same time, the radical imagination continues to express itself indirectly in dreams, fantasies, transgression, and illness. Because of this latter fact, the psyche cannot be fully absorbed into even the most completely integrated society, either of the archaic or the futuristic sort. As we have noted, "people will always dream, they will always want to transgress the social norm." Finally, a prominent manifestation of closure is repetition, not only the well-known repetitiveness of psychopathology but that of normal character and of cultural practices as well—especially the ritualistic practices of traditional societies. Repetition, we must not forget, has its adaptive side.

I would argue once again, however, that Castoriadis's rhetoric concerning the "Darwinian" moment outstrips what can be supported by the content of his argument; his position, in short, appears more extreme than it is. For humankind is only partly "unfit for life." To be sure, because human infants are born relatively premature and instinctually underendowed and, as Castoriadis stresses, because of their enlarged imagination, the human psyche is, in the first instance, adaptationally afunctional. They cannot survive in isolation. But this only means that the helpless and dependent human child requires years of formation (German: *Bildung;* Greek: *paideia*), first in the family and later in the institutions of the larger society, to become socialized and acculturated. As I argued earlier, it does not follow from the fact that the psyche "can never generate" sociability "out of itself" that it is "in no way 'predestinated *[sic]* by nature" for socialization. Again, all that follows is that a "facilitating environment"—institutions, as Castoriadis would say—are necessary for that socialization to unfold.

In light of Castoriadis's comments concerning Darwinism, a further point needs to be made. For humans, as Castoriadis well knows, culture takes over the work of adaptation that, in the broadest possible sense, in the lower species was performed by *Instinkt.* Culture is, so to speak, our peculiar collective organ of adaptation. The very condition that makes a period of extended dependency and culture necessary for humans also makes it possible. In other words, the human drive is malleable precisely because it is unspecialized and adaptationally inefficient. Put another way, human children not only require a period of extended dependency because of their instinctual underendowment and resulting helplessness, they are also educable during that period because of the relative plasticity of those very drives. Thus, the very factors that make humans "unfit for life," in the first instance, make that human life, qua a cultural life, possible one step removed, that is, after socialization. It is doubtful, however, whether this form of adaptation through culture could be shown to be "efficient" in the Darwinian sense. (We can no longer refer to the survival of the species with confidence.) As Castoriadis knows—but sometimes forgets during interludes of rhetorical excess—the human being is neither a sick animal nor a rational animal per se; because of the specific nature of the human psyche, we have an equal potential for both sickness and rationality. The nature of the drive and the imaginary, in short, makes culture and (individual and collective) pathology coequal possibilities for the human animal.

Castoriadis uses the concept of closure—which "means that what is thought cannot be put into question in its essential features"—to elucidate further the notion of heteronomy. Although the emergence of language makes it "possible in every human society to pose questions," heteronomous (or closed) societies impose severe limitations on how far that questioning can go. A heteronomous society, like all societies, must of course admit utilitarian questions pertaining to the well-being of the group, for example, "Was there really a lion on the edge of the village yesterday?" It cannot, however, tolerate questions concerning the "idols of the tribe," in the broadest possible sense of the term, that is, "the axioms of its social institution, its rules of inference and its criteria for making deductions." For example, one could not ask, "Does the earth really lie on the back of a great tortoise?" Because the sacred core of a closed society is structurally insulated from criticism through an arrangement of implicit and explicit taboos, it is systematically impossible to say or think certain things. For example,

in a consistent Hebrew society, no one can ask: Is the Law just? To pose the question would be just as absurd as to say, in Orwell's *1984:* 'Big Brother is ungood,' which was to become, in the final perfect phase of Newspeak, a pure and simple grammatical absurdity. Now, it happens that, in the *Old Testament,* Justice is one of God's names. God has given the Law. How, psychically *and* linguistically, could one say that the Law is unjust? These are the ultimate axioms which are neither questioned nor capable of being questioned.[134]

"Reflection," as opposed to the first-level order of "thinking," occurs "when thought turns back upon itself and interrogates itself not only about its particular contents, but also about its presuppositions and its foundations." Authentic reflection, by its very nature, must ultimately encompass the "putting into question of the socially instituted representations" of the tribe.[135]

It has already been noted that the vast majority of societies and the individuals living within those societies have existed in a state of collective and individual closure; heteronomous society is undoubtedly the historical norm. Indeed, only twice in history, according to Castoriadis, has a rupture occurred that broke through that state of closure and put the fundamental representations of the tribe into question, namely, "in Ancient Greece for the first time, then in Western Europe beginning at the end of the High Middle Ages." And both these ruptures were characterized by the simultaneous "birth of a public political space and by the creation of free enquiry, of unlimited interrogation."[136] Castoriadis argues therefore that the birth of philosophy and the birth of democracy are coincidental in ancient Greece. This is not to say that the pre-Socratic philosophers were explicitly democratic theorists, which they obviously were not. But "when Thales and others begin saying that what the Greeks tell are nice stories, but what *truly is [. . .],*" this critical procedure could, in principle, be generalized from the fundamental constituents of the physical world to the core legitimations of the tribe.

With respect to modern Europe, Castoriadis views Freud as one of the major figures in this historical struggle against closure, the "project of autonomy." Freud, like Plato, "made the most radical attempts to pursue the interrogation and critique of tacit presuppositions to the end . . . [and] never *gave up* this pursuit."[137] When he spoke of bringing the plague to America, Freud was indicating that his psychoanalytic investigations could not be confined to the purely psychological realm, but had devastating implications for the central myths of New World optimism, progressivism, and utilitarianism. Psychoanalysis put "into question . . . all instituted representations concerning the marvelous innocence of the child, the sexual life of man, his altruism and his goodness, his unalloyed and clearly defined belonging to one or the other sex etc. And representations concerning

sexuality are obviously a cornerstone of the edifice of the social institution."[138] With his discovery of a method for systematically interrogating the unconscious, Freud affected a fundamentally new breach
in the closure of heteronomous societies.

As I indicated above, one of the facts that makes Habermas's attack
on Castoriadis so perplexing is the affinity, indeed almost identity,
between his central notion of the "project of enlightenment" and
Castoriadis's idea of the "project of autonomy." Habermas wants to
answer the question that defined Max Weber's intellectual career—
that is, can the "cultural phenomena [which] have appeared" in the
West claim "*universal* significance and value"?—in the affirmative,
while, at the same time, avoiding the Eurocentrism, with its imperial-
ist implications, that plagued nineteenth-century philosophy of history and classical anthropology. He believes he has found a solution
in the formal, and therefore allegedly culturally neutral, phenomenon of decentration. His thesis is that Western rationality can claim
superiority over premodern worldviews in the very modest and restricted sense that the former's worldview has been decentered, that
is, differentiated into the cognitive-instrumental, moral-legal, and expressive-aesthetic spheres. I will only mention the problem of
whether formalism itself is not a specifically modern value that would
appear alien to most traditional societies. The real problem, however, lies elsewhere: on close inspection Habermas does not praise
that decentration itself on strictly formal grounds but because it, in
turn, makes possible the achievement of another, more substantive
good, namely, an "open society." Thus, despite his claim to argue for
the "project of enlightenment" and the relative superiority of modern Western rationality over premodern worldviews on strictly formal
grounds, ultimately, Habermas appeals to the same substantive ur-
norm as Castoriadis: "The dimension of 'closed' versus 'open' seems
to provide a context-independent standard for the rationality of
worldviews."[139] The institutionalization of the differentiation of an
external world, a social world, and an inner world and the forms of
cognitive-instrumental, moral-legal, and expressive-aesthetic cognition that correspond to them are a necessary precondition for the
penetration and criticism of the sacred realm that characterizes
closed societies. The autonomous critique of dogmatic tradition,

which is structurally impossible in closed societies, not the formal conditions that make it possible, constitutes the ultimate value. Furthermore, far from being a formal and "context-independent standard for the rationality of worldviews," the notion of an open society, insofar as it excludes all societies constructed on a sacred core, which is to say, the vast majority of societies that have existed historically, carries with it enormous substantive content. While the notion of an open or autonomous society must be defended, the immense problems involved in such a defense cannot be avoided by retreating into formalism.

The Progressive Uses of Regression

Freud chooses to conclude *The Interpretation of Dreams,* his magnum opus, with a consideration of the relation between dreams and the future—a topic that, needless to say, has an important bearing on utopian speculation. Dreams, he tells us, do not provide us with prophetic knowledge of the future, as many premodern cultures believed. Rather, "it would be truer to say . . . that they give us knowledge of the past. For dreams are derived from the past in every sense." He goes on to say, however, that "the ancient belief that dreams foretell the future is not wholly devoid of truth. By picturing our wishes as fulfilled, dreams are after all leading us into the future. But this future, which the dreams picture as the present, has been molded by this indestructible wish into a perfect likeness of the past."[140] The last sentence of this passage, of course, represents the immanentist-conservative (in the strict sense) strand of Freud's thinking at its strongest: there is no way to escape the indestructible power of the past. A different passage, however, in the same chapter, suggests another, less conservative (in the literal sense) approach to the tendency of the mind "to work in a *backward* direction"; indeed, it points to a certain progressive function for regressive phenomena. Freud distinguishes three terms: (1) A "need" is an "accumulation of tension" arising in the psyche owing to somatic processes "which need not concern us here."[141] (2) An "experience of satisfaction" is, by definition, the pleasurable relief of that tension, brought about by the intervention of an external agent. When an experience of satisfaction occurs, "a mnemic image" of that experience "remains associated thenceforward with the memory trace of the excitation produced by the need." (3) A "wish"[142] occurs on the basis of this "link" between the need and the memory of satisfaction. When a similar need occurs in the future, the association between the original need and the experience of satisfaction becomes cathected, and this representation of the need as fulfilled constitutes the wish. It is important to stress "that only a wish is able to set the [psychic] apparatus in motion"; for good or for ill, for creativity or pathology, a wish is the ultimate source of all psychic motion.

At the point where the wish has been cathected/represented, two courses become possible. The first is the short, regressive, and autistic path of the pleasure principle, that is, the attempt to establish what Freud terms "perceptual identity" in a hallucinatory manner: "An impulse of this kind is what we call a wish; the reappearance of the perception is the fulfillment of the wish; and the shortest path to fulfillment of the wish is a path leading directly from the excitation produced by the need to a complete cathexis of the perception."[143] The second course is the long path of the reality principle. At the point where the wish is cathected/represented, "the activity of a second system" (the ego) can intervene, "not allow mnemic cathexis to proceed" all the way backward "as far as perception" and confirm the wish as fulfilled. This second system would, in other words, arrest the backward movement of the psyche so that it would not proceed as far as hallucinatory wish fulfillment. It would instead initiate a progressive movement of the psyche by diverting "the excitation from the need along a roundabout path which ultimately, by means of voluntary movement, [would alter] the external world in such a way that it [would become] possible to arrive at a real perception of the object of satisfaction."[144] The backward motion of the psyche reversed, satisfaction of the wish can be sought through action in the public, intersubjectively mediated world. This process requires the "translation" of the private, imagistically encoded wish into an intersubjectively articulated form so that it can be pursued in the external world. The backward movement, however, and this must be stressed, is essential for retrieving the wish in the first place, for it is in this way that "the *recherche du temps perdu* becomes the vehicle of future liberation."

These considerations throw additional light on the two systematically related problems in Habermas's work that I have been trying to elucidate: the deficiencies of his Freud interpretation and his difficulty in assimilating the utopian impulses of the early Frankfurt school. The problems become particularly apparent in a somewhat unexpected forum, namely, the Habermas-Gadamer debate.[145] A central point of contention in this debate, which, in my opinion, remains one of the most important exchanges in postwar philosophy, is the interpretation of psychoanalysis. The controversy unfolds along two separate but thoroughly interrelated axes, the philosophical and the political. The philosophical content concerns "the scope of hermeneutical reflection," Gadamer's thesis being that, because of the unsurpassability of human linguisticality *(Sprachlichkeit),* the scope of hermeneutical reflection is universal:

The phenomenon of understanding, then, shows the universality of human linguisticality as a limitless medium that carries *everything* within it—not only the 'culture' that has been handed down to us through language, but absolutely everything—because everything (in the world and out of it) is included in the realm of 'understandings' and understandability in which we move.[146]

Against Gadamer's linguistic monism, Habermas raises the objection that language is not an ultimate, self-sufficient *factum,* unlimited in its scope, but is itself subject to, and constrained by, factors operating behind its back, for example, labor and power. Language is not only a medium of communication and truth but of miscommunication, which is systematically caused by the forces impinging on it. Habermas argues, therefore, against the hermeneutical claim to universality, that a framework is necessary that would include not only language but labor and domination as well. Such a framework would make possible a form of critique, as opposed to pure hermeneutics, that could explain the distortions caused by labor and power on understanding. And Habermas takes psychoanalysis, which explains the distortions caused by the unconscious on the self-understanding of the patient in order to eliminate those distortions, as a primary example of that form of critique; indeed, he maintains that psychoanalysis' particular brand of "explanatory understanding" serves to "refute the hermeneutic claim to universality."[147]

Gadamer, in turn, grants Habermas that there are indeed factors operating on language and that critique, similar to the one Habermas describes, is therefore necessary. His rejoinder is, and this is the crucial point, that as critique itself can only take place in language—as we have access to the forces acting on language only through the medium of language and do not have access to them in themselves—it is subordinate to hermeneutics, and hermeneutics retains its privileged status as the ultimate discipline: "Habermas sees the critique of ideology as the means of unmasking the 'deceptions of language.' But this critique, of course, is in itself a linguistic act of reflection."[148] This is parallel to the idea, which Habermas makes a centerpiece of his Freud interpretation, that as we have access to the unconscious only through its linguistic derivatives and not in itself, the unconscious must already be linguistic. My thesis is that, with respect to their interpretations of psychoanalysis, Gadamer is correct and Habermas cannot refute him. That is, despite Habermas's intentions, because of the truncated nature of his Freud interpretation, which, by denying the distinction between thing-representations and word-representations, thoroughly linguistifies the unconscious, he does not have the resources to refute Gadamer. Like Gadamer, he finally decides "in favor of the perspective of a lifeworld intersubjectively shared by participants" and gives up "biological or physicalistic third-person descriptions of the organic substratum."[149] Because he does not provide an alternative to take up the conceptual work of those third-person descriptions, that is, of the analyst who possesses knowledge of psychoanalytic theory and technique, Habermas loses the moment of explanatory science (and critique) altogether, and his position becomes structurally indistinguishable from Gadamer's. Ultimately, Habermas's linguistic monism—"an idealism of lingual life," as Ricoeur calls it—is as thoroughgoing as Gadamer's, and he does not grant the forces acting behind the back of language any real independence. The Otherness of the unconscious is in name only.

My thesis receives some added reinforcement from two unexpected claims of Gadamer's. The first is that "the unconscious motive does not represent a clear and fully articulable boundary for hermeneutical theory: it falls within the larger perimeter of hermeneutics," which means that psychoanalysis does not pose an ultimate challenge to the hermeneutical claim to universality. The second is that he learned this from Lacan, the other major linguistic reformulator of Freud, besides Habermas.[150] Even if the second claim is disingenuous, as some suspect, it is nevertheless thoroughly coherent.

The political correlate of the hermeneutical claim to universality is Gadamer's attempt to rehabilitate tradition. He criticizes the Enlightenment's own prejudice that all prejudices are objectionable in the sense of being "false judgments." He argues that, because of the finitude of human nature, all human understanding in the first instance presupposes prejudices, not necessarily in the pejorative sense of errors but in the sense of prejudgments *(Vorurteile)*.[151] Indeed, "the historicity of our existence entails that prejudices, in the literal sense of the word, constitute the initial directedness of our whole ability to experience. Prejudices are biases of our openness to the world. They are simply conditions whereby we experience something—whereby what we encounter says something to us."[152] To be sure, these initial prejudices may subsequently prove to be unfounded, but it was the mistake of the Enlightenment to assume that all prejudices are illegitimate and ideological as such. Likewise, it was also a mistake to assume that all forms of authority and tradition are simply ideologically disguised forms of power and domination. Gadamer argues that ultimately authority is not based on "blind obedience . . . but on recognition and knowledge. . . . The recognition of authority is always connected with the idea that what authority states is not irrational and arbitrary, but can be seen, in principle, to be true," for example, as in the case of the teacher, the superior, and the expert.[153] Finally, the Enlightenment's attempt to formulate a method that would escape the prejudices of tradition and be capable of objectifying tradition so as to distinguish between legitimate and illegitimate authority was itself an illusory prejudice of modernity, which violated the finitude of human understanding in a characteristically modern fashion.

Against these arguments, Habermas raises the following objection. Although Gadamer grants the distinction between legitimate authority based on "insight and knowledge" and illegitimate authority based on deception and coercion, because he repudiates all extrahermeneutical forms of systematic explanation, he cannot maintain the distinction. Since Descartes posited his evil genius, the move that gave modern philosophy its radicality, we moderns know too well that systematic deception is a possibility. Gadamer, however, makes no attempt to provide a means of distinguishing "insight and knowledge" on the one hand and deceptive insight or systematic delusion on the other. To put it differently, because of "the ontological priority of linguistic tradition over all forms of critique,"[154] he cannot identify when the preexisting consensus that constitutes tradition and makes understanding possible is in fact reasonable or "the result of pseudo-communication."[155] Habermas argues, therefore, that only a theory of systematically distorted communication that translates the Cartesian problematic of systematic deception into the linguistic notion of systematically distorted communication and that takes a regulative idea of undistorted communication as its point of reference can allow the distinction to be made. And he has, as is well known, attempted to develop this theory of systemically distorted communication through the development of a notion of the ideal-speech situation, in which all extralinguistic forms of coercion and power would be removed from the process of reaching understanding. A consensus reached under such conditions of unlimited and unconstrained communication would be, by definition, unprejudiced.

What, then, do these considerations have to do with our subject, the role of the transgressive wish and utopian speculation in psychoanalysis and Critical Theory? The answer is to be found in Ricoeur's reflections on the Habermas-Gadamer debate. In a characteristically nonsectarian gesture of hermeneutical charity and dialectical mediation, Ricoeur tries to develop a third position, which would preserve the truth content of the two positions in the by no means conclusive exchange. He begins with the observation that Gadamer's and Habermas's positions seem to offer two antinomian options for "the fundamental gesture of philosophy":

Is this gesture an avowal of the historical conditions to which all human understanding is subsumed under the reign of finitude? Or rather is it, in the last analysis, an act of defiance, a critical gesture, relentlessly repeated and indefinitely turned against 'false consciousness,' against communication which conceals the permanent exercise of domination and violence?

Ricoeur proceeds, however, to question the opposition itself: "But is it really so? Is it not the alternative itself that must be challenged?"[156] He attempts to sublate the apparent antinomy between a conservative hermeneutics of the past, oriented toward a consensus that precedes us, and an emancipatory critique of ideology, oriented toward a future consensus that is yet to be achieved, through an examination of their relations to temporality. In each case, the relation to past and future is not so unambiguous as it at first appears. First, with respect to Gadamer, we must state the obvious point, which nevertheless needs restating because of Gadamer's failure to appreciate it sufficiently: critique is itself a tradition, indeed our modern tradition. Ricoeur's central criticism of Gadamer, however, focuses on the major deficiency in Gadamer's retrospectively oriented, tradition-preserving hermeneutic. Like Habermas, he argues that it lacks the resources for critique and probes the hermeneutical tradition to determine where such resources might be extrapolated from it. He locates one such point in the consequences of the move from the older romantic hermeneutics to the newer hermeneutics of the text. Whereas the older romantic hermeneutics attempted to directly recapture the past, the subjective intentions of the author behind the text, textual hermeneutics seeks to discover "the sort of *world* opened up by" the text or the "mode of being unfolded in front of it." Even to understand a text, one must *"redescribe"* it in terms of its possibilities. The encounter with the text therefore requires imaginative playfulness on the part of the reader—and Ricoeur specifically praises Gadamer's "magnificent pages on *play*"—not only with respect to "mode[s] of possibility," the "power-to-be" contained in the text itself, but with respect to the reader's own subjectivity as well. To unlock the possible worlds inherent in the text, the reader must "unrealize" himself or herself and permit the "imaginative variation of [the] ego" to emerge. "The metamorphosis of the world in play is also the playful metamorphosis of the ego." Ricoeur's thesis is that textual hermeneutics is expanded into the critique of ideology with the addition of the "subversive force of the imaginary."[157] This means that the given reality can be measured—criticized, if you will—against the possibilities of different (individual and collective) realities envisaged by the imaginary.

While true, the point is sorely inadequate; the free play of the imaginary, though absolutely essential, can only be a first step in the critique. The products of the imaginary, the imagos of a different reality, once envisaged, must themselves be scrutinized to determine which are justifiable and workable images and which are not, which are defendable and undefendable phantasms, as it were. The normative question that plagues hermeneutics remains unresolved.

Ricoeur's criticisms of Habermas's future-oriented "eschatology of nonviolence,"[158] as one might expect, move in the opposite direction. Whereas Habermas, through his regulative ideal of communication free from domination, can answer the normative question, that is, can specify the conditions under which a legitimate consensus could be formulated and under which an imago could be validated, that consensus runs the risk of being empty. As we have noted, this "emptiness" is, in one sense, intentional and results from the deliberate proceduralism, which is to say, formalism, of his position. We can grant Habermas his absolutely legitimate apprehensions about the dangers of prescriptive utopianism and his insistence that "an equivalent for what was once meant by the idea of the good life" cannot be inferred "from the formal concept of reason" and nevertheless raise the following question: where would the (individual and collective) contents come from that would be debated in a future, nonviolent democratic decision-making process, the imagos of a different order, and how would they enter that process? Except for his discussion of the resources of meaning sedimented in the lifeworld,[159] Habermas fails to take up this question in a systematic fashion. Ricoeur, on the other hand, has a strong answer:

The task of the hermeneutics of tradition is to remind the critique of ideology that man can project his emancipation and anticipate an unlimited and unconstrained communication only on the basis of the creative reinterpretation of cultural heritage. . . . He who is unable to reinterpret his past may also be incapable of projecting concretely his interest in emancipation.[160]

The fact that the memory of past experiences of emancipation such as the Exodus would provide the material for those imagos and that the eradication of those memories would most likely mean the end of an interest in emancipation leads Ricoeur to reject the false "antinomy between an ontology of prior understanding and an eschatology of freedom . . . : as if it were necessary to choose between reminiscence and hope!"[161] Progress, on both the individual and the collective level, does not proceed directly, in a rectilinear fashion, but through the circuitous reworking of the past.

It will be objected, no doubt, that Habermas's scheme, precisely because it is formal and empty, can accommodate this retrospective content. This is precisely the point as well as the problem: it can only accommodate, it is only compatible with, these phenomena. Because of his uneasiness with regressive phenomena, the workings of the imaginary and of the relation between the imaginary and rational discourse do not enter systematically into his analysis. To be sure, the early Habermas, the Habermas of *Knowledge and Human Interests,* in language reminiscent of Adorno's notion of exact fantasy, spoke of the good as an exact fantasy: "The 'good' is neither a convention nor an essence, but the result of fantasy. But it must be fantasied so exactly that it corresponds to and articulates a fundamental interest: the interest in that measure of emancipation that historically is objectively possible under given and manipulable conditions."[162] The point is correct. However, as I have tried to show, because he denies the distinction between word-representations and thing-representations and overly linguistifies the unconscious, Habermas, as early as *Knowledge and Human Interests,* lacks the theoretical resources to conceptualize fantasy adequately.

5

Sublimation: A Frontier Concept

A Lacuna in Psychoanalytic Theory

Thus far I have attempted to address a number of problems from within what can be called, broadly speaking, the Freudian paradigm, which is characterized by a particular task. At the same time as Freudian psychoanalysis espouses a genetic theory of the ego and the more socialized products of the human mind—including psychoanalytic theory and practice—it also wants to claim, indeed, must claim, a degree of freedom for the ego and those products vis-à-vis the genetic, that is, infantile, instinctual, and unconscious, material from which they arose. Without that degree of freedom—note, I do not say absolute freedom—it becomes impossible to speak of anything like objectivity or validity. Contrary to the vulgarized view, Freudian theory does not seek to debunk the achievements of the human mind by demonstrating their genetic origins; rather it seeks to explicate those achievements in light of the genetic conditions from which they arose. In order to account for the process through which the genetic material is transformed and that degree of freedom achieved, the notion of sublimation, or its conceptual equivalent, is necessitated by the logic of the entire undertaking. As Laplanche and Pontalis have observed, "in the psycho-analytic literature the concept of sublimation is frequently called upon; the idea indeed answers a basic need of the Freudian doctrine and it is hard to see how it could be dispensed with."[1] We have noted also that, with the discovery of the pervasiveness of unconscious forces in mental life, the question of distortion *(Entstellung)* became a central epistemological problem for psychoanalytic theory. Again, a notion of sublimation or its conceptual equivalent is required to explain how those distorting forces can be sufficiently absorbed so that they do not nullify the more advanced forms of mentation.

Clinically, the significance of sublimation is twofold. From the side of the patient, it would be difficult to conceptualize an alternative fate for the drives that are unloosed from their habitual moorings in the course of an analysis, and hence the nature and course of the "cure," without a theory of sublimation. And from the other side of the couch, only a concept of the analyst's sublimation can allow us to identify what he or she has to offer to the treatment beyond countertransference to the patient.

Turning to the arguments of this book, I have discussed a number of problems, all of which point in the direction of a theory of sublimation for their solution. We began with a discussion of the ubiquitousness of the perverse-utopian wish in psychic life and asked what an alternative disposition for it might be, besides the unmediated idealization of transgression, on the one hand, and conformity to constrictive normality, on the other. We also considered a whole nexus of concepts—the free intercourse between the systems, the nonviolent unity of the self, and mindfulness of nature in the subject—in an attempt to provide more specificity to that third alternative. What each of these concepts represents, I would maintain, is an attempt to delineate "*another relation* between the conscious and the unconscious," which would comprise "*another attitude* of the subject with respect to himself or herself," to use Castoriadis's formulations. As such, each concept also requires a theory of sublimation to account for the process through which that different relation could be established.

To consider another closely connected problem, a concept of sublimation is needed to counter the postmodern critique of reason and the subject. As we will see, insofar as it is formulated with the aid of psychoanalysis, that critique consists in a totalization of the genetic point of view; it maintains that ego and reason do not, to any significant extent, transcend the conditions of their origins but are, to use

Lacan's term, simply effects of those conditions. Against this, I will try to show that a theory of sublimation, because it detotalizes the genetic point of view, can counter that critique. Moreover, if the goal for philosophy remains, as Merleau-Ponty argued, the integration of the irrational into an expanded conception of rationality, then sublimation is a central process through which that integration proceeds.

Finally, a theory of sublimation can be of some assistance in shielding the psychoanalytic project, and Critical Theory after the suspension of the utopian motif, from the soullessness of one-sided enlightenment. Already in the *Phaedrus,* Socrates, who was certainly no opponent of enlightenment, "has no time for" the arid demythologizers, the sophists who simply debunk the traditional myths by reducing them to natural causes. Against the sobriety of an overly rationalistic enlightenment, he argues that without the proper type of mania—a "divine" as opposed to an "evil" mania—poetic creativity, erotic life, and even knowledge would be deprived of their vitality.[2] Similarly, Ricoeur raises the crucial question for the psychoanalytic project itself: what is the fate of "the mytho-poetic core of imagination" after the psychoanalytic *askesis* (ascetic discipline) in disillusionment and the disconsolate acceptance of Ananke?[3] I would answer that only a theory of sublimation that could delineate an alternative deployment of unconscious material—that is, of the imaginary—and could explain how the ego could in fact deepen its relation with the id could satisfactorily answer this question. Without such a theory, psychoanalysis would indeed stand condemned of abstract disenchantment—of "joyless reformism," as it were.

Laplanche and Pontalis also point out, however, that while an idea of sublimation appears indispensable for Freudian theory, "the lack of a coherent theory of sublimation remains one of the lacunae in psycho-analytic thought."[4] Already in Freud's writings, where the term is demanded by the overall logic of his position and is adduced at crucial junctures, this indispensable theoretical term was never elaborated adequately; it remains, as Ricoeur puts it, both "fundamental and episodic" in Freud's thinking.[5]

The Totalization of the Hermeneutics of Suspicion

Ricoeur introduced the term "the masters of suspicion"[6] to refer to Marx, Nietzsche, and Freud and the form of critique they developed to unmask the illusory dimension of a number of our mental products, such as morality, religion, law, art, and so on. This hermeneutics of suspicion employed a genetic mode of explanation that sought to demonstrate that the manifest content of these mental products was in fact the epiphenomena of a more fundamental, latent substratum: that is, material conditions for Marx, the biologically rooted will to power for Nietzsche, and drive-related wishes for Freud. Two of these masters of suspicion, Marx and Freud, relying on nineteenth-century conceptions of positivism, remained relatively confident—if not downright complacent—about the scientific validity of the theories they employed to conduct their critiques of illusion and never attempted to subject their own standpoints, which were themselves products of the mind, to systematic critique. In other words they did not turn the weapons of suspicion against themselves.[7] Nietzsche, the third master of suspicion, however, did make such a move and, in this respect, not only differed fundamentally from the others but prefigured much of the current, postmodern discourse. In "a final," self-cannibalizing "unmasking,"[8] Nietzsche was willing to embrace the consequence that his standpoint is as radically perspectival as all those positions he seeks to unmask—and every bit as contingent and no more privileged. And, as I indicated, this sort of "radicalized critique of reason,"[9] which has become "[suspicious] of the masters of suspicion"[10] and attempts to debunk them with their own critical weapons, has become prevalent today and can be observed in the various "postmodern" philosophers who have grown deeply skeptical about the foundations of Western rationality and science. Indeed, suspicion about suspicion, which amounts to the totalization of suspicion, can be taken as one of the hallmarks of the postmodern turn.

As Foucault has written in one of the canonical texts of this movement, "It is with these techniques of interpretation, in return, that we must question these interpreters who were Freud, Nietzsche, and Marx." He describes this process as a "perpetual play of mirrors," which can arrive at the "breaking point of interpretation" where "the interpreter himself"—that is, the practitioner of suspicion—disappears.[11] Foucault is quite explicit, as the reference to mirrors already suggests, about the fact that this dissolution of the subject tends toward madness:

What is in question at the breaking point of interpretation, in this convergence of interpretation toward a point that renders it impossible, could well be something like the experience of madness—experience against which Nietzsche struggled and by which he was fascinated, experience against which Freud himself, all his life, had wrestled, not without anguish. This experience of madness would be the penalty for a movement of interpretation which approached the infinity of its center, and which collapsed, calcinated.[12]

For Foucault, however, the specter of madness is—at least from the philosophical point of view—not in itself problematic. On the contrary, it is programmatically welcomed. He maintains that the recognition of the impossibility of the transcendental project, by means of which the limits and legitimacy of the philosophical subject, reason and language, were to have been simultaneously established, is "one of the fundamental structures of contemporary thought"[13] and that this recognition compels the philosophical subject to "transgress" those limits and to seek the extrarational "opening where [rationality's] being surges forth, where it is already completely lost, completely overflowing itself."[14] Foucault argues that "the mad philosopher" discovers "the transgression of his philosophical being" not as extrinsic, "not outside his language . . . , but at the inner core of its possibilities."[15] Pushed to the limits, the transcendental program leads to its own dissolution, and that dissolution, in turn, raises the specter of madness.

The conjunction between the collapse of the transcendental program and the threat of madness is, moreover, consistent with, if the reverse of, the inaugural experience of modern philosophy. Bernstein correctly observes that the quest for indubitable foundations for knowledge, introduced into modern philosophy by Descartes, was motivated by the attempt to combat anxieties of an essentially psychotic nature. Descartes formulated his philosophy in a "hyperbolic" confrontation with a distinctly paranoid possibility of delusion that is so thoroughly totalized and systematic that it cannot even be recognized as delusion, which is to say, in confrontation with the possibility that dreams and waking life, psychosis and nonpsychosis, delirium and rational thought cannot be distinguished from one another.[16] It is also undoubtedly true, as Hannah Arendt has written, that this anxiety, indeed this nightmare, was intimately connected with the loss of the traditional security and authority of the medieval worldview—a loss that bares comparison with end-of-the-world fantasies that often accompany the onset of clinical psychosis—and the rise of the modern, scientific worldview, in which the testimony of one's senses and everyday experience could no longer be trusted.[17] Concerning this "Cartesian anxiety," Bernstein writes:

> Reading the *Meditations* as a journey of the soul helps us to appreciate that Descartes' search for a foundation or Archimedean point is more than a device to solve metaphysical and epistemological problems. It is the quest for some fixed point, some stable rock upon which we can secure our lives against the vicissitudes that constantly threaten us. The specter that hovers in the background of this journey is not just radical epistemological skepticism but the dread of madness and chaos where nothing is fixed, where we can neither touch bottom nor support ourselves on the surface. With a chilling clarity Descartes leads us with an apparent and ineluctable necessity to a grand and seductive Either/Or. *Either* there is some support for our being, a fixed foundation for our knowledge, *or* we cannot escape the forces of darkness that envelop us with madness, with intellectual and moral chaos.[18]

Despite its apparent philosophical radicalism and opposition to foundationalism, postmodern skepticism is often still enthralled by this seemingly ineluctable "Either/Or." As we have seen with Foucault, it is assumed that *either* strong foundations exist *or* we are confronted with madness; as the collective historico-philosophical learning process has taught us that strong foundations are unobtainable, madness is in fact the outcome. I would argue, however, that a still more radical alternative exists to the uncompromising "Either/Or" and that it can be provided by a theory of sublimation.

Let me argue my point by considering some recent developments in the philosophy of science. A fundamental tenet of the tradition that, prior to the Kuhnian upheaval, had played the dominate role in Anglo-American philosophy of science can be traced to Kant's distinction between questions of fact, *quid facti,* and questions of legitimacy or validity, *quid juris*.[19] What might be called the Kantian tradition in the philosophy of science has always insisted that a sharp distinction—a stringent "Either/Or"—be maintained between these two questions and that the level of a theory's verification be kept completely insulated from considerations concerning the factual conditions that generated that theory, that is, the level of discovery.[20]

An example that is often adduced to illustrate this distinction concerns the discovery of geometry in Egypt. The Egyptians discovered certain geometrical laws empirically and pragmatically, through trial-and-error efforts to reidentify their fields, each year, after the flooding of the Nile. It is argued, however, that the validity of those geometric laws has nothing to do with the empirical motivations and practices that led to their discovery nor with their pragmatic usefulness; validity can only be established by completely independent procedures, namely, the proofs of Euclid. The Kantian insistence on a strict separation between genesis and validity is born out of the fear that the introduction of genetic questions (historicism, sociologism, psychologism, anthropologism, economism, and so on) into the consideration of a theory's validity would have two undesirable consequences. First, it could jeopardize the validity of that particular theory—that is, the theory could not be maintained to be valid unconditionally, independent of the contingent conditions that produced it. Second, it could threaten the very notion of validity.

The Kantian tradition tended to view any attempt to comprehend theories genetically—and a fortiori the masters of suspicion—as a threat to the very notion of scientific validity that could open the floodgates of irrationalism.[21] While their apprehension was not entirely unfounded, the Kantians unfortunately dealt with it in a phobic manner: that is to say, rather than attempting to understand the complex and fascinating relationship between genesis and validity—to think "genesis and validity in their simultaneous unity and difference"[22]—they simply suppressed questions of genesis in their investigations, for fear of losing the concept of validity altogether.

However, with the publication of Kuhn's *Structure of Scientific Revolutions*,[23] which demonstrated the uneliminable role that historical and political, which is to say, empirico-genetic, factors inevitably play in the nodal episodes in the development of science, and with the development of the "postempiricist" philosophy of science that followed from it, the very thing the Kantian tradition sought to prevent came to pass: a recognition that the question of the validity of theories cannot unequivocally be separated from the question of their genesis; the two are unavoidably intermingled—especially in the human sciences. This, in turn, helped to engender not only the surge of interest in the history of science over the past two decades—of which the dramatic proliferation of Freud studies is certainly a part—but the postmodern critique of scientific rationality as well. However, where the old philosophy of science tended to exclude the question of genesis from its investigations completely, the new history, anthropology, and politics of science is in danger of losing sight of the question of validity in a bad infinity of research into the empirical interests and power stratagems that produced particular theories and disciplines. Owing to a central and productive tension in his position, Freud has become something of a crucial case for this entire issue.

As he is both a major figure in, and a defender of, the Western scientific tradition and, at the same time, a master of suspicion, who opened up the Pandora's box of the unconscious, psychic reality, and transference, Freud is a favorite target for the totalized critique of reason.[24] On the one hand, he can be viewed as a champion of the Enlightenment, who sought to extend the scientific conquest of nature to a domain that had previously remained uncharted and to expand the very notion of rationality in the process. It can also be argued, on the other hand, that contrary to his intentions and self-understanding, Freud's discovery of the unconscious unleashed a process that engulfed the very "project of enlightenment" and undermined the notion of scientific rationality he was seeking to advance. In this case, the critics of the Enlightenment—often through a "psychoanalytic" critique of psychoanalytic theory and practice—use Freud's discoveries in order to subvert his intentions; in short, they read Freud against Freud. The attempt is made to show that Freud's rationalism was a compromise formation that cannot be maintained against the consequences of his own discoveries.[25] Moreover, it is sometimes argued in this context that Freud, the bourgeois, did not have the courage to pursue the meaning of his discoveries to their ultimate conclusion but tried to contain their most subversive consequences within the framework of nineteenth-century positivist science—a positivism that was, in fact, challenged by those discoveries, and that can only be viewed as extremely crude by contemporary standards of scientific reflection.

Thus, for example, on the theoretical level, Samuel Weber argues that Lacan and Derrida "have put into question the status of Freud's discourse itself . . . by posing the problem of a theory that, in deriving the functions of consciousness from the conflictual dynamics of the unconscious, cannot but dislocate the conceptions of cognition and of truth on which theory has traditionally depended." Weber argues that the identification of the genetic sources of the theory in the unconscious of the theorist and the distortions *(Entstellungen)* those sources produce in the theoretical product—which are parallel to the distortions the dream work produces in the manifest content of the dream—jeopardize the validity of the theory itself, at least as it has traditionally been conceived. Granting the existence of these distorting forces, we must, nevertheless, ask the question that Weber never addresses: how does it remain possible—and it must remain possible—after Freud, to distinguish between a theory, which, admittedly, can never entirely "escape the effects of what it endeavors to think,"[26] and a dream, a neurotic symptom, a lapsus, or any other psychic production, which cannot claim cognitive validity? Weber shows what a dream and a theory have in common but not what makes them different. To be sure, after Freud's intervention in the history of rationality, "the conceptions of cognition and of truth" will necessarily be different from those of the "inherited logic-ontology."[27] But they will remain (modified) conceptions of cognition and truth nonetheless. It is this reconstructed concept of cognition and truth that does not appear in the postmodern reading of Freud.

Similarly, I would maintain that such ideas can often be discerned behind much of the recent "pathographical"[28] scrutiny of Freud's biography and the *Case Histories*—especially that of Dora—which seeks to uncover Freud's own psychopathology and countertransference to his patients in order to demonstrate how they distort his theorizing and clinical practice. While I in no way mean to deny that there is much to be criticized in the *Case Histories*—especially

Dora—the tacit assumption behind this scrutiny is often that, in order for psychoanalytic theory and clinical practice not to be invalidated, Freud must be shown to have achieved the status of a disembodied, transcendental thinking machine, from whom all genetic traces of childhood, the unconscious, and impulse have been eradicated.

It should be pointed out that these endeavors represent a form of Kantianism in reverse: like Kantianism, they assume, as Habermas has put it, that "the devil resides in the internal relationships between genesis and validity" and that, if the validity of a theory is to be defended, that "devil must be exorcised." [29] However, whereas the Kantians think that such an exorcism can be exhaustively carried out, the postmodern skeptics do not. To put it differently: they accept the Kantian requirement for a solution, namely, the absolute segregation of questions of validity from question of fact; then, in order to debunk the theory in question, and perhaps the question of validity in general, they attempt to demonstrate that that requirement cannot be fulfilled. The alternative strategy I propose contests the Kantian requirement of an absolute separation between genesis and validity itself, at least in its purist form. In its place, following Castoriadis, I will argue for a theory of sublimation that would attempt to elucidate the process through which genetic material, with all its contingency, privacy, and particularity, is transformed into cultural objects—paintings, political constitutions, mathematical proofs, musical compositions, scientific theories, or what have you—that can rightfully claim public validity in their respective domains. Freud, we should note, counted this phenomenon of transformation among "the most fascinating secrets of human nature." [30]

At least the outlines of such a theory are suggested in Freud's monograph on Leonardo da Vinci, which, after all, is the closest thing he wrote to a treatise on sublimation. Strange as it may sound, "Leonardo" can be viewed as Freud's analogue to the *Critique of Pure Reason* in the specific sense that in it Freud, at least by implication, explicates the conditions of the possibility of the validity of psychoanalysis as his "science." Indeed, the reader has the impression that, in certain important respects, in talking about Leonardo—for whose intellectual independence he undoubtedly "felt a special affection" [31] and affinity—Freud is in fact talking about himself. Freud, it will be recalled, seeks to explain a particular "concurrence" in Leonardo's life, namely between the "atrophy of his sexual life," on the one hand, and "his overpowerful instinct for research,"[32] on the other. Freud's thesis is that Leonardo "had merely converted his passion into a thirst for knowledge"; Leonardo, in short, "has investigated instead of loving."[33] Freud argues that, because of the coincidence between an especially affectionate and beautiful young mother, who stimulated his sexual curiosity, on the one hand, and an absent father, who was not present to prohibit it, on the other, Leonardo did not have to repress that curiosity, which is perhaps strongest in "the most gifted" individuals. Rather, he was able to preserve it for later sublimation into his mature scientific research.

Freud enumerates three possible outcomes for the curiosity and "research," which are characteristic features of the phases of infantile sexuality, after the "wave of energetic sexual repression" that terminates that phase sets in. In the first case, "research shares the fate of sexuality": both are inhibited, and "the free activity of intelligence may be limited for the whole of the subject's lifetime." In the second case, while "intellectual development is sufficiently strong to resist the sexual repression which has hold of it," it does not emerge unscathed from the struggle with repression: thinking itself becomes a substitute for sexual activity and assumes a "compulsive brooding" character. Hamlet is obviously the prototype. Furthermore, "the interminable character" of this sort of thinking—to which Freud would no doubt compare the interminable ruminations of perennial philosophy—results from its origins in infantile sexuality; young researchers, because their "own sexual constitution has not yet reached the point of being able to produce babies," cannot answer the question they are investigating—"where do babies come from?"—and thereby bring their research to a fruitful conclusion. Finally, "in virtue of a special disposition . . . which is the rarest and most perfect," the third type—of which Leonardo is a "model instance"—"escapes both inhibition of thought and neurotic compulsive thinking." Because of "the complete difference in the underlying psychical process," which to this day has never been satisfactorily spelled out, "the instinct can operate freely in the service of intellectual interest."[34]

Freud, in effect, fashions an unlikely marriage of Kant and Little Hans, by tracing the capacity to think for oneself, the Kantian demand of the Enlightenment, to the fate of infantile sexual curiosity. Freud dates the origins of intellectual independence and skepticism toward external authority, which was no less strong in him than it was in Leonardo, from a particular experience of disillusionment, namely, when children are lied to about the nature of sexuality. After "they energetically reject the fable of the stork," children "often feel in serious opposition to adults," are loath to forgive them for the betrayal, and begin to "investigate along their own lines."[35] With respect to Leonardo, then, owing in part to the particular familial constellation of his childhood, he was to become "the first modern natural scientist," which is to say, "the first man since the time of the Greeks to probe the secrets of nature while relying solely on observation and his own judgment." (Cf. Freud's equally groundbreaking ability to "probe the secrets" of inner nature "scientifically.") Indeed, Leonardo's maxim, " *'He who appeals to authority when there is a difference of opinion works with his memory rather than with his reason,'* " is prototypical of the Enlightenment outlook. Freud interprets Leonardo's teaching that "authority should be looked down on and that the imitation of the 'Ancients' should be repudiated" by tracing it to the "concrete individual experience" of Leonardo's childhood. Whereas for "most human beings . . ." the need for support from an authority of some sort is so compelling that their world begins to totter if that authority is not present, Leonardo, because of the scientifically propitious conditions of his *vaterlos*[36] childhood "could dispense with that support." The "boldness and independence" of Leonardo's "later scientific research," in short, presupposed "the existence of infantile sexual researches uninhibited by his father, and was a prolongation of them with the sexual element excluded." (We will question below the manner and extent to which the sexual element is excluded.) "In the highest sublimation attainable by man," Leonardo was able to transform the experience of his childhood, in which "authority simply correspond[ed] to his father, and nature [to] the tender and kindly mother who had nourished him," into his mature scientific achievements.[37]

Interestingly enough, Anzieu, in his study of Freud's self-analysis, observes a different but nonetheless similar "concurrence" with

Freud's own life. Comparing Freud to his Victorian male contemporaries, Anzieu notes: "While libertine in their acts, [those contemporaries] were inhibited in thought and speech. Freud, on the other hand, was reserved when it came to doing, and transgressive when it came to knowing." Anzieu goes on to ask, "What economy of the psyche can have supported him in this position?"[38] He argues that Freud, like Leonardo, "did not need to resort to neurotic repression in order to control" his sexual instinct; "it was enough for him to represent it to himself and to identify it." He refers to this "particular type of sublimation," in which the sexual instinct achieves "knowledge of its workings as an instinct," as "reflexive" in contrast to the more common "expressive" type of sublimation that can be found in the arts, for example.[39] Indeed, Anzieu's book itself can be seen as a model for the type of research I am suggesting. It is a monumental investigation of the process of reflexive sublimation by means of which Freud grabbed hold of and articulated the unconscious forces that were determining him from behind (or below) and laid the foundations of psychoanalysis. Furthermore, while Anzieu presents a thoroughly nonidealized picture of Freud, which does not underrate the extent of Freud's considerable neurosis in the least, it is thoroughly nonpathographic in its intent. Unlike the pathographer—and the Foucauldian genealogist—who "seeks to blacken the radiant and drag the sublime into the dust,"[40] Anzieu seeks to make the "the great man's achievements intelligible,"[41] as Freud himself had done with Leonardo.[42]

Furthermore, a pathographic approach not only presents a valet's point of view, which does nothing to distinguish the great individual from the rest of us, but also involves a conceptual difficulty, which, in fact, is simply the mirror opposite of the hagiographic. In attempting to reduce individuals' achievements to their pathology, pathographers leave themselves exposed to the tu quoque objection: the tables can always be turned on them, and the validity of their pathographical critique can be reduced to their own pathology, thus opening an infinite regress of gossip and countergossip. For example, the defender of Freud could easily point to the element of disappointment in a formerly idealized object, in whom "no vestige of human weakness or imperfection"[43] could be tolerated, so palpable in Masson and Swayles, in order to discredit their critiques of Freud.

Such a move, however, not only would be uncollegial but would be conceptually untenable: at some point the arguments must be considered on their own grounds or this infinite regress of gossip and countergossip, which is still scandalized by the ubiquitousness and unruliness of the instincts in human affairs, is opened up with no possibility of adjudication. For the postmodern skeptic, of course, this infinite regress simply makes the point: there is no firm ground to stand on, the skeptic's included.

A Reason for the Lacuna

Ricoeur and Castoriadis point to the same basic reason for the lack of an adequate theory of sublimation in psychoanalysis: the phenomenon of sublimation cannot be satisfactorily accounted for exclusively on intrapsychic grounds. Sublimation is, as Loewald notes, like "pulling oneself up by one's bootstraps,"[44] and the individual does not have the resources available for this "imperative urge and impossible task" from within the intrapsychic realm alone but must draw on extrapsychic social reality as well. A theory of sublimation would, by its very nature, overstep the bounds of the strictly intrapsychic standpoint. Most analysts, perhaps out of the legitimate fear of retreating, like so many of the revisionist schools of psychotherapy, from Freud's momentous discovery of psychic reality, have been reluctant to take this step.

Ricoeur, for example, argues that the Freudian archeology of the subject, which analyzes the subject into its genetic components, cannot stand on its own but must be supplemented by a Hegelian-style teleology of the cultural realm, which is to say, a realm that obeys a logic independent of that of the intrapsychic domain. A theory of sublimation, then, would attempt to explain how those genetic components become linked up with the matrix of cultural objects: it would, in other words, provide "a suitable theoretical instrument to render intelligible the absolutely primal dialectic between desire and the other than desire."[45] Ricocur admits, however, that such a procedure steps "completely outside of a psychoanalytic problematic." Freud, he points out, "expressly stated that the discipline he founded is not a synthesis but an analysis, that is, a process of breaking down into elements and of tracing back to origins, and that psychoanalysis is not to be completed by psychosynthesis."[46] Although it might be objected that Freud's suspicion of synthesis belongs predominately to his prestructural writings,[47] and although it should be pointed out that already in 1911 Freud stated it was time to bring "the psychological significance of the real world into the structure of our theories,"[48] Ricoeur's basic point is nevertheless well taken: although analysis qua analysis "cannot be *understood,* [even] in its strictly 'regressive' structure, except by contrast with a teleology of consciousness . . . which analysis intrinsically refers to,"[49] it cannot provide that teleology with its own internal resources but must look elsewhere. Furthermore, in a quasi-quantitative argument, Ricoeur maintains that the very *"disproportion"*[50] between the internal, intrapsychic transformations of desire, which are relatively few, and the large variety of forms sublimation can assume indicates that the object of sublimation must come from the outside and that the process cannot be exhaustively accounted for in terms of "the economics of desire"[51] alone.

Likewise, Castoriadis maintains that psychoanalysis can of necessity provide only a "partial" account of many of its most fundamental concepts—for example, "the establishment of the reality principle," "the resolution of the Oedipus Complex," or "the sublimation of the drives"—because these concepts "have a double existence, being rooted also in a field which lies beyond the scope of psychoanalysis, the social-historical field."[52] Thus he argues, for example, that psychoanalysis cannot provide an account of the incest taboo, which is an extrapsychic social institution, but only of the way the psyche encounters it, as already preconstituted, and more or less adequately internalizes it. He asserts, moreover, that Freud's "epigones have allowed the terrain" delineated by the concept of sublimation "to lie fallow," precisely because an adequate exploration of the concept would entail an excursion out of the intrapsychic into the social-historical realm.[53] In order to combat "the sociological lethargy of psychoanalysts and the psychoanalytic lethargy of sociologists,"[54] that is, to combat the reduction of the social reality to psychic reality and vice versa, Castoriadis posits the existence of two equally primordial and irreducible realms: the social imaginary, which includes institutions, language, and history; and the psychic imaginary, which, as we have seen, consists primarily in fantasies. Again, a theory of sublimation would account for the mediation between these two irreducible realms.

Freud's most sustained efforts to describe how a social institution derives from the dynamics of intrapsychic life were, of course, directed at religion. The reductionistic shortcomings of his approach are encapsulated in his well-known formula that whereas "obsessive-compulsive neurosis" constitutes "an individual religiosity," religion can be viewed as "a universal obsessive-compulsive neurosis." [55] By equating the two, however, Freud utterly fails to appreciate the significance of the fact that the first is "individual" and the second "universal." As the "individual" sphere and the "universal" sphere are structured according to different principles, this makes for a qualitative difference between the two realms. While religion undoubtedly fulfills a function "in the individual unconscious," all the psyche can produce on its own are "private phantasies, not institutions." Even the prophet who successfully founds a new religion and who, perhaps more than anyone, can successfully impose his or her private fantasies on a significant number of individuals, must articulate his or her vision with public symbols. For the prophet to succeed, moreover, "favourable social conditions must have shaped, over an indefinite area, the unconscious of [those] individuals and have prepared them for these 'good tidings.' " Otherwise, prophetic "discourse [would] remain a personal hallucination or the credo of an ephemeral sect." Castoriadis points out, furthermore, that the prophet does not create the new religion ex nihilo but that "all the religions whose genesis we know are transformations of earlier religions," which is to say, they are parasitical on preexisting institutions. Indeed, even the myth of origins that Freud presents in *Totem and Taboo* does not pertain to what is originary but presupposes previously existing social institutions: "the murder of the father is not the inaugural act of society but a reply to castration (and what is the latter if not an anticipated parrying?), just as the community of brothers, as an institution succeeding the absolute power of the father, is a revolution rather than initial institution." [56] The instituted is, in short, already there.

The interaction between the intrapsychic sphere and the cultural sphere in the process of sublimation might be elucidated if we apply to it Freud's analogy of the entrepreneur and the capitalist, which he employed to explain the relationship between the dream wish and the day's residue.[57] My idea is the following: what I have been calling the genetic or archeological material, which is analogous to the private dream wish, could be seen as the industrious entrepreneur who is constantly on the lookout for opportunities through which to realize his or her ideas. The public matrix of cultural objects—"the noematic correlates of sublimation"[58]—which is divided into different disciplinary domains, could be seen as the capitalist who provides those opportunities. The difference between the matrix of cultural objects and the day's residue, which is its analogue, however, is that the former is far more determinate: unlike the day's residue, that matrix does not provide relatively unstructured material on which the entrepreneur can opportunistically impose ideas with little restraint, as he or she can in the case of hallucinatory wish fulfillment. Rather, each domain of that matrix possesses a highly determinate grammar of its own, as it were, which is at once resistant and supple. It is resistant in that every domain at a given stage of its development prescribes certain rules and therefore possibilities as well as limits of possibilities those private thoughts must accept if they are to become valid public expressions:[59] "If dreams remain a private expression lost in the solitude of sleep, it is because they lack the mediation of the artisan's work that embodies the fantasy in a solid material and communicates it to a public."[60] But it is also supple in that, once mastered and internalized, that grammar provides the means for shaping and transforming those private thoughts into articulate expressions. Part of the distinct pleasure associated with creativity results from having made that suppleness one's own. It should be pointed out, moreover, that geniuses are precisely those individuals who transform the *"rules* and *norms"* of the grammar of their discipline so that "other figures of the thinkable," seeable, hearable, and so on, come into relief.[61] A theory of sublimation, then, would attempt to comprehend, as it were, the interaction between the entrepreneur and the capitalist in the terms I have been describing.

Let me try to make my point with an illustration. Mary Gedo, in her admirable book on Picasso,[62] gives an account of the creation of *Guernica,* undeniably one of the most important works of the twentieth century in which crucial personal, political and aesthetic material is condensed. The composition was preceded by what Picasso himself described as the worst period of his life.[63] Although he had finally been able to disentangle himself from the relationship with his wife, Olga, and affect a painful separation from her, he had less luck with his mistress, Maria-Thérèse. Despite the fact that his love, which had been predominately physical to begin with, for this, his most ordinary and least challenging mistress, had dissipated, he was nevertheless unable to leave her. His rage at not being able to separate was compounded when she gave birth to a little girl, which, Gedo argues, rekindled all the fury Picasso had experienced at the birth of his sister at the age of three. Picasso sank into a period of depression that was so severe he could hardly work and had to be patiently coaxed out of bed each morning. The creative paralysis had begun to lift, however—owing in part to his meeting Dora Maar— shortly before Franco's attack on the Spanish village. The bombing, in turn, served to galvanize Picasso's creative energies into a period of intense productivity. Gedo gives what is, to my mind, a compelling account of the intrapsychic sources of this masterpiece. Where some critics have suggested that Picasso discovered the images for the painting in actual photographs of the bombed village itself, Gedo, using certain important clues in the work, argues that Picasso also "possessed a source deep within himself for this imagery, for he had once witnessed a tragedy which paralleled the devastation of Guernica: the earthquake which rocked Malaga for three days in 1884, when the artist was three."[64] Moreover, it was in the midst of these events in Malaga that Picasso's sister was born. Gedo's thesis, then, is the following: the three-year-old Picasso, furious at the birth of his sister, believed that he was the "earthshaker" whose rage had caused the destruction. When it came to fulfilling his commission for the Spanish Republican Pavilion at the Paris International Exposition of Arts and Techniques, he retrieved from the depths of his psyche this image of crumbling buildings, contorted bulls and horses, and terrified men, women, and children scrambling for their lives and transformed it into *Guernica*, thus synthesizing, among other things, the sexual and aggressive childhood material behind his current depression with contemporary political subject matter.

Donald Kuspit has pointed out,[65] however, that this predominately genetic account ignores the other side, namely, everything that was happening in the art world in general at that time—for example, the decline of classical cubism—as well as in the internal development of Picasso's own work. But this observation, while true, does not constitute a criticism of the legitimacy and content of Gedo's approach. Rather, it defines a task: an adequate account of the genesis of *Guernica* would seek to explain how the genetic material from Picasso's inner world, which Gedo has so skillfully unearthed, became linked up not only with the immanent aesthetic development of painting but with the political and historical events of the time, to create one of the most important cultural objects of the century. This task is no less difficult than it is essential.

Similarly, an adequate account of the founding of psychoanalysis would have to explain how Freud drew on the vast variety of cultural resources available to him in his day—Helmholtzian science, Brentano's philosophy, *Gymnasium* classicism, contemporary neurology and psychiatry, sexology, German romanticism, hypnosis, Yiddish humor, archeology, ethnology, and so on—to give expression to his intrapsychic preoccupations, conflicts, and dramas and forge a new discipline. A work like Sulloway's,[66] although enormously scholarly and informative, remains small-minded from the theoretical point of view, like so much intellectual history that is preoccupied with tracing influences. In demonstrating a variety of (biological) influences on Freud and attempting to diminish the originality of Freud's achievement by reducing it to the sum total of those influences, it misses the most important point: the synthetic-sublimatory act of creation. Freud, like the opportunistic entrepreneur, exploited those resources and transformed them into a cultural object—psychoanalysis—that, while it may have been prefigured, had never existed before.[67]

Castoriadis's Polemic against Roustang

What is at stake in a theory of sublimation, both philosophically and practically, becomes particularly clear in Castoriadis's polemic against Roustang. Written in 1976, Roustang's book, *Dire Mastery*,[68] represents an attempt by one of the former members of Lacan's circle to come to terms with the degeneration of the Lacanian movement. Castoriadis argues, however, that, because of Roustang's unresolved ambivalence as a lapsed Lacanian, he actually "manages to use what he criticizes in order to justify it, and what he sees in order to go on not seeing it."[69] Roustang's thesis is that the degeneration of the Lacanians, although monstrous and deplorable, was nonetheless inevitable. Using examples from the undeniably unsettling history of the psychoanalytic movement as well as certain antitranscendental motifs from poststructuralist philosophy, he apologetically maintains that such deterioration is the unavoidable fate of all psychoanalytic associations (and, by implication, perhaps of all groups in general). They can never master their archaic, intrapsychic and familial origins to any significant degree. Rather, they are doomed a priori to reenact continuously and monotonously the drama of the primal horde, which is, in fact, their essence. All appearance of progress in rationality, maturity, and autonomy is just that—appearance. In general, the principle of immanence can never be surmounted, and we are forever lashed to the weary wheel of being. In keeping with Kojève's interpretation of Hegel, whose extremely partial reading influenced an entire generation of French intellectuals, the dialectic is arrested at the master-slave relationship, which Roustang applies to the analyst-analysand and mentor-disciple relationships. As the tie between master and slave cannot be sublated into mutual recognition to any meaningful extent, the situation of domination and subservience that obtained between Lacan, the primal father, and his horde of disciples is hypostatized as inevitable.

The entire issue turns on the question of the resolution of the transference and, more particularly, of the resolution of the transference in the training analysis. The transference, a ubiquitous feature of all social relationships, represents, in its most general aspect, the importation of unconscious material from the past, centering primarily on archaic incestuous imagos and scenarios, into the present and the projection of that material onto current situations. To the extent the transference dominates experience, our apprehension of present reality will be distorted by those imagos and scenarios from a heteronomous past that is not our own and, insofar as Freud equated pathology with atavistic infantilism, by our pathology. In analysis, the transference material is projected onto the person of the analyst where, because of the intentionally artificial nature of the psychoanalytic setting, it can be isolated, elaborated, analyzed, and resolved. The technique assumes that insofar as the transference is concerned, extrapsychic reality functions primarily as a projective screen for genetic, intrapsychic material.

With respect to social relations, to the degree that we remain under the sway of the transference, we will be prevented from treating ourselves or others as autonomous adults. Our self- and object-representations will be distorted by archaic parental and familial imagos so that we will continue to perceive the world through the eyes of a relatively helpless, dependent, and, therefore, restricted child. The resolution of the transference, then, within the analytic setting, is an essential condition for a relatively undistorted apprehension of reality and for the establishment and maintenance of mature, autonomous relationships. Conversely, if the transference is in principle unresolvable, our relation to truth and maturity would be forever compromised.

The argument for the inescapability of the transference presents the psychoanalytic variation on the theme of the totalized critique of reason. If there is nothing outside the transference, no ground exists, however minimal—no "scrap of independence,"[70] to use Freud's felicitous phrase—on which autonomous thinking and speaking could take place. Every thought and utterance would be so hopelessly enmeshed in the distorting effects of the transference that it would be impossible to distinguish between a theory *about* the transference, or about anything for that matter, and the transference itself. Such a distinction is, in short, the necessary precondition for maintaining the possibility of valid theory and thought in any meaningful sense. Roustang denies in effect the distinction between fantasy, projection, and delirium, on the one side, and valid thought and speech, on the other, when he defines "theory [as] the shared delirium of several people." This definition "leaves us," as Castoriadis observes, "only with a choice between frank psychosis and a psychosis parcelled out and filled in by reference to a 'theory,' "[71] which, while it may be less terrifying because of its shared nature, is psychosis nonetheless.

Along similar lines, Roustang also maintains that the relation between the lordship of the master and the bondage of the disciple has its source in the mutual need of both, master no less than disciple, " 'not to become mad.' " Much as Lacan sees the ego as a symptom, indeed the "the human symptom *par excellence*," [72] Roustang views both thinking and sociation (which he equates with hierarchical domination) only in terms of their symptomatic-defensive function; they are, in short, epiphenomena of psychic processes. Both the group and its theory, as Castoriadis observes, "provide a prop in reality which staves off collapse; in a word, they are a screen against psychosis."[73]

It is important to recognize that Castoriadis's "refutation" of Roustang, together with his argument for a necessary moment of transcendentality in human experience, does not constitute a strict philosophical demonstration on a par with, let us say, a Kantian transcendental deduction. Nor could it, given his philosophical self-understanding. Rather, it proceeds obliquely, as it must, and contains both empirical and dialectical elements. To begin with, Castoriadis asserts that, while it is not uncommon, it is simply not the case historically that all mentor-disciple relationships have ended in blind subservience, with the mentor stifling the disciple's creativity and autonomy and the disciple slavishly repeating the master's teaching:

Socrates never stifled Plato, and Plato never presented Aristotle with the mere choice between repetition and silence. Fichte did not drive Schelling to suicide, and Schelling did nothing to prevent Hegel from taking up an independent standpoint. . . . If this was how things were, there would have been no science, no philosophy, no thought in any field: we would be condemned to go on repeating Thales while hiding the evidence of millions of intervening suicides.[74]

Furthermore, the internalization of a mentor, as Chasseguet-Smirgel stresses, far from being opposed to the disciple's creativity and autonomy, is in fact often an essential medium of the *Bildungsprozess* in and through which that autonomy and creativity are achieved.

Similarly, Castoriadis argues that, clinically, "experience amply shows that a resolution [of the transference] 'sufficient from the standpoint of use/need' " often occurs in analysis and that despite the analyst's "exorbitant power" deriving from the transference and "opportunities for abusing" it, "such abuse is," surprisingly enough, "relatively rare."[75] Everything turns on the qualifying phrase "sufficient from the standpoint of use/need" *(pros ten chreian ikanos),* which Castoriadis takes from Aristotle's *Nichomachean Ethics* (V, 5), and which lies at the heart of his entire position. If this Aristotelian notion is "obscured, the door opens for a series of sophisms and paralogisms, both in the psychoanalytic field and in the field of activity, of *making/doing* in general." The concept is needed to forestall "the mirage of absolute Knowledge, of a perfectly conscious Ego, of total mastery." Castoriadis's thesis is that Roustang, like all skeptics, ancient, modern, and postmodern, is in fact a latent absolutist and that his psychoanalytically formulated skepticism rests on a tacit absolutist requirement, namely, the complete resolution of the transference. The skeptic presupposes the absolutist requirement only to show it cannot be fulfilled: "if we take [the resolution of the transference] *haplos* (absolutely) then it might be claimed that it is impossible, like the 'resolution of the Oedipus complex'—or the renunciation of the omnipotence of thought." Castoriadis argues, however, that "it is a lamentable sophism"—and I would add, Roustang's fundamental mistake—to infer from this that the transference is therefore never resolved to any essential extent. The same goes, *mutatis mutandis,* for the relations between the conscious and the unconscious."[76] Not without an air of disappointment, the skeptic, like the injured child who cannot endure the de-idealization of his or her omnipotent parents—the first absolute foundations for knowledge—insists that if we cannot have it all, we have nothing. But, as Wellmer has noted, "Freud's (or Nietzsche's) discoveries that desire (or the will to power) has always embedded itself as a nonintelligible force *within* rational argument and moral consciousness" are distressing "only if we *start out* with rationalist idealizations" and with the assumption that they should not be there in the first place.[77] It can be asked, of course, where this by no means self-evident idealizing assumption itself comes from.

Castoriadis argues that Roustang, "since he has put aside the question of sublimation, . . . lacks psychoanalytic terms in which to situate thought and the relation of the thinker to himself and to what he thinks (except, of course, inasfar as he see this as a matter of 'projection', 'phantazising,' and so on)."[78] That is to say, Roustang lacks the terms to situate his own standpoint as an analyst and a psychoanalytic theorist. This, in turn, makes it impossible for him to conceptualize the resolution of the transference "sufficient from the standpoint of use/need" in the training analysis and hence to conceptualize the possible validity of psychoanalytic theory and practice, which epistemologically, as it were, presupposes the adequate resolution of that transference. The transference in the training analysis can only be sufficiently resolved to the extent that the future analyst's desire is sublimated, for "psychoanalysis itself exists, in its 'subjective' aspect (for the psychoanalyst), as sublimation; that is, as a de-eroticized and desexualized investment (both narcissistic and trans-substantiated) of an activity and elucidation which are something essentially *other* than any psychic 'object' or 'representation of an object.' "[79] Thus, while "the *subject* who has become analyst may have a 'desire, perhaps to eat his patients, kill them, copulate with them, turn them into excrement, make them objects at his disposal (which turns them into 'slaves'/disciples),"[80] he is only an analyst to the extent that he has concurrently sublimated those desires, which remain at his disposal to aid in understanding the patients' fantasy lives, into a consistent investment in knowledge and in fostering the patients' autonomy. This is not to say that analysts must be purified of all countertransference toward their patients. It is only to say that countertransference, which may indeed provide a crucial source of material for their analyzing activity, is on a different level than, must be strictly distinguished from, and must be subordinated to, that analyzing activity itself. And this is not to say that analysts (and patients) do not derive pleasure from the activity of analysis—of understanding. It is only to say that this pleasure is of a different sort than organ pleasure, the immediate discharge pleasure of the drives. We return to the question of pleasure below.[81]

It might be objected against Castoriadis, however, that his criterion of sufficiency from the standpoint of use/need is too weak to refute the skeptical claims being made, to refute, specifically, the possibility of systematic and totalized deception. As its source in the *Nichomachean Ethics* suggests, this criterion comes from the practico-poetic plane of making and doing, and hence of practical reason, *phronesis,* not from the theoretical plane from which this skeptical objection is being raised. It constitutes, in short, an empirical refutation of a transcendental claim. Indeed, Castoriadis acknowledges that his argument will not satisfy the demands of "transcendental purism." However, it is precisely those purist demands—which remain in the register of the Absolute, which are "finally incoherent" in their "rigorous abstraction," and which the skeptic tacitly continues to employ—that he wants to contest.[82]

This brings us to the dialectical element of his position. As he cannot proceed directly and demonstrably in the manner of a transcendental deduction, for this would presuppose the legitimacy of the very purism he is contesting, Castoriadis must proceed indirectly, "aporetically and dialectically."[83] He elucidates his position, which, as it necessarily lacks an absolute starting point, must begin *in medias res*—in the middle of history, in the middle of language, in the middle of the transference, and so on—by rejecting two equally unmaintainable theoretical extremes, the "algorithmic and the ineffable,"[84] that is, absolute knowledge, on the one side, and radical relativism, on the other.

The rejection of absolute knowledge, after Nietzsche, Marx, Freud, Wittgenstein, and Dewey, ought already to have been incorporated into the learning experience of modernity and hence have become perfunctory by now. But owing to the rhetorical strategy of postmodernism, which has insufficiently worked through the problematic of the Absolute, and which continuously raises the specter of absolute knowledge as a rhetorical straw man—for example, the transparent Cartesian ego, totally stable meaning, pure presence, and so on—this has not been the case. As Habermas has observed, the postmodern skeptics are still "living in the shadow of the 'last philosopher' (Hegel)." Instead of truly relinquishing the Absolute, they continue to battle "against the 'strong' concepts of theory, truth and system that have actually belonged to the past for over a century and a half" and thereby remain compulsively bound to it. That is to say, they still believe that to claim any validity for thought or action, reason, "under the penalty of demise," must "hold on to [the] goals of metaphysics classically pursued from Parmenides to Hegel."[85] The pressing item on the current philosophical agenda, however, is not to refute a claim to absolute knowledge *that no one is making,* but to elucidate postmetaphysical forms of thought, speech, and action that can claim validity without an appeal to the Absolute. Unlike the postmodern skeptic, then, who is immobilized by insisting on the criterion of the Absolute while denying its attainability, Castoriadis is really prepared to give it up.

On the other side, Castoriadis's argument against radical relativism is twofold. First, relativism turns out to be a form of absolutism not only in the criteriological sense we have been considering but in another, more substantive sense as well: "It claims to be capable of dealing exhaustively [that is, absolutely] with its subject-matter by enumerating the relations in which this is enfolded."[86] By purporting to give an exhaustive account of its subject matter in terms of the genetic conditions that produced it, it eliminates the "gap" between those conditions and the subject matter and thereby also eliminates the possibility of truth, history, and creativity every bit as much as absolutism does. Secondly, Castoriadis raises the traditional paradoxes of self-referentiality against the skeptics, with the difference that now, having the discoveries of Freud at their disposal, they can bring new insights to bear on this traditional philosophical *topos.* Thus, in what might be called *reductio ad excrementum,* Castoriadis argues that, on the basis of Roustang's definition of theory as the "shared delirium of several," the "theory" of cloacal birth, a universal fantasy of childhood,[87] should be counted as an excellent theory: "Roustang, if he were consistent, ought to say: birth takes place by way of the anus. For the phantasy of anal birth is virtually universal; it is the 'delirium', not of 'several', but of almost everyone." It is essential to distinguish between the statement "almost all children imagine that birth takes place by way of the anus" from the statement "birth takes place by way of the anus," for this distinction amounts to the difference between theory and fantasy, truth and falsity. Psychoanalytic theory is not on the same level as, "is *not* one more variant of 'infantile theories of sexuality,' " but "it is *thought about* 'infantile theories' and many other things, and as such its existence depends on the extent to which *there is* a primary and essential otherness which distinguishes phantasy from reality, representation under the control of pleasure/unpleasure from truth, the psyche as a radical imagination from the social-world as the *other* of the psyche."[88] Indeed, these parallel distinctions must hold to a sufficient degree even for us to have access to the truth of our own finitude and to make the claim that they do not hold absolutely. Without these distinctions, not only would "psychoanalysis . . . be a senseless noise in its discourse" but it would be "a fraud in its activity" as well.[89] Because of the practico-clinical dimension of psychoanalysis, that is, because it treats suffering human beings, psychoanalytic skeptics are caught in a far more pernicious "performative contradiction" than their philosophical counterparts. They must be prepared to embrace not only the statement "I am a liar" but "I am a quack" as well; they must be content, that is, to stutter and stammer not only in their theoretical formulations but in their interventions from behind the couch as well.

To summarize, we cannot prove Q.E.D. that we are not totally deluded; we can only show the impossibility of maintaining that we are. That impossibility, coupled with the impossibility of absolute knowledge, defines our starting point for self-elucidation as finite beings in medias res.

Castoriadis formulates the empirical-transcendental antinomy, which has preoccupied the philosophical tradition from the Greeks through Karl-Otto Apel, and which we have been approaching here from different angles, in the following way: "Actual man is caught up in the determination of the actual world [including the determination of inner nature], where there exists only causes and effects, not truth, and value, or their opposites. And yet this assertion claims to be true—even while it remains actual." He argues that, purist claims to the contrary notwithstanding, the philosophical tradition, to the extent it has "resolved" this dilemma, has done so only by "positing a postulate of a fact of reason" in various forms.[90] The postmodern skeptic would, of course, like to maintain that Freud's discovery of the unconscious and transference have fatally exacerbated this perennial antinomy and added a fatal weapon to the skeptical arsenal.

Castoriadis argues, however, that what psychoanalysis has in fact done is make "possible a new approach to that *enigmatic and antinomial coalescence* of the empirical and the transcendental which is already present in the most rudimentary utterance as soon as the latter claims to be true."[91] While psychoanalysis is undeniably an empirical and not a transcendental psychology in the Kantian sense, it is an empirical psychology with a transcendental twist, as it were.

To begin with, Castoriadis, as we have already mentioned, rejects transcendental purism as a chimera: with respect to the transcendental ego, he argues that, although it can be posited, the I = I is an empty abstraction that "never has and never will produce anything other than the silent and useless self-evidence of the *cogito sum,* the immediate certainty of existing as a thinking substance, which cannot legitimately express itself in thought."[92] At the same time, however, he also argues that the empirical ego has a transcendental dimension as "one of its moments," namely, "the always present possibility of redirecting the gaze, of abstracting from any particular content, of bracketing everything, including oneself except inasmuch as the self is this capacity that springs forth as presence and absolute proximity at the very moment it places itself at a distance from itself." Granted, this gaze—the "observing ego," to use psychoanalytic terminology—can never assume the position of the "absolute spectator," outside of history, language, and the transference, and survey the totality, including the totality of the subject, all at one time. Nevertheless, insofar as it possesses the ability *in principle* to direct and redirect its gaze at any given content at any given time, the subject possesses a "spark outside of time," a moment of "nondimensionality,"[93] that is, a moment of transcendentality. The fundamental mistake of traditional transcendental philosophy is to hypostatize this necessary transcendental moment into a transcendental subject.

To be sure, because it is an empirical science, psychoanalysis will never satisfy the demands of a transcendental purism. But, as an empirical science, it nonetheless investigates the peculiar fact of the mind's variable capacity to transcend its merely empirical existence through the process of sublimation. Whereas first philosophy sought to found reason on nothing outside of itself and ended up positing only a *factum* of reason, psychoanalysis, as an unapologetically founded science, can, without a bad conscience, accept this fact of reason—"this pure fact [of] how we are"—as its starting point and proceed to elucidate its functioning. Or, to put it differently: Kant insisted on an absolute separation of *quid facti* and *quid juris* and, in an act of transcendental desperation, was forced to posit an utterly contingent "lucky accident" to account for the relation between them, to account, that is, for the "fit" between the mental and the extramental. Psychoanalysis, which as a developmental science rejects such a strict separation, offers a theory of sublimation to account for the mediation between the two dimensions. To make the empirical statement "that sublimation is a possible destiny of the drive is to say that the existence *de facto* of the psychic individual is the opening up *de jure* of the possibility of truth."[94] The human drive, while it has its "source" in a "somatic process which occurs in an organ or in a part of the body,"[95] has, as one of its essential vicissitudes, the capacity to find satisfaction in the desexualized objects/nonobjects of the extrapsychic, which is to say, the socially and historically mediated world.

The "divine Plato," whom Freud credits with having discovered sublimation,[96] has Diotima argue, albeit in an overly ascetic and idealistic direction,[97] that the mutability of Eros—which, it should be noted, is an intermediary[98]—and its ability to cathect nonempirical objects provides the immanent "ladder" within the empirical domain, that is, within inner nature, by means of which one can pull oneself out of the pure immanence of the totality of empirical determination. Indeed, as Plato realized in the *Symposium* and even more in the *Phaedrus,* and as Freud only came to realize after his fateful encounter with Dora, while the drives, with all of their power to cause distortion *(Entstellung),* can pose the severest obstacles to rationality and truth, they can, to the same degree, also function as the dynamic vehicle for insight. Thus, in the postscript to *Dora,* Freud reformulated his attitude toward the transference. Earlier he had seen the transference as "the greatest obstacle to psycho-analysis," which had to be circumvented, as the Kantians want to circumvent the *quid facti,* in order for the treatment to proceed and for insight to be achieved. After Dora he came to view the transference, *if handled properly,* as the very medium by which the analysis can advance, indeed, as its "most powerful ally."[99] It can become the vehicle by which the relation of the ego to the id is deepened.

David James has argued that Socrates had already recognized this fact: although he did not systematically formulate it in a doctrine of technique, Socrates, no less than the analyst, self-consciously and intentionally engaged his interlocutor's transference to initiate and promote the progress of the dialogue and the quest for truth.[100] His *daimon* exercised veto power over prospective interlocutors who did not possess the requisite Eros for the dialogical encounter; his *daimon,* as it were, decided on the question of analyzability. Indeed, without their transference to Socrates, an entire cohort of young Athenian aristocrats, including Plato himself, would not have become passionate about philosophy, and we would not have the founding texts of Western philosophy. While, ultimately, only "the force of the better argument" ought to count in adjudicating truth claims, only a consideration of transference and sublimation can explain how one comes to accede to "the unforced force"[101] of the better argument as binding; indeed, they are needed to explain why one would enter into serious discourse and not want to contradict oneself, either formally or performatively, in the first place.

Loewald, the Inveterate Dialectician

Loewald, with his characteristic feel for the inner tensions of psychoanalytic theory, observes that the concept of sublimation is "at once privileged and suspect" for the psychoanalyst. It is privileged insofar as "we take for granted the uniqueness of our psychic life and development; the value of man's imagination and thought, creativity and civilization, the worth of cultural pursuits—of morality, religion, the arts and sciences, and philosophy—and of an organized, self-reflective conduct of personal life and life in society." At the same time, sublimation is suspect insofar as analysts, despite the advances of ego psychology, continue to view the more "differentiated or 'further advanced' modes of psychic life as *defensive,* even illusory in nature, as concealment of more or less intriguing, fanciful embellishments of the elementary, true psychic reality of instinctual-unconscious life."[102] This second attitude toward sublimation, from which none of us is entirely free, can be traced back as far as the introduction of the term in psychoanalytic thinking when, in 1897, Freud referred to sublimations "as psychical facades constructed in order to bar the way to memories" of "primal scenes," that is, of historically true events. These facades, moreover, were meant to serve the purposes of "self-exoneration."[103] This attitude toward sublimation is exactly parallel to the tendency to understand the ego not as a structure that possesses defense as one of its functions but as a defensive structure as such, that is, "a structure designed, as it were, to disguise or impede the true psychic reality represented by the id."[104] It can also lead to the idealization of the lower, earthy and sexual domain as the authentic realm of existence in comparison to the presumed dissemblances and rationalizations of sublimated activity. Loewald suggests that something akin to this second attitude influenced Freud's rejection of the German distinction, current in his day, between culture *(Kultur)* and civilization *(Zivilisation)*. Whereas culture pertained to morality, education, the humanities, and the arts, that is, the so-called higher things, and "had elitist overtones," civilization referred to "the more earthbound, practical accomplishments of mankind," such as agriculture and technology. For Freud, the distinction "was tainted by just those pretensions that make sublimation suspect" as well.[105] As we will see, similar suspicions color Adorno's hostility toward the idea of sublimation.

A typical strategy to resolve the ambivalence, which is suggested by the inner logic of the problematic, consists in construing sublimation itself as a process that allows for a high degree of instinctual expression. This, as we have seen, was already Freud's strategy in the Leonardo monograph, and it received its canonical formulation in Fenichel's classic text, *The Psychoanalytic Theory of Neurosis.* In that work, Fenichel introduces a distinction between "successful" defenses, on the one side, and "unsuccessful" or "pathogenic" defenses, on the other. While in the case of the successful defenses, which Fenichel more or less equates with sublimation, the "aim or the object (or both) is changed without blocking an adequate discharge" of the drive, in the case of the pathogenic defenses, "the libido of the original impulse is held in check by a high countercathexis. . . . The countercathexes do not change the warded-off instincts into anything else; rather they suppress them . . . , thereby causing them to lose connection with the remainder of the personality."[106] Although Loewald is in complete sympathy with a distinction between a process that dams up and a process that organizes and channels instinctual life, he finds Fenichel's particular solution naive and inadequate. In this judgment he is correct. The greatness of the book notwithstanding, Fenichel works within a framework that is not simply antecedent to the postwar advances in separation-individuation and object-relations theory but that is not even sufficiently cognizant of the advances in ego psychology of his own day. The question of the "successful" versus the "unsuccessful" deployment of the drives cannot be adequately addressed with the resources of drive theory alone but requires a more differentiated theoretical scheme.

Loewald's approach to the problem of sublimation, on the other hand, follows from, indeed is one crucial aspect of, his theoretical project in general: to integrate the findings of separation-individuation theory into classical theory. This approach leads him to question the presuppositions deriving from classical theory, especially those pertaining to the nature of pleasure, that have determined the way the question of sublimation has traditionally been posed. Like Kohut, Loewald notes how little affinity or appreciation Freud had for "archaic narcissistic states" and how it was only with great reluctance that he finally unequivocally acknowledged the existence of a "primal state where id-ego and external world are not differentiated." Loewald, as opposed to Freud, wholeheartedly embraces the existence of an original unity, which is simultaneously a unity of the id and the ego and of the mother and the child. He reinterprets a broad range of traditional psychoanalytic topics, including the incest taboo, religion, primary and secondary processes, and the nature of interpretation, in terms of a quasi-Hegelian dynamic consisting in the rupture of that original unity and the reestablishment of a more differentiated unity—note again, I do not say complete unity—on a higher level of integration. Indeed, elaborating on "a side of Freud's conception of sexuality that he generally kept under wraps,"[107] Loewald even interprets sexuality, and sublimation, in terms of this scheme.

We have seen that a suspicion of the opposition between the "higher" realm of cultural achievements and the "lower" realm of earthly sexuality has tended to haunt the discussion of sublimation. Loewald attempts to undercut this opposition by developing some remarks in the Leonardo essay in which Freud argues that originally the higher and the lower, the divine and the sexual, were one and only became separated at a later date. Freud writes,

Originally the genitals were the pride and hope of living beings; they were worshipped as gods and transmitted the divine nature of their functions to all newly learned human activities. As a result of the sublimation of their basic nature there arose innumerable divinities; and at the same time when the connection between official religions and sexual activity was already hidden from the general consciousness, secret cults devoted themselves to keeping it alive among a number of initiates. In the course of cultural development so much of the divine and sacred was ultimately extracted from sexuality that the exhausted remnant fell into contempt.[108]

Not only does sexuality become depreciated when it is demoted downward after its severance from the divine, but the divine, which becomes increasingly disembodied, suffers from a depletion of vitality to the same extent. They are, in short, mutually impoverished: "The discontents of civilization include not only the starvation and denigration of instinctual life but, one must conclude, the impoverishment of the divine, of spirituality, as well." It is precisely this impoverishment that allows the death instinct to exercise "its silent power."[109]

While agreeing with Freud's claim that sexuality is *"il primo motore"* ("the driving force")[110] of all cultural activity, Loewald wants to go further. His thesis is that, in authentic sublimation, the split between the spiritual and the sexual is, at least, no longer dominant and, at best, overcome—indeed, the two are reconciled. In genuine sublimation, "the original unity" of the lowest and the highest is restored through symbolization, that is, through a process of "symbolic *linkage* which constitutes what we call meaning." In this process, something of the original "oneness of instinctual-spiritual experience" is restored "as connection." The difference, however, is that the "new synthetic organization" achieved in sublimation is a differentiated as opposed to an undifferentiated unity. That is to say, "the elements we call *instinctual* and *deinstinctualized* each acquire a measure of autonomy without losing the other."[111] This means, moreover, that the unity of the self is not achieved by the exclusion of the "lower" from the "higher" but through their integration.

There are several conclusions to be drawn from this analysis. The first pertains to the presuppositions concerning unmasking that have determined the psychoanalytic suspicion of sublimation (as well as the poststructuralist attack on psychoanalysis itself). In Loewald's view, the task of psychoanalysis "is not to uncover the truth of objective reality behind illusive higher levels of experience (so that the genitals and their power would constitute the true unadorned reality hidden beneath the disguising symbol of a god)." Rather, "by juxtaposing the two elements of an original unity and emphasizing the one hidden and defended against, psychoanalysis aims at showing their hidden linkage."[112]

The second conclusion concerns the problematic of the regulation of tension and its relation to pleasure. According to this analysis, we must assume that, whereas direct instinctual satisfaction involves a discharge and that defenses such as repression and reaction formation involve "countercathexis," sublimation, as it consists in higher forms of integration, involves "hypercathexis," that is, in an increase in tension.[113] Furthermore, as we must also assume that sublimation is in some sense pleasurable, this raises the question of "pleasurable tensions," a question that exploded in Freud's face in "The Economic Problem of Masochism"[114] and became the fundamental aporia for his entire theory of pleasure. We will return to this question shortly.

The theoretical means for conceptualizing the possible sublimatory reconciliation of sexuality and spirituality, of the drives and reason, as well the more comprehensive reconciliation of subject and object, are to be found in Freud's post-1914 *depth psychology of the ego,* which is to say, in his theory of the ego that developed out of the introduction of the concept of narcissism. Curiously enough, it is to be found in precisely the same theory that critics of the ego use to debunk it because of its narcissistic genesis. (By *depth psychology of the ego,* Loewald means the "analysis of the ego in terms of the ge-

netic-dynamic construction of psychic organization or structure"
rather than the more superficial investigation of "ego functions, defenses, and adaptation.") Indeed, a proper understanding of this theory should serve to dispel the not uncommon opinion that Freud's
career was itself split between the pre-1923 theorist of the unconscious and the drives and the post-1923 ego psychologist. With the
discovery of the narcissistic dimension of ego formation, that is, with
the discovery that sexuality encompasses "not only object relations
but also the cohesive fabric of intrapsychic structure . . . , *libido theory
and ego theory become inseparable*." Moreover, the discovery that sexuality pertains not only to the relation between subject and object but
also to "the internal relations and interactions constituting the organization of the subject as a psychic entity or structured unit" entails a
"widening of the definition of sexuality [that] culminated in Freud's
concept of eros."[115] The crucial passage linking the narcissistic formation of the ego via internalization with sublimation occurs in *The
Ego and the Id:*

The transformation of object-libido into narcissistic libido which thus takes
place obviously implies an abandonment of sexual aims, a desexualization—
a kind of sublimation, therefore. Indeed the question arises, and deserves
careful consideration, whether this is not the universal road to sublimation,
whether all sublimation does not take place through the mediation of the
ego, which begins by changing sexual object-libido into narcissistic libido
and then perhaps goes on to give it another aim.[116]

Loewald's reading of this passage, and his own position, turn on the
interpretation of the phrase "an abandonment of sexual aims, a desexualization." He argues that it involves a desexualization and an
abandonment of sexual aims only insofar as sexuality is presumed to
pertain to object choice alone: it "involves 'desexualization' in the
sense that it is no longer the external object, whether 'out there' or
in fantasy, that is desired." However, Loewald goes on to argue that
the "narcissistic libido," which results from the transformation of the
object in the process of internalization—that is, results from "an
internalizing transformation of passion or desire"—"is still libido";
the ego in fact "is held together by libidinal, erotic bonds which in
their basic nature are not different from those bonds obtaining in
object relations." This is what Freud refers to with his suggestively

paradoxical term "desexualized Eros." What can be viewed from one angle as a desexualization can be viewed from another as a broadening of sexuality from the "original narrow sense of sexual object-cathexis" into the widened sense of "the life or love instinct, of eros."[117] As opposed to Hartmann's notion of neutralization[118]—which would reinstate the original opposition of ego and id—this means, among other things, that the energy employed in sublimatory processes remains sexual, albeit in a widened sense. Loewald's thesis is that the sublimatory formation of the ego through the internalizing transformation of object libido into narcissistic libido constitutes a form of reconciliation between the ego and the drives.

That such an internalization is perhaps the universal road to sublimation has consequences for both the subject and the object and for their relation to each other. As the ego is itself formed through the sublimatory transformation of object libido into narcissistic libido, the consequences on the side of the subject are more obvious. Loewald argues, however, that, as "objects and aims in the external world change their character . . . [when] they are imbued with a changed cathexis," this process also has consequences on the side of the object: not only does "the shadow of the object fall on the ego," as Freud originally observed, but "the shadow of the altered ego falls on objects and object relations" as well. Because the process of sublimation narrows the "gulf . . . between object world and self," Loewald views it as "a kind of reconciliation of the subject-object dichotomy." In authentic sublimation, the "alienating differentiation" that was created with the rupture of the original unity of the mother-infant dyad "is being reversed in such a way that a fresh unity is created by an act of uniting." Genuine sublimation "involves an internal re-creative return toward that matrix."[119] As opposed to the undifferentiated original unity, however, this restored unity now comprises a "*differentiated unity* (a manifold) that captures separateness in the act of uniting, and unity in the act of separating." Indeed, in language that invites comparison with Wellmer's attempt to reinterpret ego identity in terms of Adorno's notion of "the nonviolent togetherness of the manifold," Loewald speaks of sublimation as resulting in "the nonrepressive organization of the ego."

He maintains, moreover, that the distinctive pleasure characteristic of sublimatory accomplishments can be understood as a "celebration" of this reconciliation. The " 'manic' element" often associated with sublimation would therefore not be a denial, or at least "not only" a denial, "but an affirmation of unity as well." While Loewald agrees with Hartmann's observation that sublimation (qua internalization) plays a decisive role in the mastery of reality, as we have noted, he qualifies the notion of mastery in a way that has crucial theoretical and political ramifications. In a move that could have helped Adorno out of his aporetic impasse, Loewald introduces a distinction between "mastery" as "domination," that is, as the domination of inner nature by the imperious subject (cf. Freud's image of draining the Zuider Zee), and "mastery" as "coming to grips with." One assumes that, in "coming to grips with," the imperious subject is itself civilized, which is to say, simultaneously decentered and naturalized.[120]

The question of the nature of the pleasure that characterizes sublimation, indeed of the nature of pleasure in general,[121] leads us into the deepest aporia of Freud's economic approach and challenges one of its fundamental assumptions, namely, the constancy hypothesis to which he had adhered since the *Project*.[122] Freud's most severe formulation equating pleasure with tension reduction, the one that appears to set the pleasure principle unavoidably at "loggerheads" with the reality principle and, thereby, to preclude the possibility of a fulfilled life, occurs in *Civilization and Its Discontents*. Citing Goethe, and undoubtedly taking the orgasm as the prototype, Freud argues that happiness "is not included in the plan of 'Creation'. What we call happiness in the strictest sense comes from the (preferably sudden) satisfaction of needs which have been damned up to a high degree, and it is from its nature only possible as an episodic phenomenon. . . . We are so made that we can derive intense enjoyment only from a contrast and very little from a state of things." Because happiness requires extension over time, and because the pleasure principle, "which decides the purpose of life," can only provide an "episodic" release that cannot issue into a "state of things," it appears that "our possibilities of happiness are already restricted by our constitution."[123] Both Loewald and Ricoeur point out that Freud at least tacitly recognizes the problem and makes a distinction between pleasure *(Lust)* and satisfaction *(Befriedigung)* in an attempt to deal with it. However, because he tries to derive the concept of satisfaction from his restricted notion of pleasure as tension reduction—via the notion of aim inhibition, for example—he can never arrive at an adequate account of satisfaction.

To avoid Freud's impasse, Loewald follows Winnicott and introduces a distinction between "climactic" and "nonclimactic" pleasure. Indeed, he points out that at least the possibility of "nonclimactic" pleasures is already admitted in a decisive passage from "The Economic Problem of Masochism" in which Freud's economic thinking is pushed to the breaking point. Freud refuses to accept the inescapable implication of his equation of pleasure with tension reduction, namely, that the pleasure principle would coincide with the death instinct; "but such a view," he declares without much support, "cannot be correct." As a result, he is forced to admit the existence of pleasurable tension and to retreat from his strictly quantitative definition of pleasure: "It seems that in the series of feelings of tension we have a direct sense of the increase and decrease of amounts of stimulus, and it cannot be doubted that there are pleasurable tensions and unpleasurable relaxations of tension. The state of sexual excitation is the most striking example of a pleasurable increase of stimulus of this sort, but it is not the only one." He goes on to concede that these pleasures "depend, not on this quantitative factor, but on some characteristic of it which can only be described as a qualitative one." While he tries to save the quantitative approach by stretching it in the direction of rhythm—"perhaps it is the rhythm, the temporal sequence of changes, rises and falls in the quantity of stimulus"—he finally admits that psychology, at its current level of development, knows very little about it. He is, in short, unable to elaborate a different concept of pleasure any further and ends his reflections with "We do not know."[124]

In his paper "The Location of Cultural Experience," Winnicott remarks that "Freud did not have a place in his topography of the mind for the experience of things cultural." Like Laplanche and Pontalis, he notes that, although Freud "used the word 'sublimation' to point the way to the place where cultural experience is meaningful,"[125] he did not delineate the nature of that space in sufficient detail. For Winnicott, of course, it coincides with the realm of transitional phenomenon, which begins with the mother-infant matrix, unfolds through the transitional object and play, and is ultimately "diffused . . . over the whole cultural field."[126] In childhood, transitional experience is characterized by a unique form of subject-object relation that is neither strictly merger nor strictly separation. Instead, from the point of view of the infant, and with the help of an empathic adult, the question of whether the transitional object belongs to "inner reality or outer reality," of whether it is created or found, *"is not to be formulated."* (In this respect, as Loewald notes, the transitional object can be compared with Kohut's notion of *selfobject*.) And something of this suspension of the question of inner versus outer reality, of this "separation that is not a separation but a form of union," of this "distanced nearness" (Adorno), returns in cultural activity, which is akin to play, and explains its enormous significance in human life; it provides relief "from the strain of relating inner and outer reality . . . that no human being is free from."[127] In Loewald's terminology, it restores the unity of the original situation but with a higher degree of differentiation. The pleasure, moreover, that accompanies transitional activity, though undoubtedly powerful, is distinct from the pleasure attendant to instinctual discharge. The sort of satisfaction we assume the infant experiences when lost in play "is retained in the intense experiencing that belongs to the arts and to religion and to imaginative living, and to creative scientific work."[128] Most significantly for our purposes, "it is to be noted that the phenomena that I am describing have no climax. This distinguishes them from phenomena that have instinctual backing, where the orgiastic element plays an essential part, and where satisfactions are closely linked with climax." Winnicott offers "the 'electricity' that seems to generate *[sic]* in meaningful or intimate contact, that is a feature, for instance, when two people are in love" as an example of nonclimactic pleasure. This flow of electricity is something that, while it can undulate, oscillate, and vibrate, that is, can have a rhythm, can nevertheless be extended over time. Furthermore, the fact that these phenomena "have infinite variability, contrasting with the relative stereotypy of" climactic pleasures, would help to explain the flexibility of transitional phenomena and aesthetic pursuits as opposed to the relative rigidity of the fetish and the perversions we noted above.[129]

The foregoing considerations require the formulation of what Loewald terms a "*revised* pleasure principle,"[130] that is, a pleasure principle that would not only take account of but assign a central place to pleasurable tensions. The revision of the pleasure principle would, in turn, necessarily require a revision of the constancy hypothesis as well. The existence of pleasurable tensions does not merely amount to a bothersome anomaly that must be explained away to save the economic model and its equation of pleasure with tension reduction. On the contrary, this so-called anomaly points to a more profound topic that must be provided with a comprehensive and positive account in psychoanalytic theory, namely, the necessary existence of an anti-entropic force in psychic life. Freud recognized very early, in the *Project*—for example, in the discussion of bound energy—that the logic of his entire position demanded such a force. Indeed, how else could he even account for the existence of the ego and thinking itself? Nevertheless, throughout his career, he seems to have approached such a force only with great resistance. I already cited Loewald's observation that "Freud seems to have felt much less at home" with the life instinct "than he did with the death instinct" and only introduced the notion of Eros when he "could no longer circumvent it." We also noted that, as the death instinct had in fact been there *in nuce* since the introduction of the constancy hypothesis, it was the introduction of the life instinct that constituted the "true and unsettling innovation in psychoanalytic theory." Loewald argues, then, that "if there were such a thing as a life instinct, its 'aim' " would be satisfaction not through the discharge of tension but "through the attainment of higher, more differentiated unities, in which tension is not eliminated but 'bound.' " This would be "satisfaction of a different kind."[131] A fundamental presupposition that skews Freud's entire analysis in this respect is that constancy can only be achieved through a complete elimination of tension to a state of absolute rest.[132] He fails to appreciate the extent to which tension, bound energy, can itself produce stability and cannot therefore adequately conceptualize Eros—"the builder of cities"[133] and "preserver of all things"[134]—nor the constancy and pleasure attached to it.[135]

Concluding Remarks: Sublimation and the Nature of Postconventional Identity

This book has presented a case for a sustained reengagement with psychoanalytic discourse within contemporary Critical Theory. I have sought to demonstrate that such an encounter would be productive not only in reopening a dimension of Critical Theory that was largely closed with the Habermasian turn but in addressing some of the outstanding problems of both the first and second generations of the Frankfurt school as well. Indeed, with respect to one particular question, the nature of the postconventional self, our investigations of Habermas and Adorno have produced largely convergent results. Habermas, it will be recalled, maintained that whatever vestige of utopian speculation about the good life might be permitted today could not be directed at questions of substantive content. Rather, it would have to focus on the fortunate "balance among [the] moments" of individual (and collective) identity that might be possible to achieve: What desirable modes of integration might a postconventional self assume? I argued that while this was a correct question, Habermas, because he had abandoned psychoanalytic theory, had denied himself the resources to explore it adequately. In the first place, by substantially softening the Freudian notion of the unconscious and thereby reducing the heterogeneity among the moments of the self, he had made the problem of the integration of those moments too easy. At the same time—and for the same reason—he had deprived himself of the means of conceptualizing a sufficiently robust notion of the self. The vitality of the self is generally proportional to the extent it has integrated the disavowed, split-off, and heterogeneous parts of the psyche—the parts that the rigidly integrated, conventional personality simply seeks to repress. To the extent, therefore, that Habermas reduces the heterogeneity of those elements of the psyche, he also reduces the degree of foreignness by which a postconventional self might enrich itself.

The question of postconventional identity was also an outstanding item at the end of our discussion of Adorno. Wellmer argued, as we saw, that although "Adorno himself set the open forms of modern art in relation to a form of subjectivity which no longer corresponds to the rigid unity of the bourgeois subject," he could not take his thought "one step further" and consider those less rigidly integrated forms of subjectivity. My claim is that a theory of sublimation such as Loewald's—which does not envision a spiritualistic transcendence of inner nature but a fully embodied integration of the ego and the drives—could have assisted Adorno in taking that step. Such a step, moreover, might have provided the alluring notion of the "mind-fulness of nature in the subject" with some content. However, not only does Adorno share the common psychoanalytic suspicion of sublimation as a form of defensive, idealizing deception, discussed by Loewald, but he also has good historical-political considerations to reenforce that suspicion as well. Adorno's general distrust of "false reconciliation" in a world where "the whole is the untrue," a distrust that permeates his entire philosophy—indeed, his suspicion of any-thing that smacks of a "beautiful whole" [136]—applies to "false recon-ciliation" in the case of the individual psyche. He argues that "the well-integrated personality" of the Hartmann era, itself the psychoan-alytic counterpart to the "go-getter" of the Eisenhower (and Ade-nauer) years, constitutes "a false reconciliation with an unreconciled world, and would presumably amount in the last analysis to an 'iden-tification with the aggressor', a mere character-mask of subordina-tion." [137] Moreover, under the current conditions of an antagonistic society, psychic integration is not even a functionally obtainable goal from the standpoint of the economics of intrapsychic life; it remains an ideological illusion: "But in an irrational society the ego cannot perform at all adequately the function allotted to it by that society. The ego is necessarily burdened with psychic tasks that are irreconcil-able with the psychoanalytic conception of the ego." [138]

Adorno's more specific criticisms of sublimation are directed at a not uncommon utilitarian interpretation of it. He argues that the criterion of the "socially useful . . . is rather innocently dragged in" [139] from the outside to distinguish sublimation from other less desirable forms of instinctual expression. To the extent that this is true, and it certainly is in a number of the more superficial discussions of sublimation (including some of Freud's), it would indeed inject an unreflected conformism into the heart of the concept itself. It does not follow, however, that the concept of sublimation must be rejected entirely, for it is possible to formulate less crudely utilitarian, more refined interpretations of it. Surely, Adorno cannot mean to dismiss altogether the social value of even the most negative works. After all, he does not praise Beckett's *Endgame* as *art pour l'art* nor as individualist existential drama. An explication of the social value of a negative work such as *Endgame* could have led Adorno to consider a nonutilitarian account of sublimation. But because of the polemical context in which he was writing, he never attempted to develop a more adequate concept of sublimation. Instead, he only continued to insist that "every 'image of man' is ideology except the negative one," and that every anticipatory representation of "a more human existence" must be "damaged rather than harmonious." [140]

Yet, as always, there exist opposing tendencies in his thinking. Without referring to it by name, Adorno makes use of the concept of sublimation in his theoretical dispute with idealism. However, just as he never extrapolated from his analysis of aesthetic synthesis, so he never used the results of his "refutation of idealism" to address the possibility of new forms of subjectivity. His thesis is that the sexual impulse, which is excised by Kant's philosophy in order to achieve the transcendental purity of its argument and the autonomy of the moral law, must be reintroduced as an "addendum" [141] to make good the deficits of Kantian moral theory. Indeed, the idea of freedom itself "feeds upon . . . the archaic impulse not yet steered by the solid I," which is in fact solidified in and through the subjugation of that impulse. The impulse is, in turn, "banished to the zone of unfree bondage to nature" in the process. However, it continues to "echo" in the concept of spontaneity, which is "the philosophical concept that does most to exalt freedom as a mode of conduct above empirical existence." That is to say, the archaic impulse reverberates in the very concept that "means to prove its freedom" through the "control and ultimate destruction" of it. [142]

Kant removed "the genetical moment from the philosophy of morals" to prevent "his own insight that in the phenomenal world all

motivations are motivations of the empirical, psychological ego"
from clashing with "the transcendental principle." However, he was
then stuck with the problem of how the empirically cleansed moral
law could be effective. It is only because the ego is "not something
immediate" but mediated—that it "has branched off from the diffuse
energy of the libido" and is therefore a derivative of inner nature,
however remote—that can help to explain the effectiveness of the
moral law.[143] Adorno argues, moreover, that the will, which is supposed to constitute the mediating faculty between the supersensible
and the sensible in the Kantian scheme and to account thereby for
that effectiveness, in fact amounts to "a no-man's-land between subject and object," which as such cannot mediate between the two. As
a result, Kant cannot provide content for his notion of the "causality
of freedom," which remains simply an "oxymoron." Only the ego's
sublimated derivation from the drive can provide a mediation between the transcendental and empirical self and thereby account for
the causality of freedom.

It is at this point that the "addendum," the impulse, must be introduced to rectify the deficit in the Kantian scheme. Whereas the will
is "a no-man's-land," the addendum, as an impulse, as Freud maintained, is a frontier entity on the border between the mental and the
physical. This means that, as "it denies the Cartesian dualism of *res
extensa* and *res cogitans,*" the "addendum has an aspect which under
rationalistic rules is irrational." But it also means that, because it is
"instrumental and somatic in one," the impulse represents "a phase
in which the dualism of extramental and intramental was not yet
thoroughly consolidated . . . nor [is] ontologically ultimate" and thus
contains the conditions of "the will's transition to practice" and of
the extension of freedom to "the realm of experience." Indeed,
Adorno wants to go even further. Despite his repudiation of utopian
speculation, he maintains that the "phantasm" contained in the frontier status of the drive "is the phantasm of reconciling nature and
mind," and that this reconciliation "is not as alien to reason" as it
would appear in idealist philosophy. The addendum is simply the
necessary reintroduction of "that which was eliminated" from the
Kantian scheme in its excessive abstraction; "without it, there would
be no real will at all." Adorno is correct in his assertion that the
addendum "is a flash of light between the poles of something long

past, something grown but unrecognizable, and that which some day might come true."[144] He would have needed, however, a developed concept of sublimation to transform that flash of light into the steady illumination of a theory.

Adorno's correct disdain for therapeutically abetted adaptation to a bad reality, an adaptation that forgets "the world is deeply ailing,"[145] prevents him from reflectively appropriating the concept of sublimation, which he in fact uses, and causes him to forget one of his most important insights concerning unmediated social deviance. Like Loewald, he knows full well that the dissociation of the instincts from thinking results in the rationalist atrophy of thought: "But if the impulses are not at once preserved and surpassed in the thought which has escaped their sway, then there will be no knowledge at all, and the thought that murders the wish that fathered it will be overtaken by the revenge of stupidity."[146] This atrophy pertains especially to thought's critical function, for "anticipatory desire"[147]—fantasy, the imaginary—is a primary source of that function. But, again, because of his hostility toward "amelioristic" psychoanalysis that seeks to "transform [the drives] into socially desirable achievements,"[148] he does not pursue the question of how those drives are "at once preserved and surpassed in thought," that is, how they are sublimated.

His antipathy to sublimation becomes even more pronounced when he turns to art: "Artists do not sublimate." The supposedly incidental remark that directly follows this provocative statement reveals the motivation for it: "Incidentally, legitimate works of art are today without exception socially undesired." Because he equates sublimation with pacified social conformity, and because the important contemporary works of art are, by their very nature, neither pacified nor socially desirable in any conventional sense, Adorno is led to reject the notion of sublimation. Adorno is in fact polemicizing against the conservative guardians of high culture and beautiful appearance whom he lumps together with the psychoanalysts: "To anything sublimated [artists] oppose idiosyncrasies. They are implacable toward aesthetes, indifferent to a carefully-tended environment, and in tastefully-conducted lives they recognize diminished reactions against pressures to diminution as surely as do the psychologists, by whom [the artists] are themselves misunderstood." Adorno must be reminded, however, that while serious contemporary art is "socially undesirable" and represents a rebellion against a deeply ailing world, not every rebellion against that world constitutes legitimate art. Indeed, many forms of rebellions just self-destructively repeat the pathology against which they are protesting. Adorno supplies the missing *differentia specifica,* however, when he compares the symptom and the work of art. Whereas both stem from the same instinctual material and constitute a protest against painful reality, artistic "expression negates reality by holding up to it what is unlike it, but it never denies reality; it looks straight in the eye the conflict that results blindly in the symptom." [149] And the change of function that allows for the truth orientation of the work of art, as opposed to the blindness and repetitiveness of the symptom, requires a transformation, a sublimation, of the instinctual material from which they both spring.

A harmoniously integrated self and life history, as envisioned in the classical bourgeois ideal of *Erfahrung,* are undoubtedly impossible today. And, for reasons we have considered, they are for the most part undesirable as well. Nevertheless, even Adorno recognized that the fragmented characters in Beckett's work—which along with Schoenberg's oeuvre constitutes his paradigm for "legitimate" art— make reference to an integrated self, however obliquely, in the same way "consonance survives atonal harmony." [150] Indeed, *Endgame* is a protest in the name of that consonance. Whereas Habermas would like to explore this postconventional consonance, as it were, but has deprived himself of the resources to do it adequately, Adorno's apprehension about the false harmony of the bourgeois ego and classical bourgeois art has inhibited him from examining the question at all. A concept of the noncoercive integration of the self, however, is not only a necessity for countering postmodernism's manic and one-sided celebration of generalized dissolution and dispersion, it is also a *desideratum* for Critical Theory. As I have tried to show, this desideratum emerges from the immanent development of both the first and second generations of the Frankfurt school itself. And grappling with both the perennial questions and the more recent developments in psychoanalysis would, as I have also tried to show, be one of the most productive ways to pursue it.

Notes

Introduction

1. Quoted in Martin Jay, *The Dialectical Imagination: A History of the Frankfurt School and the Institute of Social Research, 1923–1950* (Boston: Little, Brown, 1973), 102. The question itself had originally been put to Lowenthal by Ernst Kris, one of the major émigré analysts in New York.

2. See Leo Lowenthal, *An Unmastered Past: The Autobiographical Reflections of Leo Lowenthal,* ed. Martin Jay (Berkeley: University of California Press, 1987), 51; Karen Brecht et al., *"Here Life Goes on in a Most Peculiar Way . . .": Psychoanalysis before and after 1933,* trans. Christine Trollope (Hamburg: Kellner Verlag, 1985), 56ff.; and Jay, *The Dialectical Imagination,* 86ff. Horkheimer, it should be noted, was also instrumental in establishing the Sigmund Freud Institute in Frankfurt after World War II.

3. Lowenthal, *An Unmastered Past,* 51.

4. Jay, *The Dialectical Imagination,* 87.

5. Ibid., 105.

6. It could be argued that Foucault was involved in a similar quest in *Madness and Civilization* with his tendency to valorize madness as the good Other of excluding modern rationality. I believe it could also be shown that, despite his rejection of the repressive hypothesis, he never abandoned this search completely. Foucault's dilemma was the following: because he never revised his diagnosis of the repressive nature of modern reason and its subject, he was constantly tempted to valorize those phenomena that transgress it, i.e., madness, perversion, criminality, terror, and so on. However, after *Madness and Civilization,* he became too sophisticated, both theoretically and politically, to affirm those transgressive phenomena *directly*. In a future publication, I hope to show that the various revisions and equivocations in his theory resulted, in part, from his attempt to hedge this dilemma. Indeed, I believe he rejected the repressive hypothesis in an attempt to rid himself of the entire problematic. Finally, I also believe that Foucault's ambivalence concerning Freud, which

Forrester has exhaustively documented, can be traced to this same fundamental problematic. See John Forrester, "Michel Foucault and the History of Psychoanalysis," in *The Seductions of Psychoanalysis: Freud, Lacan and Derrida* (New York: Cambridge University Press, 1989), 286–316.

Derrida, in a paper commemorating the twentieth anniversary of the publication of *Madness and Civilization,* has also addressed Foucault's thoroughgoing ambivalence—his "interminable and inexhaustible *fort/da*"—toward Freud. (Jacques Derrida, " 'To Do Justice to Freud': The History of Madness in the Age of Psychoanalysis," trans. Pascale-Anne Brault and Michael Nass, *Critical Inquiry* 20 [Winter 1994] 254.)

7. Hans Loewald attempts to distinguish between mastery as the nonviolent "coming to terms with" and mastery as domination. I am convinced that the concept of nondomineering mastery, like the concept of sublimation, is essential to the Freudian project. See *Sublimation: Inquiries into Theoretical Psychoanalysis* (New Haven: Yale University Press, 1988). See also Adorno's notion of *Aufarbeitung* in "What Does Coming to Terms With Mean?" in *Bitburg in Moral and Political Perspective,* ed. Geoffrey Hartmann (Bloomington: Indiana University Press, 1986).

8. See Cornelius Castoriadis, "Fait et à Faire," *Revue européenne des sciences sociales* 27, no. 86 (1989): 471.

9. Sigmund Freud, "Female Sexuality," vol. 21 of *The Standard Edition of the Complete Psychological Works of Sigmund Freud,* trans. James Strachey (London: Hogarth Press, 1975), 226. In subsequent citations, *Standard Edition* is abbreviated S.E.

10. Hans Loewald, "The Waning of the Oedipus Complex," in *Papers on Psychoanalysis* (New Haven: Yale University Press, 1980), 386. Loewald's paper should be read in conjunction with another classic of the same period: André Green, "The Analyst, Symbolization and Absence in the Analytic Setting" (1975). Both these papers indicate that, by the seventies, analysts were grappling with the significance of Klein, Winnicott, Mahler, and Kohut for classical theory. As Green puts it, "I think that one of the main contradictions which the analyst faces today is the necessity (and the difficulty) of making a body of interpretations (which derive from the work of Freud and of classical analysis) coexist and harmonize with the clinical experience and the theory of the last twenty years" (p. 32). Green's article appears in André Green, *On Private Madness* (Madison, CT: International Universities Press, 1986), 30–59.

11. See Heinz Kohut, "Forms and Transformations of Narcissism," *Journal of the American Psychoanalytic Association* 14 (April 1966): 243ff.

12. See, for example, Otto Fenichel, "A Critique of the Death Drive," in *The Collected Papers of Otto Fenichel* (New York: W. W. Norton, 1953), 363–72.

13. Loewald, "The Waning of the Oedipus Complex," 402.

14. It is now clear that Freud's discussion of the prospects for atheism was too optimistic, because he underestimated the strength of that striving. And because he miscalculated the tenacity of the drive for identification and merger, he failed to consider possible alternative destinies for it in a postreligious world. Just as the Aeschylean *polis* had to find a place for the Furies, so modern secular society must give these strivings their due.

15. See Jürgen Habermas, "Science and Technology as 'Ideology,' " in *Toward a Rational Society: Student Protest, Science, and Politics,* trans. Jeremey J. Shapiro (Boston: Beacon Press, 1970), 99.

16. See especially the programmatic statement in Jürgen Habermas, "Modernity— An Incomplete Project," in *The Anti-Aesthetic: Essays on Postmodern Culture,* ed. Hal Foster (Port Townsend, WA: Bay Press, 1983), 3–15. The essay also appeared under the title "Modernity versus Postmodernity," in *New German Critique* 22 (winter 1981). See also Richard Bernstein's introduction to *Habermas and Modernity,* ed. Richard. J. Bernstein (Cambridge, MA: MIT Press, 1985), 1–34.

17. I would argue that one of the rhetorical advantages that poststructuralism has in the controversy with critical theory is its *apparent* radicalism.

18. Sigmund Freud, *The Interpretation of Dreams* (1900), S.E., vol. 5, 603.

19. Cornelius Castoriadis, "The Retreat from Autonomy: Post-Modernism and the Generalization of Conformity," *Thesis Eleven* 31 (1992): 20.

20. One symptom of this atrophy of the political imagination is a comment that has surfaced regularly since 1989, representing Taiwan as our ideal polis. In fact, it has been suggested that a desirable outcome for eastern Europe and the Middle East would be a society resembling this technocapitalist wasteland.

21. The synthesis, I believe, also helps to explain the appeal of Hegel and Beethoven.

22. Albrecht Wellmer, "The Dialectic of Modernism and Postmodernism: The Critique of Reason since Adorno," in *The Persistence of Modernity: Essays on Aesthetics, Ethics, and Postmodernism,* trans. David Midgley, (Cambridge, MA: MIT Press, 1991), 58–59.

23. Maurice Merleau-Ponty, "Hegel's Existentialism," in *Sense and Nonsense,* trans. Hubert L. Dreyfus and Patricia Allen Dreyfus (Evanston, IL: Northwestern University Press, 1964), 63. Moreover, because it does not identify reason as such with *Verstand* but, as Merleau-Ponty puts it in the same passage, seeks to furnish a reason "broader than the understanding," this approach is not forced to vilify rationality as instrumental reason, technique, logocentrism, identifying thought, or what have you. For an attempt to redress the balance in the relationship of Hegel to Nietzsche, see Elliot Jurist, *The Familiar Is Unknown: Philosophy, Culture, and Agency in Hegel and Nietzsche* (Cambridge, MA: MIT Press, forthcoming).

24. Significantly, it is in a discussion of Foucault's *Madness and Civilization* that Habermas endorses the conception of " 'reason' proper to German Idealism" that sought to enter a dialogue with its "split-off" Other, namely, madness. Foucault, of course, thought that this sort of dialogue between reason and *folie* took place in the late Middle Ages and early Renaissance before the Great Confinement and the constitution of modern rationality. See Jürgen Habermas, *The Philosophical Discourse of Modernity,* trans. Frederick G. Lawrence (Cambridge, MA: MIT Press, 1987), 412, no. 3.

25. Significantly, Critical Theory's retreat from Freud roughly coincided with the explosion of interest in psychoanalysis in France in the seventies, where Freud had been resisted for some time. This was, of course, due largely to the enormous impact

of Lacan, without whom we would not have had such gems of French psychoanalysis as Laplanche and Pontalis's *The Language of Psychoanalysis*, Ricoeur's *Freud and Philosophy*, André Green's *On Private Madness*, and even Castoriadis's *The Imaginary Institution of Society*. As a result of Lacan's "provocation," Freud now constitutes a major point of reference for French intellectual life. The tendency in France, however, has been to read Freud through Heidegger and thereby appropriate him—against his intentions, I would say—for the anti-Enlightenment program of poststructuralism. It is therefore a pity that Critical Theory was vacating the psychoanalytic field at precisely the same time these developments were taking place in France. See Sherry Turkle, *Psychoanalytic Politics: Freud's French Revolution* (New York: Basic Books, 1978), chap. 1; Marion Michel Oliner, *Cultivating Freud's Garden in France* (New York: Jason Aronson, 1988), chaps. 2 and 3; Elisabeth Roudnesco, *Jacques Lacan & Co.: A History of Psychoanalysis in France, 1925–1985*, trans. Jeffrey Mehlman (Chicago: University of Chicago Press, 1990), chap. 5.

26. See especially Peter Dews, "Adorno, Post-Structuralism, and the Critique of Identity," *New Left Review* 157 (May/June 1986): 28–44, and *The Logics of Disintegration: Post-Structuralist Thought and the Claims of Critical Theory* (London: Verso Books, 1987).

27. Theodor W. Adorno, *Negative Dialectics*, trans. E. B. Ashton (New York: Seabury Press, 1973), 35. Robert Pippin also observes, "I think [Habermas's] attention to self-referential paradoxes, typical of many attacks on relativism, is far too abstract to avoid the counter-charge that he is begging the very question at issue" (*Modernism as a Philosophical Problem* [Cambridge, MA: Basil Blackwell, 1991], 184, n. 8). See also Martin Jay, "The Debate over Performative Contradiction: Habermas versus the Poststructuralists," in *Philosophical Interventions in the Unfinished Project of Modernity*, ed. Axel Honneth et al. (Cambridge, MA: MIT Press: 1992), 261–79.

28. Theodor W. Adorno, *Minima Moralia*, trans. E. F. N. Jephchott (London: New Left Books, 1974), 392.

29. Hans-Georg Gadamer, *Truth and Method*, trans. Garrett Barden and John Cumming (New York: Seabury Press, 1975), 308.

30. Quoted in Pippin, *Modernism as a Philosophical Problem*, 148.

31. The Nietzschean attempt to celebrate this groundlessness as a condition of emancipation strikes me as a case of manic denial, to use Melanie Klein's terminology. Adorno, it might be said, at least advanced to the depressive position and had the decency to be melancholy at the prospect of totalized groundlessness. This difference is already apparent in Lyotard's early article on Adorno. See Jean-François Lyotard, "Adorno as the Devil," *Telos* 19 (spring 1974): 128–37.

32. Habermas's own political strategy, moreover, requires a more extensive analysis of the darker dimensions of the psyche, if only to deal with the forces that oppose his position. Whether we like it or not, if the call for "constitutional patriotism," based on "abstract procedures and principles," is not to remain a mere "moral ought" in Hegel's sense, alternative dispositions for the narcissistic impulse toward identification, omnipotence, and merger must be found. This impulse, which was formerly fulfilled by religion and communism and today is gratifying itself in the sudden recrudescence of nationalist and chauvinist movements, must be extensively examined. See Jürgen Habermas, "Neoconservative Cultural Criticism in the United States and West Germany" and "Historical Consciousness and Post-Traditional Identity: The

Federal Republic's Orientation to the West," in *The New Conservatism: Cultural Criticism and the Historians' Debate*, ed. and trans. Shierry Weber Nicholson (Cambridge, MA: MIT Press, 1989).

33. See David Ingram, "Habermas on Aesthetics and Rationality: Completing the Project of Enlightenment," *New German Critique* 55 (spring/summer 1991): 67–103. On Habermas's relation to aesthetic modernism in general, see Martin Jay, "Habermas and Modernism," in *Habermas and Modernity*, 125–39.

34. Habermas, *The Philosophical Discourse of Modernity*, 106.

35. "While it has been [psychoanalysis'] intent to penetrate unconscious mentality with the light of rational understanding, it also has been and is its intent to uncover the irrational unconscious sources and forces motivating and organizing conscious and rational mental processes. In the course of these explorations, unconscious processes became accessible to rational understanding, and at the same time rational thought itself and our rational experience of the world as an 'object world' became problematic. In the conceptualization and investigation of the Oedipus complex and of transference, it became apparent that not only the neurotic's libidinal object is 'unrealistic' in that its objectivity is contaminated and distorted by transference. In normality as well, object relations as established in the oedipal period contribute to the constitution of the contemporary libidinal object. In other words, the contemporary libidinal object, even if freed of the gross transference distortions seen in neurosis (which helped us to see the ubiquitous phenomenon of transference), is 'unrealistic' or contains 'irrational' elements. If this is so, objectivity, rationality, and reality themselves are not what we thought them to be, not absolute states of mind and the world that would be independent of and unaffected by the generative process-structures of the mind and world" (Loewald, "The Waning of the Oedipus Complex," 402).

36. Sigmund Freud, *The Psychopathology of Everyday Life* (1901), S.E., vol. 6, 259.

37. David Macey, *Lacan in Contexts* (London: Verso Books, 1988), 280, n. 81.

38. G. W. F. Hegel, *Phenomenology of Spirit*, trans. A. V. Miller (Oxford: Clarendon Press, 1977 [1807]), 9.

39. Sigmund Freud, *Beyond the Pleasure Principle* (1920), S.E., vol. 18, 52.

40. The person who has done the most sustained and creative work in this area is, of course, Castoriadis with his notion of "the project of autonomy." See especially Cornelius Castoriadis, *The Imaginary Institution of Society*, trans. Kathleen Blamey (Cambridge, MA: MIT Press, 1987), 101ff.; "The State of the Subject Today," trans. David Ames Curtis, *American Imago* 46 (winter 1989): 371–412; and "Power, Politics and Autonomy," in *Philosophy, Politics, Autonomy: Essays in Political Philosophy*, trans. David Ames Curtis (New York: Oxford University Press, 1991), 143–74.

41. Sigmund Freud, *Inhibitions, Symptoms and Anxiety* (1926), S.E., vol. 20, 98.

42. Castoriadis, *The Imaginary Institution of Society*, 104.

43. The polemics against the centered, transparent Cartesian subject strike me as a red herring, given the fact that it would be virtually impossible to identify anyone defending those ideas today.

44. All of the quotations in this paragraph are from Luc Ferry and Alain Renaut, *Heidegger and Modernity*, trans. Franklin Philip (Chicago: University of Chicago Press, 1990), 17. It even seems that the wholesale attack on the metaphysics of subjectivity has exhausted itself within French Heideggerianism and that a new examination of the topic is under way. See Eduardo Cadava, et al., ed. *Who Comes after the Subject?*, (New York: Routledge, 1991).

Chapter 1

1. Sigmund Freud, *Civilization and Its Discontents* (1930), S.E., vol. 21, 114–15.

2. Sigmund Freud, *The Future of an Illusion* (1927), S.E., vol. 21, 2. This relatively impartial account should be contrasted with the more impassioned discussion of the achievements of civilization that Freud gave in the opening pages of "Thoughts for the Times on War and Death" (1915), S.E., vol. 14, some twelve years earlier.

3. Freud, *Future of an Illusion*, 10.

4. Ibid., 6.

5. Ibid., 15.

6. Freud, *Civilization and Its Discontents*, 95–96.

7. For the considerable influence of Hobbes on Freud, see Edwin R. Wallace IV, *Freud and Anthropology: A History and Reappraisal* (New York: International Universities Press, 1983).

8. Max Horkheimer and Theodor Adorno, *Dialectic of Enlightenment*, trans. John Cumming (New York: Herder and Herder, 1972), 57.

9. Ibid., 54.

10. See Jürgen Habermas, "Psychic Thermidor and the Rebirth of Rebellious Subjectivity," in *Habermas and Modernity*, ed. Richard Bernstein (Cambridge, MA: MIT Press, 1985), 74ff.

11. Herbert Marcuse, *Eros and Civilization: A Philosophical Inquiry into Freud* (Boston: Beacon Press, 1966), 4.

12. Ibid., 7.

13. Ibid., 5.

14. Ibid., 129.

15. Herbert Marcuse, "The End of Utopia," in *Five Lectures: Psychoanalysis, Politics and Utopia*, trans. Jeremy J. Shapiro and Shierry M. Weber (Boston: Beacon Press, 1970), 62–82.

16. See Herbert Marcuse, *An Essay on Liberation* (Boston: Beacon Press, 1969).

17. Marcuse, "The End of Utopia," 62, 64.

18. Marcuse, *Eros and Civilization*, chap. 1.

19. Ibid., 4.

20. Ibid., 17.

21. Ibid., 147.

22. Ibid., 34.

23. Ibid., 35.

24. Ibid., 88.

25. Karl Marx, *Capital*, vol. 3 (1894), ed. Friedrich Engels (Moscow: Progress Publishers, 1971), 820.

26. Marcuse, *Eros and Civilization*, 129.

27. Ibid., 139.

28. Ibid., 35.

29. Ibid., 132.

30. See Roy Schafer, "The Psychoanalytic Vision of Reality," in *A New Language for Psychoanalysis* (New Haven: Yale University Press, 1976), 35ff.

31. Hannah Arendt, *The Human Condition* (Chicago: University of Chicago Press, 1973), 133.

32. Aristotle, *Politics*, 1253b30–1254a18.

33. Marcuse, *Eros and Civilization*, 156.

34. In his important essay on Walter Benjamin, Habermas makes a similar distinction between the natural right tradition, which sought dignity and justice, and the utopian tradition, which aimed at happiness. See "Walter Benjamin: Consciousness-Raising or Rescuing Critique," in *Philosophical-Political Profiles,* trans. Frederick G. Lawrence (Cambridge, MA: MIT Press, 1983), 156. In this context, see also Bernard Yack, *The Longing for Total Revolution: Philosophic Sources of Social Discontent from Rousseau to Marx and Nietzsche* (Princeton: Princeton University Press, 1986).

35. Freud, *Future of an Illusion*, 8.

36. Marcuse, *Eros and Civilization,* 46–47.

37. See Sigmund Freud, *Three Essays on the Theory of Sexuality* (1905), S.E., vol. 7, 208ff. It should be pointed out that the hypostatization of psychosexual stages into a strict teleological scheme with genitality as its culmination was not so much the work of Freud but of Abraham, and it was then taken over by Reich, Fenichel, and Balint. See

Martin S. Bergmann, *The Anatomy of Loving: The Story of Man's Quest to Know What Love Is* (New York: Columbia University Press, 1987), chap. 16. Moreover, Chasseguet-Smirgel has made the point that the idealization of genitality can itself become another utopian illusion; see "Some Thoughts on the Ego Ideal: A Contribution to the Study of the 'Illness of Ideality,' " *The Psychoanalytic Quarterly* 45, no. 3 (1976): 355.

38. Marcuse, *Eros and Civilization,* 37–38.

39. Ibid., 39.

40. Ibid., 41.

41. Ibid., p. 48.

42. See Chapter 3, below.

43. Marcuse, *Eros and Civilization,* 33.

44. Ibid., 49–50.

45. Ibid., 139.

46. Ibid., 50.

47. Sigmund Freud, "Formulations on the Two Principles of Mental Functioning" (1911), S.E., vol. 12, 222.

48. Marcuse, *Eros and Civilization,* 19.

49. Ibid., 142.

50. Ibid., 151.

51. Ibid., 19.

52. Karl Marx, *Grundrisse: Introduction to the Critique of Political Economy,* trans. Martin Nicolaus (Baltimore: Penguin Books, 1973), 706.

53. Marcuse, *Eros and Civilization,* 152.

54. Ibid., 201.

55. Ibid., 253.

56. Ibid., 215.

57. Ibid., 197.

58. Ibid., 159.

59. Ibid., 160.

60. Ibid., 161.

61. Simone Sternberg, "The Mother Tongue and Mother's Tongue," in *Psychoanalytic Approaches to the Resistant and Difficult Patient,* ed. Herbert S. Strean (New York: Haworth Press, 1985), 63.

62. Cf. The discussion of the Siren episode in Chapter 3.

63. Marcuse, *Eros and Civilization,* 166.

64. Ibid., 166–67.

65. Ibid., 169.

66. Nancy Chodorow also criticizes Marcuse's theory in terms of its treatment of narcissism, but she develops these criticisms from a different perspective than the one I employ. See "Beyond Drive Theory: Object Relations and the Limits of Radical Individualism," in *Feminism and Psychoanalytic Theory* (New Haven: Yale University Press, 1989), 114–53.

67. Marcuse, *Eros and Civilization,* 171.

68. Ibid., 25.

69. Ibid., 142.

70. Hans Loewald, "Ego and Reality," in *Papers on Psychoanalysis,* 3–20.

71. Marcuse, *Eros and Civilization,* 76.

72. We will see that Chasseguet-Smirgel views the attempt to reunite with the archaic mother *in an unmediated fashion* as the source of much contemporary political and cultural barbarism.

73. Marcuse, *Eros and Civilization,* 230.

74. For the significance of the father in the separation-individuation process, see two important articles by Ernest Abelin, "The Role of the Father in the Separation-Individuation Process," in *Separation-Individuation: Essays in Honor of Margaret Mahler,* ed. John McDevitt and Calvin Settlage (New York: International Universities Press, 1971), 229–52; and "Triangulation, the Role of the Father and the Origins of Core Gender Identity during the Rapprochement Subphase," in *Rapprochement: The Critical Subphase of Separation-Individuation,* ed. Ruth Lax, Sheldon Bach, and J. Alexis Burland (New York: Jason Aronson, 1980), 151–70. For a different but convergent perspective, see also Jacques Lacan, "The Signification of the Phallus," in *Ecrits: A Selection,* trans. Alan Sheridan (New York: W. W. Norton, 1977), 281–91.

75. Marcuse, *Eros and Civilization,* 230. Chasseguet-Smirgel makes the interesting observation that Freud turned his attention to the topics of death and female sexuality during the same period of his life. She suggests that, for him, both contain the threat of opacity, engulfment, and unfathomability: "Freud's fears about fusion with the mother in oblivion were, probably, activated at the onset of his cancer. The final duality of the instincts is often associated with Freud's illness. But his major writings on femininity are contemporary with the introduction of the death instinct and carry

the undeniable stamp of death" ("The Femininity of the Analyst in Professional Practice," in *Sexuality and Mind: The Role of the Father and the Mother in the Psyche* [New York: New York University Press, 1986], 39).

76. Loewald, "Ego and Reality," 7.

77. Marcuse, *Eros and Civilization*, 49.

78. Ibid., 76.

79. Ibid., 111.

80. Ibid., 109–10.

81. Ibid., 109, 112.

82. Ibid., 112.

83. This fact lends credence to well-known psychoanalytic observations concerning the narcissistic core of Greek culture. See especially Freud, *Three Essays*, 149, n. 1; and Hans Sachs, "The Delay of the Machine Age," *Psychoanalytic Quarterly* 2 (1933): 420ff.

84. Aristotle, *Nicomachean Ethics*, 1178b24.

85. Aristotle, *Metaphysics*, 1072b14–15.

86. Ibid., 1072a28–b5.

87. Ibid., 1172b27.

88. See Richard J. Bernstein, "Reconciliation/Rupture," in *The New Constellation: The Ethical-Political Horizons of Modernity/Postmodernity* (Cambridge, MA: MIT Press, 1992), 293–322.

89. Marcuse, *Eros and Civilization*, 191.

90. Ibid., 231.

91. Walter Benjamin, "Theses on the Philosophy of History," in *Illuminations*, ed. Hannah Arendt, trans. Harry Zohn (New York: Schocken Books, 1968), 262 (Marcuse's translation).

92. Paul Ricoeur, *Freud and Philosophy: An Essay on Interpretation*, trans. Denis Savage (New Haven: Yale University Press, 1970), 372.

93. Castoriadis, *The Imaginary Institution of Society*, 311.

94. See Joyce McDougall, *Theaters of the Mind: Illusion and Truth on the Psychoanalytic Stage* (New York: Basic Books, 1985), 248.

95. Joyce McDougall, *A Plea for a Measure of Abnormality* (New York: International Universities Press, 1980), 67.

96. It is a central thesis of Robert Stoller's work that sexual perversions represent an attempt to triumph over trauma. In this it coincides with much recent research that suggests that compulsive perverse activity is often the result of childhood sexual abuse and represents an attempt to master that trauma retrospectively. See Robert Stoller, *Perversions: The Erotic Form of Hatred* (New York: Pantheon Books, 1975).

97. Freud, *Three Essays*, 163, 165.

98. Sigmund Freud, "An Outline of Psychoanalysis" (1940), S.E., vol. 23, 205.

99. Jean Laplanche and J.-B. Pontalis, *The Language of Psychoanalysis,* trans. Donald Nicholson-Smith (New York: W. W. Norton, 1974), 118. See Sigmund Freud, "Fetishism" (1927), S.E., vol. 21, 152–57; "An Outline of Psychoanalysis," 141–208; and "Splitting of the Ego in the Process of Defense" (1940), S.E., vol. 23, 275–78.

100. Sigmund Freud, "The Loss of Reality in Neurosis and Psychosis" (1924), S.E., vol. 19, 185.

101. Freud, "The Infantile Genital Organization," 144.

102. Sigmund Freud, "Some Psychical Consequences of the Anatomical Distinction between the Sexes" (1925), S.E., vol. 19, 253.

103. Freud, "Fetishism," 153–54. It should be noted that, while actual fetishism generally pertains to men, both sexes can employ innumerable perverse strategies to cope with the anxieties surrounding sexual difference. See Louise J. Kaplan, *Female Perversions: The Temptations of Emma Bovary,* (New York: Doubleday, 1991).

104. Ibid., 153.

105. For this reason, Laplanche and Pontalis suggest that another term—perhaps Freud's own "repudiation" *(Verwerfung)* or Lacan's "foreclosure" *(forclusion)*—be reserved to designate this strictly psychotic, outright rejection of reality, and that "disavowal" be reserved for another purpose.

106. Freud, "Fetishism," 154 (emphasis added).

107. Freud, "An Outline of Psychoanalysis," 203.

108. The extent to which Freud hoarded theoretical terms and reemployed early concepts later in his life provides evidence for his own claim that human beings are loath to give anything up.

109. Freud, "An Outline of Psychoanalysis," 201.

110. Janine Chasseguet-Smirgel, "Perversion, Idealization and Sublimation," *The International Journal of Psycho-Analysis* 55, pt. 3 (1974): 350.

111. See Chasseguet-Smirgel, "The Femininity of the Analyst," 30.

112. Sigmund Freud, *Inhibitions, Symptoms and Anxiety* (1926), S.E., vol. 20, 154–55.

113. Janine Chasseguet-Smirgel, "Freud and Female Sexuality: The Consideration of Some Blind Spots in the Exploration of the 'Dark Continent,' " in *Sexuality and Mind*, 21.

114. Sigmund Freud, "On Narcissism: An Introduction" (1914), S.E., vol. 14, 100. It will undoubtedly be objected that the notions of primary narcissism and symbiosis have been thoroughly discredited by infant research. I hope to show in a future publication, however, that, while recent research has taught us the infant comes into the world with far more adaptive equipment than we had formerly assumed, the wholesale rejection of symbiosis is nevertheless unfounded. What remains to be worked out is the dialectic of two opposing forces, namely, the allure of reality and the pull of symbiosis.

115. Chasseguet-Smirgel, "The Femininity of the Analyst," 30. Because the male can in fact reenter the woman's body with his penis, Chasseguet-Smirgel takes mother-son incest as the paradigmatic—and also the most tabooed and therefore infrequent—form of incest. She argues, however, that all forms of incest, including father-daughter, involve fantasies of fusion with the primary object. Furthermore, the threat of engulfment by the mother is compounded for the little girl owing to her primary identification with the parent of the same sex.

116. Chasseguet-Smirgel, "Perversion, Idealization and Sublimation," 350.

117. The term is Little Hans's. See Sigmund Freud, *Analysis of a Phobia in a Five-Year-Old Boy* (1909), S.E., vol. 10, 3–152.

118. It is interesting to note that, in an unusual twist on the customary oedipal logic, Chasseguet-Smirgel, following Grunberger, maintains that the ultimate source of the interdiction against incest is not the prohibiting father but the boy himself. Sensing his inability to carry out the incestuous act because of his physiological immaturity, the little boy projects the prohibition onto the father. It is thus a case of denying "I cannot do it" by maintaining "He will not permit me to do it." Unfortunately, as far as I am aware, she has never elaborated the implications, which would have to be substantial, of this revision for a psychoanalytic theory of the origins of authority and law.

119. See Sigmund Freud, *The Ego and the Id* (1923), S.E., vol. 19, 34.

120. See Janine Chasseguet-Smirgel, *The Ego Ideal: A Psychoanalytic Essay on the Malady of the Ideal*, trans. Paul Barrows (New York: W. W. Norton, 1985), 76–77.

121. Sigmund Freud, *Beyond the Pleasure Principle* (1920), S.E., vol. 18, 10.

122. Chasseguet-Smirgel, "Some Thoughts on the Ego Ideal," 351.

123. This attitude of defensive idealization and jealous superiority is nicely captured in a derogatory slang expression employed by French youth to connote uninspired parental lovemaking: namely, *l'amour à la papa*, which, roughly translated, means "the old man's way of doing it." Chasseguet-Smirgel, "Perversion, Idealization and Sublimation," 351.

124. See McDougall, *Theaters of the Mind*, chap. 11.

125. McDougall, *Plea for a Measure of Abnormality*, 67.

126. Ibid., 69.

127. Ibid., 210.

128. Ibid., 69.

129. See Sigmund Freud, "The Infantile Genital Organization" (1923), S.E., vol. 18, 141–48; "The Economic Problem of Masochism" (1924), S.E., vol. 19, 157–72; "Some Psychical Consequences of the Anatomical Distinction between the Sexes," 243–60; "Fetishism," (1927), S.E., vol. 21, 149–58; and "Splitting of the Ego in the Process of Defense" (1940), S.E., vol. 33, 271–78.

130. Freud, "The Loss of Reality in Neurosis and Psychosis" (1924), S.E., vol. 14, 185.

131. McDougall borrows the term from Wilfred Bion. See Wilfred Bion, *Learning From Experience* (London: Heinemann, 1962), 74–75.

132. Unless otherwise specified, all of the quotes from McDougall in the preceding paragraph are from *Plea for a Measure of Abnormality,* 73ff.

133. Sigmund Freud, "Pyscho-Analytic Notes on an Autobiographical Account of a Case of Paranoia" (1911), S.E., vol. 12, 71.

134. McDougall, *Plea for a Measure of Abnormality,* 81. Cf. Freud's notion of ritual as a "motor hallucination" (*Totem and Taboo,* 84).

135. McDougall, *Plea for a Measure of Abnormality,* 81.

136. Ibid., 188.

137. Ibid., 159.

138. "Freud," of course, "did not delve into the problematical questions of the infant's archaic sexual experience and fantasies and their potential effect on the later oedipal constellation" (ibid., 249).

139. Ibid., 150.

140. Ibid., 147.

141. Ibid., 185. See also Phyllis Greenacre, "The Fetish and the Transitional Object" (1969) and "The Transitional Object and the Fetish: With Special Reference to the Role of Illusion" (1970), both in *Emotional Growth: Psychoanalytic Studies of the Gifted and a Great Variety of Other Individuals,* vol. 1 (New York: International Universities Press, 1971).

142. McDougall, *Plea for a Measure of Abnormality,* 171. This distinction helps to elucidate the singular accomplishment of Claude Lanzmann's film *Shoah.* In an effort to avoid denial, other works on the Holocaust have tended to overwhelm the audience with images of bulldozed corpses, acts of unspeakable brutality, and hellish smokestacks, which have had the cumulative effect of paralyzing the viewers' capacity to think and to fantasize. In contrast, the inexplicit and restrained visual approach of Lanzmann's masterpiece, combined with the oral testimony of its subjects, allows

the viewer the "imaginative space" and stimulation to fantasize and think about the unimaginable.

143. Janine Chasseguet-Smirgel, "Perversion and the Universal Law," in *Creativity and Perversion* (New York: W. W. Norton, 1984), 11–12. See also Sigmund Freud, "On Transformations of Instinct as Exemplified in Anal Eroticism" (1917), S.E., vol. 17, 127–33.

144. Janine Chasseguet-Smirgel, "A Psychoanalytic Study of Falsehood," in *Creativity and Perversion,* 75.

145. Chasseguet-Smirgel, "Perversion, Idealization and Sublimation," 356.

146. Chasseguet-Smirgel, "Perversion and the Universal Law," 2.

147. Janine Chasseguet-Smirgel, "Aestheticism, Creation and Perversion," in *Creativity and Perversion,* 90.

148. Chasseguet-Smirgel, "A Psychoanalytic Study of Falsehood," 68.

149. Chasseguet-Smirgel, "The Femininity of the Analyst," 35.

150. Quoted in *Plea for a Measure of Abnormality,* 249.

151. Chasseguet-Smirgel, "Perversion and the Universal Law," 6.

152. Janine Chasseguet-Smirgel, "Reflexions on the Connexions between Perversions and Sadism," *The International Journal of Psycho-Analysis* 59, pt. 1 (1978): 32.

153. Janine Chasseguet-Smirgel, "The Archaic Matrix of the Oedipus Complex," in *Sexuality and Mind,* 77.

154. Chasseguet-Smirgel, "Perversion and the Universal Law," 2.

155. Ibid., 6.

156. Chasseguet-Smirgel, "Reflexions on the Connexions between Perversions and Sadism," 30, 33. See also Sheldin Bach and Lester Schwartz, "A Dream of the Marquis de Sade: Psychoanalytic Reflections on Narcissistic Trauma, Decompensation, and the Reconstitution of a Delusional Self," *Journal of the American Psychoanalytic Association* 20, no. 3 (July 1972): 451–75.

157. McDougall, *Plea for a Measure of Abnormality,* 162.

158. See Robert Waelder, "The Principle of Multiple Function: Observations on Overdetermination in Psychoanalysis," in *Psychoanalysis—Observation, Theory, Application: Selected Papers of Robert Waelder,* ed. Samuel A. Guttman (New York: International Universities Press, 1976), 57–67.

159. McDougall, *Plea for a Measure of Abnormality,* 404.

160. Ibid., 295.

161. Ibid., 204.

162. McDougall, *Theaters of the Mind*, 280.

163. McDougall, *Plea for a Measure of Abnormality*, 151–52.

164. See Freud, "Formulations on the Two Principles of Mental Functioning" (1911), S.E., vol. 12, 224.

165. McDougall, *Plea for a Measure of Abnormality*, 209.

166. See Chasseguet-Smirgel, *The Ego Ideal*, 115.

167. Joyce McDougall, "Perversions and Deviations in the Psychoanalytic Attitude: Their Effect on Theory and Practice," in *Perversions and Near-Perversions in Clinical Practice. New Psychoanalytic Perspectives*, ed. Gerald I. Fogel and Wayne A. Myers (New Haven: Yale University Press, 1991), 176–203.

168. Ibid., 196.

169. Ibid., 196–97.

170. Chasseguet-Smirgel, *Creativity and Perversion*, 1.

171. Ibid., 1–2.

172. Ibid., 12.

173. I would suggest the following reason for Freud's difficulty in distinguishing between the superego and the ego ideal. Both the idealizing function and the interdictory function—while they have distinct histories and logics— converge in the successful resolution of the Oedipus complex. Thus, in the following passage, Freud identifies the "ego ideal or super-ego" as the product of the oedipal phase: *"The broad general outcome of the sexual phase dominated by the Oedipus complex may, therefore, be taken to be the forming of a precipitate in the ego, consisting of these two identifications* [with the parents] *in some way united with each other. This modification of the ego retains its special position; it confronts the other contents of the ego as an ego ideal or super-ego"* (emphasis in the original). Despite the identification of the ego ideal and super-ego in this passage, Freud goes on to write that the successful resolution of the Oedipus complex has two components. The first is negative—the interdiction. The little boy renounces his incestous wishes because of the fear of castration. He internalizes the maxim, "You *may not be like this* [like your father]—that is, you may not do all that he does; some things are his prerogative" (the super-ego). The second is positive—the identification with the father. In this case, the motive for renouncing his desire for the mother is the promise that some day the boy will have a mature woman for himself. The maxim here is: "You *ought to be like this* [like your father]," which is to say, "if you grow up and mature, you can be like your father and have—with the exception of possessing the mother—prerogatives like his" (the ego ideal). Through this identification, "the infantile ego . . . borrowed strength to [renounce its oedipal desires and erect the incest barrier], so to speak, from the father, and this loan was an extraordinarily momentous act" (*The Ego and the Id* [1923], S.E., vol. 19, 34).

174. Chasseguet-Smirgel, *The Ego Ideal*, 1; see also pp. 220ff.

175. Freud, *The Ego and the Id*, 34, 35; and Chasseguet-Smirgel, *The Ego Ideal*, 76–77.

176. Sigmund Freud, *Group Psychology and the Analysis of the Ego* (1921), S.E., vol. 18, 109–10.

177. Sigmund Freud, "On Narcissism" (1914), S.E., vol. 14, 94.

178. Sigmund Freud, "Types of Onset of Neurosis" (1912), S.E., vol. 12, 235. I am grateful to Donald Kaplan for calling my attention to this important concept in Freud.

179. Freud, "On Narcissism," 94. Unlike some psychoanalytic authors, Chasseguet-Smirgel rejects the notion of ideal ego—as opposed to the ego ideal—which, while present in Freud, is confused and never systematically employed. I think it might be useful, however, to retain this term precisely to mark the distinction Chasseguet-Smirgel wants to emphasize, namely, between the evolutionary and the regressive means of pursuing the lost perfection of childhood. The term "ego ideal" would be reserved for designating the projected *telos* of the evolutionary route for pursuing childhood perfection. And the "ideal ego," as Nunberg uses it in the classical formulation, would be reserved for the regressive goal of returning to the "as-yet-unorganized ego which feels as one with the id [and the object]" and which, therefore, "corresponds to an ideal condition." Nunberg goes on to observe that "in certain catatonic and manic attacks, in a number of those psychoses which lead to mental deterioration, and also to a certain though lesser degree in neuroses, the individual achieves such an ideal condition, in which he grants himself everything pleasurable and rejects everything unpleasurable. . . . When this ideal is again attained in the illness, the patient, in spite of his suffering and feelings of inferiority, feels more or less omnipotent and endowed with magic powers" (Herman Nunberg, *Principles of Psychoanalysis: Their Application to the Neuroses,* trans. Madlyn Kahr and Sidney Kahr [New York: International Universities Press, 1955], 126). The ideal ego could be fruitfully compared to Kohut's notion of the grandiose self. See Heinz Kohut, *The Analysis of the Self: A Systematic Approach to the Psychoanalytic Treatment of Narcissistic Personality Disorders* (New York: International Universities Press, 1971), and *The Restoration of the Self* (New York: International Universities Press, 1977). See also Jacques Lacan, *The Seminar of Jacques Lacan,* book 1, *Freud's Papers on Technique (1953–54),* trans. John Forrester (New York: W. W. Norton, 1988), 129–42.

180. Freud, "On Narcissism," 94, 100.

181. Chasseguet-Smirgel, "Some Thoughts on the Ego Ideal," 345.

182. Walter Benjamin uses the motto "the origin is the goal," taken from Karl Kraus, to introduce thesis 14 of his "Theses on the Philosophy of History," *Illuminations,* ed. Hannah Arendt, trans. Harry Zohn (New York: Schocken Books, 1968) 261.

183. Chasseguet-Smirgel, "Some Thoughts on the Ego Ideal," 4.

184. Sigmund Freud, *Totem and Taboo* (1913), S.E., vol. 13, 90.

185. Chasseguet-Smirgel, "Some Thoughts on the Ego Ideal, 351; see also her *Ego Ideal,* 30, and Ricoeur, *Freud and Philosophy,* 186.

186. Freud, "On Narcissism," 100.

187. Chasseguet-Smirgel, "Freud and Female Sexuality," 82.

188. Chasseguet-Smirgel, "Perversion, Idealization and Sublimation," 350.

189. Sigmund Freud, *Beyond the Pleasure Principle* (1920), S.E., vol. 18, 15.

190. Chasseguet-Smirgel, "Some Thoughts on the Ego Ideal," 352.

191. Ibid., 348.

192. Janine Chasseguet-Smirgel, "Narcissism and Group Psychology," in *Creativity and Perversion,* 55–56. Although I am criticizing Chasseguet-Smirgel's position, there is, nevertheless, one point I must stress. She is one of the few contemporary analysts who continues to theorize in the "grand tradition," which seems largely to have atrophied within mainstream psychoanalysis. By that I mean, like Freud in his cultural writings, she continues to bring the discoveries of clinical psychoanalysis to bear on the major political, social, and cultural issues of our day.

193. Janine Chasseguet-Smirgel, introduction to *Sexuality and Mind,* 4.

194. Janine Chasseguet-Smirgel, "The Paradox of the Freudian Method," in *Sexuality and Mind,* 139. Her earlier book on politics, written with Bela Grunberger in the wake of the events of 1968, was much more polemical and strident: *Freud or Marx: Psychoanalysis and Illusion,* trans. Clair Pajaczkowska (London: Free Association Books, 1968).

195. Chasseguet-Smirgel, *The Ego Ideal,* 76.

196. See, for example, Freud, *The Ego and the Id,* 48–49.

197. Ibid., 53.

198. Ricoeur, *Freud and Philosophy,* 447.

199. Ibid., 449. Both Piaget and Jacobson makes similar points, from very different perspectives, about the inadequacy of the superego as a moral agent. See Edith Jacobson, *The Self and the Object World* (New York: International Universities Press, 1964), 127; and Jean Piaget, *The Moral Judgement of the Child,* trans. Marjorie Gabain (New York: Free Press, 1965), 369–70.

200. Janine Chasseguet-Smirgel, "Thinking and the Superego: Some Interrelations," in *The Psychoanalytic Core: Essays in Honor of Leo Rangell, M.D.,* ed. Harold Blum et al. (Madison, CT: International Universities Press, 1989), 207.

201. In a similar vein, she writes that "there is no 'great man'—artist, scholar, writer or thinker—who has not had some model, some mentor, some spiritual father. It is as if, in the realm of creativity, the most beautiful unusual flower is that which also has its roots deep in the soil of tradition. The great innovators have known the inspiration of being with those on whom they have projected their ego ideal and whom they wish to resemble" (*The Ego Ideal,* 99–100). While the role of tradition in forming the creative genius should in no way be underestimated, Chasseguet-Smirgel fails to recognize the other, equally important side, namely, the patricidal element in all genius, which exists side by side with the element of mentorship. In addition to learning from, and elaborating the work of, their respective mentors, Aristotle overthrew Plato and Socrates, Beethoven overthrew Mozart and Haydn, and Hegel overthrew Kant.

202. See, for example, Chasseguet-Smirgel, "Perversion and the Universal Law," 5ff.

203. See, for example, Freud, *Future of an Illusion,* chap. 7.

204. The terms are Christopher Lasch's. See *The Minimal Self: Psychic Survival in Troubled Times* (New York: W. W. Norton, 1984).

205. Ricoeur, *Freud and Philosophy,* 330, 332.

206. Ibid., 263.

207. Ibid., 324–25.

208. Heinz Kohut, *How Does Analysis Cure?* ed. A. Goldberg (Chicago: University of Chicago Press, 1984), 54.

209. Freud, *Civilization and Its Discontents,* 76.

210. Ricoeur, *Freud and Philosophy,* 238, 327.

211. Freud, *Future of an Illusion,* 49.

212. Ricoeur, *Freud and Philosophy,* 334.

213. Kohut is consistent in simultaneously affirming the positive aspects of narcissism and challenging Freud's adherence to the scientific paradigm.

214. Ricoeur, *Freud and Philosophy,* 332.

215. Ibid., 310.

216. Freud, "Thoughts," 291.

217. Sigmund Freud, "On Transience" (1916), S.E., vol. 14, 307.

218. Freud, "Mourning and Melancholia," 245.

219. Freud, "On Transience," 306–307.

220. Freud, "Thoughts," 290.

221. Ricoeur, *Freud and Philosophy,* 322.

222. This is one of the main respects, I believe, in which Ricoeur's work can be seen as "an internal discussion or debate with Herbert Marcuse" (*Freud and Philosophy,* 462).

Excursus

1. Quoted in Martin Jay, *Adorno* (London: Fontana Books, 1984), 86.

2. See G. W. F. Hegel, "Absolute Freedom and Terror," in *Phenomenology of Spirit,* 355ff.

3. Adorno, *Negative Dialectics,* 146–47.

4. Castoriadis, "The Retreat from Autonomy," 20.

5. See Axel Honneth, *The Critique of Power: Reflective Stages in a Critical Social Theory,* trans. Kenneth Baynes (Cambridge, MA: MIT Press, 1991), chaps. 4–6.

6. See Helmut Dubiel, *Theory and Politics: Studies in the Development of Critical Theory,* trans. Benjamin Gregg (Cambridge, MA: MIT Press, 1985), 18–21.

7. Theodor W. Adorno, "Subject and Object," in *The Essential Frankfurt School Reader,* ed. Andrew Arato and Eike Gebhardt (New York: Urizen Books, 1978), 503.

8. See Yack, *The Longing for Total Revolution.*

9. Adorno, *Minima Moralia,* 247. Something of the "standpoint of redemption" remains in Habermas's conception of the ideal-speech situation. Only the ideal-speech situation, which is *counterfactually* posited but never empirically achieved, is capable of illuminating the actual distortions in worldly communication.

10. See Theodor W. Adorno, "Resignation," *Telos* 35 (spring 1978).

11. Adorno, *Minima Moralia,* 247.

12. See Jürgen Habermas, "Labor and Interaction: Remarks on Hegel's Jena *Philosophy of Mind,*" in *Theory and Practice,* trans. John Viertel (Boston: Beacon Press, 1973), 142–69, and *Knowledge and Human Interests.*

13. Albrecht Wellmer, "Communications and Emancipation: Reflections on the Linguistic Turn in Critical Theory," in *On Critical Theory,* ed. John O'Neill (New York: Seabury Press, 1976), 245.

14. Habermas, "Walter Benjamin," 158.

15. Jürgen Habermas "The Entwinement of Myth and Enlightenment: Horkheimer and Adorno," in *The Philosophical Discourse of Modernity,* 117.

16. See Leo Lowenthal, "The Utopian Motif Is Suspended," in *An Unmastered Past,* 237–48.

17. Jürgen Habermas, "A Philosophico-Political Profile," in *Habermas: Autonomy and Solidarity: Interviews with Jürgen Habermas,* ed. Peter Dews (London: New Left Books, 1986), 188.

18. Thomas McCarthy, *The Critical Theory of Jürgen Habermas* (Cambridge, MA: MIT Press, 1978), 195.

19. Habermas, *Knowledge and Human Interests,* 214.

20. See Jürgen Habermas, "A Postscript to *Knowledge and Human Interests,*" *Philosophy of Social Science* 3 (1973): 182ff.; McCarthy, *The Critical Theory of Jürgen Habermas,* 94, 272ff.; and Honneth, *The Critique of Power,* 278ff.

21. Freud, *The Ego and the Id*, 13ff., 60ff. Cf. Piaget's discussion of the affective and cognitive unconscious: "Affectivity is characterized by its energic composition, with charges distributed over one object or another (cathexis), positively or negatively. The cognitive aspect of conduct, on the contrary, is characterized by its structure, whether it be elementary schemata, concrete classification, operations seriation, etc., or the logic of propositions with their different 'function' " ("The Affective Unconscious and the Cognitive Unconscious," *Journal of the American Psychoanalytic Association* 21, no. 2 [1973]: 250).

22. Honneth, *The Critique of Power*, 284. See also Hans Joas, "The Unhappy Marriage of Hermeneutics and Functionalism" and "Complexity and Democracy: Or the Seducements of Systems Theory," in *The Theory of Communicative Action*, ed. Axel Honneth and Hans Joas (London: Polity Press, 1991).

23. See especially the programmatic statement in Jürgen Habermas, "Modernity—An Incomplete Project," 3–15. The essay also appeared under the title "Modernity versus Postmodernity," in *New German Critique* 22 (winter 1981). See Richard J. Bernstein's introduction to *Habermas and Modernity*, 1–34.

24. Thomas McCarthy asks whether Piaget's and Kohlberg's theories can carry the quasi-foundational load Habermas places on them: "In the face of these problems and open questions, Habermas would, it seems, be well advised to adopt a much more tentative and critical posture towards cognitive developmental theories than he has to date. They certainly cannot be appealed to as providing confirmation of his universality claims. In the present state of affairs, perhaps, the most they can be said to offer is 'a heuristic guide and encouragement' " ("Rationality and Relativism: Habermas's 'Overcoming' of Hermeneutics," in *Habermas: Critical Debates*, ed. John B. Thompson and David Held [Cambridge, MA: MIT Press, 1982], 72.

25. Max Horkheimer and Theodor Adorno, *Dialectic of Enlightenment*, 231.

26. Honneth, *The Critique of Power*, 281.

27. Habermas, "Walter Benjamin," 157.

28. Ibid., 158.

29. On the latter point, see David Ingram, "Habermas on Aesthetics and Rationality: Completing the Project of Enlightenment," *New German Critique* 55 (spring/summer 1991): 67–103. On Habermas's relation to aesthetic modernism in general, see Martin Jay, "Habermas and Modernism," in *Habermas and Modernity*, 125–39.

30. For a recent discussion of the thesis that self-determination is the fundamental norm of modernity and modernist culture, see Robert B. Pippen, *Modernism as a Philosophical Problem* (Cambridge, MA: Basil Blackwell, 1991).

31. Jürgen Habermas, "Theodor Adorno: The Primal History of Subjectivity—Self-Affirmation Gone Wild," in *Philosophical-Political Profiles*, 108.

32. Habermas, *The Theory of Communicative Action*, 390; Albrecht Wellmer, "Truth, Semblance and Reconciliation: Adorno's Aesthetic Redemption of Modernity," trans. Maeve Cooke, *Telos* 62 (winter 1984–85): 98ff; Seyla Benhabib, *Critique, Norm, and Utopia*, 213ff.

33. Jay, *The Dialectical Imagination*, chap. 5.

34. Herbert Marcuse, "On Hedonism," in *Negations: Essays in Critical Theory*, trans. Jeremy J. Shapiro (Boston: Beacon Press, 1968), 159–200.

35. Jürgen Habermas, "Moral Development and Ego Identity," in *Communication and the Evolution of Society*, trans. Thomas McCarthy (Boston: Beacon Press, 1979), 93.

36. Freud, *Inhibitions, Symptoms and Anxiety* (1926), S.E., vol. 20, 98.

37. Habermas, "Moral Development and Ego Identity," 78.

38. *Habermas: Critical Debates*, 235.

39. Ibid., 262.

40. Habermas, "Moral Development and Ego Identity," 93.

41. See Habermas, *Knowledge and Human Interests*, chaps. 10–12.

Chapter 2

1. Sigmund Freud, "A Difficulty in the Path of Psycho-Analysis" (1917), S.E., vol. 17, 143 (emphasis in the original).

2. Sigmund Freud, S.E., vol. 13, 275–78.

3. Sigmund Freud, *New Introductory Lectures on Psycho-Analysis* (1933), S.E., vol. 22, 80 (translation altered).

4. Jacques Lacan, "in a series of virtuoso exegeses," dissolves the problem by inverting the generally accepted meaning of the dictum. See Peter Dews, *The Logics of Disintegration*, 86. For an example, see Lacan, "The Freudian Thing," in *Ecrits*, 128.

5. Sigmund Freud, *Introductory Lectures on Psycho-Analysis, XVIII*, S.E., vol. 16, 284–85. See also Freud, "A Difficulty in the Path of Psycho-Analysis," passim.

6. Adorno, "Sociology and Psychology," 88.

7. Ricoeur, *Freud and Philosophy*, 426.

8. Philip Rieff, *Freud: The Mind of the Moralist* (Chicago: University of Chicago Press, 1979), chap. 9; and Kohut, *How Does Analysis Cure?* 54.

9. Cf. Habermas's attempt to formulate a minimalist progressive philosophy of history qua a collective learning theory through a discussion of the Rationality Debate. See *The Theory of Communicative Action*, vol. 1 of *Reason and the Rationalization of Society*, trans. Thomas McCarthy (Boston: Beacon Press, 1984), 143ff.

10. All of the quotes in the preceding paragraph come from Freud, "Animism, Magic and the Omnipotence of Thoughts," which is the third chapter of *Totem and Taboo* (1913), S.E., vol. 13, 75–99.

11. See Ricoeur, *Freud and Philosophy*, 236ff.

12. See Castoriadis, *The Imaginary Institution of Society*, 107; and Jürgen Habermas, "Toward a Reconstruction of Historical Materialism," in *Communication and the Evolution of Society*, 154.

13. Freud, *Future of an Illusion* (1927), S.E., vol. 21, 30–31.

14. The influence of Feuerbach on Freud has not been adequately appreciated. See Wallace, *Freud and Anthropology*, 12–15.

15. "The key to illusion is the harshness of life, which is barely tolerable for man, since he not only understands and feels pain but yearns for consolation as a result of his innate narcissism" (Paul Ricoeur, "Psychoanalysis and the Movement of Contemporary Culture," in *The Conflict of Interpretations: Essays on Hermeneutics* [Evanston, IL: Northwestern University Press, 1974], 131).

16. Ricoeur, *Freud and Philosophy*, 332.

17. Ibid., 72.

18. Castoriadis, "Psychoanalysis: Project and Elucidation," in *Crossroads in the Labyrinth*, trans. Kate Soper and Martin H. Ryle (Cambridge, MA: MIT Press, 1984), 63.

19. See Castoriadis, "Psychoanalysis: Project and Elucidation," 62–63.

20. Winnicott makes the following observation, which is pertinent in this context: "We can share a respect for *illusory experience*, and if we wish we may collect together and form a group on the basis of the similarity of our illusory experiences. This is a natural root of grouping among human beings. Yet it is a hall-mark of madness when an adult puts too powerful a claim on the credulity of others, forcing them to acknowledge a sharing of illusion that is not their own" ("Transitional Objects and Transitional Phenomena," in *Through Paediatrics to Psycho-Analysis*, ed. M. Masud R. Khan [New York: Basic Books, 1975], 231). See also Piaget, *The Moral Judgement of the Child*, 276ff.

21. See G. W. F. Hegel, *The Philosophy of Right*, trans. T. M. Knox (Oxford: Clarendon Press, 1942), addition paragraph 182.

22. See Albrecht Wellmer, "Model of Freedom in the Modern World," *The Philosophical Forum* 21, nos. 1–2 (winter 1989–90): pp 228ff.

23. For Freud's extensive knowledge of Hobbes, see Wallace, *Freud and Anthropology*, 54–55, n. 18.

24. Ricoeur, *Freud and Philosophy*, 327.

25. Freud, *Civilization and Its Discontents* (1930), S.E., vol. 30, 72.

26. Freud, *Future of an Illusion*, 49.

27. Ibid., 54.

28. Ricoeur, *Freud and Philosophy*, 33.

29. Freud, *Future of an Illusion*, 43.

30. See Sigmund Freud, "Lecture XXXV: The Question of a Weltanschauung," *New Introductory Lectures*, 176.

31. Freud, *Future of an Illusion*, 53.

32. Ibid., 54.

33. Ibid., 53.

34. Ricoeur, "Psychoanalysis and the Movement of Contemporary Culture," 150.

35. Cf. Lacan's linguistic reformulation of Groddeck's position: "This passion of the signifier now becomes a new dimension of the human condition in that it is not only man who speaks, but that in man and through man *it* speaks (*ça parle*), that his nature is woven by effects in which is to be found the structure of language, of which he becomes the material, and that therefore there resounds in him, beyond what could be conceived of by a psychology of ideas, the relation of speech" ("The Signification of the Phallus," 284).

36. Freud, *The Ego and the Id* (1923), S.E., vol. 19, 23. It is interesting, given the genealogy of poststructuralism, that Freud traces the term back past Groddeck to Nietzsche, whom Groddeck "no doubt followed."

37. See especially chap. 5, S.E., vol. 19, 48–59.

38. Freud, *The Ego and the Id*, 56. Cf. "[T]he therapeutic efforts of psycho-analysis . . . [are], indeed, to strengthen the ego, to make it more independent of the super-ego, to widen its field of perception and enlarge its organization, so that it can appropriate fresh portions of the id. Where id was, there ego shall be. It is a work of culture—not unlike the draining of the Zuider Zee" (*New Introductory Lectures* [1933], S.E., vol. 22, 80).

39. Freud, *The Ego and the Id*, 25.

40. Ibid., 56.

41. Freud, *Three Essays*, 134.

42. Freud, *The Ego and the Id*, 25.

43. See Sigmund Freud, "Neurosis and Psychosis" (1924), S.E., vol. 19, 149ff., and "The Loss of Reality in Neurosis and Psychosis," 183ff.

44. Freud, *The Ego and the Id*, 55–56.

45. Cf. Hartmann's concept of "biological solipsism" in *Ego Psychology and the Problem of Adaptation*, trans. David Rapaport (New York: International Universities Press, 1964), 33.

46. Freud, *The Ego and the Id*, 30.

47. Ibid., 55–56.

48. Ibid., 56.

49. Ibid., 25. It would be safe to say that contemporary analysts of various schools tend to agree that the transference is the central vehicle of the treatment.

50. It could also be argued that, insofar as morality is introduced into the psyche through the relationship with the parents in the Oedipus complex, the truth in the normative sense is also introduced via the medium of libido—and aggression— which is to say, instinctually.

51. See S.E., vol. 14, 249 ff.

52. Freud, *The Ego and the Id*, 28–29.

53. Ibid., 30. I will return to the question of the ego's deepening its relations with the id later when I examine Loewald's position on sublimation.

54. Ibid., 46.

55. Freud, *Three Essays* (1905), S.E., vol. 7, 218. The section in which this term is to be found was added to the *Three Essays* after the formulation of the theory of narcissism in 1914.

56. Freud, "On Narcissism" (1914), S.E., vol. 14, 75.

57. While the sexual drive later become reactively autonomous, it originally "leans on" self-preservative functions and is, hence, derivative from them; e.g., autoerotic thumb sucking leans on the nutritive function of drinking.

58. Jean Laplanche and J.-B. Pontalis, *The Language of Psychoanalysis*, trans. Donald Nicholson-Smith (New York: W. W. Norton, 1974), 147.

59. Freud, *Beyond the Pleasure Principle* (1920), S.E., vol. 18, 52.

60. For example, "Our views have from the very first been *dualistic,* and to-day they are even more definitely dualistic than before—now that we describe the opposition as being, not between ego-instincts and sexual instincts but between life instincts and death instincts. Jung's libido theory is on the contrary monistic" (Freud, *Beyond the Pleasure Principle*, 53).

61. Freud, "On Narcissism," 76. See also Freud, *Beyond the Pleasure Principle*, 52–53.

62. Freud, *Beyond the Pleasure Principle*, 53.

63. Freud, *The Ego and the Id*, 55.

64. Freud, *Inhibitions, Symptoms and Anxiety* (1926), S.E., vol. 20, 95.

65. Ibid., 97.

66. Freud, *New Introductory Lectures*, 79.

67. Ibid., 79.

68. Hartmann, as Macey points out, makes the modest claim that he is merely making a "systematic presentation" of certain unelaborated "motifs" in Freud and attempting a "mutual adjustment of some hypotheses in the field." However, the shift in emphasis from Freud's structural theory to Hartmann's ego psychology can, despite their subtlety, be substantial indeed, and the current topic is a case in point. I am suggesting that Freud, who did not employ the notions of "structuralization" and "neutralization," presents a much more fluid conception of the relations between the psychic agencies. I would also argue from the other side that Freud's structural theory was already an ego psychology—a fact Lacan chooses to ignore for polemical reasons—but one with considerable differences from Hartmann's—a fact Hartmann obscures for similarly polemical reasons, albeit in a less strident fashion. See Heinz Hartmann, "Some Comments on the Psychoanalytic Theory of the Ego" (1950), in *Essays on Ego Psychology* (New York: International Universities Press, 1965), 113–17.

69. See Samuel Weber, *The Legend of Freud* (Minneapolis: University of Minnesota Press, 1983), 8ff.

70. Sigmund Freud, "On the History of the Psycho-Analytic Movement" (1914), S.E., vol. 14, 52.

71. Sigmund Freud, *The Interpretation of Dreams* (1990), S.E., vol. 5, 490, 499.

72. Ibid., 499.

73. Weber, *The Legend of Freud*, 12. See also Freud, *The Interpretation of Dreams*, 490; *New Introductory Lectures*, 161, n. 1.

74. Freud, *Totem and Taboo*, 95. In the "Rat Man" case, Freud criticizes his earlier theory of obsessive neurosis in terms of its excessive striving for unification: "This definition [of obsessional ideas] now seems to me to be open to criticism upon formal grounds, though its component elements are unobjectionable. It was aiming too much at unification, and took as its model the practice of obsessional neurotics themselves, when, with their characteristic liking for indeterminateness, they heap together under the name of 'obsessional ideas' the most heterogeneous psychical structures" (*Notes upon a Case of Obsessional Neurosis* [1909], S.E., vol. 10, 221).

75. Weber, *The Legend of Freud*, 13.

76. Ibid., 13

77. Freud, "On the History of the Psycho-Analytic Movement," 15.

78. Weber, *The Legend of Freud*, 15

79. See Lawrence Friedman, "Conflict and Synthesis in Freud's Theory of the Mind," *International Review of Psycho-Analysis* 4 (1977): 155–70. Hartmann's claim that he was not adding anything new to Freud's theory but simply systematizing it indicates that he did not appreciate this crucial point.

80. Adorno, *Negative Dialectics,* 165.

81. Freud, *Inhibitions, Symptoms and Anxiety,* 97.

82. Freud, *The Ego and the Id,* 25. There is something peculiar about this argument, for even if the ego *began* as a part of the id, once it has been differentiated, it can no longer be said that it is "identical" with the id. It should also be pointed out that Hartmann argues that the ego cannot be simply "a developmental by-product of the influence of reality on the instinctual drives," but, even on purely conceptual grounds, it must possess a partly independent origin ("Some Comments on the Psychoanalytic Theory of the Ego," 119).

83. Freud, *Inhibitions, Symptoms and Anxiety,* 97.

84. Ibid., 97.

85. Ibid., 97.

86. Freud, *New Introductory Lectures,* 79.

87. Ibid., 58.

88. Historically, Richard Sterba was the first to identify the therapeutic split of the ego in psychoanalysis. See "The Fate of the Ego in Analytic Therapy," *The International Journal of Psycho-Analysis* 15 (1935): 177–126.

89. Freud *New Introductory Lectures,* 58–59.

90. Ibid., 80.

91. Freud, "Splitting of the Ego in the Process of Defense," 276.

92. Freud, *New Introductory Lectures,* 76. In a footnote to this passage, Strachey points out that, while Freud did not thematize the notion of the synthetic function until his later period, it seems to have been implicit in his earliest psychoanalytic writing, for example, in the notion of "incompatible" ideas that was common during the Breuer period.

93. Freud, *Inhibitions, Symptoms and Anxiety,* 98. See also Loewald, *Sublimation,* 18ff.

94. Both Loewald and Castoriadis trace the synthetic function of the ego to an earlier, indeed the earliest, developmental phase of primary narcissism or primary autism. They both argue that the synthetic function of the ego derives from the unity of that original position and represents an attempt to "constantly reestablish" it (Loewald). See Loewald, "Ego and Reality," 11–12; and Castoriadis, *The Imaginary Institution of Society,* 294ff.

95. Castoriadis, *The Imaginary Institution of Society,* 299.

96. Freud, "Splitting of the Ego in the Process of Defense," 276.

97. Castoriadis, *The Imaginary Institution of Society,* 298.

98. Horkheimer and Adorno, *Dialectic of Enlightenment,* 27.

99. Freud, *The Ego and the Id,* 40.

100. Sigmund Freud, "The Unconscious" (1915), S.E., vol. 14, 194.

101. Freud, *Inhibitions, Symptoms and Anxiety,* 91.

102. Ibid., 98.

103. Ibid., 98.

104. Sigmund Freud, "Lines of Advance in Psycho-Analytic Therapy" (1919), S.E., vol. 17, 161.

105. Freud, *New Introductory Lectures,* 80.

106. Castoriadis, *The Imaginary Institution of Society,* 104.

107. Freud, *New Introductory Lectures,* 80.

108. Castoriadis, *The Imaginary Institution of Society,* 104.

Chapter 3

1. Stanley Cavell, "Freud and Philosophy: A Fragment," *Critical Inquiry* 13, no. 2 (winter 1987): 391.

2. See Martin Jay, *The Dialectical Imagination,* chap. 3. Castoriadis makes the following similar but broader point: "Without prejudice to the new depth dimension revealed by Freud, this is the program proposed by philosophical reflection on the individual for the past 25 centuries, at once the assumption and the outcome of ethics as it has been viewed by Plato and the Stoics, Spinoza or Kant. (It is of immense importance in itself . . . that Freud proposes an effective way to attain what, for philosophers, had remained an 'ideal' accessible through abstract knowledge.)" (*The Imaginary Institution of Society,* 102).

3. See Michel Foucault, "What Is Enlightenment?" *The Foucault Reader,* ed. Paul Rabinow (New York: Pantheon Books, 1984), 32–51; Jürgen Habermas, "Taking Aim at the Heart of the Present," in *Foucault: A Critical Reader,* ed. David Couzens Hoy (New York: Basil Blackwell, 1986), 103–9; Hubert Dreyfus and Paul Rabinow, "What Is Maturity? Habermas and Foucault on 'What Is Enlightenment?' " in *Foucault: A Critical Reader,* 109–23.

4. Popper observes that in the opening paragraph of "What Is Enlightenment?" Kant "is saying something personal. . . . It is part of his own history. Brought up in near poverty, in the narrow outlook of Pietism—a severe German version of Puritanism—his own life was a story of emancipation through knowledge. In later years he used to look back with horror to what he called 'the slavery of childhood,' his period of tutelage" (*Conjectures and Refutations: The Growth of Scientific Knowledge* [New York: Basic Books, 1965], 177).

5. See Immanuel Kant, *Groundwork of the Metaphysics of Morals*, trans. J. J. Paton (New York: Harper Torchbooks, 1964), 100.

6. Laplanche and J.-B. Pontalis, *The Language of Psychoanalysis*, 363.

7. Cornelius Castoriadis, "The First Institution of Society," *Free Associations* 12 (1988): 42.

8. Ibid., 41. Castoriadis believes that this "rupture" occurred twice in history, with the ancient Greeks and with modernity.

9. Sigmund Freud, "Family Romances" (1909), S.E., vol. 9, 237. In the same passage Freud notes, "Indeed, the whole progress of society rests upon the opposition between successive generations."

10. See Wallace, *Freud and Anthropology*, 25.

11. Freud, *New Introductory Lectures* (1933), S.E., vol. 22, 80 (translation altered).

12. "The Freudian school in its heroic period . . . used to call for a ruthless criticism of the super-ego as something truly heteronomous and alien to the ego. The super-ego was recognized, then, as blindly, unconsciously internalized social coercion" (Adorno, *Negative Dialectics*, 272).

13. Freud, *The Ego and the Id* (1923), S.E., vol. 19, 56.

14. Lacan, Seminar I, 16.

15. Jacques Derrida, "Structure, Sign and Play," in *The Structuralist Controversy: The Languages of Criticism and the Sciences of Man*, ed. Richard Macksey and Eugenio Donato (Baltimore: Johns Hopkins University Press, 1972), 248.

16. Despite the subversive aura that has surrounded Lacan throughout his career, Dews makes the following point concerning the possibility of critique within Lacan's framework: "Despite the profundity and ingenuity of Lacan's theoretical reconstruction of psychoanalysis, such a conclusion clearly eliminates the—albeit ambivalent—potential for critique of modern society and culture which was built into Freud's original model. Despite Lacan's suspicion of all forms of naturalism and essentialism, in a curious sense, his interpretation of psychoanalysis as concerned with the relation between the subject and language *as such*, returns psychoanalysis to a historical and political vacuum ultimately no less debilitating than the most crudely naturalistic interpretation of Freud" (Dews, *Logics of Disintegration*, 108).

17. Jacques Lacan, "Some Reflections on the Ego," *The International Journal of Psycho-Analysis* 34 (1953): 13.

18. Karl Marx, *Grundrisse*, 83.

19. Jacques Lacan, *The Seminar of Jacques Lacan*, book 2, *The Ego in Freud's Theory and in the Technique of Psychoanalysis 1954–1955*, trans. Sylvana Tomaselli (New York: W. W. Norton, 1988), 5–6. Cf. Adorno's observation that "the prebourgeois order does not yet know psychology, the oversocialized one knows it no longer" ("Sociology and Psychology," 95).

20. Lacan, *Seminar II*, 5.

21. Ibid., 4.

22. Lacan, *Seminar I*, 16.

23. Lacan, "Some Reflections on the Ego," 17. Lacan would jettison this humanist rhetoric when he later discovered Lévi-Strauss's structuralism.

24. Lacan, *Seminar II*, 3.

25. Freud, *The Interpretation of Dreams* (1900), S.E., Vol. 5, 603; and Lacan, *Seminar II*, 43. It should be pointed out that, despite the innovations of ego psychology and the structural model in the twenties, and the theoretical reorientation brought about by those innovations, Freud uses the very same phrase to describe the id in "An Outline of Psycho-Analysis," thirty-eight years after *The Interpretation of Dreams*. See S.E., vol. 23, 197. And it is this phrase that Lacan points to when explicating "the excentricity of the subject in relation to the ego," which is to say, the decentration of the ego (*Seminar II*, 44ff.). The fact that Freud repeats the phrase in his last work gives credence to Lacan's claim that Freud did not de-essentialize the position of the unconscious or the id vis-à-vis the ego with the structural model (or second topography, as the French refer to it), as the ego psychologists claim. The repeated phrase can certainly be cited to support the position that the ego is dominated by the id every bit as much as consciousness was dominated by the unconscious in the topographical model. To do so, however, and to ignore other countervailing passages in Freud, which we have examined, would not only be an injustice to a Freud interpretation, but—and more importantly—would also be an injustice to the very important substantive problem at hand.

26. Lacan, *Seminar II*, 11.

27. Ibid., 148.

28. Freud, *Inhibitions, Symptoms and Anxiety* (1926), S.E., vol. 20, 145–46.

29. Lacan, "Some Reflections on the Ego," 14.

30. Jacques Lacan, "The Mirror Stage," in *Ecrits*, 4.

31. Lacan, *Seminar II*, 50.

32. Lacan, "The Mirror Stage," 1.

33. Ibid., 2.

34. Ibid., 4.

35. Lacan, "Some Reflections on the Ego," 12.

36. Lacan, *Seminar II*, 10.

37. With respect to reification, it is difficult to understand why the decentered subject is preferable to the ego, when the subject is identified as an equally reified,

cybernetic "circuit." Indeed, it is hard to reconcile the early Lacan's antireification rhetoric with his fascination with the machine. See *Seminar II*, 79ff.

38. Lacan, *Seminar II*, 10, 44.

39. "People tell us about the autonomous ego, about the sane part of the ego, about the ego which must be strengthened, about the ego which isn't sufficiently strong to support us in doing an analysis, about the ego which should be the ally of the analyst, the ally of the analyst's ego, etc. You see the two *egos*, arm in arm, the analyst's ego and that of the subject, in fact subordinated to the other in this so-called alliance. Nothing in experience gives us the faintest hint of it, since precisely the contrary takes place—it is at the level of the ego that all the resistances occur. One really does wonder where they could start if not from this ego" (*Seminar II*, 68). See also Lacan, *Seminar I*, 16.

40. Lacan, "The Mirror Stage," 2. Lacan's discussion of the orthopedic nature of the ego is close to Adorno's comparison of the subject's protective shell to the rhinoceros's armor (*Negative Dialectics*, 180).

41. Lacan, "The Mirror Stage," 2.

42. Lacan, *Seminar II*, 167.

43. Manfred Frank, *What Is Neostructuralism?* trans. Sabina Wilke and Richard Gray (Minneapolis: University of Minnesota Press, 1989), 297.

44. Lacan, *Seminar II*, 168.

45. Jacques Lacan, "Aggressivity in Psychoanalysis," in *Ecrits*, 17.

46. Ibid., 22.

47. Ibid., 21.

48. Lacan, "Some Reflections on the Ego," 9.

49. Jacques Lacan, "Agency of the Letter in the Unconscious," in *Ecrits*, 21.

50. (Freud, *Beyond the Pleasure Principle* [1920], S.E., vol. 18, 53).

51. See Ricoeur, *Freud and Philosophy*, 319.

52. See Loewald, *Sublimation*, 30. Ricoeur makes the same point: "Strangely enough, Freud has a more finely developed conception of the evils that are 'the burden of existence' than he has of pleasure" (*Freud and Philosophy*, 322–23).

53. Freud, *Group Psychology and the Analysis of the Ego* (1921), S.E., vol. 18, 92.

54. Lacan, *Seminar II*, 79.

55. Sigmund Freud, S.E., vol. 33, 243.

56. See Lacan, *Seminar II,* 70ff.

57. Heinz Hartmann, "Theory of the Ego," *Essays on Ego Psychology: Selected Problems in Psychoanalytic Theory* (New York: International Universities Press, 1964), 138–39.

58. Paul Ricoeur, "The Question of the Subject: The Challenge of Semiology," in *The Conflict of Interpretations: Essays on Hermeneutics,* ed. Don Ihde (Evanston, IL: Northwestern University Press, 1974), 243.

59. Ibid., 241–42.

60. Foucault challenges even this in his exchange with Derrida. See "My Body, This Paper, This Fire," trans. Geoffrey Bennington, *Oxford Literary Review* 4 (1979): 9–28.

61. Ricoeur, "The Question of the Subject," 241.

62. Ricoeur, *Freud and Philosophy,* 421.

63. Ibid., 421.

64. For this entire paragraph, see Ricoeur, "The Question of the Subject," 242ff. For this entire discussion, see also Ricoeur, *Freud and Philosophy,* 379ff.

65. Ricoeur, *Freud and Philosophy,* 422.

66. Ricoeur, "The Question of the Subject," 241. With respect to the question of the *practical* termination of analysis, which is in principle an infinite project, Castoriadis makes the following absolutely crucial point: "In a word: the mirage of absolute Knowledge, of a perfectly conscious Ego, of total mastery, is ever-present, and always determinant; and this is true whether the possibility of lucid *making/doing* is affirmed, or bitterly denied. 'Resolution of the transference'; if we take this phrase *haplos* (absolutely) then it might be claimed that it is impossible, like the 'resolution of the Oedipus complex'—or the renunciation of the omnipotence of thoughts. . . . But it is a lamentable sophism to infer from this that the transference is therefore *never* resolved to *any essential extent*. The same goes, *mutatis mutandis* for the relations between the conscious and the unconscious" (Castoriadis, *Crossroads in the Labyrinth,* 108).

67. See Ricoeur, *Freud and Philosophy,* 378–79; Lacan, *Seminar II,* 70ff.

68. Ricoeur, "The Question of the Subject," 244.

69. See Richard J. Bernstein, *Beyond Objectivism and Relativism: Science, Hermeneutics, and Praxis* (Philadelphia: University of Pennsylvania Press, 1983).

70. Descartes, of course, adopted the principle that whenever an idea could be doubted, it should be assumed false; he inferred, in other words, the actuality of deception from the possibility of deception. It is often forgotten, however, that this principle was adopted provisionally, *on methodological grounds,* to discover

whether there were any facts that could survive his hyperbolic doubt. Descartes did not maintain that, whenever the possibility of doubt exists, the idea is in fact false.

71. Cf. Habermas's observation: "A theory of linguistic communication that wanted to bring Benjamin's insights back into a materialist theory of social evolution would need to conceive two of Benjamin's theses together. I am thinking of the assertion that 'there is a sphere of human agreement that is nonviolent to the extent that it is wholly inaccessible to violence: the proper sphere of "mutual understanding," language.' And I am thinking of the warning that belongs with this: '. . . pessimism all along the line. Absolutely . . . , but above all mistrust, mistrust, and again mistrust in all reciprocal understanding between classes, between nations, between individuals. And unconditional trust only in I. G. Farben and the peaceful perfection of the Luftwaffe' " ("Walter Benjamin," *The Philosophical Discourse of Modernity: Twelve Lectures,* trans. Frederick Lawrence (Cambridge, MA: The MIT Press, 1987), 158–59).

72. See Jürgen Habermas, *The Philosophical Discourse of Modernity,* chap. 5. In this section, I am indebted to the work of Peter Dews, who has demonstrated both the degree of convergence between Adorno and poststructuralism as well as Adorno's ultimate difference from the poststructuralists'. See "Adorno, Post-Structuralism and the Critique of Identity," *New Left Review* 157 (May/June 1986), and *The Logics of Disintegration.*

73. See Elisabeth Roudinesco, *Jacques Lacan & Co.,* 287ff.; Ed Casey and J. Melvin Woody, "Hegel, Heidegger, Lacan: Dialectic of Desire," in *Interpreting Lacan.* Psychiatry and the Humanities, vol. 6, ed. Joseph H. Smith, M.D., and William Kerrigan (New Haven: Yale University Press, 1983), 88ff.

74. Adorno, *Negative Dialectics,* 226n.

75. Ibid., 15.

76. Horkheimer and Adorno, *Dialectic of Enlightenment,* xiii.

77. Ibid., xvi.

78. Habermas, *The Philosophical Discourse of Modernity,* 119. One could ask whether Habermas's position, which assumes the possibility of a universal theory that is at the same time fallibilistic at its basis, is any less aporetic than Adorno's.

79. Dews, "Adorno, Post-Structuralism and the Critique of Identity," 36.

80. Horkheimer and Adorno, *Dialectic of Enlightenment,* 40 [translation altered].

81. Adorno, "Sociology and Psychology," 95.

82. Adorno, *Negative Dialectics,* 250.

83. Ibid., 299.

84. Horkheimer and Adorno, *Dialectic of Enlightenment,* 87.

85. See Hegel, *The Philosophy of Right,* pars. 182–256.

86. See Max Weber on *oikos* production: *Economy and Society: An Outline in Interpretive Sociology,* ed. Guenther Roth and Claus Wittich, trans. Ephraim Fischoff et al. (New York: Bedminster Press, 1968) 1:370ff.

87. Lawrence Stone, *The Family, Sex and Marriage in England, 1500–1800* (New York: Harper & Row, 1977), passim.

88. See Christopher Lasch, *Haven in a Heartless World: The Family Besieged* (New York: Basic Books, 1977).

89. See Hegel, *The Philosophy of Right,* pars. 158–81. See also Max Horkheimer, "Authority and the Family," in *Critical Theory: Selected Essays,* trans. Matthew O'Connell et al. (New York: Seabury Press, 1972), 47–128.

90. See Axel Honneth, *The Critique of Power,* 73ff.

91. Max Horkheimer, "Traditional and Critical Theory," in *Critical Theory,* 236–37. For a critique of this position, see Jessica Benjamin, "The End of Internalization: Adorno's Social Psychology," *Telos* 32 (1977): 27–41.

92. See Jürgen Habermas, *Legitimation Crisis,* trans. Thomas McCarthy (Boston: Beacon Press, 1975), 122ff.

93. Horkheimer, "Traditional and Critical Theory," 235–37.

94. Adorno, "Sociology and Psychology," 93.

95. Ibid., 95.

96. Adorno, *Minima Moralia,* 17–18.

97. Adorno, "Sociology and Psychology," 95.

98. See also Herbert Marcuse, "The Obsolescence of the Freudian Concept of Man," in *Five Lectures,* 44–61.

99. Adorno, *Minima Moralia,* 49.

100. See Adorno, "Sociology and Psychology," 89.

101. See, for example, Anna Freud, "The Widening Scope of Indications for Psychoanalysis," *Journal of the American Psychoanalytic Association* 2 (1954): 607ff.; Leo Stone, same volume, 567ff.

102. Adorno, *Minima Moralia,* 72.

103. Habermas, *The Philosophical Discourse of Modernity,* 110.

104. Ibid., 23.

105. Horkheimer and Adorno, *Dialectic of Enlightenment,* 57.

106. Ibid., 5.

107. See Honneth, *The Critique of Power*, 40–41.

108. Horkheimer and Adorno, *Dialectic of Enlightenment*, 7–8.

109. Ibid., 9.

110. Ibid., 10.

111. Ibid., 14.

112. Ibid., 9.

113. Ibid., 10.

114. Ibid., 84.

115. Ibid., 7, 14.

116. Ibid., 9.

117. Ibid., 9.

118. Ibid., 81.

119. Ibid., 84.

120. Ibid., 83.

121. Ibid., 87.

122. It is interesting to note that Lacan sees the mirror phase, with its infinite regress, as an alternative to the transcendental unity of apperception. This means there is no fundamental unity. See Lacan, *Seminar II*, 55.

123. Horkheimer and Adorno, *Dialectic of Enlightenment*, 82.

124. Ibid., 84.

125. Ibid., 82.

126. Theodor Adorno, "Subject and Object," 499.

127. Horkheimer and Adorno, *Dialectic of Enlightenment*, 87.

128. Ibid., 83.

129. This is one of the many reasons why, at the same time as we must retain the "preponderance of the object" (Adorno), "it is no longer possible to think in terms of that which founds and that which is founded; we must rather think in terms of interchange, reversibility" (Castoriadis, "The Sayable and the Unsayable," in *Crossroads in the Labyrinth*, 122).

130. Horkheimer and Adorno, *Dialectic of Enlightenment*, 32.

131. Ibid., 12.

132. Ibid., 11.

133. Ibid., 16. "The animal to be devoured must be evil. The sublimation of this anthropological schema extends all the way to epistemology. Idealism—most explicitly Fichte—gives unconscious sway to the ideology that the not-I, *l'autrui*, and finally all that reminds us of nature is inferior, and so the unity of the self-preserving thought may devour it without misgivings. The system justifies the principle of the thought as much as it increases the appetite. The system is the belly turned mind, and rage is the mark of each and every idealism. It disfigures even Kant's humanism and refutes the aura of higher and nobler things in which he knew how to garb it" (Adorno, *Negative Dialectics*, 22–23).

134. Horkheimer and Adorno, *Dialectic of Enlightenment*, 46.

135. Ibid., 32

136. Margaret Mahler defines the "fear of reengulfment" as fear of "regression to a symbiotic state from which the toddler has only recently individuated (emerged). The fear of reengulfment is the defense against the perpetual longing of the human being for reunion with the erstwhile symbiotic mother, a longing that threatens individual entity and identity and, therefore, has to be warded off even beyond childhood" (*On Human Symbiosis and the Vicissitudes of Individuation* [New York: International Universities Press, 1968], 290).

137. Horkheimer and Adorno, *Dialectic of Enlightenment*, 47

138. Ibid., 46

139. See Margaret S. Mahler, Fred Pine, and Anni Bergman, *The Psychological Birth of the Human Infant: Symbiosis and Individuation* (New York: Basic Books, 1975).

140. Horkheimer and Adorno, *Dialectic of Enlightenment*, 47.

141. Ibid., 55.

142. Ibid., 32, 33.

143. Ibid., 33. "According to that theory—and dialectically enough—the repressing agent, the compulsive mechanism, is one with the I, the organon of freedom" (Adorno, *Negative Dialectics*, 223).

144. Horkheimer and Adorno, *Dialectic of Enlightenment*, 31.

145. Ibid., 33.

146. Ibid., 59. For a reference to the "Semitic element" in the *Odyssey*, see 61 n. 14.

147. Ibid., 34.

148. Ibid., 34. Cf. "If we press that idea to its necessary conclusion, we are led to emphasize the privileged character of masochism in human sexuality. The analysis, in its

very content, of an essential fantasy—the 'primal scene'—would illustrate it well: the child, impotent in his crib, is Ulysses tied to the mast or Tantalus, on whom is imposed the spectacle of parental sexuality" (Jean Laplanche, *Life and Death in Psychoanalysis,* trans. Jeffrey Mehlman [Baltimore: Johns Hopkins University Press, 1976], 102).

149. Ibid., 57. Cf. "The feeling of happiness derived from the satisfaction of a wild instinctual impulse untamed by the ego is incomparably more intense than that derived from sating an instinct that has been tamed. The irresistibility of perverse instincts, and perhaps the attraction in general of forbidden things, finds an economic explanation here" (Freud, *Civilization and Its Discontents,* 79).

150. Ibid., 54.

151. Ibid., 88.

152. Ibid., 54.

153. Ibid., 54–55.

154. See Loewald, *Sublimation,* 17.

155. Martin Jay has called my attention to the fact that there is also a strong anti-Hegelian tendency in *Dialectic of Enlightenment* owing to the influence of Walter Benjamin, whose resent death cast an enormous shadow over the project. For the influence of Benjamin on Adorno, see also Susan Buck-Morss, *The Origin of Negative Dialectics: Theodor W. Adorno, Walter Benjamin, and the Frankfurt Institute,* (New York: The Free Press, 1977).

156. While the inner logic of these two crucial terms obviously invites exploration, no one, to my knowledge, has carried out a detailed examination of the relation between them.

157. Horkheimer and Adorno, *Dialectic of Enlightenment,* 57.

158. "Novalis' definition, according to which all philosophy is homesickness, holds true only if this longing is not dissolved into the phantasm of a lost remote antiquity, but represents the homeland, nature itself, as wrested from myth" (Horkheimer and Adorno, *Dialectic of Enlightenment,* 78).

159. Ibid., 55. Cf. "Indeed, happiness is nothing other than being encompassed, an after-image of the original shelter within the mother" (Adorno, *Minima Moralia,* 112).

160. Marcuse, *Eros and Civilization,* 168.

161. See Frank, *What is Neostructuralism?* 316.

162. Adorno, *Negative Dialectics,* 240. This is the clinical counterpart, as it were, to Adorno's philosophical refusal to hypostatize disunity, which is only the obverse of hypostatizing unity: "The illusion of taking direct hold of the Many would be a mimetic regression, as much a recoil into mythology, into the horror of the diffuse, as the thinking of the One, the imitation of blind nature by repressing it, ends at the opposite pole in mythical domination. The self-reflection of enlightenment is not its revocation; it is corrupted into revocation only for the sake of today's status quo.

Even the self-critical turn of unitarian thinking depends on concepts, on congealed syntheses. The tendency of synthesizing acts is reversible by reflection upon what they do to the Many. Unity alone transcends unity" (Adorno, *Negative Dialectics,* 148).

163. Adorno, *Minima Moralia,* 60.

164. Ibid., 73.

165. Adorno, *Negative Dialectics,* 256.

166. Adorno, *Minima Moralia,* 50.

167. Albrecht Wellmer, "Reason, Utopia and the *Dialectic of Enlightenment,*" in *Habermas and Modernity.*

168. Albrecht Wellmer, "Truth, Semblance, Reconciliation" and "The Dialectic of Modernism and Postmodernism: The Critique of Reason since Adorno" are both collected in *The Persistence of Modernity.*

169. Wellmer, *The Persistence of Modernity,* vii.

170. Wellmer, "The Dialectic of Modernism and Postmodernism," 73.

171. Cf. Adorno's comments on the *intrinsic* relation of philosophy to aesthetics in *Negative Dialectics,* 15.

172. Wellmer, "Reason, Utopia, and the *Dialectic of Enlightenment,*" 48.

173. Wellmer, "Truth, Semblance and Reconciliation," 14.

174. Wellmer, "The Dialectic of Modernism and Postmodernism," 63.

175. Wellmer, "Truth, Semblance and Reconciliation," 19.

176. Ibid., 20–21.

177. Ibid., 20.

178. Wellmer, "The Dialectic of Modernism and Postmodernism," 57.

179. Freud, *The Ego and the Id* (1923), S.E., vol. 19, 56.

180. Wellmer, "The Dialectic of Modernism and Postmodernism," 18. Wellmer makes the important observation that the discovery of the Other of the subject and reason, "which [was] in any case not as new as all that," appears as a *"discovery"*—and as a traumatic disappointment—"only if we *start out* with [the] rationalist idealizations" that it should not be there in the first place. Postmodern skepticism, like all forms of skepticism, begins with an unfounded demand for the Absolute in various forms—for example, the complete stability of meaning, transparency of the ego, exhaustibility of translation, separation of power and knowledge, rationality of paradigm changes, resolution of the transference—only to show, in a demonstration that oscillates between gleefulness and despondency, that it cannot be fulfilled. "The

philosophy of total unmasking is," in short, "fed by the same rationalistic metaphysics that it claims to be destroying." It would be more fruitful, and take us deeper, to question the demand for the Absolute in the first place, that is, to really question the metaphysical tradition. See also Habermas, *The Philosophical Discourse of Modernity,* 408, n. 28; Castoriadis, *Crossroads in the Labyrinth,* xiii; and Bernstein, *Beyond Objectivism and Relativism,* pt. 1.

181. Wellmer, "The Dialectic of Modernism and Postmodernism," 57.

182. Ibid., 60.

183. Ibid., 61.

184. Jürgen Habermas, *Knowledge and Human Interests,* 312.

185. Wellmer, "The Dialectic of Modernism and Postmodernism," 73–74.

186. It should be pointed out that Lacan, with his thesis that "the unconscious is structured like a language," attempts to combine the psychological and the linguistic critiques of the subject. Indeed, this attempt can be seen as defining his project. Drawing on the resources of structuralism for his return to Freud, he attempts to reinterpret the psychological decentering of the subject as a linguistic decentering of the subject.

187. Wellmer, "The Dialectic of Modernism and Postmodernism," 64.

188. Ibid., 74.

189. Ibid., 57.

190. Ibid., 65.

191. Ibid., 65.

192. Ibid., 67.

193. Ibid., 67.

194. Ibid., 66.

195. Ibid., 71.

196. Ibid., 80.

197. Ibid., 80.

198. Horkheimer and Adorno, *Dialectic of Enlightenment,* 82.

199. Wellmer, "The Dialectic of Modernism and Postmodernism," 81.

200. See Bernstein, *Beyond Objectivism and Relativism,* 51ff.

201. Wellmer, "The Dialectic of Modernism and Postmodernism," 83.

202. Wellmer, "Truth, Semblance, Reconciliation," 2.

203. Habermas, *The Theory of Communicative Action*, 390.

204. Benhabib, *Critique, Norm, and Utopia*, 213ff.

205. Wellmer, "Reason, Utopia, and the *Dialectic of Enlightenment*," 49.

206. Adorno, "Subject and Object," 500.

207. Wellmer, "The Dialectic of Modernism and Postmodernism," 238, n. 70. It should also be pointed out that the problem of reference is no less problematic for the philosophy of language than the problem of perception was for the philosophy of the subject. Indeed, it is exactly parallel. Whereas in the former it is a question of how language "hooks up" with the world, in the latter it is a question of how consciousness registers external reality.

208. Wellmer, "Truth, Semblance, Reconciliation," 20.

209. Wellmer, "The Dialectic of Modernism and Postmodernism," 89.

210. Ibid., 53.

211. Wellmer, "Reason, Utopia, and the *Dialectic of Enlightenment*," 49.

212. Wellmer, "The Dialectic of Modernism and Postmodernism," 76–77.

213. Wellmer, "Truth, Semblance, Reconciliation," 20.

214. Wellmer, "The Dialectic of Modernism and Postmodernism," 84.

215. The early Foucault argued that, as it is impossible to remain within the frontier region, which is the region of transcendental thinking in the broadest sense of the term, the philosopher ought to intentionally transgress the limits of language and scandalously embrace his or her madness. See Michel Foucault, "A Preface to Transgression," in *Language, Counter-Memory, Practice: Selected Essays and Interviews by Michel Foucault,* trans. Donald Bouchard and Sherry Simon (Ithaca, NY: Cornell University Press, 1977), 29ff.

216. Sigmund Freud, "Instincts and Their Vicissitudes" (1915), S.E., vol. 14, 121–22.

Chapter 4

1. Jürgen Habermas, *Knowledge and Human Interests*, chaps. 10–12.

2. See Albrecht Wellmer, "Communications and Emancipation: Reflections on the Linguistic Turn in Critical Theory," in *On Critical Theory*, 231–62.

3. It is significant that the excursus on Castoriadis immediately follows a chapter entitled "An Alternative Way out of the Philosophy of the Subject: Communicative versus Subject-Centered Reason," in *The Philosophical Discourse of Modernity*, 294–326.

4. See Joel Whitebook, "The Problem of Nature in Habermas," *Telos* 40 (summer 1979): 41–69; and Jürgen Habermas, "A Reply to My Critics," in *Habermas: Critical Debates*, 238ff.

5. It is interesting to note that, according to Castoriadis, the two topics that "radically question inherited logic and ontology" and demand new, radicalized forms of thinking are "the auto-organization of living organisms and the unconscious," that is, biology and psychoanalysis. These are two areas where the application of Habermas's philosophical program has of necessity not produced its most conspicuous successes. See Castoriadis, *The Imaginary Institution of Society*, 340.

6. Habermas, "Appendix: Knowledge and Human Interests: A General Perspective," in *Knowledge and Human Interests*, 314.

7. Castoriadis, *The Imaginary Institution of Society*, 333.

8. Cornelius Castoriadis, "Modern Science and Philosophical Interrogation," in *Crossroads in the Labyrinth*, 168–69.

9. Castoriadis, *The Imaginary Institution of Society*, 274.

10. Castoriadis, *Crossroads in the Labyrinth*, xx. Castoriadis's notion of the psychic imaginary can be compared to Hannah Arendt's notion of natality, which she too used to combat historical determinism and account for the possibility of radically new beginnings in history. See Arendt, *The Human Condition*.

11. Castoriadis, *The Imaginary Institution of Society*, 311.

12. Ibid., 281.

13. Ibid., 282.

14. Ibid., 282.

15. Ibid., 282.

16. Ibid., 283.

17. Ibid., 285.

18. Ibid., 298.

19. Ibid., 291.

20. Ibid., 294.

21. Ibid., 283.

22. For Castoriadis, as distinct from Habermas, the monadic pole of the psyche is a source of individuation. As a kind of Aristotelian prime matter that cannot be exhaustively informed by the socialization process and therefore resists complete absorption into the common world *(kosmos koinos)*, it "assures the individual a singular identity" (Castoriadis, *The Imaginary Institution of Society*, 302).

23. Castoriadis, *The Imaginary Institution of Society*, 297.

24. Ibid., 302.

25. Ibid., 299.

26. Janine Chasseguet-Smirgel, "Some Thoughts on the Ego Ideal," 345.

27. Castoriadis, *The Imaginary Institution of Society*, 299.

28. This was pointed out to me by Albrecht Wellmer.

29. Kant, *The Critique of Pure Reason*, Avii (Kemp Smith translation).

30. See Hegel, *Phenomenology of Spirit*, 355–64.

31. Laplanche and Pontalis, *The Language of Psychoanalysis*, 29–32.

32. Castoriadis, "Modern Science and Philosophical Interrogation," 217ff.

33. Castoriadis, *The Imaginary Institution of Society*, 290.

34. Ibid., 290.

35. Ibid., 316.

36. Ibid., 298, 301.

37. Ibid., 300–301.

38. Ibid., 298.

39. Ibid., 273.

40. Ibid., 302.

41. Ibid., 302.

42. Beginning with the posit of primary autism, Castoriadis is shackled with all the insoluble dilemmas that confronted Freud's notion of primary narcissism and that are, as Laplanche has argued, simply the insurmountable aporia of Cartesian solipsism recast in psychoanalytic terms. On the assumption of a totally closed monadic starting point, with complete and utter irrelation between internal consciousness and the external world, there is no way out: it is as impossible for Freud to distinguish between perceptions and hallucinations as it was for Descartes to distinguish between veridical and adventitious ideas. See Laplanche, *Life and Death in Psychoanalysis*, trans. Jeffrey Mehlman (Baltimore: Johns Hopkins University Press, 1976), 70ff, and *New Foundations for Psychoanalysis*, trans. David Macey (New York: Basil Blackwell, 1989), 75.

43. Freud, "Formulations on the Two Principles of Mental Functioning" (1911), S.E. vol. 12, 219.

44. Castoriadis, *The Imaginary Institution of Society*, 311.

45. See D. W. Winnicott, *The Maturational Process and the Facilitating Environment: Studies in the Theory of Emotional Development* (New York: International Universities Press, 1965), 223, 239.

46. Castoriadis, *The Imaginary Institution of Society,* 300.

47. See Marion Michel Oliner, *Cultivating Freud's Garden in France* (New York: Jason Aranson, 1988), 13.

48. Castoriadis, *The Imaginary Institution of Society,* 276, 301.

49. Ibid., 274.

50. Hans Loewald, "Primary Process, Secondary Process, and Language," in *Papers on Psychoanalysis,* 184. Consider also: "We consider these to be the older, primary processes, the residues of a phase of development in which they were the only kind of mental process" (Freud, "Formulations on the Two Principles of Mental Functioning" [1911], S.E., vol. 12, 219).

51. Habermas, *Knowledge and Human Interests,* 241. I would like to point out that this passage equates the domain of words with the domain of the symbolic as such and thereby denies the existence of a semiotic realm that is larger than, but inclusive of, the linguistic. As we will see, the attempt to identify a signifying function that exceeds the scope of language in the strict sense is at the heart of Ricoeur's analysis of the linguisticality of the unconscious. See Ricoeur, *Freud and Philosophy,* 398–99. See also Paul Ricoeur, "Image and Language in Psychoanalysis," *Psychoanalysis and Language,* Psychiatry and the Humanities, vol. 3, ed. Joseph H. Smith, M.D. (New Haven: Yale University Press, 1978), 314ff.

52. Freud, "The Unconscious" (1915), S.E., vol. 14, 201–2.

53. Freud, *The Interpretation of Dreams* (1900), S.E., vol. 5, 340.

54. See Ricoeur, "Image and Language in Psychoanalysis," 303.

55. Habermas, *Knowledge and Human Interests,* 238. Cf. Jacques Lacan, "The Function and Field of Speech and Language in Psychoanalysis," in *Écrits,* 32, and "The Agency of the Letter in the Unconscious," 148–49.

56. Jean Laplanche and Serge Leclaire, "The Unconscious: A Psychoanalytic Study," *Yale French Studies,* no. 46 (1971): 176. (It is made clear that Laplanche wrote these lines.)

57. Freud, *The Interpretation of Dreams* (1900), S.E., vol. 5, 1.

58. Lacan, "The Agency of the Letter in the Unconscious," 159.

59. Ricoeur, *Freud and Philosophy,* 59ff.

60. Dews, *The Logics of Disintegration,* 74. Consider also: "And we fail to pursue the question further as long as we cling to the illusion that the signifier answers to the function of representing the signified, or better, that the signifier has to answer for

its existence in the name of any signification whatever" (Lacan, "The Agency of the Letter in the Unconscious," 150).

61. Lacan, "The Agency of the Letter in the Unconscious," 160.

62. Wellmer speaks of "a 'coherence' beyond the compulsion to systematize" ("The Dialectic of Modernism and Postmodernism," 82).

63. Dews, *The Logics of Disintegration*, 74.

64. Lacan, "The Agency of the Letter in the Unconscious," 149. On Lacan's scientism, see François Roustang, *The Lacanian Delusion,* trans. Greg Sims (New York: Oxford University Press, 1990), chap. 2.

65. Jean-François Lyotard, "The Dream-work Does Not Think," in *The Lyotard Reader,* ed. Andrew Benjamin (Cambridge, MA: Basil Blackwell, 1989), 19–21.

66. "How are we to arrive at a knowledge of the unconscious? It is of course only as something conscious that we know it, after it has undergone transformation or translation into something conscious. Psycho-analytic work shows us every day that translation of this kind is possible" (Freud, "The Unconscious" [1915], S.E., vol. 14, 166).

67. Habermas, *Knowledge and Human Interests,* 241. I must leave aside for now the critical question of whether Habermas, or any of the linguistic reinterpreters of Freud for that matter, can adequately account for the dynamic, economic, and affective elements involved in analysis—for example, working through—within the theoretical confines of their linguistic reformulations.

68. Ibid., 258.

69. Ibid., 223–34.

70. Freud, "The Unconscious" (1915), S.E., vol. 14, 190.

71. Habermas, *Knowledge and Human Interests,* 239.

72. Freud, *The Interpretation of Dreams* (1900), S.E., vol. 5, 534. This idea provides the rationale for the use of the couch in psychoanalytic practice. The recumbent position and reduction of external stimuli to a minimum are meant to engender a sleeplike state in the patient, in which the mind will begin to work in "a backward direction" as it does in sleep. Through this process of regression, the analysand is able to experience and capture the images of unconscious mentation. At this point, however, the analogy with the dreams ceases: the experiencing of those images is not, as it is in a dream, an end in itself; for the therapeutic process to proceed, the mind must reverse its direction and the images must be put into words.

73. Freud, *The Interpretation of Dreams* (1900), S.E., vol. 5, 534.

74. Habermas, *Knowledge and Human Interests,* 256.

75. See Freud, "Instincts and Their Vicissitudes" (1915), S.E., vol. 14, 122.

76. Ibid., 121–22.

77. See William I. Grossman, "Hierarchies, Boundaries and Representations in a Freudian Model of Mental Organization," *Journal of the American Psychoanalytic Association* 40, no. 1 (1992): 27–62.

78. Castoriadis, *Crossroads in the Labyrinth*, 107, n. 11.

79. Ricoeur notes in *Freud and Philosophy*, "The most difficult notion of all is the idea of an 'energy' that is transformed into meaning. . . . Nothing, consequently, is firmly settled in this area; indeed, it may be that the entire matter must be redone, possibly with the help of energy schemata quite different from Freud's. . . . The intersection of the 'natural' and the 'signifying' is the point where the instinctual drives are 'represented' by affects and ideas" (p. 395). It should also be pointed out that Ricoeur himself provides an explanation of the hierarchy of forms of representation in Freud that perhaps makes Freud more coherent than he actually is; see p. 398.

80. See, among others, Ricoeur, *Freud and Philosophy*, 134ff.; Laplanche and Pontalis, *The Language of Psychoanalysis*, 200–201, 203–4, 223–24, 364–65; and James Strachey's editorial note to Freud, "Instincts and Their Vicissitudes" (1915), S.E., vol. 14, 112.

81. Yosef Hayim Yerushalmi, "The Moses of Freud and the Moses of Schoenberg: On Words, Idolatry, and Psychoanalysis," *The Psychoanalytic Study of the Child*, vol. 47 (New Haven: Yale University Press, 1992): 15.

82. Ibid., 11.

83. Freud, *The Interpretation of Dreams* (1900), S.E., vol. 5, 525. Bowie has made the following observation: "But to say this is not at all to say that linguistic forms saturate the psychoanalytic domain, and that the analyst who conducts his explorations in words can expect to find nothing other than words at the end of his quest. For Freud language had as its crowning capacity that of ushering the theorist and the therapist to the threshold of another world, and that world—which for 'the unconscious' was an appropriate shorthand designation—mattered because it was the mute, unstoppable and unappeasable inwardness of human desire. The unconscious was the fountainhead of psychoanalytic thinking, and it was verbal as soon as it made any form of public appearance. But the fact that its outward effects were discursive ones did not mean that it was itself a discourse or imaginable only by pretending it was. . . . The history of the term 'unconscious' in Freud's writings is long and complicated. But if the metapsychological paper 'The Unconscious' (1915) is thought of as occupying a special place in that history, it cannot be doubted that the question 'where do words stop?' was of central importance to Freud in his attempts to model the psychical apparatus." (Malcolm Bowie, *Lacan* [Cambridge, MA.: Harvard University Press, 1991], 49).

84. "In the end we are left with words. Books extolling silence are written in words. Philosophers must use words to describe the limitations" (Yerushalmi, "The Moses of Freud and the Moses of Schoenberg," 18).

85. Freud, *The Question of Lay Analysis* (1926), S.E., vol. 20, 186–87.

86. Sigmund Freud, *Group Psychology and the Analysis of the Ego* (1921), S.E., vol. 18, 111.

87. Quoted in Yerushalmi, "The Moses of Freud and the Moses of Schoenberg," 13.

88. Habermas, *Knowledge and Human Interests*, 214, 217.

89. Ibid., 229. Consider also: "Seen from the analyst's perspective [the reconstruction] remains mere knowledge 'for us,' until its communication turns into enlightenment—that is, the knowledge 'for it,' for the patient's consciousness: 'On that particular matter our knowledge will then have becomes *his* knowledge as well.' Freud calls the common endeavor that overcomes this gap between communication and enlightenment 'working-through.' Working-through designates the dynamic component of a cognitive activity that leads to recognition only against resistance" (pp. 230–31). Compare this passage to one from Ricoeur: "Thus analysis does not consist in replacing ignorance by knowledge but in provoking a work of consciousness by means of work on resistances" ("Technique and Nontechnique in Interpretation," 180).

90. Habermas, *Knowledge and Human Interests*, 250. Consider also: "For these metapsychological categories and connections were not only *discovered* under determinate conditions of specifically sheltered communication, they cannot even be *explicated* independently of this context. The conditions of this communication are thus the conditions of the possibility of analytic knowledge for both partners, doctor and patient, likewise" (p. 252).

91. Ricoeur, *Freud and Philosophy*, 363–64. Interestingly, the reason André Green cites for his break with Lacan was the lack of appreciation for affect and for the body in the latter's theory. See the introduction to *On Private Madness*, 6ff; "Conceptions of Affect," in *On Private Madness*, 174–213; and "Logic of Lacan's object a and Freudian Theory: Convergences and Questions," in *Interpreting Lacan*, 166–92.

92. Ricoeur, *Freud and Philosophy*, 430ff. Compare Habermas's statement regarding the rejection of traditional metapsychology: "The hydraulic model and its reliance on a mechanics of instinctual energy has only a metaphorical character, even for Freud himself. In any case, one cannot have both the analytic instrument of depth hermeneutics and a theory of drives formulated in quasi-physicalist concepts" ("Questions and Counterquestions," in *Habermas and Modernity*, 212).

93. Ricoeur, "The Question of the Subject," 244.

94. Ricoeur, *Freud and Philosophy*, 104.

95. Ricoeur, "Technique and Nontechnique in Interpretation," in *The Conflict of Interpretations*, 183.

96. Ibid., 184–85.

97. Other important work terms in Freud's vocabulary include the work of mourning *(Trauerarbeit)* and working-through *(Durcharbeiten)*.

98. Ricoeur, *Freud and Philosophy*, 407–8. Habermas, because he is concerned with the critique of instrumental reason, is eager, of course, to differentiate psychoanalysis from positivist science constituted with an interest in technical control. Ricoeur, however, attempts to delineate a meaning of technique that is not linked with domina-

tion and adaptation: "All the techniques which come out of the psychology of the observation of behavior are, in the last resort, aimed toward adaptation for the sake of domination. What is at stake in analysis is access to true discourse, and that is quite different from adaptation, the tactic by which the scandal of psychoanalysis has been hastily undermined and rendered socially acceptable. For who knows where a single true discourse may lead with respect to the established order, i.e., with respect to the idealized discourse of established disorder? Psychoanalysis seems to me to be linked, rather, to the express will to bracket the question of adaptation, which is the question inevitably posed by others, that is, by existing society on the basis and foundation of its reified ideals and the mendacious relationship between the idealized profession of its beliefs and the effective reality of its practical relationships" ("Technique and Nontechnique in Interpretation," 188).

99. Sigmund Freud, "On Psychotherapy" (1905), S.E., vol. 7, 267.

100. Ricoeur, "Technique and Nontechnique in Interpretation," 183. In "A Postscript to *Knowledge and Human Interests,*" *Philosophy of Social Science*, 163–83, Habermas admits, as we have noted, in response to his critiques, that he had conflated two notions of reflection in that work. The first is the Kantian-epistemological notion that "denotes the reflexion upon the conditions of general abilities of a knowing, speaking and acting subject as such." The second is a Hegelian notion that "denotes the reflexion upon unconsciously produced constraints to which a determinate subject (or a determinate group of subjects, or a determinate species) succumbs in the process of self-formation. The latter, which also contains a moment of epistemological reflection, aims at "the critical dissolution of subjectively constituted pseudo-objectivity. . . . [I]n other words, [it] contains the idea of an *analytical emancipation* from *objective illusions.*" While the Hegelian program of emancipation through genetic self-reflection is much closer to the psychoanalytic project, it nevertheless lacks a notion of technique, and therefore Ricoeur's point concerning the difference between psychoanalysis and the philosophy of reflection remains valid.

101. Ricoeur, *Freud and Philosophy*, 413.

102. Ibid., 403, 405.

103. Habermas, *The Philosophical Discourse of Modernity*, 333–34.

104. Habermas, "A Postscript to *Knowledge and Human Interests*," 170.

105. Habermas, *The Philosophical Discourse of Modernity*, 334.

106. Winnicott, "Transitional Objects and Transitional Phenomena," 240.

107. Habermas, "Moral Development and Ego Identity," 91.

108. Habermas, *The Philosophical Discourse of Modernity*, 334.

109. Ricoeur, "Image and Language in Psychoanalysis," 312.

110. Ricoeur, *Freud and Philosophy*, 398–99.

111. Cornelius Castoriadis, *"Fait et à Faire,"* *Revue européenne des sciences sociales* 27, no. 86 (1989): 474.

112. Ricoeur, "Image and Language in Psychoanalysis," 293, 311.

113. See Ricoeur, *Freud and Philosophy*, 400ff., and "Image and Language in Psychoanalysis," 312.

114. Joel Whitebook, "Intersubjectivity and the Monadic Core of the Psyche," *Revue européenne des sciences sociales* 27, no. 86 (1989), 225–45.

115. See Castoriadis, *The Imaginary Institution of Society*, 342; *Crossroads in the Labyrinth*, 169; and "The Greek Polis and the Creation of Democracy," *Graduate Faculty Philosophy Journal* 9 (fall 1983): 85.

116. Kant, *Critique of Judgement*, trans. J. C. Meredith (Oxford: Oxford University Press, 1952), 23.

117. Castoriadis, *"Fait et à Faire,"* 462.

118. Castoriadis, *Crossroads in the Labyrinth*, 77.

119. Freud, *Future of an Illusion* (1927), S.E., vol. 21, 55.

120. See Heinz Hartmann, "On the Reality Principle," in *Essays on Ego Psychology* (New York: International Universities Press, 1965), 264. See also Hartmann, *Ego Psychology and the Problem of Adaptation*.

121. Castoriadis, *"Fait et à Faire,"* 472.

122. Castoriadis, *The Imaginary Institution of Society*, 275.

123. Ibid., 343.

124. Ricoeur, *Freud and Philosophy*, 455–57.

125. Castoriadis, *"Fait et à Faire,"* 462.

126. Ibid., 461–62.

127. Ibid., 474.

128. Ibid., 462–63.

129. Cornelius Castoriadis, "Imagination, Logic, Reflection," *American Imago* 49 (1992): 20.

130. Ibid., 20

131. Castoriadis, *"Fait et à Faire,"* 475.

132. Castoriadis, "Imagination, Logic, Reflection," 22.

133. Ibid., 24.

134. Ibid., 25–26.

135. Ibid., 29.

136. Castoriadis, "The First Institution of Society," 41. See also his "The Greek Polis and the Creation of Democracy," 81–123.

137. Castoriadis, *The Imaginary Institution of Society,* 104.

138. Castoriadis, "Imagination, Logic, Reflection" 28.

139. Habermas, *Theory of Communicative Action,* vol. 1, 62.

140. Freud, *The Interpretation of Dreams* (1900), S.E., vol. 5, 621.

141. Ibid., 598.

142. As Laplanche and Pontalis correctly point out, by translating Freud's *Wunsch* as *désir,* Lacan tries to smuggle in his synthesis of Freud and Hegel linguistically, as it were. For *désir,* or "desire," is much closer to the Hegelian *Begierde* than to the Freudian *Wunsch.* Whereas the former has strongly private connotations, the latter is already intersubjective, and by using the same term for both Lacan obscures the difference. But, of course, this is his intention. See *The Language of Psychoanalysis,* 482–83.

143. Freud, *The Interpretation of Dreams* (1900), S.E., vol. 5, 566.

144. Ibid., 598–99.

145. See Hans-Georg Gadamer, "The Universality of the Hermeneutical Problem," "On the Scope and Function of Hermeneutical Reflection," in *Philosophical Hermeneutics,* trans. and ed. David Linge (Berkeley: University of California Press, 1976) and *Truth and Method,* xviff; Jürgen Habermas, *On the Logic of the Social Sciences,* trans. Shierry Weber Nicholsen and Jerry A. Stark (Cambridge, MA: MIT Press, 1988), chap. 8, and "The Hermeneutic Claim to Universality," in *Contemporary Hermeneutics: Hermeneutics as Method, Philosophy and Critique,* ed. Josef Bleicher (Boston: Routledge and Kegan Paul, 1980).

146. Gadamer, "On the Scope and Function of Hermeneutical Reflection," 25.

147. Habermas, "The Hermeneutic Claim to Universality," 190.

148. Gadamer, "On the Scope and Function of Hermeneutical Reflection," 30.

149. Habermas, "Questions and Counterquestions," 213. There is a legitimate concern with respect to the analyst's presumption to know something beyond the second-person perspective of a partner in dialogue. It is often feared that any claim to specialized knowledge, and the asymmetrical relationship resulting from it, will lead to an omniscient and authoritarian attitude on the part of the analyst. If, however, the analyst's mastery of psychoanalytic technique is necessary for transforming a social encounter into a psychoanalytic process, and if, at the same time, the dangers of the *"sujet supposé savoir,"* to use Lacan's term, are to be avoided, then a nonauthoritarian interpretation of the analyst's privileged knowledge must be forthcoming. Following Joyce McDougall, I would suggest the analogy with a stage manager is particularly apt in this context. What the analyst knows how to do is manage—and resolutely

protect—the stage of the analytic setting so that the drama of the transference can unfold with as little outside interference as possible. Then, as the drama unfolds, the analyst and patient as partners can try to decipher its meaning together. (See Joyce McDougall, *Theaters of the Mind.*)

150. Gadamer, "On the Scope and Function of Hermeneutical Reflection," 41.

151. Gadamer, *Truth and Method*, 242.

152. Gadamer, "The Universality of the Hermeneutical Problem," 9.

153. Gadamer, *Truth and Method*, 248–49.

154. Habermas, "The Hermeneutic Claim to Universality," 204.

155. Ibid., 205.

156. Paul Ricoeur, "Hermeneutics and the Critique of Ideology," in *From Text to Action: Essays in Hermeneutics II,* trans. Kathleen Blamey and John B. Thompson (Evanston, IL: Northwestern University Press, 1991), 270.

157. Ricoeur, "Hermeneutics and the Critique of Ideology," 300–301. See also Ricoeur, "The Function of Fiction in Shaping Reality," in *A Ricoeur Reader: Reflection and Imagination,* ed. Mario Valdes (Toronto: University of Toronto Press, 1991), 117–36.

158. Ricoeur, "Hermeneutics and the Critique of Ideology," 295.

159. See Habermas, *The Theory of Communicative Action,* vol. 2, *Lifeworld and System: A Critique of Functionalist Reason,* trans. Thomas McCarthy (Boston: Beacon Press, 1984), chap. 7, "System and Lifeworld."

160. Ricoeur, "Hermeneutics and the Critique of Ideology," 303–4.

161. Ibid., 306. Cf. Wellmer's observation concerning Adorno: "The theological motif interacts with the sensualist one to produce a utopian perspective in which the hope of redemption is nourished by the yearning for a lost paradise" ("Truth, Semblance, Reconciliation," 12).

162. Habermas, *Knowledge and Human Interests,* 288.

Chapter 5

1. Laplanche and Pontalis, *The Language of Psychoanalysis,* 433.

2. See Socrates, *Phaedrus,* 229c–230b, 244–245c (Hackforth translation). Martha Nussbaum argues that the doctrine of divine madness in the *Phaedrus* represents a recantation of Plato's ascetic view of sublimation in the *Symposium,* namely, the ascent on Diotima's ladder. She maintains that, as opposed to the *Symposium* (and the *Republic*), in which Plato had advocated the merits of *sophrosune,* rational self-mastery, in the *Phaedrus,* he had come to appreciate the *intrinsic* value of the "non-intellectual

elements." See *The Fragility of Goodness: Luck and Ethics in Greek Tragedy and Philosophy* (New York: Cambridge University Press, 1986), chaps. 5–7. Nussbaum's reading of Plato is immensely suggestive for the psychoanalytic theory of sublimation, in which a similar tension has existed historically. On the one side, one finds Hartmann's ascetic notion of "neutralization," in which the drives seem to be left behind altogether. On the other, there is Loewald, who praises sexuality precisely because of its connection with the divine and its indispensability for creativity. See also Ricoeur's discussion of Plato's notion *thumos* (spiritedness), which can be on the side of reason or of irrationality, and which can serve as the mediator between *Bios* and *Logos* (Ricoeur, *Freud and Philosophy*, 506); and Green, "Passions and Their Vicissitudes."

3. Ricoeur, *Freud and Philosophy*, 35. Ricoeur, who is a religious believer, is to be admired for the intellectual courage displayed in his Freud study. One of the fundamental questions that motivates the entire investigation is what, if anything, survives the Freudian critique of religion?

4. Laplanche and Pontalis, *The Language of Psychoanalysis*, 433. The absence of such a theory is not simply the result of the relative disfavor into which the concept of sublimation has fallen in recent years, owing, I suspect, to the general and, in my opinion, unfounded hostility toward energic modes of explanation. Consider, for example, "I find it difficult to continue to believe in Freud's libido theory, as it was informed by a now obsolete psychobiology. Consequently, it is also difficult for me to be comfortable with the term *sublimation*. For sublimation is traditionally linked to libido theory, as in the taming of instinctual passion, a diversion from a 'lower' (instinctual) aim to a 'higher' (cultural) aim. Again, I find myself distracted by these connotations of language, and wish that there were a fresh term that one could substitute" (Arnold Modell, review of *Sublimation*, by Hans Loewald, *Psychoanalytic Quarterly* 60, no. 3 [1991]: 468).

5. Ricoeur, *Freud and Philosophy*, 484.

6. Ibid., 33.

7. "Having recognized religious doctrines as illusions, we are at once faced by a further question: may not other cultural assets of which we hold a high opinion and by which we let our lives be ruled be of a similar nature? Must not the assumptions that determine our political regulations be called illusions as well? And is it not the case that in our civilization the relations between the sexes are disturbed by an erotic illusion or a number of such illusions? And once our suspicion has been aroused, we should not shrink from asking too whether our conviction that we can learn something about external reality through the use of observation and reasoning in scientific work—whether this conviction has any better foundation. Nothing ought to keep us from directing our observation to our own selves or from applying our thought to criticism of itself. In this field a number of investigations open out before us, whose results could not but be decisive for the construction of a *'Weltanschauung'*. We surmise, moreover, that such an effort would not be wasted and that it would at least in part justify our suspicion. But the author does not dispose of the means for undertaking so comprehensive a task; his needs must confine his work to following out one only of these illusions—namely, that of religion" (Freud, *Future of an Illusion* [1927], S.E., vol. 21, 34).

8. Habermas, "The Entwinement of Myth and Enlightenment," 23.

9. Jürgen Habermas, *The Philosophical Discourse of Modernity*, 203.

10. Richard Rorty, "Habermas and Lyotard on Postmodernity," in *Habermas and Modernity*, 161. See also Peter Sloterdijk, *Critique of Cynical Reason*, trans. Michael Eldred (Minneapolis: University of Minnesota Press, 1987).

11. Michel Foucault, "Nietzsche, Freud, and Marx," in *Transforming the Hermeneutical Contexts: Freud and Nietzsche to Nancy*, ed. Gayle Ormiston and Alan Schrift (Albany: State University New York Press, 1990), 61–64. Cf. Lacan's use of the mirror, with its infinite regression of reflection, as an alternative "foundational" structure for the ego.

12. Foucault, "Nietzsche, Freud, and Marx," 64.

13. Michel Foucault, "A Preface to Transgression," 42.

14. Ibid., 43.

15. Ibid., 44.

16. The controversy between Foucault and Derrida concerning Descartes and madness is both confusing and revealing. The apparent point at issue is whether Descartes—and via him modern rationality—excluded madness in its foundational act. Derrida argues that, through the "audacity" of introducing the evil genius, Descartes did indeed include the possibility of madness in the foundations of modern rationalism. Foucault, on the other hand, argues that the positing of the evil genius was not audacious enough, because it leaves intact an experiencing subject that can be systematically deluded; by retaining this intact subject, the possibility of madness was excluded in the founding of modern rationality. The point, however, is that Derrida and Foucault never seem to join issues adequately, because they each assume a different concept of madness. For Derrida, it was sufficient for Descartes to consider the possibility of totalized delusion; Derrida, in short, equates madness with paranoid or hallucinatory psychosis. Foucault, on the other hand, equates madness with the complete fragmentation of the subject, and, given this equation, Descartes indeed did not go far enough. See Jacques Derrida, "The Cogito and the History of Madness," and Michel Foucault, "My Body, This Paper, This Fire."

17. See Arendt, *The Human Condition*, 273ff.

18. Bernstein, *Beyond Objectivism and Relativism*, 18. Hannah Arendt makes a similar observation concerning the two phantasms that launched the Cartesian quest for certainty: "Descartes' philosophy is haunted by two nightmares which in a sense became the nightmares of the whole modern age, not because this age was so deeply influenced by Cartesian philosophy, but because their emergence was almost inescapable once the true implications of the modern world were understood. These nightmares are very simple and very well known. In the one, the reality of the world as well as of human life, is doubted; if neither the senses nor common sense nor reason can be trusted, then it may well be that all we take for reality is only a dream. The other concerns the general human condition as it was revealed by the new discoveries and the impossibility of man to trust his sense and his reason; under these circumstances it seems, indeed, much more likely that an evil spirit, a *Dieu trompeur*, wilfully and spitefully betrays man than that God is the ruler of the universe. The consummate devilry of this evil spirit would consist in having created a creature

which harbors a notion of truth only to bestow on it such other faculties that it will never be able to reach any truth, never be able to be certain of anything" (*The Human Condition*, 277).

19. Kant, *The Critique of Pure Reason*, 120.

20. Considered psychologically, the demand for a strict separation between *quid facti* and *quid juris* is a form of isolation: the contaminated empirical should never touch the pure transcendental. As such, it points to the obsessive roots of philosophy.

21. Interestingly, Adorno likens Husserl, who with his polemic against psychologism is a militant Kantian, to Freud, whom Adorno, here at least, takes as a genetic reductionist. Adorno's thesis is that both men, albeit coming at the issue from opposite directions, could not grasp social reality: "Husserl's campaign against psychologism—which coincides in time exactly with the early beginnings of psychoanalysis—the doctrine of logical absolutism which at all levels separates the validity of intellectual constructs from their genesis and fetishizes the former, is only the obverse side of an approach that sees nothing but the genesis, not its relation to objectivity, and ultimately abolishes the very notion of truth in favour of the reproduction of the existent. The two extreme opposites, both conceived, significantly, amidst the apologetics of an obsolously semi-feudal Austria, ultimately converge. The status quo is either hypostatized as the content of 'intentions' or protected against all criticism by the further subordination of such criticism to psychology" (Adorno, "Sociology and Psychology," 93).

22. Adorno, "Sociology and Psychology," 93.

23. Thomas S. Kuhn, *The Structure of Scientific Revolutions*, 2d ed. (Chicago: University of Chicago Press, 1970).

24. It is true, of course, that all the great figures in the scientific tradition, from Thales to the present, were both rationalists and masters of suspicion. Each figure in the process of enlightenment is a master of suspicion insofar as he or she criticizes, in the name of reason, the previous stage achieved by enlightenment as mythological. But each enlightener, in turn, subsequently succumbs to the critique of illusion when his or her position is attacked as mythological and replaced by another purportedly more rational one. What is unique today is the claim that this process has exhausted itself and that there is no next move.

25. So-called French Freud follows the same general strategy as antihumanist philosophy, namely, to hyperbolically radicalize classical figures of German thought. See Ferry and Renaut, *French Philosophy of the Sixties: An Essay on Antihumanism*, 19ff.

26. Weber, *The Legend of Freud*, xvi.

27. Castoriadis, *The Imaginary Institution of Society*, 248.

28. Sigmund Freud, "Leonardo da Vinci and a Memory of His Childhood" (1910), S.E., vol. 11, 130.

29. Habermas, "The Entwinement of Myth and Enlightenment," 30.

30. Freud, "Leonardo," 130.

31. Ibid., 130.

32. Ibid., 88.

33. Ibid., 23–25.

34. Ibid., 79–80. Admittedly, the question must be raised to what extent Freud's account of Leonardo's nonrepressive sublimation of sexuality is itself idealized. Freud acknowledges that Leonardo could not picture the physiology of the sexual act in an undistorted fashion and that his thinking was marked by obsessive constrictions, both of which would suggest conflict in Leonardo's attitude toward sexuality. Freud, however, never considers the challenge these facts pose to his account of Leonardo's sublimation.

35. Ibid., 78–79.

36. See Alexander Mitscherlich, *Society Without the Father: A Contribution to Social Psychology,* trans. Eric Mosbacher (New York: Schocken Books, 1970).

37. Freud, "Leonardo" (1910), S.E., vol. 11, 122–23.

38. Didier Anzieu, *Freud's Self Analysis,* trans. Peter Graham (Madison, CT: International Universities Press, 1986), 51.

39. Anzieu argues that "reflexive as opposed to more common sublimations, which are expressive, produce quantitatively only a partial and insufficient discharge of instinctual energy. There remains an appreciable instinctual residue which is bound neither in thought by reflexive work, nor by repression into a neurotic symptomatology. The residue tends to discharge itself in the body, in the form of more or less hypochondriacal disorders, fatigues, and mobile, highly variable functional disorders never affecting the same organ for a very great length of time. We have already seen, and shall see again, that this was precisely Freud's case" (*Freud's Self Analysis,* 52). We shall return to the connection between sublimation and discharge below.

40. This quote comes from Schiller and is cited by Freud in "Leonardo," 63.

41. Freud, "Leonardo" (1910), S.E., vol. 11, 130.

42. I would add, moreover, that what Freud says about pathography in general often applies to the pathographical accounts of his life: "Pathography does not in the least aim at making the great man's achievements intelligible; and surely no one should be blamed for not carrying out something he has never promised to do. The real motives for the opposition are different. We can discover them if we bear in mind that biographers are fixated on their heroes in a quite special way. In many cases they have chosen their hero as the subject of their studies because—for reasons of their personal emotional life—they have felt a special affection for him from the very first. They then devote their energies to a task of idealization, aimed at enrolling the great man among the class of their infantile models—at reviving in him, perhaps, the child's idea of his father. To gratify this wish they obliterate the individual features of their subject's physiognomy; they smooth over the traces of his life's struggles with internal and external resistances, and they tolerate in him no vestige of human weakness or imperfection. They thus present us with what is in fact a cold, strange, ideal figure, instead of a human being to whom we might feel ourselves distantly related.

That they should do this is regrettable, for they thereby sacrifice truth to an illusion, and for the sake of their infantile phantasies abandon the opportunity of penetrating the most fascinating secrets of nature" (Freud, "Leonardo" [1910], S.E., vol. 11, 130).

43. Ibid., 130.

44. Loewald, *Sublimation*, 82.

45. Ricoeur, *Freud and Philosophy*, 490.

46. Ibid., 460.

47. It should be noted that Freud explicitly objected to active technical efforts at promoting psychosynthesis, which he believed was "achieved during analytic treatment without our intervention, automatically an inevitably." He did not object to synthesis as such. It should also be pointed out that these objections occurred in the context of his arguments with the psychoanalytic dissidents, who advocated such a synthesis, in the years prior to the First World War, that is, before the structural model: "The well-founded comparison of medical psycho-analytic activity with a chemical procedure might suggest a new direction for our therapy. We have *analyzed* the patient—that is, separated his mental processes into their elementary constituents and demonstrated these instinctual elements in him singly and in isolation; what could be more natural than to expect that we should also help him to make a new and better combination of them? You know that this demand has actually been put forward. We have been told that after an analysis of a sick mind a synthesis of it must follow. And, close upon this, concern has been expressed that the patient might be given too much analysis and too little synthesis; and there has then followed a move to put all the weight on this synthesis as the main factor in the psychotherapeutic effect, to see in it a kind of restoration of something that had been destroyed— destroyed, as it were, by vivisection. . . . But I cannot think . . . that any new task is set us by this psycho-synthesis. If I allow myself to be frank and uncivil I should say it was nothing but an empty phrase" (Freud, "Lines of Advance in Psycho-Analytic Therapy" [1919], S.E., vol. 17, 160–61).

48. Freud, "Formulations on the Two Principles of Mental Functioning" (1911), S.E., vol. 12, 218.

49. Ricoeur, *Freud and Philosophy*, 473.

50. Ibid., 500.

51. Ibid., 497. Castoriadis makes the same point concerning a purely intrapsychic approach somewhat more flamboyantly: "In this way, the same corporeal constitution, the same sexuality, the same Eros and Thanatos, the same oral, anal, genital drives always and everywhere at work, are held to produce, depending on unknown minor and external accidents, sometimes polygamy, sometimes monogamy, sometimes boomerangs and sometimes atomic bombs, sometimes a God-King and sometimes a people's assembly, sometimes shamans and sometimes psychoanalysts, sometimes the glorification and official consecration of masculine homosexuality and sometimes the destruction of Sodom by heaven-sent fire. In the name of the scientific and rigorous mind, one ends up once again with this scientific monstrosity

as a consequence: constant factors produce variable effects" (Castoriadis, *The Imaginary Institution of Society*, 316).

52. Castoriadis, "Epilegomena to a Theory of the Soul," in *Crossroads in the Labyrinth*, 36.

53. Castoriadis, "Psychoanalysis: Project and Elucidation," 95.

54. Castoriadis, *"Fait et á Faire,"* 475.

55. Freud, "Obsessive Actions and Religious Practices" (1907), S.E., vol. 9, 126–27.

56. Castoriadis, *The Imaginary Institution of Society*, 144–45.

57. See Freud, *The Interpretation of Dreams* (1900), S.E., vol. 5, 561.

58. Ricoeur, *Freud and Philosophy*, 519.

59. After all, "the musical thinking of *Tristan*," as Castoriadis has observed, "could not be said in the language of the *Well-Tempered Clavier*" (Castoriadis, *The Imaginary Institution of Society*, 126).

60. Ricoeur, *Freud and Philosophy*, 522.

61. Castoriadis, *Crossroads in the Labyrinth*, xx.

62. Mary Gedo, *Picasso: Art as Autobiography* (Chicago: University of Chicago Press, 1980).

63. Ibid., 166.

64. Ibid., 178.

65. Personal communication. Cf. "With their assumption of an analogy between dreaming and artistic creation, psychoanalysts, like all positivists, vastly overrate the moment of fiction in art. The projection that occurs in the creative process is not at all the decisive moment in works of art; equally important are idiom, material, and, above all, the product itself; the latter being virtually ignored by psychoanalysts" (Theodor W. Adorno, *Aesthetic Theory*, trans. C. Lenhardt, ed. Gretel Adorno and Rolf Tiedemann [New York: Routledge and Keagan Paul, 1986], 12).

66. Frank J. Sulloway, *Freud: Biologist of the Mind: Beyond the Psychoanalytic Legend* (New York: Basic Books, 1979). Paul Robinson makes the following observation in his discussion of Sulloway: "But there is a more fundamental, and subtle consideration: the elements of a theory never add up to the theory itself. In judging a theory's originality one must do more than compile a list of those components that can be traced to earlier sources. One must also assess the structural power of the conceptual whole into which the components have been fitted. In this respect, Freud's achievement can be usefully compared to the intellectual syntheses created by Marx or Darwin. Numerous scholars have shown that all the components of Darwin's theory of natural selection and of Marx's theory of historical materialism had been anticipated by earlier thinkers. But Marx and Darwin have been rightly judged great innovators because they were

the first to shape those ideas into a rigorous and comprehensive whole." (*Freud and His Critics*, [Berkeley: University of California Press, 1993], 75.)

67. Castoriadis, who believes in radical creation, makes the point even more strongly: "Freud occupied, as founder, a unique and unrepeatable movement by which psychoanalysis was *instituted*. The words 'I found . . .' were uttered, in this domain, once and for all, and they were uttered, as always in the case of an authentic foundation, without any need for their being made explicit—so that any repetition of them is a pretentious and derisory camouflage of a non-foundation. Nobody else, since the time of the Greeks (not even Marx), has been such a founder of a quasi-absolute innovation (Galileo was carrying forward something which had long been evolving)" ("Psychoanalysis: Project and Elucidation," 74).

68. François Roustang, *Dire Mastery: Discipleship from Freud to Lacan,* trans. Ned Lukacher (Baltimore: Johns Hopkins University Press, 1982).

69. Castoriadis, "Psychoanalysis: Project and Elucidation," 48.

70. Sigmund Freud, *Group Psychology and the Analysis of the Ego* (1921), S.E., vol. 18, 129.

71. Castoriadis, "Psychoanalysis: Project and Elucidation," 48.

72. Jacques Lacan, *Seminar I,* 16.

73. Castoriadis, "Psychoanalysis: Project and Elucidation," 50.

74. Ibid., 64–65.

75. Ibid., 67.

76. Ibid., 108, n. 18.

77. Albrecht Wellmer, "The Dialectic of Modernism and Postmodernism," 59.

78. Castoriadis, "Psychoanalysis: Project and Elucidation," 79.

79. Ibid., 95. On the controversial question of whether sublimation involves the aim or the object of the drive, Castoriadis argues that it involves both, as he must if he is going to maintain his theory of sublimation as the mediator between the psychic imaginary and socio-historical reality. See *The Imaginary Institution of Society,* 313–14.

80. Castoriadis, "Psychoanalysis: Project and Elucidation," 112, n. 47.

81. To his credit, Roustang wrote one of the finest critiques of Lacan some ten years after the publication of *Dire Mastery.* In *The Lacanian Delusion,* he offers a precise analysis of both the transference dynamics that Lacan skillfully manipulated to keep his followers subordinated to him and of the rhetorical tricks he employed to disguise the basic weakness of his theory. In so doing, Roustang offers an exemplary confirmation of Castoriadis's claims concerning the possibility of sublimation. See Roustang, *The Lacanian Delusion.*

82. Castoriadis, "Epilegomena to a Theory of the Soul," 37.

83. See ibid., 34.

84. Castoriadis, "Psychoanalysis: Project and Elucidation," 72. Cf. Bernstein's ineluctable Either/Or above.

85. Habermas, *The Philosophical Discourse of Modernity*, 408, n. 28.

86. Castoriadis, preface to *Crossroads in the Labyrinth*, xxiii.

87. See Freud, "On the Sexual Theories of Children" (1908), S.E., vol. 9, 219–20.

88. Castoriadis, "Psychoanalysis: Project and Elucidation," 90.

89. Castoriadis, "Epilegomena to a Theory of the Soul," 36.

90. Ibid., 35.

91. Ibid., 37 (emphasis added).

92. Castoriadis, *The Imaginary Institution of Society*, 106.

93. Ibid., 105. See also Castoriadis's "Epilegomena to a Theory of the Soul," 36.

94. Castoriadis, "Epilegomena to a Theory of the Soul," 37.

95. Freud, "Instincts and Their Vicissitudes" (1915), S.E., vol. 14, 121–23.

96. Freud, *Three Essays* (1905), S.E., vol. 7, 134; see also Martin S. Bergmann, "Platonic Love, Transference Love, and Love in Real Life," *Journal of the American Psychoanalytic Association* 30, no. 1 (1982): 87ff.

97. See Nussbaum, *The Fragility of Goodness*, 176ff.

98. See *Symposium*, 202A–203B.

99. Sigmund Freud, "Fragments of an Analysis of a Case of Hysteria" (1905), S.E., vol. 7, 117.

100. David James, unpublished dissertation. He argues that, while it was never explicitly set down in anything resembling Freud's *Papers on Technique*, Socrates' erotic technique was every bit as much a technique for handling the transference as Freud's.

101. Habermas, "The Entwinement of Myth and Enlightenment," 107.

102. Loewald, *Sublimation*, 1 (emphasis added).

103. Freud, Draft L, 248, and Letter 61, 247, both in "Extracts from the Fliess Paper" (1950), S.E., vol. 1.

104. Loewald, *Sublimation*, 4. Cf. the criticisms of Lacan's notion of *mésconnaisance* above. This passage is also consistent with Loewald's earlier reinterpretation of the

relation between the ego and reality in terms of separation-individuation theory: "The following formulation, at this point, seems justified: The relationship of ego to reality is not primarily one of defense against an outer force thrust upon the ego, originally unrelated to it. The relatedness between ego and reality, or objects, does not develop from an originally unrelated coexistence of two separate entities that come into contact with each other, but on the contrary from a unitary whole that differentiates into distinct parts. Mother and baby do not get together and develop a relationship, but the baby is born, becomes detached from the mother, and thus a relatedness between two parts that were originally one becomes possible" (Loewald, "Ego and Reality," 11).

105. Loewald, *Sublimation,* 6, n. 3. Chasseguet-Smirgel argues that the difference between aestheticizing pseudosublimation and true sublimation is that, whereas in the former the instinctual element is disguised and covered over with idealizations, in the latter it is elaborated and shines through in the work; see *The Ego Ideal,* 103ff.

106. Otto Fenichel, *The Psychoanalytic Theory of Neurosis* (New York: W. W. Norton, 1945), 141–43.

107. Loewald, *Sublimation,* 11.

108. Freud, "Leonardo" (1910), S.E., vol. 11, 97. See also Freud's discussion, written roughly at the same time, of the ambivalent meaning of "taboo" as both "sacred" and "unclean": *Totem and Taboo* (1913), S.E., vol. 13, chap. 11.

109. Loewald, *Sublimation,* 11.

110. Freud, "Leonardo" (1910), S.E., vol. 11, 74.

111. Two possible misunderstandings of Loewald's position must be anticipated. First, he is not making an ontological claim about an original state of absolute presence. Rather, he is making a psychological claim about the experience of unity in early development. And it might be the case that experience provides the psychological source for the metaphysical wish for presence. Second, he is not arguing that sublimation achieves a state of complete reconciliation à la Hegel. He is arguing, instead, that it consists in a higher—but always *relatively* higher—level of integration, in which the opposition between the so-called earthly and the spiritual is diminished to a degree.

112. Loewald, *Sublimation,* 13. Loewald also uses this notion of the creation of new synthetic organizations to account for the transition from primary process, consisting in thing-representations, to secondary process, consisting in word-representations, and to explain thereby the "mutative" nature of interpretation: through language, interpretation creates higher levels of integration. See Loewald, "Primary Process, Secondary Process, and Language."

113. Loewald, *Sublimation,* 41.

114. Freud, "The Economic Problem of Masochism" (1924), S.E., vol. 19, 160.

115. Loewald, *Sublimation,* 16 (emphasis added).

116. Freud, *The Ego and the Id* (1923), S.E., vol. 19, 30.

117. Loewald, *Sublimation*, 18–19.

118. Heinz Hartmann, "Notes on the Theory of Sublimation" (1955), in *Essays on Ego Psychology*. See also Ernst Kris, "Neutralization and Sublimation: Observations on Young Children" (1955), in *The Selected Papers of Ernst Kris* (New Haven: Yale University Press, 1955), 151–71.

119. See Freud, *Beyond the Pleasure Principle* (1920), S.E., vol. 18, 57–58. This claim recalls Aristophanes' account, in the *Symposium* of love as the restoration of an original unity, which Freud takes as a point of departure for his analysis of Eros in *Beyond the Pleasure Principle*.

120. Alesandro Ferrara points out, moreover, that the notion of coming to grips "with internal reality . . . must not be confused with conformity to the prevailing social expectations" ("Postmodern Eudaimonia," *Praxis International* 11, no. 4 [January 1992]: 395).

121. "Must we not also doubt our most confident assertions about pleasure? Throughout, we have regarded pleasure as the 'watchman over life'; as such, can it express merely the reduction of tensions? If pleasure is connected with life, and not solely with death, must it not be something more than the psychical sign of the reduction of tensions? Indeed, do we ultimately know what pleasure means?" (Ricoeur, *Freud and Philosophy*, 310).

122. As early as 1905, Freud, in trying to account for the apparently pleasurable tension of sexual arousal, noted the fundamentally problematic character of the question of pleasure: "Everything relating to the problem of pleasure and unpleasure touches upon one of the sorest spots of present-day psychology" (*Three Essays*, [1905], S.E., vol. 7, 209).

123. Sigmund Freud, S.E., vol. 21, 76–77. See Paul Ricoeur: "What is the meaning, in Freud's works, of this disparity between the diversity of suffering and the monotony of enjoyment? Does Freud stand in need of completion on this point? Must we somehow distinguish as many degrees of satisfaction as there are degrees of suffering? Must we restore the dialectic of pleasure, sketched by Plato in the *Philebus*, or even the dialectic of pleasure and happiness in the manner of Aristotle's *Ethics*? Or does the pessimism of pleasure make us admit that man's capacity for suffering is richer than his power of enjoyment? In the face of manifold suffering, does man's only recourse lie in unvaried enjoyment and in bearing the excess of suffering with resignation. I am inclined to think that the whole of Freud's work tends toward the second hypothesis" (*Freud and Philosophy*, 323–24). See also Alesandro Ferrara, "Postmodern Eudaimonia," 390.

124. Sigmund Freud, S.E., vol. 19, 160. Consider also: "The raising of these tensions is in general felt as unpleasure and their lowering as *pleasure*. It is probable, however, that what is felt as pleasure or unpleasure is not the *absolute* height of this tension but something in the rhythm of the changes in them. . . . An action by the ego is as it should be if it satisfies simultaneously the demands of the id, of the super-ego and of reality—that is to say, if it is able to reconcile their demands with one another" (*An Outline of Psycho-Analysis* [1940], S.E., vol. 23, 146). See also Ricoeur, *Freud and Philosophy*, 319–22, and Laplanche, *Life and Death in Psychoanalysis*, 103ff.

125. Winnicott, "The Location of Cultural Experience" (1967), in *Playing and Reality* (London: Tavistock Publications, 1971), 95.

126. Winnicott, "Transitional Objects and Transitional Phenomena," 233. In addition to the fact that Freud did not work with children, the reason he could not find his way to the concept of the transitional object was perhaps because of a Kantian, dichotomizing tendency in his thinking, that is, a tendency to conceptualize things in terms of rigid oppositions: e.g., the pleasure principle and the reality principle, primary processes and secondary processes, conscious and unconscious, id and ego, and so on. There is, however, another countertendency in his thinking, which can be traced from Freud's early notion of the *Zwischenreich* (the "in-between realm"), which appears in "Extracts from the Fliess Paper," to his later notion of frontier concepts, such as the ego and the drives. This potentially fertile countertendency has yet to be explored in depth.

127. Winnicott, "Transitional Objects and Transitional Phenomena," 240.

128. Ibid., 242.

129. Winnicott, "The Location of Cultural Experience," 98.

130. Loewald, *Sublimation*, 29.

131. Ibid., 26. See also Ricoeur, *Freud and Philosophy*, 320.

132. On this point and, in general, for his discussion of the deep conceptual problems with Freud's theory of the death instinct, see Sulloway, *Freud: Biologist of the Mind*, 393ff.

133. W. H. Auden, "In Memoriam of Sigmund Freud," *International Review of Psycho-Analysis* 1 (1974): 4.

134. Freud, "Leonardo" (1910), S.E., vol. 11, 70.

135. "Thus we have the sketch of an answer: that which escapes the principle of constancy is Eros itself, the disturber of sleep, the 'breaker of the peace.' However, doesn't this proposition destroy the hypothesis that lies at the origin of psychoanalysis, namely that the psychical apparatus is regulated quasi-automatically by the principle of constancy?" (Ricoeur, *Freud and Philosophy*, 320).

136. See Laplanche and Pontalis's entry on sublimation in *The Language of Psychoanalysis*, 433.

137. Adorno, "Sociology and Psychology," 83.

138. Ibid., 87.

139. Ibid., 87.

140. Ibid., 86.

141. Adorno, *Negative Dialectics*, 226ff.

142. Ibid., 221–22.

143. Ibid., 271.

144. Ibid., 228–29.

145. Adorno, *Minima Moralia,* 200.

146. Ibid., 122.

147. Ibid., 123.

148. Ibid., 213.

149. Ibid., 213

150. Theodor W. Adorno, "Trying to Understand *Endgame,*" in *Notes to Literature,* vol. 1, trans. Shierry Weber Nicholsen (New York: Columbia University Press, 1991), 248.

Bibliography

Abelin, Ernest. "The Role of the Father in the Separation-Individuation Process." *Separation-Individuation: Essays in Honor of Margaret Mahler.* Ed. John McDevitt and Calvin Settlage. New York: International Universities Press, 1971.

Abelin, Ernest. "Triangulation, the Role of the Father and the Origins of Core Gender Identity during the Rapprochement Subphase." *Rapprochement: The Critical Subphase of Separation-Individuation.* Ed. Ruth Lax, Sheldin Bach, and J. Alexis Burland. New York: Jason Aronson, 1980.

Adorno, Theodor W. "Sociology and Psychology." Trans. Irving N. Wohlfarth. *New Left Review* 47 (January–February 1968): 79–97.

Adorno, Theodor W. *Negative Dialectics.* Trans. E. B. Ashton. New York: Seabury Press, 1973.

Adorno, Theodor W. *Minima Moralia: Reflections from Damaged Life.* Trans. E. F. N. Jephchott. London: New Left Books, 1974.

Adorno, Theodor W. "Resignation." *Telos* 35 (spring 1978): 165–68.

Adorno, Theodor W. "Subject and Object." *The Essential Frankfurt School Reader.* Ed. Andrew Arato and Eike Gebhardt. New York: Urizen Books, 1978.

Adorno, Theodor W. *Aesthetic Theory.* Trans. C. Lenhardt. Ed. Gretel Adorno and Rolf Tiedemann. New York: Routledge and Kegan Paul, 1986.

Adorno, Theodor W. "What Does Coming to Terms With the Past Mean?" *Bitburg in Moral and Political Perspective.* Ed. Geoffrey Hartmann. Bloomington: Indiana University Press, 1986.

Adorno, Theodor W. "Trying to Understand *Endgame.*" Vol. 1, *Notes to Literature.* Trans. Shierry Weber Nicholsen. New York: Columbia University Press, 1991.

Anzieu, Didier. *Freud's Self Analysis.* Trans. Peter Graham. Madison, CT: International Universities Press, 1986.

Arendt, Hannah. *The Human Condition.* Chicago: University of Chicago Press, 1973.

Aristotle. *Metaphysics. The Basic Works of Aristotle.* Ed. Richard McKeon. New York: Random House, 1941.

Aristotle. *Nicomachean Ethics.* Trans. Martin Ostwald. New York: The Liberal Arts Press, 1962.

Aristotle. *Politics. See* Aristotle 1941.

Auden, W. H. "In Memoriam of Sigmund Freud." *International Review of Psycho-Analysis* 1 (1974): 1–3.

Bach, Sheldin, and Lester Schwartz. "A Dream of the Marquis de Sade: Psychoanalytic Reflections on Narcissistic Trauma, Decompensation, and the Reconstitution of a Delusional Self." *Journal of the American Psychoanalytic Association* 20, no. 3 (July 1972): 451–75.

Benhabib, Seyla. *Critique, Norm, and Utopia: A Study of the Foundations of Critical Theory.* New York: Columbia University Press, 1986.

Benjamin, Jessica. "The End of Internalization: Adorno's Social Psychology," *Telos* 32 (1977): 27–41.

Benjamin, Walter. "Theses on the Philosophy of History." *Illuminations.* Ed. Hannah Arendt. Trans. Harry Zohn. New York: Schocken Books, 1968.

Bergmann, Martin S. "Platonic Love, Transference Love, and Love in Real Life." *Journal of the American Psychoanalytic Association* 30, no. 1 (1982): 87–111.

Bergmann, Martin S. *The Anatomy of Loving: The Story of Man's Quest to Know What Love Is.* New York: Columbia University Press, 1987.

Bernstein, Richard J. *Beyond Objectivism and Relativism: Science, Hermeneutics, and Praxis.* Philadelphia: University of Pennsylvania Press, 1983.

Bernstein, Richard J. "Reconciliation/Rupture." *The New Constellation: The Ethical-Political Horizons of Modernity/Postmodernity.* Cambridge, MA: MIT Press, 1992.

Bernstein, Richard J., ed. Introduction to *Habermas and Modernity.* Cambridge, MA: MIT Press, 1985.

Bowie, Malcolm. *Lacan.* Cambridge, MA: Harvard University Press, 1991.

Bion, Wilfred R. *Learning from Experience.* London: Heinemann, 1962. Reprint. New York: Jason Aronson, 1983.

Brecht, Karen, et al., eds. *"Here Life Goes on in a Most Peculiar Way . . . :" Psychoanalysis before and after 1933.* Trans. Christine Trollope. Hamburg: Kellner Verlag, 1985.

Buck-Morss, Susan. *The Origin of Negative Dialectics: Theodor W. Adorno, Walter Benjamin, and the Frankfurt Institute.* New York: The Free Press, 1977.

Cadava, Eduardo et al., eds. *Who Comes after the Subject?* New York: Routledge, 1991.

Casey, Ed, and J. Melvin Woody. "Hegel, Heidegger, Lacan: Dialectic of Desire." *Interpreting Lacan*. Psychiatry and the Humanities, vol. 6. Ed. Joseph H. Smith, M.D., and William Kerrigan. New Haven: Yale University Press, 1983.

Castoriadis, Cornelius. "Epilegomena to a Theory of the Soul." *Crossroads in the Labyrinth*. Trans. Kate Soper and Martin H. Ryle. Cambridge, MA: MIT Press, 1984.

Castoriadis, Cornelius. "Modern Science and Philosophical Interrogation." *Crossroads in the Labyrinth*. *See* Castoriadis 1984.

Castoriadis, Cornelius. "Psychoanalysis: Project and Elucidation." *Crossroads in the Labyrinth*. *See* Castoriadis 1984.

Castoriadis, Cornelius. "The Sayable and the Unsayable." *Crossroads in the Labyrinth*. *See* Castoriadis 1984.

Castoriadis, Cornelius. *The Imaginary Institution of Society*. Trans. Kathleen Blamey. Cambridge, MA: MIT Press, 1987.

Castoriadis, Cornelius. "The First Institution of Society." *Free Associations* 12 (1988): 40–51.

Castoriadis, Cornelius. "Fait et à Faire." *Revue européenne des sciences sociales* 27, no. 86 (1989): 457–514.

Castoriadis, Cornelius. "The State of the Subject Today." Trans. David Ames Curtis. *American Imago* 46 (winter 1989): 371–412.

Castoriadis, Cornelius. "The Greek Polis and the Creation of Democracy." *Philosophy, Politics, Autonomy: Essays in Political Philosophy*. Trans. David Ames Curtis. New York: Oxford University Press, 1991. (First published in *Graduate Faculty Philosophy Journal* 9 [fall 1983]: 79–115.)

Castoriadis, Cornelius. "Power, Politics and Autonomy." *Philosophy, Politics, Autonomy*. *See* Castoriadis 1991.

Castoriadis, Cornelius. "Imagination, Logic, Reflection." *American Imago*. 49 (1992): 3–33.

Castoriadis, Cornelius. "The Retreat From Autonomy: Post-Modernism and the Generalization of Conformity." *Thesis Eleven* 31 (1992): 15–23.

Cavell, Stanley. "Freud and Philosophy: A Fragment." *Critical Inquiry* 13, no. 2 (winter 1987): 386–93.

Chasseguet-Smirgel, Janine. "Perversion, Idealization and Sublimation." *The International Journal of Psycho-Analysis* 55, pt. 3 (1974): 349–63.

Chasseguet-Smirgel, Janine. "Some Thoughts on the Ego Ideal: A Contribution to the Study of the 'Illness of Ideality.'" *The Psychoanalytic Quarterly* 45, no. 3 (1976): 345–73.

Chasseguet-Smirgel, Janine. "Reflections on the Connections between Perversions and Sadism." *The International Journal of Psycho-Analysis* 59, pt. 1 (1978): 27–35.

Chasseguet-Smirgel, Janine. "Aestheticism, Creation and Perversion." *Creativity and Perversion.* New York: W. W. Norton, 1984.

Chasseguet-Smirgel, Janine. "Narcissism and Group Psychology." *Creativity and Perversion. See Chasseguet-Smirgel 1984.*

Chasseguet-Smirgel, Janine. "Perversion and the Universal Law." *Creativity and Perversion. See* Chasseguet-Smirgel 1984.

Chasseguet-Smirgel, Janine. "A Psychoanalytic Study of Falsehood." *Creativity and Perversion. See* Chasseguet-Smirgel 1984.

Chasseguet-Smirgel, Janine. *The Ego Ideal: A Psychoanalytic Essay on the Malady of the Ideal.* Trans. Paul Barrows. New York: W. W. Norton, 1985.

Chasseguet-Smirgel, Janine. "The Archaic Matrix of the Oedipus Complex." *Sexuality and Mind: The Role of the Father and Mother in the Psyche.* New York: New York University Press, 1986.

Chasseguet-Smirgel, Janine. "The Femininity of the Analyst in Professional Practice." *Sexuality and Mind. See* Chasseguet-Smirgel 1986.

Chasseguet-Smirgel, Janine. "Freud and Female Sexuality: The Consideration of Some Blind Spots in the Exploration of the 'Dark Continent.' " *Sexuality and the Mind. See* Chasseguet-Smirgel 1986.

Chasseguet-Smirgel, Janine. "The Paradox of the Freudian Method." *Sexuality and Mind. See* Chasseguet-Smirgel 1986.

Chasseguet-Smirgel, Janine. "Thinking and the Superego: Some Interrelations." *The Psychoanalytic Core: Essays in Honor of Leo Rangell, M.D.* Ed. Harold Blum et al. Madison, CT: International Universities Press, 1989.

Chasseguet-Smirgel, Janine, and Bela Grunberger. *Freud or Reich?: Psychoanalysis and Illusion.* Trans. Clair Pajaczkowska. London: Free Association Books, 1968.

Chodorow, Nancy J. "Beyond Drive Theory: Object Relations and the Limits of Radical Individualism." *Feminism and Psychoanalytic Theory.* New Haven: Yale University Press, 1989.

Derrida, Jacques. "Structure, Sign and Play." *The Structuralist Controversy: The Languages of Criticism and the Sciences of Man.* Ed. Richard Macksey and Eugenio Donato. Baltimore: Johns Hopkins University Press, 1972.

Derrida, Jacques. "The Cogito and the History of Madness." *Writing and Difference.* Trans. Alan Bass. Chicago: University of Chicago Press, 1978.

Derrida, Jacques. " 'To Do Justice to Freud' " The History of Madness in the Age of Psychoanalysis." Trans. Pascale-Anne Brault and Michael Nass. *Critical Inquiry* 20 (Winter 1994) 227–66.

Dews, Peter. "Adorno, Post-Structuralism, and the Critique of Identity." *New Left Review* 157 (May/June 1986): 28–44.

Dews, Peter. *The Logics of Disintegration: Post-Structuralist Thought and the Claims of Critical Theory.* London: Verso Books, 1987.

Dreyfus, Hubert, and Paul Rabinow. "What Is Maturity? Habermas and Foucault on 'What is Enlightenment?' " *Foucault: A Critical Reader.* Ed. David Couzens Hoy. New York: Basil Blackwell, 1986.

Dubiel, Helmut. *Theory and Politics: Studies in the Development of Critical Theory.* Trans. B. Gregg. Cambridge, MA: MIT Press, 1985.

Fenichel, Otto, M.D. *The Psychoanalytic Theory of Neurosis.* New York: W. W. Norton, 1945.

Fenichel, Otto, M. D. "A Critique of the Death Drive." *The Collected Papers of Otto Fenichel.* New York: W. W. Norton, 1953.

Ferrara, Alesandro. "Postmodern Eudaimonia." *Praxis International* 11, no. 4 (January 1992): 387–411.

Ferry, Luc, and Alain Renaut. *French Philosophy of the Sixties: An Essay on Antihumanism.* Trans. Mary H. S. Cattani. Amherst, MA: University of Massachusetts Press, 1990.

Ferry, Luc, and Alain Renaut. *Heidegger and Modernity.* Trans. Franklin Philip. Chicago: University of Chicago Press, 1990.

Forrester, John. "Michel Foucault and the History of Psychoanalysis." *The Seductions of Psychoanalysis: Freud, Lacan and Derrida.* Cambridge Studies in French. New York: Cambridge University Press, 1989.

Foucault, Michel. *Madness and Civilization: A History of Insanity in the Age of Reason.* Trans. Richard Howard. New York: Pantheon Books, 1965.

Foucault, Michel. "A Preface to Transgression." *Language, Counter-Memory, Practice: Selected Essays and Interviews by Michel Foucault.* Ed. Donald Bouchard. Trans. Donald Bouchard and Sherry Simon. Ithaca, NY: Cornell University Press, 1977.

Foucault, Michel. "What Is Enlightenment?" *The Foucault Reader.* Ed. Paul Rabinow. New York: Pantheon Books, 1984.

Foucault, Michel. "Nietzsche, Freud, and Marx." *Transforming the Hermeneutical Contexts: Freud and Nietzsche to Nancy.* Ed. Gayle Ormiston and Alan Schrift. Albany: State University of New York Press, 1990.

Foucault, Michel. "My Body, This Paper, This Fire." Trans. Geoffrey Bennington. *Oxford Literary Review* 4 (1979): 5–28.

Frank, Manfred. *What is Neostructuralism?* Trans. Sabina Wilke and Richard Gray. Minneapolis: University of Minnesota Press, 1989.

Freud, Anna. "The Widening Scope of Indications for Psychoanalysis." *Journal of the American Psychoanalytic Association* 2, no. 4 (1954): 607–20.

Friedman, Lawrence. "Conflict and Synthesis in Freud's Theory of the Mind." *International Review of Psycho-Analysis* 4 (1977): 155–70.

Gadamer, Hans-Georg. *Truth and Method.* Trans. Garrett Barden and John Cumming. New York: Seabury Press, 1975.

Gadamer, Hans-Georg. "On the Scope and Function of Hermeneutical Reflection." *Philosophical Hermeneutics.* Trans. and ed. David Linge. Berkeley: University of California Press, 1976.

Gadamer, Hans-Georg. "The Universality of the Hermeneutical Problem." *Philosophical Hermeneutics. See* Gadamer 1976.

Gedo, Mary M. *Picasso: Art as Autobiography.* Chicago: University of Chicago Press, 1980.

Green, André. "The Logic of Lacan's object *a* and Freudian Theory: Convergences and Questions." *Interpreting Lacan. See* Casey and Woody, 1983.

Green, André. "The Analyst, Symbolization and Absence in the Analytic Setting" (1975). *On Private Madness.* Madison, CT: International Universities Press, 1986.

Green, André. "Conceptions of Affect." *On Private Madness. See* Green 1986.

Green, André. Introduction to *On Private Madness. See* Green 1986.

Green, André. "Passions and Their Vicissitudes." *On Private Madness. See* Green 1986.

Greenacre, Phyllis. "The Fetish and the Transitional Object" (1969). Vol. 1. *Emotional Growth: Psychoanalytic Studies of the Gifted and a Great Variety of Other Individuals.* New York: International Universities Press, 1971.

Greenacre, Phyllis. "The Transitional Object and the Fetish: With Special Reference to the Role of Illusion" (1970). *Emotional Growth. See* Greenacre 1971.

Grossman, William I. "Hierarchies, Boundaries and Representations in a Freudian Model of Mental Organization." *Journal of the American Psychoanalytic Association* 40, no. 1 (1992): 27–59.

Habermas, Jürgen. "Science and Technology as 'Ideology.' " *Toward a Rational Society: Student Protest, Science, and Politics.* Trans. Jeremy J. Shapiro. Boston: Beacon Press, 1970.

Habermas, Jürgen. *Knowledge and Human Interests.* Trans. Jeremy J. Shapiro. Boston: Beacon Press, 1971.

Habermas, Jürgen. "Labor and Interaction: Remarks on Hegel's *Jena Philosophy of Mind." Theory and Practice.* Trans. John Viertel. Boston: Beacon Press, 1973.

Habermas, Jürgen. "A Postscript to *Knowledge and Human Interests.*" *Philosophy of Social Science* 3 (1973): 157–89.

Habermas, Jürgen. *Legitimation Crisis.* Trans. Thomas McCarthy. Boston: Beacon Press, 1975.

Habermas, Jürgen. "Moral Development and Ego Identity." *Communication and the Evolution of Society.* Trans. Thomas McCarthy. Boston: Beacon Press, 1979.

Habermas, Jürgen. "Toward a Reconstruction of Historical Materialism." *Communication and the Evolution of Society. See* Habermas 1979.

Habermas, Jürgen. "The Hermeneutic Claim to Universality." *Contemporary Hermeneutics: Hermeneutics as Method, Philosophy and Critique.* Ed. Josef Bleicher. Boston: Routledge and Kegan Paul, 1980.

Habermas, Jürgen. "A Reply to My Critics." *Habermas: Critical Debates.* Ed. John Thompson and David Held. Cambridge, MA: MIT Press, 1982.

Habermas, Jürgen. "Modernity—An Incomplete Project." *The Anti-Aesthetic: Essays on Postmodern Culture.* Ed. Hal Foster. Port Townsend, WA: Bay Press, 1983. (First published as "Modernity versus Postmodernity." *New German Critique* 22 [winter 1981]: 3–18.)

Habermas, Jürgen. "Theodor Adorno: The Primal History of Subjectivity—Self-Affirmation Gone Wild." *Philosophical-Political Profiles.* Trans. Frederick G. Lawrence. Cambridge, MA: MIT Press, 1983.

Habermas, Jürgen. "Walter Benjamin: Consciousness-Raising or Rescuing Critique." *Philosophical-Political Profiles. See* Habermas, 1983.

Habermas, Jürgen. *The Theory of Communicative Action.* Vol. 1, *Reason and the Rationalization of Society.* Trans. Thomas McCarthy. Boston: Beacon Press, 1984a.

Habermas, Jürgen. *The Theory of Communicative Action.* Vol. 2, *Lifeworld and System: A Critique of Functionalist Reason.* Trans. Thomas McCarthy. Boston: Beacon Press, 1984b.

Habermas, Jürgen. "Psychic Thermidor and the Rebirth of Rebellious Subjectivity." *Habermas and Modernity. See* Bernstein 1985.

Habermas, Jürgen. "Questions and Counterquestions." *Habermas and Modernity. See* Bernstein 1985.

Habermas, Jürgen. "A Philosophico-Political Profile." *Habermas: Autonomy and Solidarity: Interviews with Jürgen Habermas.* Ed. Peter Dews. London: New Left Books, 1986.

Habermas, Jürgen. "Taking Aim at the Heart of the Present." *Foucault: A Critical Reader. See* Dreyfus 1986.

Habermas, Jürgen. "An Alternative Way out of the Philosophy of the Subject: Communicative versus Subject-Centered Reason." *The Philosophical Discourse of Modernity:*

Twelve Lectures. Trans. Frederick G. Lawrence. Cambridge, MA: MIT Press, 1987.

Habermas, Jürgen. "The Entwinement of Myth and Enlightenment." *The Philosophical Discourse of Modernity. See* Habermas 1987. (First published in *New German Critique* 26 [spring/summer 1982]: 13–30).

Habermas, Jürgen. *"Excursus on Cornelius Castoriadis: The Imaginary Institution." The Philosophical Discourse of Modernity. See* Habermas 1987.

Habermas, Jürgen. *On the Logic of the Social Sciences.* Trans. Shierry Weber Nicholsen and Jerry A. Stark. Cambridge, MA: MIT Press, 1988.

Habermas, Jürgen. "Historical Consciousness and Post-Traditional Identity: The Federal Republic's Orientation to the West." *The New Conservatism: Cultural Criticism and the Historians' Debate.* Ed. and trans. Shierry Weber Nicholsen. Cambridge, MA: MIT Press, 1989.

Habermas, Jürgen. "Neoconservative Cultural Criticism in the United States and West Germany." *The New Conservatism. See* Habermas 1989.

Hartmann, Heinz. *Ego Psychology and the Problem of Adaptation.* Journal of the American Psychoanalytic Association Monograph Series. No. 1. Trans. David Rapaport. New York: International Universities Press, 1964.

Hartmann, Heinz. "Notes on the Theory of Sublimation" (1955). *Essays on Ego Psychology.* Selected Problems in Psychoanalytic Theory. New York: International Universities Press, 1965.

Hartmann, Heinz. "On the Reality Principle" (1956). *Essays on Ego Psychology. See* Hartmann 1965.

Hartmann, Heinz. "Comments on the Psychoanalytic Theory of the Ego" (1950). *Essays on Ego Psychology. See* Hartmann 1965.

Hegel, G. W. F. *The Philosophy of Right.* Trans. T. M. Knox. Oxford: Clarendon Press, 1942.

Hegel, G. W. F. *Phenomenology of Spirit.* Trans. A. V. Miller. Oxford: Clarendon Press, 1977.

Honneth, Axel. *The Critique of Power: Reflective Stages in a Critical Social Theory.* Trans. Kenneth Baynes. Cambridge, MA: MIT Press, 1991.

Horkheimer, Max. "Authority and the Family." *Critical Theory: Selected Essays.* Trans. Matthew O'Connell et al. New York: Seabury Press, 1972.

Horkheimer, Max. "Traditional and Critical Theory." *Critical Theory. See* Horkheimer 1972.

Horkheimer, Max, and Theodor W. Adorno. *The Dialectic of Enlightenment.* Trans. John Cumming. New York: Herder and Herder, 1972.

Ingram, David. "Habermas on Aesthetics and Rationality: Completing the Project of Enlightenment." *New German Critique* 55 (spring/summer 1991): 67–103.

Jacobson, Edith. *The Self and the Object World.* Journal of the American Psychoanalytic Association Monograph Series. No. 2. New York: International Universities Press, 1964.

James, David. *Socrates' Erotic Art and Freud's Psychoanalytic Technique.* Ph.D. diss. The Graduate Faculty of The New School For Social Research, 1993.

Jay, Martin. *The Dialectical Imagination: A History of the Frankfurt School and the Institute of Social Research, 1923–1950.* New York: Little, Brown, 1973.

Jay, Martin. *Adorno.* London: Fontana Books, 1984.

Jay, Martin. "Habermas and Modernism." *Habermas and Modernity. See* Bernstein 1985.

Jay, Martin. "The Debate over Performative Contradiction: Habermas versus the Poststructuralists." *Philosophical Interventions in the Unfinished Project of Modernity.* Ed. Axel Honneth et al. Cambridge, MA: MIT Press, 1992.

Joas, Hans. "Complexity and Democracy: Or the Seducements of Systems Theory." *The Theory of Communicative Action.* Ed. Axel Honneth and Hans Joas. London: Polity Press, 1991.

Joas, Hans. "The Unhappy Marriage of Hermeneutics and Functionalism." *The Theory of Communicative Action. See* Joas, 1991.

Jurist, Elliot. *The Familiar Is Unknown: Philosophy, Culture and Agency in Hegel and Nietzsche.* Cambridge, MA: MIT Press, forthcoming.

Kant, Immanuel. *Critique of Judgement.* Trans. J. C. Meredith. Oxford: Oxford University Press, 1952.

Kant, Immanuel. *Groundwork of the Metaphysics of Morals.* Trans. J. J. Paton. New York: Harper Torchbooks, 1964.

Kant, Immanuel. *The Critique of Pure Reason.* Trans. N. K. Smith. New York: St. Martin's Press, 1965.

Kaplan, Louise J. *Female Perversions: The Temptations of Emma Bovary.* New York: Doubleday, 1991.

Kohut, Heinz. "Forms and Transformations of Narcissism." *Journal of the American Psychoanalytic Association* 14, no. 2 (April 1966): 243–72.

Kohut, Heinz. *The Analysis of the Self: A Systematic Approach to the Psychoanalytic Treatment of Narcissistic Personality Disorders.* New York: International Universities Press, 1971.

Kohut, Heinz. *The Restoration of the Self.* New York: International Universities Press, 1977.

Kohut, Heinz. *How Does Analysis Cure?* Ed. A. Goldberg. Chicago: University of Chicago Press, 1984.

Kris, Ernst. "Neutralization and Sublimation: Observations on Young Children." *The Selected Papers of Ernst Kris*. New Haven: Yale University Press, 1955.

Kuhn, Thomas S. *The Structure of Scientific Revolutions*. 2d ed. Chicago: University of Chicago Press, 1970.

Lacan, Jacques. "Some Reflections on the Ego." *The International Journal of Psycho-Analysis* 34 (1953): 11–17.

Lacan, Jacques. "The Agency of the Letter in the Unconscious." *Ecrits: A Selection*. Trans. Alan Sheridan. New York: W. W. Norton, 1977.

Lacan, Jacques. "Aggressivity in Psychoanalysis." *Ecrits. See* Lacan 1977.

Lacan, Jacques. "The Freudian Thing." *Ecrits. See* Lacan 1977.

Lacan, Jacques. "The Function and Field of Speech and Language in Psychoanalysis." *Ecrits. See* Lacan 1977.

Lacan, Jacques. "The Mirror Stage." *Ecrits. See* Lacan 1977.

Lacan, Jacques. "The Signification of the Phallus." *Ecrits. See* Lacan 1977.

Lacan, Jacques. *The Seminar of Jacques Lacan*. Ed. Jacques-Alain Miller. Book 1, *Freud's Papers on Technique (1953–54)*. Trans. John Forrester. New York: W. W. Norton, 1988.

Lacan, Jacques. *The Seminar of Jacques Lacan*. Ed. Jacques-Alain Miller. Book 2, *The Ego in Freud's Theory and in the Technique of Psychoanalysis 1954–1955*. Trans. Sylvana Tomaselli. New York: W. W. Norton, 1988.

Laplanche, Jean. *Life and Death in Psychoanalysis*. Trans. Jeffrey Mehlman. Baltimore: Johns Hopkins University Press, 1976.

Laplanche, Jean. *New Foundations for Psychoanalysis*. Trans. David Macey. New York: Basil Blackwell, 1989.

Laplanche, Jean, and Serge Leclaire. "The Unconscious: A Psychoanalytic Study." *Yale French Studies*, no. 46 (1971).

Laplanche, Jean, and J.-B. Pontalis. *The Language of Psychoanalysis*. Trans. Donald Nicholson-Smith. New York: W. W. Norton, 1974.

Lasch, Christopher. *Haven in a Heartless World: The Family Besieged*. New York: Basic Books, 1977.

Lasch, Christopher. *The Minimal Self: Psychic Survival in Troubled Times*. New York: W. W. Norton, 1984.

Loewald, Hans. "Ego and Reality." *Papers on Psychoanalysis*. New Haven, CT: Yale University Press, 1980.

Loewald, Hans. "Primary Process, Secondary Process, and Language." *Papers on Psychoanalysis. See* Loewald 1980.

Loewald, Hans. "The Waning of the Oedipus Complex." *Papers on Psychoanalysis. See* Loewald 1980.

Loewald, Hans. *Sublimation: Inquiries into Theoretical Psychoanalysis.* New Haven, CT: Yale University Press, 1988.

Lowenthal, Leo. "The Utopian Motif Is Suspended." *An Unmastered Past: The Autobiographical Reflections of Leo Lowenthal.* Ed. Martin Jay. Berkeley: University of California Press, 1987.

Lyotard, Jean-Françiois. "Adorno as the Devil." *Telos* 19 (spring 1974): 128–37.

Lyotard, Jean-François. "The Dream-work Does Not Think." *The Lyotard Reader.* Ed. Andrew Benjamin. Cambridge, MA: Basil Blackwell, 1989.

Macey, David. *Lacan in Contexts.* London: Verso Books, 1988.

Mahler, Margaret S. *On Human Symbiosis and the Vicissitudes of Individuation.* New York: International Universities Press, 1968.

Mahler, Margaret S., Fred Pine, and Anni Bergman. *The Psychological Birth of the Human Infant: Symbiosis and Individuation.* New York: Basic Books, 1975.

Marcuse, Herbert. *Eros and Civilization: A Philosophical Inquiry into Freud.* Boston: Beacon Press, 1966.

Marcuse, Herbert. "On Hedonism." *Negations: Essays in Critical Theory.* Trans. Jeremy J. Shapiro. Boston: Beacon Press, 1968.

Marcuse, Herbert. *An Essay on Liberation.* Boston: Beacon Press, 1969.

Marcuse, Herbert. "The End of Utopia." *Five Lectures: Psychoanalysis, Politics and Utopia.* Trans. Jeremy J. Shapiro and Shierry M. Weber. Boston: Beacon Press, 1970.

Marcuse, Herbert. "The Obsolescence of the Freudian Concept of Man." *Five Lectures. See* Marcuse 1970.

Marx, Karl. *Capital.* Vol. 3. Ed. Friedrich Engels. Moscow: Progress Publishers, 1971.

Marx, Karl. *Grundrisse: Introduction to a Critique of Political Economy.* Trans. Martin Nicolaus. Baltimore: Penguin Books, 1973.

McCarthy, Thomas A. *The Critical Theory of Jürgen Habermas.* Cambridge, MA: MIT Press, 1978.

McCarthy, Thomas A. "Rationality and Relativism: Habermas's 'Overcoming' of Hermeneutics." *Habermas: Critical Debates. See* Habermas 1982.

McDougall, Joyce. *A Plea for a Measure of Abnormality.* New York: International Universities Press, 1980.

McDougall, Joyce. *Theaters of the Mind: Illusion and Truth on the Psychoanalytic Stage.* New York: Basic Books, 1985.

McDougall, Joyce. "Perversions and Deviations in the Psychoanalytic Attitude: Their Effect on Theory and Practice." *Perversions and Near-Perversions in Clinical Practice.* New Psychoanalytic Perspectives. Ed. Gerald I. Fogel and Wayne A. Myers. New Haven: Yale University Press, 1991.

Merleau-Ponty, Maurice. "Hegel's Existentialism." *Sense and Non-sense.* Trans. Hubert L. Dreyfus and Patricia Allen Dreyfus. Evanston, IL: Northwestern University Press, 1964.

Mitscherlich, Alexander. *Society without the Father: A Contribution to Social Psychology.* Trans. Eric Mosbacher. New York: Schocken Books, 1970. Reprint. New York: HarperPerennial, 1991.

Modell, Arnold H. Review of *Sublimation: Inquiries into Theoretical Psychoanalysis,* by Hans Loewald. *Psychoanalytic Quarterly* 60, no. 3 (1991): 467–70.

Nunberg, Herman. *Principles of Psychoanalysis: Their Application to the Neuroses.* Trans. Madlyn Kahr and Sidney Kahr. New York: International Universities Press, 1955.

Nussbaum, Martha Craven. *The Fragility of Goodness: Luck and Ethics in Greek Tragedy and Philosophy.* New York: Cambridge University Press, 1986.

Oliner, Marion Michel. *Cultivating Freud's Garden in France.* New York: Jason Aronson, 1988.

Piaget, Jean. *The Moral Judgement of the Child.* Trans. Marjorie Gabain. New York: Free Press, 1965.

Piaget, Jean. "The Affective Unconscious and the Cognitive Unconscious." *Journal of the American Psychoanalytic Association* 21, no. 2 (1973): 249–61.

Pippin, Robert B. *Modernism as a Philosophical Problem.* Cambridge, MA: Basil Blackwell, 1991.

Plato. *Symposium.* Trans. Walter Hamilton. London: Penguin Books, 1951.

Popper, Sir Karl Raimund. *Conjectures and Refutations: The Growth of Scientific Knowledge.* 2d. ed. New York: Basic Books, 1965.

Ricoeur, Paul. *Freud and Philosophy: An Essay on Interpretation.* Trans. Denis Savage. New Haven: Yale University Press, 1970.

Ricoeur, Paul. "Psychoanalysis and the Movement of Contemporary Culture." *The Conflict of Interpretations: Essays on Hermeneutics.* Ed. Don Ihde. Evanston, IL: Northwestern University Press, 1974.

Ricoeur, Paul. "The Question of the Subject: The Challenge of Semiology." *The Conflict of Interpretations. See* Ricoeur 1974.

Ricoeur, Paul. "Technique and Nontechnique in Interpretation." *The Conflict of Interpretations. See* Ricoeur 1974.

Ricoeur, Paul. "Image and Language in Psychoanalysis." *Psychoanalysis and Language.* Psychiatry and the Humanities, vol. 3. Ed. Joseph H. Smith, M.D. New Haven: Yale University Press, 1978.

Ricoeur, Paul. "The Function of Fiction in Shaping Reality." *A Ricoeur Reader: Reflection and Imagination.* Ed. Mario Valdes. Toronto: University of Toronto Press, 1991.

Ricoeur, Paul. "Hermeneutics and the Critique of Ideology." *From Text to Action: Essays in Hermeneutics II.* Trans. Kathleen Blamey and John B. Thompson. Evanston, IL: Northwestern University Press, 1991.

Rieff, Philip. *Freud: The Mind of the Moralist.* 3d. ed. Chicago: University of Chicago Press, 1979.

Robinson, Paul. *Freud and His Critics.* Berkeley: University of California Press, 1993.

Rorty, Richard. "Habermas and Lyotard on Postmodernity." *Habermas and Modernity. See* Bernstein 1985.

Roudnesco, Elisabeth. *Jacques Lacan & Co.: A History of Psychoanalysis in France, 1925–1985.* Trans. Jeffrey Mehlman. Chicago: University of Chicago Press, 1990.

Roustang, François. *Dire Mastery: Discipleship from Freud to Lacan.* Trans. Ned Lukacher. Baltimore: Johns Hopkins University Press, 1982.

Roustang, François. *The Lacanian Delusion.* Trans. Greg Sims. New York: Oxford University Press, 1990.

Sachs, Hans. "The Delay of the Machine Age," *Psychoanalytic Quarterly,* 2 (1933): 404–23.

Schafer, Roy. "The Psychoanalytic Vision of Reality." *A New Language for Psychoanalysis.* New Haven: Yale University Press, 1976.

Sloterdijk, Peter. *Critique of Cynical Reason.* Trans. Michael Eldred. Minneapolis: University of Minnesota Press, 1987.

Sterba, Richard. "The Fate of the Ego in Analytic Therapy." *The International Journal of Psycho-Analysis* 15 (1935): 117–26.

Sternberg, Simone. "The Mother Tongue and Mother's Tongue." *Psychoanalytic Approaches to the Resistant and Difficult Patient.* Ed. Herbert S. Strean. New York: Haworth Press, 1985.

Stoller, Robert. *Perversions: The Erotic Form of Hatred.* New York: Pantheon Books, 1975.

Strachey, James. Editor's note to "Instincts and Their Vicissitudes." *See* Sigmund Freud 1915b.

Sulloway, Frank J. *Freud: Biologist of the Mind: Beyond the Psychoanalytic Legend.* New York: Basic Books, 1979.

Turkle, Sherry. *Psychoanalytic Politics: Freud's French Revolution.* New York: Basic Books, 1978.

Waelder, Robert. "The Principle of Multiple Function: Observations on Overdetermination in Psychoanalysis." *Psychoanalysis—Observation, Theory, Application: Selected Papers of Robert Waelder.* Ed. Samuel A. Guttman. New York: International Universities Press, 1976.

Wallace, Edwin R., IV. *Freud and Anthropology: A History and Reappraisal.* New York: International Universities Press: 1983.

Weber, Max. *Economy and Society: An Outline of Interpretive Sociology.* Ed. Guenther Roth and Claus Wittich. Trans. Ephraim Fischoff et al. New York: Bedminster Press, 1968. Reprint. Berkeley: University of California Press, 1978.

Weber, Samuel. *The Legend of Freud.* Minneapolis: University of Minnesota Press, 1983.

Wellmer, Albrecht. "Communication and Emancipation: Reflections on the Linguistic Turn in Critical Theory." *On Critical Theory.* Ed. John O'Neill. New York: Seabury Press, 1976.

Wellmer, Albrecht. "Reason, Utopia and the *Dialectic of Enlightenment.*" *Habermas and Modernity. See* Bernstein 1985.

Wellmer, Albrecht. "Models of Freedom in the Modern World." *The Philosophical Forum* 21, nos. 1–2 (winter 1989–90): 227–52.

Wellmer, Albrecht. "The Dialectic of Modernism and Postmodernism: The Critique of Reason since Adorno." *The Persistence of Modernity: Essays on Aesthetics, Ethics, and Postmodernism.* Trans. David Midgley. Cambridge, MA: MIT Press, 1991.

Wellmer, Albrecht. "Truth, Semblance and Reconciliation: Adorno's Aesthetic Redemption of Modernity." *The Persistence of Modernity. See* Wellmer 1991. (First published *Telos* 62 [winter 1984–85]: 89–94. Trans. Maeve Cooke.)

Whitebook, Joel. "The Problem of Nature in Habermas." *Telos* 40 (summer 1979): 41–69.

Whitebook, Joel. "Intersubjectivity and the Monadic Core of the Psyche: Castoriadis and Habermas on the Unconscious." *Revue européenne des sciences socials* 27, no. 86 (1989): 225–45.

Winnicott, D. W. *The Maturational Process and the Facilitating Environment: Studies in the Theory of Emotional Development.* New York: International Universities Press, 1965.

Winnicott, D. W. "The Location of Cultural Experience." *Playing and Reality.* London: Tavistock Publications, 1971.

Winnicott, D. W. "Transitional Objects and Transitional Phenomena." *Through Paediatrics to Psycho-Analysis.* Intro. M. Masud R. Khan. New York: Basic Books, 1975. (First published as *Collected Papers: Through Paediatrics to Psycho-Analysis.* New York: Basic Books, 1958.)

Yack, Bernard. *The Longing for Total Revolution: Philosophic Sources of Social Discontent from Rousseau to Marx and Nietzsche.* Princeton: Princeton University Press, 1986.

Yerushalmi, Yosef Hayim. "The Moses of Freud and the Moses of Schoenberg: On Words, Idolatry, and Psychoanalysis." *The Psychoanalytic Study of the Child,* vol. 47. New Haven: Yale University Press, 1992.

Works by Sigmund Freud

All works by Sigmund Freud are taken from *The Standard Edition of the Complete Psychological Works of Sigmund Freud.* 24 vols. Trans. James Strachey. London: Hogarth Press, 1975.

Freud, Sigmund. *The Interpretation of Dreams* (1900). Vols. 4 and 5.

Freud, Sigmund. *The Psychopathology of Everyday Life* (1901). Vol. 6.

Freud, Sigmund. "On Psychotherapy" (1905a). Vol. 7.

Freud, Sigmund. *Three Essays on the Theory of Sexuality* (1905b). Vol. 7.

Freud, Sigmund. "Fragment of an Analysis of a Case of Hysteria" (1905c). Vol. 7.

Freud, Sigmund. "Obsessive Actions and Religious Practices" (1907). Vol. 9.

Freud, Sigmund. "On the Sexual Theories of Children" (1908). Vol. 9.

Freud, Sigmund. "Analysis of a Phobia in a Five-Year-Old Boy" (1909). Vol. 10.

Freud, Sigmund. "Family Romances" (1909a). Vol. 9.

Freud, Sigmund. "Notes upon a Case of Obsessional Neurosis" (1909b). Vol. 10.

Freud, Sigmund. *Leonardo da Vinci and a Memory of His Childhood* (1910). Vol. 11.

Freud, Sigmund. "Formulations on the Two Principles of Mental Functioning" (1911). Vol. 12.

Freud, Sigmund. "Psycho-Analytic Notes on an Autobiographical Account of a Case of Paranoia (Dementia Paranoides)" (1911). Vol. 12.

Freud, Sigmund. "Types of Onset of Neurosis" (1912). Vol. 12.

Freud, Sigmund. *Totem and Taboo* (1913). Vol. 13.

Freud, Sigmund. "On Narcissism: An Introduction" (1914a). Vol. 14.

Freud, Sigmund. "On the History of the Psycho-Analytic Movement" (1914b). Vol. 14.

Freud, Sigmund. "Thoughts for the Times on War and Death" (1915a). Vol. 14.

Freud, Sigmund. "Instincts and Their Vicissitudes" (1915b). Vol. 14.

Freud, Sigmund. "The Unconscious" (1915c). Vol. 14.

Freud, Sigmund. "On Transience" (1916). Vol. 14.

Freud, Sigmund. *Introductory Lectures on Psycho-Analysis* (1916–1917). Vols. 15 and 16.

Freud, Sigmund. "A Difficulty in the Path of Psycho-Analysis" (1917a). Vol. 17.

Freud, Sigmund. "On Transformations of Instinct as Exemplified in Anal Eroticism" (1917b). Vol. 17.

Freud, Sigmund. "Mourning and Melancholia" (1917c). Vol. 14.

Freud, Sigmund. "Lines of Advance in Psycho-Analytic Therapy" (1919). Vol. 17.

Freud, Sigmund. *Beyond the Pleasure Principle* (1920). Vol. 18.

Freud, Sigmund. *Group Psychology and the Analysis of the Ego* (1921). Vol. 18.

Freud, Sigmund. *The Ego and the Id* (1923a). Vol. 19.

Freud, Sigmund. "The Infantile Genital Organization: An Interpolation into the Theory of Sexuality" (1923b). Vol. 19.

Freud, Sigmund. "Neurosis and Psychosis" (1924a). Vol. 19.

Freud, Sigmund. "The Economic Problem of Masochism" (1924b). Vol. 19.

Freud, Sigmund. "The Loss of Reality in Neurosis and Psychosis" (1924c). Vol. 19.

Freud, Sigmund. "Some Psychical Consequences of the Anatomical Distinction between the Sexes" (1925). Vol. 19.

Freud, Sigmund. *Inhibitions, Symptoms and Anxiety* (1926). Vol. 20.

Freud, Sigmund. *The Question of Lay Analysis* (1926). Vol. 20.

Freud, Sigmund. *The Future of an Illusion* (1927a). Vol. 21.

Freud, Sigmund. "Fetishism" (1927b). Vol. 21.

Freud, Sigmund. *Civilization and Its Discontents* (1930). Vol. 21.

Freud, Sigmund. "Female Sexuality" (1931). Vol. 21.

Freud, Sigmund. *New Introductory Lectures on Psycho-Analysis* (1933). Vol. 22.

Freud, Sigmund. "Analysis Terminable and Interminable" (1937). Vol. 23.

Freud, Sigmund. *An Outline of Psycho-Analysis* (1940a). Vol. 23.

Freud, Sigmund. "Splitting of the Ego in the Process of Defense" (1940b). Vol. 23.

Freud, Sigmund. "Extracts from the Fliess Paper" (1950). Draft L and Letter 61. Vol. 1.

Index

Studies in Contemporary German Social Thought
Thomas McCarthy, General Editor

Herbert Marcuse, *Hegel's Ontology and the Theory of Historicity*
Gil G. Noam and Thomas E. Wren, editors, *The Moral Self*
Guy Oakes, *Weber and Rickert: Concept Formation in the Cultural Sciences*
Claus Offe, *Contradictions of the Welfare State*
Claus Offe, *Disorganized Capitalism: Contemporary Transformations of Work and Politics*
Helmut Peukert, *Science, Action, and Fundamental Theology: Toward a Theology of Communicative Action*
Joachim Ritter, *Hegel and the French Revolution: Essays on the* Philosophy of Right
William E. Scheuerman, *Between the Norm and the Exception: The Frankfurt School and the Rule of Law*
Alfred Schmidt, *History and Structure: An Essay on Hegelian-Marxist and Structuralist Theories of History*
Dennis Schmidt, *The Ubiquity of the Finite: Hegel, Heidegger, and the Entitlements of Philosophy*
Carl Schmitt, *The Crisis of Parliamentary Democracy*
Carl Schmitt, *Political Romanticism*
Carl Schmitt, *Political Theology: Four Chapters on the Concept of Sovereignty*
Gary Smith, editor, *On Walter Benjamin: Critical Essays and Recollections*
Michael Theunissen, *The Other: Studies in the Social Ontology of Husserl, Heidegger, Sartre, and Buber*
Ernst Tugendhat, *Self-Consciousness and Self-Determination*
Georgia Warnke, *Justice and Interpretation*
Mark Warren, *Nietzsche and Political Thought*
Albrecht Wellmer, *The Persistence of Modernity: Essays on Aesthetics, Ethics and Postmodernism*
Joel Whitebook, *Perversion and Utopia: A Study in Psychoanalysis and Critical Theory*
Rolf Wiggershaus, *The Frankfurt School: Its History, Theories, and Political Significance*
Thomas E. Wren, editor, *The Moral Domain: Essays in the Ongoing Discussion between Philosophy and the Social Sciences*
Lambert Zuidervaart, *Adorno's Aesthetic Theory: The Redemption of Illusion*